Twentieth Century
Political Theory

Twentieth Century Political Theory

A Reader

Edited by
Stephen Eric Bronner

ROUTLEDGE
New York and London

Published in 1997 by

Routledge
29 West 35th Street
New York, NY 10001

Published in Great Britain by

Routledge
11 New Fetter Lane
London EC4P 4EE

Printed in the United States of America
Design: Jack Donner

Library of Congress Cataloging-in-Publication Data

Twentieth century political theory / ed. by Stephen Eric Bronner.
p.   cm.
Includes bibliograhical references.
ISBN 0–415–91532–5 (cl). — ISBN 0–415–91533–3 (pb)
1. Political Science—Philosophy.   I. Bronner, Stephen Eric, 1949–   .
JA71.R686 1996   96–24599
320.1—dc20
CIP

CONTENTS

PART IV
NEW SOCIAL MOVEMENTS

PART V
CONCLUSION: THE END OF HISTORY?

ACKNOWLEDGMENTS

A number of people deserve my thanks for their help in seeing this project to completion. Laurie Naranch participated in every aspect of the undertaking. Jeanne Park's assistance was invaluable. Christine Cipriani and Norma McLemore offered excellent editorial advice, and I want to express my appreciation to my friends and colleagues Pedro Caban, John Ehrenberg, Michael Forman, Micheline Ishay, Kurt Jacobsen, Chip Kreider, Sandra Marshall, John Martin, Eduardo Mendieta, and Manfred Steger for providing me with many useful suggestions and insights. Finally, however, I would like to thank Cecelia Cancellaro, without whose support and enthusiasm this book would never have seen the light of day.

Political Theory in Our Time

Political theory is experiencing a crisis of relevance. It has been divorced from analytic philosophy, sociology, ideology, political behavior, and a host of other suitors. Traditionalists celebrate the autonomy of political theory. But its political value and social function have become increasingly uncertain insofar as its practitioners have preoccupied themselves with the "idea" of politics and with various attendant lifeless abstractions such as "virtue" and "the good citizen." The classical canon, which extends from Plato to Hegel or Marx, is also tottering. There is, of course, something self-evident about the importance of these great thinkers. But none of them could possibly have anticipated the dramatic events of the twentieth century or the manner in which totalitarianism gripped a generation. Non-Western experiences and the new social movements have also exposed deep problems with the Western tradition. Marxism was furthermore not buried with Marx; conservatism did not end with Jacob Burckhardt; and liberalism continued to develop after John Stuart Mill. New worldviews have been created while old ones have been revised.

Understanding the trajectory of political theory in the twentieth century initially depends upon making sense of the profound political changes the world has experienced. Liberalism, conservatism, and anarchism were already losing their appeal prior to the outbreak of World War I. But their role became even more tenuous during the interlude between the wars, which, whatever the principled republicanism of social democracy in this period, was dominated by the now discredited mass movements of fascism and communism. World War II and the shock of the concentration camps, coupled with the vigorous struggles against imperialism, undermined faith in the Western notions of progress and instrumental reason, as well as faith in the bureaucratic state. New social movements sought to empower and build the identities of previously excluded social groups and questioned the institutional assumptions of traditional political action. Traditionalists have responded critically by merging their cultural elitism with a new commitment to the economic principles of capitalism. Indeed, with a push from the fall of communism, all sides have now seemingly embraced the liberal capitalist state.

This development has made it possible for some to ignore the new prospects for inter-nationalism, and to envision the "end of history" as the twentieth century draws to a close. But the original euphoria of 1989 has passed, and, with the successful conservative offensive initiated in the 1980s, politics has once again become ideologically charged. Distinguishing between the different expressions of liberal capitalism is now of particular importance. Public life has changed, the most fundamental values have been called into question, new concerns have entered the popular consciousness, and conflict between states has taken new forms. New developments in political theory appropriate to the needs of the next century must generate a new commitment to the formation of rational and ethical principles with which to judge events, evaluate institutions, and further the practice of freedom.

The new, however, is never mechanically divorced from the old. It remains necessary to grasp the forms political theory has taken in the twentieth century. This anthology will provide a general framework for making sense of them and will present important contributions from a variety of traditions. The book is divided into five parts, each of which is broken down into a number of topical sections. Each part surveys a particular approach usually related to some practical undertaking with essays of varying degrees of difficulty. Each also offers diverse contributions by major representatives in the history of twentieth-century political theory. Some are well known, others are less so, and there is necessarily something arbitrary about the thinkers chosen and those ignored. But the aim is clear enough. *Twentieth Century Political Theory: A Reader* hopes to offer a new international orientation to the political theory of our time and to indicate its relevance to the needs of a new world in a new milennium.

*   *   *

A hundred years does not always make a century. Our own century began in 1914 with a world war, which transformed the political landscape, and ended in 1989, when the last vestige of this earlier conflict began to crumble amid seemingly universal jubilation. World War I generated a new preoccupation with administrative planning among all of the war's most important participants. New links were forged between the state and civil society, and they impacted on all the forms of democratic theory exhibited in Part I of this anthology. New forms of mass media complemented the increasingly conformist requisites of mass production. New commercialized forms of culture profoundly transformed a liberal public sphere. The state began to set priorities in the arena of economic production and to intervene in other spheres of life as well, including what the great French historian Elie Halevy called "the organization of enthusiasm."

World War I spurred the creation of a new interventionist state. National economies everywhere began experiencing dramatic deficits in production, raw materials, and labor power. The market alone could not handle the demands of this first "total war," in which imperialism played such a vital role. Even in the aftermath of the conflict, however, little change in liberal political theory occurred. Its proponents generally retained their traditional belief in free trade, colonialism, and the notion of a "watchman state" essentially intent on protecting the public welfare and ensuring the rights of individuals to engage freely in business and public affairs. Liberals prided themselves on their pragmatism and their willingness to compromise. Nevertheless, their political weakness in Europe during the next decade derived largely from their inability to deal with the problems raised by a new era.

Liberalism was a genuinely radical ideology during the epoch of democratic revolution, which extended roughly from 1680 to 1800. Its idea of liberty was never static, and it still calls arbitrary and authoritarian institutional exercises of power into question. Especially in Europe, however, by the second half of the nineteenth century liberalism had turned into the ideology of the bourgeois gentleman committed to civil liberties and markets, if not necessarily imperialist expansion. It never really gripped the masses between the two world wars or until 1989, when communism collapsed and socialism was tarred by the same brush of failure. This was true even in England, the birthplace of liberalism, whatever the exceptional contributions of individual thinkers. A *modern* liberal tradition with broad-based popular support took hold only in the United States when the New Deal was introduced to meet the challenge of the Great Depression in 1932.

Liberalism was transformed by mixing a new belief in government assistance programs with its traditional commitment to an ideology of individual rights based on rationalist and universalist assumptions. Its identification with the market and the individual entrepreneur sagged. But its mass appeal soared until the 1980s, when conservatives mounted their assault upon "big government" and "welfare dependency." Liberalism also began to appear increasingly sclerotic in the era of the new social movements given its privileging of the universal over the particular, process over any substantive definition of public goods, and the constitution over any emotional identification with the nation as such. Thus, with the century nearing its close, the interventionist form of liberalism inherited from the 1930s came under attack by those embracing the "free market" as surely as by those concerned with reinvigorating the idea of community.

Communitarianism is a particularly sophisticated response to the crisis of liberalism. Its proponents span the ideological spectrum. Some focus on the need for voluntary associations in contrast to state-sponsored programs. Others continue to recognize the importance of state intervention as they emphasize the need for diversity and the irreducible experiences of different cultures. All are concerned, however, with the loss of what Machiavelli originally termed "civic virtue" and of public participation and debate. Communitarian thinkers have illuminated the tension between particular interests and private goods along with the primacy accorded "government" as against local control. They fear the growth of an impersonal, bureaucratic state machine and, if they deplore the corrosive effects of individualism, they also question the seemingly abstract universalist propositions of philosophical rationalism.

These criticisms articulated by communitarian political theory actually have their roots in the writings of Aristotle, Rousseau, Burke, Hegel, and Tocqueville. Values and mores are seen as the products of specific cultural developments. Most communitarians retain a commitment to the liberal state, but its value is seen in its ability to take local conditions into account, and its validity is narrowed to those societies in which it has already emerged. All communitarians are wary of attempting to export any specific ideology or institutional form of politics; they recognize the costs of such undertakings, and they retain a legitimate fear of imperialist cultural or political practices. But the criticism of liberalism also produces its own problems. Traditions assume validity in their own right, and the attack on universalism undermines the articulation of criteria for criticizing their more repressive effects. The way opens not merely for provincial notions of ethnic solidarity, but also for an assault on cosmopolitan ideals and human rights.

Interestingly enough, communitarian criticisms of liberalism were also evident in the aftermath of World War I. A feeling of alienation and longing for solidarity arose in response to four years of trench warfare. The community, whether defined in terms of class or nation, was believed to have been betrayed or "stabbed in the back." The new liberal republics of Central Europe, in particular, were seen more as the problem than as the solution. Their emphasis on political process appeared to ignore the substantive power of powerful interests. Their parliamentary institutions and competitive political parties seemed to generate only fragmentation and a paralysis of the "national will."

Conservatism could not provide a viable alternative. Its advocates had generally been committed to the reigning church and to an aristocracy whose existence and values were inspired by the reaction against the legacy of the French Revolution. Their nationalism was usually mixed with a commitment to feudal forms of hierarchy, and this made sense given the existence of so many interlocking dynasties with histories that stretched back into the impenetrable mist of the past. Amid the carnage of World War I, however, the Austro-Hungarian Empire, the Ottoman Empire, the Russian Empire, and the German Empire were cast into what Hegel called "the dustbin of history."

Traditional forms of elitism, if only for this reason, lost their appeal. Politics became identified with the "will," or the impersonal "decision," while the assault on universals such as equality and the legitimation of the state was predicated on its ability to differentiate "us" from "them" or "friend" from "enemy." The aristocracy surrendered its social dominance to "the masses," nationalism became informed by a new sense of "mission," and totalitarian ideology substituted itself for religion. Conservative political theory could subsequently offer little in the way of competition to the new totalitarian movements on the right and little appeal for even moderates on the left.

Only after Hitler and World War II would conservatives genuinely engage in an attempt to recast their thinking. The romantic nostalgia for the feudal order is now gone. The market is taken for granted, along with a somewhat elitist understanding of the need for a "liberal" society. The relatively uncritical belief in tradition and "breeding" perhaps remains. Nevertheless, particularly in the United States, the old elitism has been given a new form and a new language to meet the new conditions arising in the aftermath of the Vietnam War.

The trauma induced by that war, coupled with the collapse of the great protest movements, produced a sense of moral malaise. A shift in the international economy during the 1970s from industrial to informational products also generated new forms of material uncertainty. Affirmative action created resentment as the welfare state expanded and taxes rose. All of this combined to generate a new feeling of disillusionment with the past. The liberal worldview of the 1930s began to totter, and its opponents made the most of the situation. They called for an uncompromising assault on the counterculture of the 1960s and eventually on the welfare state itself. A defense of the canonical "Western tradition" and of "family values" became fused with a new admiration for classical liberal economic principles. The result of this strange merger is now known as neo-conservatism.

Conservatives are not alone, of course, in their hatred of the modern state. Contempt for its power has traditionally been expressed by anarchism. This enemy of the political and the traditional, of all forms of hierarchy and exploitation, once constituted an important tendency in the labor movement. But its fortunes, too, changed in the aftermath of World War I. Anarchism had always opposed the parliamentarism of social democracy and, following an initial burst of revolutionary solidarity, its proponents also became increasingly critical of the new communist regime in the USSR. The philosophical representatives of anarchism, however, were unable to offer anything resembling a concrete vision of their own. They were left with only a utopian wish to abolish the state in the name of a reinvigorated, democratic, civil society. Their romantic commitment to the self-administration of the community was genuine. Their respect for the individual and solidarity, localism and participation, was a bold response to the alienation of a modern bureaucratic order. Nevertheless, the anarchist vision of an emancipated form of social life remained hopelessly vague.

Anarchism retained its appeal only in the least economically developed nations of Europe. It played an important role in Italy and an even more important one among the anti-fascists during the Spanish Civil War. It took the form of the *kibbutzim* in Israel. But it could offer no substantial opposition to either the social democratic or the communist wings of the labor movement in the more economically advanced nations. Underground groups persisted, and terrorists bandied about its slogans in the 1950s. Then in the 1960s, anarchism experienced a certain resurgence among ultra-left students and intellectuals in Europe and the United States. Its concerns with decentralization and participation, and its emphasis on personal responsibility and freedom from outmoded cultural constraints, leaked into the organizational thinking of the new social movements and even the libertarian principles of the far right. Nevertheless, the revolutionary specter of anarchism has ever more surely receded in a mass society dominated by organized politics and increasingly complex forms of production.

*   *   *

Part II of this anthology focuses on the various forms of political theory generated by the great mass movements of this century. All had their roots in the prewar period. But World War I dramatically changed their fortunes. Each placed emphasis on the state. Each sought to deal with the tension between nationalism and internationalism. Each considered itself revolutionary, after its fashion, and retained a utopian element in its worldview. Each contributed to the new suspicion accorded bureaucracy and centralized modes of politics in the aftermath of World War II.

Social democracy arose as the dominant political expression of the labor movement during the last quarter of the nineteenth century. Orthodox Marxism was the banner under which its struggles were fought, and its activists considered themselves heirs to the

Enlightenment legacy. Social democrats were the advocates of internationalism, political democracy, and social or economic justice for their proletarian constituencies. While revolutionary in word, however, the labor movement was basically reformist in deed. Its activists painstakingly created the first democratic mass parties in European history, and its leadership gained an ever larger stake in maintaining the conditions in which labor could organize. They were also enormously successful. Socialism was the fastest-growing movement on the continent and, especially on the left, it dominated political theory around the turn of the century. Its triumph appeared inevitable.

But, for a complicated set of reasons, socialist parties supported their respective nation-states in 1914 and "betrayed" their internationalist commitments. Most of their leading political theorists may never have identified with the imperialistic war aims of their governments. But the workers paid a price for the decision of their political representatives. Among the more militant, if not the more staunch, supporters of the status quo, social democracy lost its radical aura. The labor movement was criticized on the left for compromising its principles and leading its proletarian constituency to the slaughter. At the same time, it was discredited in the eyes of moderates and castigated on the right for its republicanism and its half-hearted support of the war effort. Thus, these proletarian parties found themselves more and more often on the defensive in the aftermath of World War I.

Nonetheless, social democracy became the bulwark for the new republican regimes of Central Europe during the 1920s, and its practice became ever more estranged from its revolutionary theory. Social democrats began speaking the language of rights, and, although they opposed reactionary attempts to suppress it, they sharply criticized the increasingly authoritarian character of the Russian Revolution of 1917. Their political theory became ever more preoccupied with solidifying the connection between socialism and liberalism. Perhaps the latter has even overshadowed the former, and socialism has become more a critical idea than an actual form of practice. But the movement never succumbed to the totalitarian temptation; its problem was of a different sort. The increasingly establishmentarian practice of social democracy has left its traditional supporters increasingly uninspired, resulting in a crisis of purpose and identity that has only grown more pronounced.

This process of "embourgeoisement," or integration into capitalist society, was already well under way by the end of World War I. A new generation of the trenches had formed new attitudes quite alien to the social democratic labor movement. Writers of various political persuasions—Henri Barbusse, Bertolt Brecht, Ernest Hemingway, Ödön von Horváth, Ignazio Silone, Thomas Mann, and others—gave them artistic expression. The new generation had grown harder. Its members were ill-suited for everyday life and, perhaps in order to compensate, inclined towards revolutionary visions of the future. They were critical of individualism, humanism, and democracy. They believed that either their class or their nation had been betrayed by the prewar establishment. Indeed, this generation of the trenches fueled the new movements of the 1920s.

A "wind from the East" swept away the militants of the left. They looked with wonder to Lenin, who had transformed a small Bolshevik sect into a world-historical revolutionary force. They understood his emphasis on discipline and his unsentimental bearing. They applauded his mixture of intransigence and principle—his willingness to offend even the left wing of international social democracy—when he called upon the workers of the world to turn the international conflict among nations into an international class war. They agreed with his explanation of the war as having been generated by competition over colonies among imperialist nations under the sway of finance capital and with the support of a social-democratic "labor aristocracy." Finally, they admired his bold claim that the revolution would occur "at the weakest link in the chain," and they admired the daring he showed in making good on his prediction.

The political theory of communism was authoritarian from the beginning. It was born in 1902 with the split in Russian Social Democracy between the Mensheviks, who wished to import the democratic structure of European socialist parties, and the Bolsheviks, led by Lenin. This latter, younger group of activists essentially believed that the political authoritarianism and economic underdevelopment of the Russian Empire called for a new "vanguard party" whose military structure would enable it to operate underground and effectively organize the interests of both a tiny working class and a huge peasantry. Indeed, from the first, Lenin knew this would prove possible only by making the party accountable to neither class.

His political theory, for this reason, identified the "true" interests of the working class with those of the party and, following the seizure of power in 1917, identified the interests of the party with those of the state. Any criticism of the party, in this way, became an example of "false consciousness"—or treason—by definition. Acceptance of the "vanguard" form of party organization became, according to this same logic, a condition for all wishing to participate in the Communist International, while the policies of the "dictatorship of the proletariat" were increasingly associated with the realization of a historically preordained utopian future.

Internationalism was identified with the interests of the fledgling state and hence those of the party. The party was seen as incarnating the future, and the enormity of the party's task as justifying what Georg Lukács termed a "teleological suspension of the ethical." Individual judgment gradually became subordinated, *as a principle* of political theory, to the judgment of the organization. Even "factions" were eliminated. The party always knew better. "The party has a thousand eyes," wrote Bertolt Brecht; "we have only two."

This single-mindedness became a matter of some importance as the Soviet Union sought to industrialize at breakneck speed during the late 1920s and 1930s under the stewardship of Josef Stalin. The myth of the party intensified precisely as the demand for sacrifice increased, and massive purges were undertaken in the name of securing support for one policy or "line" and then another. In this way, Stalin transformed communist political theory into little more than a set of pronouncements created ad hoc to serve a new totalitarian order.

Fascism was always more ambivalent with respect to matters of theory. Its thinkers prized the irrational and action for its own sake. Intuition and feeling—"thinking with the blood"—informed a mystical quest for nationalism and community. This was then easily combined with a radical rejection of individualism and democracy, a preoccupation with "living dangerously," and a contempt for the inherently "inferior" enemy to generate a new elitism with a populist thrust.

The fascist worldview appealed to those soldiers who saw World War I as the defining event of their lives and who, amid the bloodshed and the drudgery, the sacrifice and the heroism, felt they had experienced a higher form of solidarity. It enabled them to hate the "defeatists" and traitors—liberals, socialists, communists, and Jews—who had either robbed them of their victory or bargained it away. Rationalism and materialism were philosophies of the cash register; they drained a people of its vitality and its will to power. War provided an alternative to a degraded form of everyday life and, so they claimed, brought out the best in them: the spirit of nationalism, the sacrifice of individuality, and the existential moment of heroism in battle. Fascism would use this mindset to create a world in which politics became identicial with a new form of war against enemies both inside and outside the state.

World War I, the "total war," gave rise to the vision of a dynamic "total state," itself identified with the cult of a heroic leader and a subservient populace stripped of its particular interests. The appeal of fascism was not limited to Italy and Germany. As surely as communism, in fact, fascism became an international phenomenon during the 1920s with more or less powerful independent parties in virtually every major nation of Europe. Fascism was never about "law and order"; it was instead about the arbitrary exercise of power and the attempt to keep the excitement of the populace at a fevered pitch. Authoritarianism, militarism, and imperialism were praised, and in every country where it existed, the fascist movement found its "scapegoat."

Only with Nazism, however, would racism utterly dominate the worldview of a movement. Nazi political philosophers turned history into a cosmological conflict between Aryan and Jew. Tolerance was identified with weakness and compromise with vacillation. Nazis saw their goal as the abolition of the enemy in order to save Christian civilization and the Aryan race—by any means necessary. Its success in this venture made Nazism *the* symbol of evil for a century not lacking in competitors for that honor.

All the dominant popular ideologies of the interwar period shared a belief in progress. Social democrats, communists, and fascists may have understood the term differently. Each, however, saw history as favoring its interests, and each considered technological development an end unto itself. Politics was understood as a competition for institutional power. All the major ideologies emphasized the party, the seizure of state power, and political "realism" in the development of new policies. Only with such concerns, it was believed, could theory inform practice.

With the end of World War II, however, the obsession with institutional power had cost theory its critical edge. Its utopian or teleological justifications had been invalidated by the concentration camps. Its reliance on instrumental reason had turned technology into, employing the phrase of David Hume, a "slave of the passions." The individual, the particular, had seemingly been sacrificed to the universalistic and totalistic pretentions of the dominant great movements and their ideologies. Nazism had been defeated. But the new choice between the eastern and western blocs created by the Cold War appeared dogmatic to many and almost meaningless for those languishing in the Third World. The time had come for political theory to reorient itself, concern itself again with subjectivity, and reinvigorate the dream of an emancipation denied by reality. It was time, in short, to reassert the radical imagination.

*   *   *

Part III of this anthology begins with a section on critical theory. Normally associated with the Institute for Social Research, which was founded in 1923 in Frankfurt, the term itself was not coined until 1937. Its mostly Jewish members fled Germany following Hitler's seizure of power, and they wrote their greatest works in exile. These studies were originally concerned with explaining why an emancipatory proletarian revolution had not occurred and why fascism had emerged within a democratic society. The "Frankfurt School" called into question the economistic and positivistic assumptions of traditional Marxism. This led to a new emphasis on the role of consciousness, which produced a groundbreaking interpretation of the "culture industry," as well as innovative developments in social psychology, aesthetics, and philosophy.

Proponents of critical theory began their reasoning with an anthropological assault on the notion of progress and the most naive assumptions of enlightenment liberalism. Progress was not seen as having produced a more reflective and moral individual or a more peaceful and just world. It had instead resulted in the domination of scientific or instrumental reason, which in turn undermined the individual capacity for reflection on both the need and the possibility for emancipation. Progress was thereby understood less as fostering autonomy than as fostering conformism and, ultimately, a totalitarian politics in which the individual was inseparable from the number inscribed on his arm. Auschwitz had become the culmination of history.

"The whole," wrote Theodor Adorno, "is untrue." Political theory no longer offered the hope of liberation. Liberalism had generated the conditions for fascism, and it continued to betray its original promise given the politics so many of its proponents pursued in the Cold War and the imperialist ambitions they harbored in Vietnam and elsewhere. By the same token, however, communism had produced a bureaucratic monster, and social democracy now reflected the interests of a proletariat ideologically integrated into the status quo. A politics of resistance would, if only for these reasons, have to take a new form, and the character of emancipation would have to change.

Critical theory began to consider aesthetic experience and sometimes even a certain form of religious experience as meaningful responses to a "real world" in which every possibility for authentic subjectivity and liberation was being absorbed by a culture industry intent on appealing to the lowest common denominator in order to secure the greatest possible profit. This perspective reflected the pessimistic assessment of traditional politics generally associated with "mass society." But other trends employed this new emphasis on aesthetics and subjectivity in order to justify a new form of cultural transformation with emancipatory forms of solidarity beyond those offered by traditional political parties and institutions. Radical students and intellectuals disgusted with the conformism of the 1950s saw the need for a reinvigorated utopian vision predicated on happiness, creativity, and freedom from convention in order to contest the motivating ideals of advanced industrial society. Indeed, this would shape the way in which critical theory was appropriated by the New Left of the 1960s.

The anti-imperialist revolutions of the "Third World" brought an explosion of revolutionary hope as well as an assault on the traditional assumptions underpinning Western hegemony. A common purpose and a reinvigorated liberalism informed the civil rights movement and the opposition to the Vietnam War in the United States. The "counterculture" resonated with utopian themes. With the collapse of the original movement in the 1970s, however, new suspicions arose concerning the manner in which the particular forms of oppression experienced by people of color, women, and gays were being veiled by universalist categories and concerns.

Poststructuralism is the expression in theory of this development in practice. "Essentialism" and the "grand narrative" are its nemeses. Categories such as the "totality" and the "universal" are seen, following Nietzsche, as harboring nothing more than the interests of particular groups seeking to dominate other groups by identifying their concerns with those of the world at large. Universalistic theories of logic or language, for example, are seen as inherently obscuring or denying the ways in which the discourse of sexism or racism conditions our understandings of women or people of color. Objectivity is an anachronism. Information banks and the media are turning the "real" into the "hyperreal." Reality itself is less a given than an artificial social construct, and every boundary, whether between fact and value or science and metaphysics, has become arbitrary. Old-fashioned beliefs in the absolute must now make way for a new relativism in which the viability of the repressed experience or "desire" assumes primacy.

A permanent revolution of subjectivity, a commitment to diversity and multiculturalism, is projected by poststructuralism. Its authentic anarchism, its radicalism, manifests itself in a challenge to all forms of authority. The indeterminacy of this position, however, has its drawbacks. It becomes impossible to make qualitative distinctions between institutions, all forms of resistance become equally legitimate, and ultimately the abdication of judgment is turned into a principle of judgment.

Conformism and radicalism, in this way, become equally legitimate responses to the "postmodern" world. As the extremes blend they can even become self-reinforcing. Certain poststructuralists, according to this logic, conveniently find themselves defending the institutional framework of liberal democracy insofar as it alone makes possible the ability to challenge "hegemonic" forms of discourse and to foster diversity. Viewing democracy as the precondition for multiculturalism makes sense. Arguing this from a poststructuralist perspective, however, creates a number of problems for the original theoretical undertaking, insofar as liberal democracy is inherently based on "essentialist" premises and not every form of particularism furthers liberal or democratic values.

Criticisms of this sort presuppose the possibility as well as the need for "thematizing" an argument or narrative. Especially in its most radical forms, however, the logic of poststructuralism makes no such concession. The finished, the consistent, and the systemic are its enemies. Resistance is identified, in fact, with the response of the particular—of subjectivity—against all attempts to categorize it. The very attempt to regulate, to classify, to organize takes the form of domination in the more consequent theorists of this tendency.

All such theoretical undertakings ignore the unique and the element of "difference" even as they ultimately deny a given "desire" in order to bolster the status quo and particular forms of domination. Insanity or alcoholism, according to this logic, lose any scientific or medical determination. These categories label certain behaviors as negative and thereby repress certain fantasies or wishes in order to preserve social stability. It is impossible to determine what a person really "is." To put it another way, any fixed meaning is always absent. Experience escapes definition and militates against every attempt to objectify it. The liberation of desire from artificial social constraints, especially those that appear definitive, is the aim of the poststructuralist enterprise, even as a new preoccupation with self-definition, or "identity," serves as a political response to the homogenizing ambitions of traditional theory.

Developing a new identity is also an important part of the struggle against imperialism. But if poststructuralism is a philosophical manifestation of Western culture's discontent with itself, postcolonial theory is an attempt by the exploited and the disenfranchised to make sense of their condition vis-à-vis a decadent and cynical advanced industrial society. Almost all forms of political theory generated over the last two hundred years are complicit in their dismissal of non-Western cultures. The world has generally been viewed through the lens of a tiny fraction of humanity. The perspective of the "other," and arguably the genuine interests of the "other" as well, have never really been part of the discussion. No wonder new demands for recognition should have arisen by those who are neither white, Christian, nor Western after the defeat of fascism and the dissolution of the colonial empires of Belgium, Britain, France, Holland, and other Western nations.

Economic progress along the Western model has produced untold misery for a great portion of the globe. The preoccupation with industrial development has contributed to imperialism, fascism, and communism. New spiritual values and practical forms of resistance are seen as having been rendered necessary by the twin poisons of imperialism and racism. And so, writing in the aftermath of World War II, Jean-Paul Sartre could argue that Jews should no longer rely on the platitudes of liberalism or humanism, but rather organize themselves around their own identity. It is no different for the "Arab" or the native seeking to contest imperialism to explode the caricature made of him or her—whether by terror or peaceful forms of noncooperation.

*   *   *

The new social movements have highlighted the unfulfilled promises of advanced industrial society, and, perhaps for this very reason, it makes sense that they should have originated in the United States. The United States' peculiar institutional structure, with its weak political parties and strong interest groups, its liberal individualism and voluntary associations, and its lack of a genuine socialist tradition and ideological preoccupation with class-consciousness, contributed to generating a "new" form of political organization in the aftermath of the 1960s.

The new social movements have fostered a new awareness of racism, sexism, and the destructive impulses of an unqualified commitment to economic and technological progress. To speak of a "new awareness," however, merely reflects the problem. Racism and sexism are nothing new and, in principle, should always have been recognized as crucial issues of concern. But in the predominantly white and male culture of the West, they generally were not. Liberals and social democrats essentially saw racism and sexism as anachronistic prejudices that were in the process of being eradicated by general forms of enlightenment. Orthodox Marxists and communists considered them subordinate to the question of class and open to solution only "after" the revolution. Conservatives either saw no real problem or viewed these prejudices as so deeply embedded that political action could not resolve them without disrupting the prevailing customs and mores.

The new social movements have dealt forthrightly with issues of racism, sexism, eurocentrism, and homophobia. Often building on poststructuralist arguments, they deny the legitimacy of privileging any particular "standpoint" over any other. Issues concerning previously excluded groups define their undertakings and culture and take on new political connotations. Concerns once considered private, such as domestic violence or abortion, have been rendered public. Prejudice is considered in terms far more radical and substantive than those inherited from earlier forms of political theory. The new social movements have indeed redefined or, at a minimum, radically broadened traditional understandings of political theory.

This is true for common notions of politics as well. The new social movements are generally considered "non-state agents" or "extra-state actors." Disgusted with the integration of the social-democratic labor movement and the authoritarian character of communism, all of the movements in some degree originally manifested a suspicion of the bureaucratic state. Institutional politics, with its traditional emphasis on parties, expertise, and bureaucratic logrolling, has given way to a new concern with grassroots democracy and the *quality* of social existence. The public sphere has been changed, and the feminist movement serves as a model for the others with its network of health clinics, rape-counseling centers, day-care activities, conferences, and the like. The new social movements have brought to the forefront what Anthony Giddens termed "life politics."

The new social movements have given modernity a new look. It can no longer be simply identified with bureaucracy, technology, and the increasingly anonymous individual confronting an ever more alienated mass society. Modernity must now be understood as also unleashing a new preoccupation with subjectivity and identity. Paradoxically, however, these quintessentially "new" social movements have had to deal with fundamentally premodern problems. Racism, patriarchy, and the instrumental domination of nature predated the emergence of modern capitalist society. All have an anthropological component and are irreducible to the demands of any given system. That is why, with the new social movements, terms such as reform and revolution lose their determinate content; often, they even become open to symbolic manipulation.

The real division within the new social movements, whatever the rhetoric, was never between reformists and revolutionaries, if only because none ever projected a coherent alternative to the status quo or a practice capable of bringing it about. It is subsequently better to speak of the tensions between an extra-institutional and an integrationist, a grassroots and a bureaucratic, a fundamentalist and a realist, tendency. Each of the new social movements is torn between the concern with cultural identity and the need to compromise with the more progressive political forces and traditions of the society they criticize.

Tensions of this sort become immediately apparent in the struggles of African-Americans. Socialism, for example, held a certain attraction for many within the African-American community during the first decades of the century. But the connection between race and class on the ideological level has generally been forced. The prejudice exhibited by so much of the white working class and the rural traditions of many in the black community, coupled with the general weakness of the socialist movement in the United States, also tended to undermine its allure. These same factors, in turn, enhanced the appeal of nationalism. The political and economic programs of nationalism's advocates have been confused and often utopian. Its emphasis on the pervasiveness of racism in the United States, however, generated new interest in Africa and concern with the establishment of a black identity.

In the South of the 1950s and 1960s, a burgeoning "civil rights" movement, organized through the churches and committed to integration, employed pacifist forms of resistance and the universalistic assumptions of a liberal society to contest the exclusion and discrimination experienced by black people throughout the United States. Its leadership would soon link criticism of the political system with a criticism of its foreign policy, especially the Vietnam War, and the economic plight of poor people. A radical and coherent vision with a mass base, if not a new institutional form with which to sustain the movement over time, was the legacy of the Rev. Dr. Martin Luther King, Jr.

Even before King's death, however, many blacks were suspicious of the important role played by whites in the civil rights movement, and the identity of the movement became an issue for groups ranging from the Student Non-Violent Coordinating Committee to The Nation of Islam. Indeed, if pacifism was called into question, so was the role Christianity played in the black community. "Black Pride" and "Black Power," a new concern with the African heritage, became issues of profound concern as eurocentrism and "white-skin privilege" came under attack.

Attempts were made to link the struggles undertaken by people of color in the United States with those under way in the former colonial territories. The revolutionary upsurge in the Third World has receded, but such cultural concerns are still strong. In fact, whatever its failings on the level of economic and political program, the emotional allure and symbolic power of identity politics has only grown with the triumph of conservatism in the 1980s and the abandonment of the broader liberal vision by white society.

The future of new social movements is increasingly a question of which will assume primacy among them: equality or difference. And in the present context, this translates into the following practical dilemma. Insofar as a new social movement insists upon an anti-institutional and strict ideological posture, its politics will become ever more symbolic and marginal to the formation of policy. Insofar as it seeks access to institutions and transforms itself into a lobbying organization or an interest group, however, the new social movement must dilute the ideological dynamism from which its mass constituency draws inspiration.

Feminism finds itself in such a situation. It was initially concerned with raising the demand for equality and reciprocity with men and bringing the neglected and ignored status of women into the public realm. A new social movement formed. Decentralized in character and anti-bureaucratic, often revolutionary in its rhetoric and radical in its demands for a change in lifestyles, it created the cultural and ideological preconditions for political action. But its loose organizational structure and anti-institutional predilections prevented the translation of its demands into legislation. For this reason, other feminist theorists with an eye on greater political efficacy called upon women to organize as an interest group and eliminate the radical rhetoric, as well as the anti-hierarchical values, associated with the social movement. Interest groups like the National Organization of Women, however, have found that they must accept existing institutional arrangements and cannot effectively contest the structural imbalance of political and economic power. Consequently, especially in England, certain Marxist and socialist feminists sought to highlight the particular plight of working-class women.

Bringing in the issue of class, however, confronts the logic of solidarity informing the new social movements and the inherently transclass understanding of identity. The particular voice is also always in danger of being lost. This indeed becomes clear for a black, lesbian, working-class woman whose identity cannot receive complete expression from any of the original groups. According to the logic of identity politics, therefore, it only makes sense that a new organization should appear with its own ideological and practical interest in perpetuating its own autonomy. This logic of fragmentation, however, has had unfortunate political implications. The left has increasingly become defined as a set of "special interests," distrust has grown among the oppressed, and the whole appears less than the sum of its parts.

The environmental movement is seen by many as offering a ray of hope. Its concern with the survival of the planet and the pollution of natural resources are often seen less as particular, or identified with a given group, than as universal in character. The instrumental exploitation of nature, the obsession with growth, the alienation of modern life, and the price paid for progress are also not merely incidental issues. A new form of ecological thinking has surely illuminated the risks inherent in turning the world into a laboratory in which the most unthinkable catastrophe can result from the seemingly most miniscule, bureaucratic decision.

But, for all that, the environmental movement is still a particular interest in a world of competing interests. Its emphasis on limiting growth and "sustainable development" is looked on with suspicion by those without jobs, who are often concentrated in the ghettos, as well as those insecure about the future of the economy. Class and race come into play when considering the ecological vision of environmentalists and the debate over economic growth. Ideas concerning the ability of industry to regulate itself, or to foster environmental policies capable of reversing the damage, also now seem incredibly optimistic given the devastating impact of deregulation on the environment. Thus, whatever the role of ecology in envisioning a livable future, its vision demands consideration within a more general context cognizant of the interplay of interests and the structural imbalances of power in modern society.

New social movements raise new questions for any political theory concerned with furthering progressive aims. Such a theory will have to confront the debilitating competition between the new social movements over increasingly scarce resources. It cannot ignore the manner in which interest groups gain a stake in maintaining their own autonomy and privileging the concerns of their particular membership. It must deal with the inherent problems in a strategy basically content with forging single-issue coalitions. It must overcome the opposition between equality and difference.

Above all, however, progressive forms of political theory must come to terms with the passing of the 1960s. Economic prospects for the future are no longer glowing, labor markets are becoming increasingly rigid, and the interventionist state is under withering attack. It is also becoming ever more evident how especially the unskilled workers within each of these groups are bearing the brunt of these changes. Identity politics and its logic of fragmentation, in short, may well become self-defeating.

The problems associated with racism and sexism and the environment, of course, have not been solved. New forms of progressive political theory must subsequently aim to determine the institutional arenas in which social movements with their particularist ideologies remain effective. At the same time, however, they must also begin to develop coherent categories—and a new "standpoint"—capable of linking the interests of working people in each group without privileging the concerns of any.

Introducing such a standpoint is impossible without challenging the ideologies of particularism and relativism. Equality must receive a new degree of ideological primacy over and against the insistence on difference. The old traditions and values with which equality has been associated, if only for this reason, retain a new relevance. Internationalism, democracy, and economic justice are those with which every genuinely progressive movement has identified. And what was true of the past will assuredly prove true of the future as well.

* * *

The crumbling of communism in 1989 brought the century to a close. Every trend in contemporary political theory now finds itself in the position of either advocating or presupposing both the liberal state and the free market. None of them has been able to articulate a viable institutional alternative to either. There is admittedly still a lingering sympathy, especially around the radical fringes, for the council or soviet. Innovations on this idea, however, have not materialized. Its advocates remain stuck in the past and unable to deal with issues pertaining to the increasing complexity of the modern economy or the ways in which individual rights can be guaranteed without a centralized authority or state.

There is also something profoundly antihistorical and even dogmatic about mechanically seeking to transplant the vision of 1905 into the 1990s. A place might exist for the council in the political theory and practice of the coming century. But if so, that place is within the structure of the existing state. The council can no longer serve as an alternative to the state.

Perhaps an alternative to the liberal capitalist state no longer exists. Did not the masses of Eastern Europe rise up against their communist oppressors in the name of liberal capitalist ideals? Is not everything associated with state planning held in contempt? Has not discontent with socialism, and even liberalism, caused the proliferation of "democratic theory"? Has not ideological politics come to an end? Does it even make sense any longer to speak of a difference between "left" and right"? If the quest for freedom has reached institutional fruition, then, in keeping with Hegel, is it not legitimate to note the "end of history"?

Such are the questions with which new forms of political theory will have to deal. Traditional issues will not disappear. But new concerns of this sort will influence the way in which they are understood. Interestingly enough, however, these new questions may actually obscure more than they illuminate.

Nationalism, ethnocentrism, and religious politics are on the rise. Poverty and authoritarianism have gripped much of Eastern Europe. Communist parties, even more ideologically bereft than they were before, control any number of these states. Complacency concerning the secular consciousness of modern society is misplaced, and ideological politics still exists. The market has lost its utopian veneer in the East and liberalism, to further or even maintain democracy, may well have to buttress itself with certain egalitarian policies of socialism. Conversely, the attack on economic equality has usually led to constraints on political participation. Indeed, just as socialism once had its authoritarian and democratic variants, so democracy has developed liberal and authoritarian forms as well.

But these issues are not pertinent only to Eastern Europe. *Qualitative* differences have also become apparent in England and the United States between the new conservatism promulgated by the followers of Margaret Thatcher and Ronald Reagan and the interventionist policies once proposed by leaders like Franklin Delano Roosevelt. Ignoring such differences necessarily occurs once history is seen as coming to an end. There is also something interesting about attempting to abolish the distinction between left and right just when conservatism has become dominant and progressive forces are in disarray.

Normative issues and distinctions of this sort are the stuff of political theory. Hegel saw the ability to distinguish between phenomena as a hallmark of intellectual progress. Universalism and particularism, planning and the market, and the rights and responsibilities of citizens are all part of modern political life. But the proportionate role each plays will have a profound impact on society. The new forms of politics advocated by representatives of the new social movements have not yet invalidated the importance of institutional power. Curtailing civil freedoms and deregulating the state will obviously affect the liberation of subjectivity and the environment. The liberal state is not an inflexible abstraction, and now more than ever it is necessary to illuminate the ways in which differences of degree can turn into differences of kind within the seemingly same institutional model. Making the necessary distinctions and defining the issues, however, can occur only by examining the traditions of the past while fashioning new ideas for the future.

Part I

PERSPECTIVES

ON DEMOCRATIC THEORY

THE LIBERAL IDEA

Liberalism inspired a new vision of what Jürgen Habermas called "the public sphere." His article in this volume, which summarizes certain themes from his seminal *Structural Tranformation of the Public Sphere*, insists upon the connection between liberal democracy and the emergence of an unrestricted public realm of free discussion. Multiple newspapers, the town meeting, and other cultural forms contested the arbitrary exercise of power by the state. In the modern period, however, things have changed. Commodification, centralization, and the march of industrial progress have undermined the emancipatory promise of the public sphere in our time. The radical democratic promises of the liberal revolutions in England, the United States, and France during the seventeenth and eighteenth centuries are being betrayed by a new form of bureaucratic capitalist society.

According to Benedetto Croce, the great Italian philosopher of history, however, liberalism retains a dynamic understanding of liberty. Given the liberal preoccupation with the rule of law, civil liberties, and individual rights, its notion of liberty is always capable of altering existing legal arrangements in a democratic order and contesting the abuses of power in an authoritarian society. Liberalism is, in short, inherently opposed to arbitrary authority and incapable of complete realization.

It is the same with democracy. In the opinion of Karl Jaspers, a psychiatrist and one of the most important figures in the development of existential philosophy, it rests on the citizenry's commitment to reason and education. Democracy is considered inherently imperfect in this selection from *The Future of Mankind*. Under extreme circumstances, in fact, it may even have to become "intolerant of intolerance itself." But its general concern is clear. It places priority on persuasion over coercion and compromise over dogmatism by giving individuals the "right" to articulate grievances against the state.

The liberal notion of justice makes this possible, and no modern work has provided a finer analysis of this concept than *A Theory of Justice*, by John Rawls. His article "Justice As Fairness" illuminates the basic themes of the book. It highlights the manner in which his idea of fairness presupposes constitutional democracy and the intuitive presuppositions underpinning it as a context for its applicability. Also illuminating the arguments of his next work, *Political Liberalism*, this article emphasizes the political rather than the purely moral character of his theory. Fairness, or the common ethical product of an "overlapping consensus," is intrinsically connected with the commitment to furthering diversity and allowing for the existence of conflicting and even incommensurable conceptions of the public good.

The purpose of political philosophy, according to Rawls, involves clarifying this consensus or uncovering new ways of resolving basic questions in a mutually acceptable way for the benefit of the most disadvantaged. It must also seek to show why certain ways of arranging institutional forms are more appropriate than others for realizing democratic values such as liberty and equality. This is possible only by making reference to tradition and those provisionally fixed convictions wherein such an arrangement, or a given notion of justice, will make sense to the public at large.

Political theory becomes rooted in political culture. It must recognize that there is no practical possibility of fully resolving disputed religious, philosophical, or moral issues. Political theory should therefore not insist on providing substantive solutions; it should deal instead with issues of process and procedure. Therein lies the basis of democracy. The identification of justice with fairness, for this reason, presupposes the notions of reciprocity and tolerance implicit in the liberal worldview from its very inception.

JÜRGEN HABERMAS

The Public Sphere

THE CONCEPT

By "the public sphere" we mean first of all a realm of our social life in which something approaching public opinion can be formed. Access is guaranteed to all citizens. A portion of the public sphere comes into being in every conversation in which private individuals assemble to form a public body. They then behave neither like business or professional people transacting private affairs, nor like members of a constitutional order subject to the legal constraints of a state bureaucracy. Citizens behave as a public body when they confer in an unrestricted fashion—that is, with the guarantee of freedom of assembly and association and the freedom to express and publish their opinions—about matters of general interest. In a large public body, this kind of communication requires specific means for transmitting information and influencing those who receive it. Today, newspapers and magazines, radio and television are the media of the public sphere. We speak of the political public sphere in contrast, for instance, to the literary one, when public discussion deals with objects connected to the activity of the state. Although state authority is, so to speak, the executor of the political public sphere, it is not a part of it. To be sure, state authority is usually considered "public" authority, but it derives its task of caring for the well-being of all citizens primarily from this aspect of the public sphere. Only when the exercise of political control is effectively subordinated to the democratic demand that information be accessible to the public, does the political public sphere win an institutionalized influence over the government through the instrument of law-making bodies. The expression *public opinion* refers to the tasks of criticism and control which a public body of citizens informally—and, in periodic elections, formally as well—practices vis-à-vis the ruling structure organized in the form of a state. Regulations demanding that certain proceedings be public [*Publizitätsvorschriften*]—for example, those providing for open court hearings—are also related to this function of public opinion. The public sphere as a sphere which mediates between society and state, in which the public organizes itself as the bearer of public opinion, accords with the principle of the public sphere—that principle of public information which one had to be fought for against the arcane policies of monarchies and which since that time has made possible the democratic control of state activities.

It is no coincidence that these concepts of the public sphere and public opinion arose for the first time only in the eighteenth century. They acquire their specific meaning from a concrete historical situation. It was at that time that the distinction of "opinion" from "opinion publique" and "public opinion" came about. Though mere opinions (cultural assumptions, normative attitudes, collective prejudices and values) seem to persist unchanged in their natural form as a kind of sediment of history, public opinion can by definition come into existence only when a reasoning public is presupposed. Public discussions about the exercise of political power which are both critical in intent and institutionally guaranteed have not always existed—they grew out of a specific phase of bourgeois society and could enter into the order of the bourgeois constitutional state only as a result of a particular constellation of interests.

HISTORY

There is no indication that European society of the high Middle Ages possessed a public sphere as a unique realm distinct from the private sphere. Nevertheless, it was not coincidental that during that period symbols of sovereignty, for instance, the princely seal, were deemed "public." At that time there existed a public representation of power. The status of the feudal lord, at whatever level of the feudal pyramid, made it unnecessary to employ the categories "public" and "private." The holder of the position represented it publicly; he showed himself, presented himself as the embodiment of an ever-present "higher" power. The concept of this representation has been maintained up to the most recent constitutional history. Regardless of the degree to which it has loosened itself from the old base, the authority of political power today still demands a representation at the highest level by a head of state. Such elements, however, derive from a prebourgeois social structure. Representation in the sense of a bourgeois public sphere, for instance, the representation of the nation or of particular mandates, has nothing to do with the medieval representative public sphere—a public sphere directly linked to the concrete existence of a ruler. As long as the prince and the estates of the realm still "are" the land, instead of merely functioning as deputies for it, they are able to "represent"; they represent their power "before" the people, instead of for the people.

The feudal authorities (Church, princes, and nobility), to which the representative public sphere was first linked, disintegrated during a long process of polarization. By the end of the eighteenth century they had broken apart into private elements on the one hand, and into public elements on the other. The position of the Church changed with the Reformation: the link to divine authority which the Church represented, that is, religion, became a private matter. So-called religious freedom came to insure what was historically the first area of private autonomy. The Church itself continued its existence as one public and legal body among others. The corresponding polarization within princely authority was visibly manifested in the separation of the public budget from the private household expenses of a ruler. The institutions of public authority, along with the bureau-cracy and the military, and in part also with the legal institutions, asserted their independence from the privatized sphere of the princely court. Finally, the feudal estates were transformed as well: the nobility became the organs of public authority, parliament, and the legal institutions; while those occupied in trades and professions, insofar as they had already established urban corporations and territorial organizations, developed into a sphere of bourgeois society which would stand apart from the state as a genuine area of private autonomy.

The representative public sphere yielded to that new sphere of "public authority" which came into being with national and territorial states. Continuous state activity (permanent administration, standing army) now corresponded to the permanence of the relationships which with the stock exchange and the press had developed within the exchange of commodities and information. Public authority consolidated into a concrete opposition for those who were merely subject to it and who at first found only a negative definition of themselves within it. These were the "private individuals" who were excluded from public authority because they held no office. "Public" no longer referred to the "representative" court of a prince endowed with authority, but rather to an institution regulated according to competence, to an apparatus endowed with a monopoly on the legal exertion of authority. Private individuals subsumed in the state at whom public authority was directed now made up the public body.

Society, now a private realm occupying a position in opposition to the state, stood on the one hand as if in clear contrast to the state. On the other hand, that society had become a concern of public interest to the degree that the production of life in the wake of the developing market economy had grown beyond the bounds of private domestic market economy had grown beyond the bounds of private domestic authority. *The bourgeois public sphere* could be understood as the sphere of private individuals assembled into a public body, which almost immediately laid claim to the officially regulated "intellectual newspapers" for use against the public authority itself. In those newspapers, and in moralistic and critical journals, they debated that public authority on the general rules of social intercourse in their fundamentally privatized yet publicly relevant sphere of labor and commodity exchange.

THE LIBERAL MODEL OF THE PUBLIC SPHERE

The medium of this debate—public discussion—was unique and without historical precedent. Hitherto the estates had negotiated agreements with their princes, settling their claims to power from case to case. This development took a different course in England, where the parliament limited royal power, than it did on the Continent, where the monarchies mediatized the estates. The Third Estate then broke with this form of power arrangement, since it could no longer establish itself as a ruling group. A division of power by means of the delineation of the rights of the nobility was no longer possible within an exchange economy—private authority over capitalist property is, after all, unpolitical. Bourgeois individuals are private individuals. As such, they do not "rule." Their claims to power vis-à-vis public authority were thus directed not against the concentration of power, which was to be "shared." Instead, their ideas infiltrated the very principle on which the existing power is based. To the principle of existing power, the bourgeois public opposed the principle of supervision—that very principle which demands that proceedings be made public [*Publizität*]. The principle of supervision is thus a means of transforming the nature of power, not merely one basis of legitimation exchanged for another.

In the first modern constitutions, the catalogues of fundamental rights were a perfect image of the liberal model of the public sphere: they guaranteed the society as a sphere of private autonomy and the restriction of public authority to a few functions. Between these two spheres, the constitutions further insured the existence of a realm of private individuals assembled into a public body who as citizens transmit the needs of bourgeois society to the state, in order, ideally, to transform political into "rational" authority within the medium of this public sphere. The general interest, which was the measure of such rationality, was then guaranteed, according to the presuppositions of a society of free commodity exchange, when the activities of private individuals in the marketplace were freed from social compulsion and from political pressure in the public sphere.

At the same time, daily political newspapers assumed an important role. In the second half of the eighteenth century, literary journalism created serious competition for the earlier news sheets, which were mere compilations of notices. Karl Bücher characterized this great development as follows: "Newspapers changed from mere institutions for the publication of news into bearers and leaders of public opinion—weapons of party politics. This transformed the newspaper business. A new element emerged between the gathering and publication of news: the editorial staff. But for the newspaper publisher it meant that he changed from a vendor of recent news to a dealer in public opinion." The publishers insured the newspapers a commercial basis, yet without commercializing them as such. The press remained an institution of the public itself, effective in the manner of a mediator and intensifier of public discussion, no longer a mere organ for the spreading of news but not yet the medium of a consumer culture.

This type of journalism can be observed above all during periods of revolution, when newspapers of the smallest political groups and organizations spring up—for instance, in Paris in 1789. Even in the Paris of 1848 every half-way eminent politician organized his club, every other his journal: 450 clubs and over 200 journals were established there between February and May alone. Until the permanent legalization of a politically functional public sphere, the appearance of a political newspaper meant joining the struggle for freedom and public opinion, and thus for the public sphere as a principle. Only with the establishment of the bourgeois constitutional state was the intellectual press relieved of the pressure of its convictions. Since then it has been able to abandon its polemical position and take advantage of the earning possibilities of a commercial undertaking. In England, France, and the United States, the transformation from a journalism of conviction to one of commerce began in the 1830s at approximately the same time. In the transition from the literary journalism of private individuals to the public services of the mass media, the public sphere was transformed by the influx of private interests, which received special prominence in the mass media.

THE PUBLIC SPHERE IN THE SOCIAL WELFARE STATE: MASS DEMOCRACY

Although the liberal model of the public sphere is still instructive today with respect to the normative claim that information be accessible to the public, it cannot be applied to the actual conditions of an industrially advanced mass democracy organized in the form of the social welfare state. In part, the liberal model had always included ideological components, but it is also in part true that the social preconditions, to which the ideological elements could at one time at least be linked, had been fundamentally transformed. The very forms in which the public sphere manifested itself, to which supporters of the liberal model could appeal for evidence, began to change with the Chartist movement in England and the February revolution in France. Because of the diffusion of press and propaganda, the public body expanded beyond the bounds of the bourgeoisie. The public body lost not only its social exclusivity; it lost in addition the coherence created by bourgeois social institutions and a relatively high standard of education. Conflicts hitherto restricted to the private sphere now intrude into the public sphere. Group needs which can expect no satisfaction from a self-regulating market now tend toward a regulation by the state. The public sphere, which must now mediate these demands, becomes a field for the competition of interests, competitions which assume the form of violent conflict. Laws which obviously have come about under the "pressure of the street" can scarcely still be understood as arising from the consensus of private individuals engaged in public discussion. They correspond in a more or less unconcealed manner to the compromise of conflicting private interests. Social organizations which deal with the state act in the political public sphere, whether through the agency of political parties or directly in connection with the public administration. With the interweaving of the public and private realms, not only do the political authorities assume certain functions in the sphere of commodity exchange and social labor, but, conversely, social powers now assume political functions. This leads to a kind of "refeudalization" of the public sphere. Large organizations strive for political compromises with the state and with one another, excluding the public sphere whenever possible. But at the same time the large organizations must assure themselves of at least plebiscitary support from the mass of the population through an apparent display of openness [demonstrative Publizität].

The political public sphere of the social welfare state is characterized by a peculiar weakening of its critical functions. At one time the process of making proceedings public [Publizität] was intended to subject persons or affairs to public reason, and to make political decisions subject to appeal before the court of public opinion. But often enough today the process of making public simply serves the arcane policies of special interests; in the form of "publicity" it wins public prestige for people or affairs, thus making them worthy of acclamation in a climate of nonpublic opinion. The very words "public relations work" [Öffentlichkeitsarbeit] betray the fact that a public sphere must first be arduously constructed case by case, a public sphere which earlier grew out of the social structure. Even the central relationship of the public, the parties, and the parliament is affected by this change in function.

Yet this trend towards the weakening of the public sphere as a principle is opposed by the extension of fundamental rights in the social welfare state. The demand that information be accessible to the public is extended from organs of the state to all organizations dealing with the state. To the degree that this is realized, a public body of organized private individuals would take the place of the now-defunct public body of private individuals who relate individually to each other. Only these organized individuals could participate effectively in the process of public communication; only they could use the channels of the public sphere which exist within parties and associations and the process of making proceedings public [*Publizität*] which was established to facilitate the dealings of organizations with the state. Political compromises would have to be legitimized through this process of public communication. The idea of the public sphere, preserved in the social welfare state mass democracy, an idea which calls for a rationalization of power through the medium of public discussion among private individuals, threatens to disintegrate with the structural transformation of the public sphere itself. It could only be realized today, on an altered basis, as a rational reorganization of social and political power under the mutual control of rival organizations committed to the public sphere in their internal structure as well as in their relations with the state and each other.

BENEDETTO CROCE

Liberty and Revolution

Liberty cannot exist without law, rights, a constitution. But law is not liberty, rather it is the framework that liberty makes for itself from time to time in which to act; it is the constitution and system of rights which liberty sets up and guarantees by the power of its will. It sets it up and pulls it down, or, as we say, reforms it, by its subsequent actions; it is always pulling down and always rebuilding to suit the new situations which arise in the course of things. Such is the life of liberty.

This being so, liberty, far from excluding revolutions, necessarily contains them, since it is itself a perpetual revolution, constantly altering, in greater or less degree, the framework of rights and constitutional arrangements in force. Social and political stability conceal beneath the superficial calm which meets our eyes a movement to be detected by the mind. When the usual rhythm of the process is intensified or accelerated, the word "revolution" springs to our lips and we talk of "legal" or "peaceful" revolutions.

Such phrases suggest an opposite idea of "illegal" or "violent" revolutions as they are called; but if we think carefully we can find no logical distinction between the two kinds. Every modification of law or of rights is accomplished by the pressure of a certain number of wills on a certain number of others; whether this pressure is harsh or gentle, whether its methods are kindly or cruel, the graduation from one to the other is continuous. The two extremes of the scale are no doubt distinct and opposite, but the distinction is only one of degree, empirical and useful for practice, not of kind, and therefore it is useless for philosophy.

The true distinction and opposition is between justifiable and unjustifiable revolutions, between legitimate and illegitimate infractions of legality; and if the latter are called revolutions, especially by those who boast of having made them, yet we feel it is a misnomer and we hesitate to use the word. If revolutions are the perpetual progress and development of liberty they are always essentially "liberal"; what is opposed to such progress and tries to reverse or retard and impede it cannot be revolution. If liberty is morality and if its development is the widening and the enriching of the individual's moral life, all that withstands this must be a defect and an evil; it must be the resistance of private passions and interests to the common interest, and its occasional and temporary victories depend on the collapse of the moral forces which oppose it. So these self-styled revolutions are properly called "reactionary" or "anarchical" according to circumstances, or perhaps "brutal folly and madness." Such have been seen in all ages and eminently again in our own, even among peoples trained in liberty and who had long prospered under its laws; they are not revolutions for they do not belong to the active life of liberty. They are part of history and have historical effects, just as disease has in the bodily life but yet is distinguishable from health.

We can define liberty by its essentially revolutionary character, very much as a German philosopher defined walking when he called it "a continuous process of falling" which, because continuous, never quite lets us down. This was in the minds of those who tried to construct a theory of modern liberalism and who understood liberty as a perpetual motion, an increasing growth and progress. But on this truth was grafted a hope not so much deduced from it as derived from a feeling of confidence in science, in culture, in the mutual understanding and respect of nations and classes, and from a corresponding ideal of ever-increasing unity and good-will among men. It was hoped that fierce and violent revolutions, bloody and ruinous, could no longer find the conditions which occasion them, and that, as the saying went, revolution would be replaced by evolution. It is not the fault of those who entertained this generous hope if it has been disappointed, any more than they could have claimed the merit if it had been fulfilled. It is a hope which, if it would sacrifice the utopian ideal of absolute perfection, should be cherished by all men of good-will as the guide and guardian of their conduct.

There are only two opposing political attitudes, the liberal and the authoritarian, however the power may be defined in which authority is placed—in autocracy, theocracy, or communism (at least in its Marxist and undemocratic form). The difference between the two attitudes is not that one excludes all liberty and the other all authority, which would be absurd; but simply that each lays a superior emphasis on a different principle. Neither side can deny the fact that both principles are necessary for human life; they cannot understand, and therefore estimate, them differently. . . . If liberty or morality is the principle of life and our essential attribute, it can and must regulate the satisfaction of those physical needs which are called economic or material, and this is its constant occupation. But in the continual stooping to control our economic needs, and by contact with them, it runs the risk of confounding ruled and ruler, of degrading liberty and identifying it with the materials which it controls, or of making it conditional and dependent on these materials. As an antidote to this we must remind ourselves that liberty is a way of life, an eternal *via docendi et agendi,* not a particular possession nor a way of solving economic problems, still less the actual or proposed solution of any particular problem. Its vitality and its eternal spontaneity belong to it in virtue of this character, just as the vitality and spontaneity of thought resides in its own infinite nature and not in any one of the finite problems which it has solved or is trying to solve.

We must make this distinction a strong and permanent logical conviction in all those who think about politics, and in our time there will be plenty in that field who think before they act and while they act; we must insinuate it in the most acceptable way, in the guise of common sense, into the many minds which are little or not at all disposed or trained to speculation. This has been achieved among some nations, and especially among the English, as can be seen from some of their customs and habits that arouse curiosity and surprise in other peoples. In England it is not surprising to hear someone, like Middleton Murry some years ago, defending communism with all the enthusiasm of a new convert, and inserting the proviso: "Provided of course there be universal freedom of speech, of association, of elections and of parliament"! This popular loyalty to liberalism in England has been slowly developed through centuries of medieval and modern history from *Magna Carta* and the embryo parliament of 1265, through the religious struggles of the seventeenth century, down to the formation of the new parties when all had become harmoniously liberal. It cannot of course be immune from the dangers of forgetfulness and decay. Other countries may perhaps acquire it with the same firmness and durability if they have learnt the lessons of a shocking and terrible experience. They will have learnt what happens to a highly civilised people, in the full tide of social, economic and moral progress facilitated by liberty, when it allows itself to be snared, stunned, overpowered and seduced, and gives away its government to some cried-up superman and to the gang which serves his fortunes or their own. A people which can find in its annals a page of this kind, if it does not forget it and knows how to read it with understanding, has a source of redemption and salvation more effective than the pages which record its positive but ancient greatness.

KARL JASPERS

The Future of Mankind

It would be folly to expect the world to be put right by a few reasonable men. To become effective and durable, reason must pervade the nations. This is why "democracy" is ineluctable. It is its purpose to bring forth reason in the collective thinking and acting of a people as well as among peoples.

What we hear today about democracy is paradoxical. All governments, whether totalitarian or free, claim to be based on the will of the people and call themselves democratic. All of them present the people as their sovereign, at least in mass meetings, national celebrations, and festive orations. As a word, "democracy" has become publicly sacrosanct, an idol of our time.

In print, however, democracy is rejected by a large body of opinion. It is described as unable to put reason into practice and thus, in fact, resulting in the worst tyranny, either by the majority or by total rule. It is said that humanity by its nature lacks reason and hence makes democracy madness.

Against this antithesis of idolizing and demonizing democracy, its real meaning can be established only by reason itself. Then, instead of glorifying or damning it, we shall examine its factuality in all its ramifications and see it as our hard, stony, but only possible road. All the basic ideas about the risks of democracy have been with us since De Tocqueville and Max Weber, but in these men we find a pained, indeed a shocked awareness of its possibilities combined with an ineradicable faith in man and his freedom. The ruthlessly critical view of these political thinkers is not directed against democracy but toward its self-improvement; for they realize that the actual course of social history and the necessity of reason itself make democracy indispensable. The human task is to surmount its risks in the unforeseeable course of history by intense, patient effort and practical, effective self-criticism.

Churchill is said to have called democracy the worst form of government, except for all others. His sense of humor found a word for the fundamental disorder of human affairs, in which democracy seems the least noxious form of government, being the only visible or conceivable way to provide opportunities for incalculable improvement by the growth of reason in the peoples themselves.

Only in small states, under favorable circumstances, can the love of home and country become one with democratic thinking. In large nations, the human ruthlessness in politics and the terrors and dangers of democracy are felt more strongly than the beauty of its challenge. Shortly before the First World War, I was present at a conversation between a Swiss jurist and Max Weber, the great German political thinker. Both men were profoundly democratic. "We must love the state," said the Swiss. "What?" replied Weber, "On top of it all one should love the monster?" But what is democracy? The notions regarding it are manifold and contradictory. But its idea is unitary. Let us try to state it in a few theses.

1. Reason can prevail reliably only if it guides the people along with their leaders, not just a few lone, aloof individuals. This is impossible unless every individual has a chance to participate in thinking and acting. Democracy, therefore, requires the whole people to be educated so as to develop everyone's thought and judgment to the limits of his natural capacity. It calls for publicity of thought, especially of news, discussions, propositions, and plans.

2. Reason does not mean possession but being on the way. Only by way of universal education can it lead to democracy as common thought and action. It follows that democracy is never in its final form but keeps changing as it is shaped. From this, in turn, follows the requirement of self-criticism. Democracy will endure only by continuing to improve.

3. In principle, reason belongs to every human being. Hence, every individual has absolute value and must never be a mere means. Each individual is irreplaceable. The objective is that everyone, according to his abilities, should be able to actualize man's innate essence, his freedom. Hence, democracy aims at equality; it seeks to give everyone equal rights, in the sense of equal opportunities. This goal, insofar as it is possible at all, including the heads of the government, must be tied to laws that have been legally enacted and can be legally amended. New conditions call for new laws; the injustice that always remains requires constant improvement in the laws.

4. Reason works by persuasion, not by force. But as force is actually present in human action, rational self-preservation must meet force with force. Democracy, therefore, employs police powers against lawbreakers, but only as authorized by law or in judicial proceedings. Thus everyone is protected from arbitrary and illegal violence by the state, secure in life and limb.

5. As a state of mind, reason is prior to all specific laws and institutions. Recognized above any laws and not subject to legislation are human rights that both bind and free all men. These human rights are not subject to legislation which, by its very nature, can be changed. Before any judgment, evaluation, and regulation of the manifold actions and qualities of men comes a liberality in the recognition of all human potentialities; before the conception, adoption, and enforcement of any law comes sensitivity to injustice and to wrong as such. Democracy defines the rights of man and tries to safeguard them against

future encroachments. It protects individuals and minorities from majority coercion. It lives by the active solicitude that makes a wrong done to one a matter of concern to all.

6. In its political actualization, reason never forgets that it is men who govern. Like the governed, they are creatures with human failings and prone to error. At some time, government even by the best of men needs checking up on. But this control, carried out by human beings, must be mutual: in the intellectual battle of opinions, in the distribution of offices, in the accounting rendered to the voters.

Democracy aims at a government of reason, through government by the people. Yet how can the people govern before they are rational?

This is a question of the means of making the popular will clear, public, and a fact. These means are the press, the assembly of all the people—in very small democracies an actual meeting of all citizens, in large ones a popular vote on previously published and extensively debated issues—and the representation of the people in elected parliamentary bodies. But what if these tools of the democratic idea turn against the idea of democracy itself? If, for instance, a parliamentary majority violates its own principles, as in the German Reichstag's suicidal enabling act of 1933? And if a plebiscite decides, by majority vote, to do away with the government of laws—as happened also in the Germany of 1933, when National Socialists, German Nationalists, and Communists agreed on this objective? What if the people freely resolve to have no more freedom? Has the majority the right to say that it will not carry any weight in the future? Has it the right to abolish democracy, to wipe out human rights, to do violence to minorities? Can it be just and lawful for a majority decision to destroy all justice and legality?

Here lies the Gordian knot that can become inextricable for democracies at some time, in some crisis. No democratic form of government can guarantee the democratic idea. And where is the authority that can cut this knot?

The trouble is that democracy, which is to evoke reason in the people, already presupposes this reason. Irrational force will not vanish until all are rational. But what if reason deserts the people?

We can distinguish between the will of a temporary majority and the people's basic, permanently ingrained, rational will. The temporary will may go astray, and a minority, perhaps only a few, may be representing the true, basic will. But in reality there is no organ of government to speak for that basic will; every institution—the head of the state and its smallest governing body, the legislature, the judiciary, the plebiscite—can fail and succumb to irrationality. We depend upon real authorities. In a democracy we depend upon majorities, on the assumption that their decisions, if proved wrong, can be corrected later. But what if the decision abolishes correction and effects destruction?

No political apparatus is capable of preventing, reliably, the use of the institutions of democracy to counter the idea of democracy. Only the enduring attitude of reason on the part of those who use these institutions can do so. The limit lies where reason itself, in the minority and in opposition to the brute force of a majority that would destroy all reason, submits and allows itself to be overwhelmed by violence. By such submission the minority opens the floodgates to the deluge of force as such (until, in the Second World War, it surpassed all previous dimensions and, by happenstance, led at the end to at least a partial restitution of the opportunities for freedom; next time the atomic war could bring about the destruction of all). Or reason, now embodied in great statesmen allied perhaps with tiny minorities would, for its part, resort to a maximum of skillful maneuvers within the framework of legality and, at the decisive moments, to brute force in order to counter its violation by the majority and by terror. This act is counter to law since it is carried out against the law-destroying actions of the formally legal majority; it cannot be justified by any institution.

Democracy, in short, can sustain itself as an actuality only if it masters in its institutions the purely rational consequences of its laws guaranteeing freedom; or, expressed differently: if it can overcome, based on the strength of its ideas, those votes that would lead to its suicide. But this is possible only through acts of those who, at critical moments, either are at the helm or reach for it. The same form of legal institutions can be used in order to save or to destroy democracy. No law and no order can anticipate what will happen at such moments. Straightforward rational consistency, jurisprudence, the different spheres of influence, the bureaucracy—all of these fail. The great statesman who, at such moments, either reveals himself as such or fails to be such, proves himself by his capacity of also winning his allies for his sense of reason at decisive instances and by the significance of the action with which he successfully brings about lasting effects.

Democracy is tolerant of all possibilities but must be able to become intolerant of intolerance itself. It is against force but must maintain itself by pitting force against force. It permits all intellectual, social, political movements but where these, through their organization and through their actions turn against the cause of democratic reason itself, there the power of the state must, for its part, be in a position to act against them. All too often, politicians and officials unworthy of democracy are tied into legal knots by the shrewd men who do away with all legality. Unable to disentangle themselves, they conceal their failure by talking, negotiating in all directions, and doing nothing. The democratic idea is lost in the hands of mere politicians who will let it die in pseudo-democratic emotionalism.

Yet all this goes to show only that democracy is built on volcanic soil and cannot be maintained by legal guarantees alone.

Democracy is dangerous as is all of human existence. The moments of great crisis in the super-powers of a particular age are decisive for world history, and at such moments democracy cannot survive just by patient bargaining, making sensible compromises, and splitting the difference. It may do so in periods of calm, but even then the breath of evil must be felt and kept in mind—even then, vigilance must be at a constant alert if the men of domocracy, instead of being paralyzed with fright in times of peril, find, in their broad horizons, their daring decisions and stick to them, moving and convincing others.

Democracy is an idea. This means that it cannot be perfect anywhere, that indeed it is beyond visualization even as an ideal. Man's reason tells him that no right, perfectible order exists in the world. The awareness of human imperfectibility is a corollary of the democratic idea.

As an idea, however, it is not weak or skeptical. It has the thoughtfulness of reason, its powerful impulse, its inspiring enthusiasm. The idea is before our eyes—never grasped, ever present yet ever elusive, and always guiding. To the realist it seems fantastic, and if we were to take its mere outline for a program of actualization, and our awareness of the impulse for real achievement, he would be right. He is wrong if he fails to perceive that any real, more than fleetingly successful achievement is bound up with the idea. But it takes broad horizons, extensive knowledge, and competent action to make the idea strong.

The word "democracy" is used today in self-justification by all states, yet the concept defies any simple definition. We must distinguish, first, between the idea of democracy and its institutions of the moment—which are almost endlessly variable, filled with the idea only to a degree, and apt to turn into configurations destructive of the idea. The idea of democracy lives out of the substance of a historic tradition extending to the everyday ethos of a people. Democracy, turned into a palpable idol in the form of a written consti- tution, is either adopted cut and dried as a panacea or a charm, or else foisted on peoples, supposedly in their own best interest. Hence the idea has had a long history, from its man- ifestations in Antiquity by way of the guild systems and Mediterranean city-states to its modern forms, which have achieved a relative measure of historically grounded stability only in countries that have long known freedom, such as Britain, the United States, the Netherlands, and Switzerland. Since the French Revolution, it has had another modern history which perverted the idea into abstract principles, with the merely rational conse- quence of institutions and actions that have over and again destroyed the idea of democ- racy as well as freedom.

Second, we must distinguish between a form of government and a way of governing. Democracy may mean one of the several forms that a state can assume, such as democracy, aristocracy, monarchy, as taught in Antiquity. Or it may mean a way of governing—what Kant calls the "republican manner of government," which has only one antithesis, i.e., despotism. Both, the democratic and despotic way of ruling, may occur in all three forms of government.

Third, we must distinguish the idea of democracy from the notion of popular sover- eignty. Identical at first, the two diverge and become opposites if the path toward reason is given up for the postulation of an absolute wisdom already in place in the actuality of the people. Now the objects of idolatry are not only specific institutions but the people them- selves, by means of their institutions. The sovereign people are imbued with the character of sanctity, as it were, as absolute princes used to be: "The people's voice is God's voice."

The true, wise, popular sovereign demands obedience, and there is no more appeal from the people's will than there ever was from that of a sovereign prince in the age of absolutism. The presupposition that there is a will as such of the people demands that it be determined what it is. It often seems to deceive itself where it expresses itself. Where is it free of deception? The answer is: either in the majority that emerges in elections, or in the minority of a vanguard which, in contrast to the confused, vacillating and manipulable multitudes, claims to know the genuine will of the people. It is men, always, who claim to rule in the name of the sovereign people, and since the sovereign people's will is absolute, the result is either a brutal assault on minorities by rulers chosen by the people to be the representative of the majority, or violation of all by a minority. From the supposed exis- tence of a popular will, which the rulers claim to represent, they further deduce the right to exterminate their opponents as rebels against the sovereign people. Such an absolute, institutionalized popular sovereignty will reject all deviation as falsehood and ill will. Rule by absolute sovereignty of the people incarnate in organizations and leaders puts an end to all discussion.

The democratic idea is the way to counter the idolization of the existing sovereignty of the people. It knows no reigning and governing sovereign, but it knows a will that must constantly evolve anew among the people in a process of self-education, in institutions which, for all their firmness and despite all checks and safeguards, remain modifiable. This way requires solidarity of the most diverse members of the community oriented toward and guided by reason. It requires, on the one hand, a liberal approach, and on the other, the inviolability of existing law. The ruling individuals who are on the way of the democratic idea are always bound by the law, while the individuals embodying popular sovereignty can, in extreme situations, rule by decree which they may breach once more since they are sovereign over law and decree.

The way of the democratic idea is an incessant struggle as a community to find truth. Everything is subject to unlimited public debate, though not based upon debate but on decisions. Whatever truth is found at any time must be decided under the pressure of the situation. In case of disagreement, provisional agreement on actions that are deemed necessary is achieved by majority vote, with the minority suspending its divergent views, knowing that in the future, in new situations, it will have another chance to put them to the test and make them prevail. Complying loyally with what are now common decisions, the minority in turn enjoys the protection of the laws and of a solidarity resting upon the common ground of the democratic idea.

The idea of democracy is sober, clear, and inspiring; the claim of absolute popular sovereignty is wild, murky, and fanaticized.

Should we avoid the word "democracy" because it invites so many interpretations and is open to so much abuse? Would not its abolition be all the more justified since the doctrine of Antiquity coined the concept as that of a form of government, alongside monarchy and aristocracy? But the abolition would be in vain and inappropriate, for the word does mean the people—all the people of a state. All of them shall get to exercise their right of thinking and acting in concert.

The only stark contrast is between democratic and despotic ways of ruling. When we speak of the idea of democracy, we mean Kant's "republican manner of government." For this, there is no better name than democracy.

Wherever a government lays claim to democracy—as all of them do nowadays—there we find the question of the alternative: of that which is not democratic. Everything "undemocratic" is rejected and each accuses the other of being ruled by a minority rather than by the people. Here, we hear, monopoly capital is in the saddle, there a party clique. Here men are subject to capitalistic exploitation, there to despotic exploitation.

Yet these alternatives are propagandistic arguments that take the particular for the whole. They refer to tangible, specific aspects. Against them, there is one sole and radical alternative that determines the totality of what we want and do, and this can only be circumscribed *ad infinitum* but not itself determined. For its primary characteristic is that it is not an alternative of antithetical doctrines. It is an alternative of the basic direction of our lives. The way of reason knows doctrines as particular means to particular ends, but it never turns into a doctrine itself and thus cannot have a doctrine for its antithesis. It resists any doctrinization—any type of confinement in definitive rigidities, in the embodiment of an absolute, or in the acrobatics of a dialectical movement.

As a way of reason, democracy refuses to be absolutized. If it is based on reason, it cannot help realizing that, while reason ought to prevail, it is actually neither all-pervasive nor certain that it can continue on its way without being limited (although it hopes to do so). Yet democracy refuses to conclude from this experience that the rule of irrationality is unchangeable, that unreasonable mankind must be forever ruled by equally unreasonable force.

Democracy does not permit us to assume that rulers are, or could or should be, superhuman. It insists that, in the nature of things, all challenges are directed at human beings, and it rejects any other legitimization, such as a certain post being a direct mandate from God, or the charisma of a person to indicate that he is a divinely instituted leader. It knows the seriousness of the responsibility connected with an office and the gifts of great men, and it respects both without idolizing them. Democracy knows that both of these must be actual if it is to thrive.

The alternative to the democratic idea is whatever seeks to shirk the task of being-human. This happened and happens in grandiose-appearing forms, in actualities making claims of divinity or of absolute knowledge. All alternatives to the way of democracy may be described, in Kant's term, as states of despotism. Even at best, they block the path of rational man; today they block the path to the rescue of mankind. In fortunate moments despots are said to have governed well, but such moments were mere accidents in the course of destruction. For it is not thus that the nations awaken: the mass of individuals achieve neither insight nor responsibility; they stay imprisoned in their particular environments—whether wretched or beautiful—under authoritarian direction; they are technically drilled, made into useful, skillful, knowledgeable tools of labor, but removed in all instances from the great, infinite process of human development.

The way of democracy, for all its errors and seeming dead ends, provides the opportunities for a majority of men to grow into thinking, responsible creatures; it does so even though its first result is a leveling that entails the risk of democracy's being perverted into one of the worst dictatorships ever known. The democratic idea has its ground in man's task of self-actualization in reason, and in the unique, irreplaceable character of every individual, and in his dignity based on his participation in reason. the failings in democratic actualization are not justified, of course, but put into perspective by the far greater failings of all other present systems. To despair of the democratic idea is to despair of man . . .

JOHN RAWLS

Justice As Fairness: Political Not Metaphysical

In this discussion I shall make some general remarks about how I now understand the conception of justice that I have called "justice as fairness" (presented in my book *A Theory of Justice*).[1] I do this because it may seem that this conception depends on philosophical claims I should like to avoid, for example, claims to universal truth, or claims about the essential nature and identity of persons. My aim is to explain why it does not. I shall first discuss what I regard as the task of political philosophy at the present time and then briefly survey how the basic intuitive ideas drawn upon in justice as fairness are combined into a political conception of justice for a constitutional democracy. Doing this will bring out how and why this conception of justice avoids certain philosophical and metaphysical claims. Briefly, the idea is that in a constitutional democracy the public conception of justice should be, so far as possible, independent of controversial philosophical and religious doctrines. Thus, to formulate such a conception, we apply the principle of toleration to philosophy itself: the public conception of justice is to be political, not metaphysical. Hence the title.

I want to put aside the question whether the text of *A Theory of Justice* supports different readings than the one I sketch here. Certainly on a number of points I have changed my views, and there are no doubt others on which my views have changed in ways that I am unaware of.[2] I recognize further that certain faults of exposition as well as obscure and ambiguous passages in *A Theory of Justice* invite misunderstanding; but I think these matters need not concern us and I shan't pursue them beyond a few footnote indications. For our purposes here, it suffices first, to show how a conception of justice with the structure and content of justice as fairness can be understood as political and not metaphysical, and second, to explain why we should look for such a conception of justice in a democratic society.

I

One thing I failed to say in *A Theory of Justice*, or failed to stress sufficiently, is that justice as fairness is intended as a political conception of justice. While a political conception of justice is, of course, a moral conception, it is a moral conception worked out for a specific kind of subject, namely, for political, social, and economic institutions. In particular, justice as fairness is framed to apply to what I have called the "basic structure" of a modern constitutional democracy.[3] (I shall use "constitutional democracy" and "democratic regime," and similar phrases interchangeably.) By this structure I mean such a society's main political, social, and economic institutions, and how they fit together into one unified system of social cooperation. Whether justice as fairness can be extended to a general political conception for different kinds of societies existing under different historical and social conditions, or whether it can be extended to a general moral conception, or a significant part thereof, are altogether separate questions. I avoid prejudging these larger questions one way or the other.

It should also be stressed that justice as fairness is not intended as the application of a general moral conception to the basic structure of society, as if this structure were simply another case to which that general moral conception is applied.[4] In this respect justice as fairness differs from traditional moral doctrines, for these are widely regarded as such general conceptions. Utilitarianism is a familiar example, since the principle of utility, however it is formulated, is usually said to hold for all kinds of subjects ranging from the actions of individuals to the law of nations. The essential point is this: as a practical political matter no general moral conception can provide a publicly recognized basis for a conception of justice in a modern democratic state. The social and historical conditions of such a state have their origins in the Wars of Religion following the Reformation and the subsequent development of the principle of toleration, and in the growth of constitutional government and the institutions of large industrial market economies. These conditions profoundly affect the requirements of a workable conception of political justice: such a conception must allow for a diversity of doctrines and the plurality of conflicting, and indeed incommensurable, conceptions of the good affirmed by the members of existing democratic societies.

Finally, to conclude these introductory remarks, since justice as fairness is intended as a political conception of justice for a democratic society, it tries to draw solely upon basic intuitive ideas that are embedded in the political institutions of a constitutional democratic regime and the public traditions of their interpretation. Justice as fairness is a political conception in part because it starts from within a certain political tradition. We hope that this political conception of justice may at least be supported by what we may call an "overlapping consensus," that is, by a consensus that includes all the opposing philosophical and religious doctrines likely to persist and to gain adherents in a more or less just constitutional democratic society.[5]

II

There are, of course, many ways in which political philosophy may be understood, and writers at different times, faced with different political and social circumstances, understand their work differently. Justice as fairness I would now understand as a reasonably systematic and practicable conception of justice for a constitutional democracy, a conception that offers an alternative to the dominant utilitarianism of our tradition of political thought. Its first task is to provide a more secure and acceptable basis for constitutional principles and basic rights and liberties than utilitarianism seems to allow.[6] The need for such a political conception arises in the following way.

There are periods, sometimes long periods, in the history of any society during which certain fundamental questions give rise to sharp and divisive political controversy, and it seems difficult, if not impossible, to find any shared basis of political agreement. Indeed, certain questions may prove intractable and may never be fully settled. One task of political philosophy in a democratic society is to focus on such questions and to examine whether some underlying basis of agreement can be uncovered and a mutually acceptable way of resolving these questions publicly established. Or if these questions cannot be fully settled, as may well be the case, perhaps the divergence of opinion can be narrowed sufficiently so that political cooperation on a basis of mutual respect can still be maintained.[7]

The course of democratic thought over the past two centuries or so makes plain that there is no agreement on the way basic institutions of a constitutional democracy should be arranged if they are to specify and secure the basic rights and liberties of citizens and answer to the claims of democratic equality when citizens are conceived as free and equal persons (as explained in the last three paragraphs of Section III). A deep disagreement exists as to how the values of liberty and equality are best realized in the basic structure of society. To simplify, we may think of this disagreement as a conflict within the tradition of democratic thought itself, between the tradition associated with Locke, which gives greater weight to what Constant called "the liberties of the moderns," freedom of thought and conscience, certain basic rights of the person and of property, and the rule of law, and the tradition associated with Rousseau, which gives greater weight to what Constant called "the liberties of the ancients," the equal political liberties and the values of public life. This is a stylized contrast and historically inaccurate, but it serves to fix ideas.

Justice as fairness tries to adjudicate between these contending traditions first, by proposing two principles of justice to serve as guidelines for how basic institutions are to realize the values of liberty and equality, and second, by specifying a point of view from which these principles can be seen as more appropriate than other familiar principles of justice to the nature of democratic citizens viewed as free and equal persons. What it means to view citizens as free and equal persons is, of course, a fundamental question and is discussed in the following sections. What must be shown is that a certain arrangement of the basic structure, certain institutional forms, are more appropriate for realizing the values of liberty and equality when citizens are conceived as such persons, that is (very briefly), as having the requisite powers of moral personality that enable them to participate in society viewed as a system of fair cooperation for mutual advantage. So to continue, the two principles of justice (mentioned above) read as follows:

1. Each person has an equal right to a fully adequate scheme of equal basic rights and liberties, which scheme is compatible with a similar scheme for all.

2. Social and economic inequalities are to satisfy two conditions: first, they must be attached to offices and positions open to all under conditions of fair equality of opportunity; and second, they must be to the greatest benefit of the least advantaged members of society. Each of these principles applies to a different part of the basic structure; and both

are concerned not only with basic rights, liberties, and opportunities, but also with the claims of equality; while the second part of the second principle underwrites the worth of these institutional guarantees.[8] The two principles together, when the first is given priority over the second, regulate the basic institutions which realize these values.[9] But these details, although important, are not our concern here.

We must now ask: how might political philosophy find a shared basis for settling such a fundamental question as that of the most appropriate institutional forms for liberty and equality? Of course, it is likely that the most that can be done is to narrow the range of public disagreement. Yet even firmly held convictions gradually change: religious toleration is now accepted, and arguments for persecution are no longer openly professed; similarly, slavery is rejected as inherently unjust, and however much the aftermath of slavery may persist in social practices and unavowed attitudes, no one is willing to defend it. We collect such settled convictions as the belief in religious toleration and the rejection of slavery and try to organize the basic ideas and principles implicit in these convictions into a coherent conception of justice. We can regard these convictions as provisional fixed points which any conception of justice must account for if it is to be reasonable for us. We look, then, to our public political culture itself, including its main institutions and the historical traditions of their interpretation, as the shared fund of implicitly recognized basic ideas and principles. The hope is that these ideas and principles can be formulated clearly enough to be combined into a conception of political justice congenial to our most firmly held convictions. We express this by saying that a political conception of justice, to be acceptable, must be in accordance with our considered convictions, at all levels of generality, on due reflection (or in what I have called "reflective equilibrium").[10]

The public political culture may be of two minds even at a very deep level. Indeed, this must be so with such an enduring controversy as that concerning the most appropriate institutional forms to realize the values of liberty and equality. This suggests that if we are to succeed in finding a basis of public agreement, we must find a new way of organizing familiar ideas and principles into a conception of political justice so that the claims in conflict, as previously understood, are seen in another light. A political conception need not be an original creation but may only articulate familiar intuitive ideas and principles so that they can be recognized as fitting together in a somewhat different way than before. Such a conception may, however, go further than this: it may organize these familiar ideas and principles by means of a more fundamental intuitive idea within the complex structure of which the other familiar intuitive ideas are then systematically connected and related. In justice as fairness, as we shall see in the next section, this more fundamental idea is that of society as a system of fair social cooperation between free and equal persons. The concern of this section is how we might find a public basis of political agreement. The point is that a conception of justice will only be able to achieve this aim if it provides a reasonable way of shaping into one coherent view the deeper bases of agreement embedded in the public political culture of a constitutional regime and acceptable to its most firmly held considered convictions.

Now suppose justice as fairness were to achieve its aim and a publicly acceptable political conception of justice is found. Then this conception provides a publicly recognized point of view from which all citizens can examine before one another whether or not their political and social institutions are just. It enables them to do this by citing what are recognized among them as valid and sufficient reasons singled out by that conception itself. Society's main institutions and how they fit together into one scheme of social cooperation can be examined on the same basis by each citizen, whatever that citizen's social position or more particular interests. It should be observed that, on this view, justification is not regarded simply as valid argument from listed premises, even should these premises be true. Rather, justification is addressed to others who disagree with us, and therefore it must always proceed from some consensus, that is, from premises that we and others publicly recognize as true; or better, publicly recognize as acceptable to us for the purpose of establishing a working agreement on the fundamental questions of political justice. It goes without saying that this agreement must be informed and uncoerced, and reached by citizens in ways consistent with their being viewed as free and equal persons.[11]

Thus, the aim of justice as fairness as a political conception is practical, and not metaphysical or epistemological. That is, it presents itself not as a conception of justice that is true, but one that can serve as a basis of informed and willing political agreement between citizens viewed as free and equal persons. This agreement when securely founded in public political and social attitudes sustains the goods of all persons and associations within a just democratic regime. To secure this agreement we try, so far as we can, to avoid disputed philosophical, as well as disputed moral and religious, questions. We do this not because these questions are unimportant or regarded with indifference,[12] but because we think them too important and recognize that there is no way to resolve them politically. The only alternative to a principle of toleration is the autocratic use of state power. Thus, justice as fairness deliberately stays on the surface, philosophically speaking. Given the profound differences in belief and conceptions of the good at least since the Reformation, we must recognize that, just as on questions of religious and moral doctrine, public agreement on the basic questions of philosophy cannot be obtained without the state's infringement of basic liberties. Philosophy as the search for truth about an independent metaphysical and moral order cannot, I believe, provide a workable and shared basis for a political conception of justice in a democratic society.

We try, then, to leave aside philosophical controversies whenever possible, and look for ways to avoid philosophy's longstanding problems. Thus, in what I have called "Kantian constructivism," we try to avoid the problem of truth and the controversy between realism and subjectivism about the status of moral and political values. This form of constructivism neither asserts nor denies these doctrines.[13] Rather, it recasts ideas from the tradition of the social contract to achieve a practicable conception of objectivity and justification founded on public agreement in judgment on due reflection. The aim is free agreement, reconciliation through public reason. And similarly, as we shall see (in Section V), a conception of the person in a political view, for example, the conception of citizens as free and equal persons, need not involve, so I believe, questions of philosophical psychology or a metaphysical doctrine of the nature of the self. No political view that depends on these deep and unresolved matters can serve as a public conception of justice in a constitutional democratic state. As I have said, we must apply the principle of toleration to philosophy itself. The hope is that, by this method of avoidance, as we might call it, existing differences between contending political views can at least be moderated, even if not entirely removed, so that social cooperation on the basis of mutual respect can be maintained. Or if this is expecting too much, this method may enable us to conceive how, given a desire for free and uncoerced agreement, a public understanding could arise consistent with the historical conditions and constraints of our social world. Until we bring ourselves to conceive how this could happen, it can't happen.

III

Let's now survey briefly some of the basic ideas that make up justice as fairness in order to show that these ideas belong to a political conception of justice. As I have indicated, the overarching fundamental intuitive idea, within which other basic intuitive ideas are systematically connected, is that of society as a fair system of cooperation between free and equal persons. Justice as fairness starts from this idea as one of the basic intuitive ideas which we take to be implicit in the public culture of a democratic society.[14] In their political thought, and in the context of public discussion of political questions, citizens do not view the social order as a fixed natural order, or as an institutional hierarchy justified by religious or aristocratic values. Here it is important to stress that from other points of view, for example, from the point of view of personal mortality, or from the point of view of members of an association, or of one's religious or philosophical doctrine, various aspects of the world and one's relation to it, may be regarded in a different way. But these other points of view are not to be introduced into political discussion.

We can make the idea of social cooperation more specific by noting three of its elements:

1. Cooperation is distinct from merely socially coordinated activity, for example, from activity coordinated by orders issued by some central authority. Cooperation is guided by publicly recognized rules and procedures which those who are cooperating accept and regard as properly regulating their conduct.

2. Cooperation involves the idea of fair terms of cooperation: these are terms that each participant may reasonably accept, provided that everyone else likewise accepts them. Fair terms of cooperation specify an idea of reciprocity or mutuality: all who are engaged in co-operation and who do their part as the rules and procedures require, are to benefit in some appropriate way as assessed by a suitable benchmark of comparison. A conception of political justice characterizes the fair terms of social cooperation. Since the primary subject of justice is the basic structure of society, this is accomplished in justice as fairness by formulating principles that specify basic rights and duties within the main institutions of society, and by regulating the institutions of background justice over time so that the benefits produced by everyone's efforts are fairly acquired and divided from one generation to the next.

3. The idea of social cooperation requires an idea of each participant's rational advantage, or good. This idea of good specifies what those who are engaged in cooperation, whether individuals, families, or associations, or even nation-states, are trying to achieve, when the scheme is viewed from their own standpoint.

Now consider the idea of the person.[15] There are, of course, many aspects of human nature that can be singled out as especially significant depending on our point of view. This is witnessed by such expressions as *homo politicus, homo oeconomicus, homo faber,* and the like. Justice as fairness starts from the idea that society is to be conceived as a fair system of cooperation and so it adopts a conception of the person to go with this idea. Since Greek times, both in philosophy and law, the concept of the person has been understood as the concept of someone who can take part in, or who can play a role in, social life, and hence exercise and respect its various rights and duties. Thus, we say that a person is someone who can be a citizen, that is, a fully cooperating member of society over a complete life. We add the phrase "over a complete life" because a society is viewed as a more or less complete and self-sufficient scheme of cooperation, making room within itself for all the necessities and activities of life, from birth until death. A society is not an association for more limited purposes; citizens do not join society voluntarily but are born into it, where, for our aims here, we assume they are to lead their lives.

Since we start within the tradition of democratic thought, we also think of citizens as free and equal persons. The basic intuitive idea is that in virtue of what we may call their moral powers, and the powers of reason, thought, and judgment connected with those powers, we say that persons are free. And in virtue of their having these powers to the requisite degree to be fully cooperating members of society, we say that persons are equal.[16] We can elaborate this conception of the person as follows. Since persons can be full participants in a fair system of social cooperation, we ascribe to them the two moral powers connected with the elements in the idea of social cooperation noted above: namely, a capacity for a sense of justice and a capacity for a conception of the good. A sense of justice is the capacity to understand, to apply, and to act from the public conception of justice which characterizes the fair terms of social cooperation. The capacity for a conception of the good is the capacity to form, to revise, and rationally to pursue a conception of one's rational advantage, or good. In the case of social cooperation, this good must not be understood narrowly but rather as a conception of what is valuable in human life. Thus, a conception of the good normally consists of a more or less determinate scheme of final ends, that is, ends we want to realize for their own sake, as well as of attachments to other persons and loyalties to various groups and associations. These attachments and loyalties give rise to affections and devotions, and therefore the flourishing of the persons and associations who are the objects of these sentiments is also part of our conception of the good. Moreover, we must also include in such a conception a view of our relation to the world—religious, philosophical, or moral—by reference to which the value and significance of our ends and attachments are understood.

In addition to having the two moral powers, the capacities for a sense of justice and a conception of the good, persons also have at any given time a particular conception of the good that they try to achieve. Since we wish to start from the idea of society as a fair system of cooperation, we assume that persons as citizens have all the capacities that enable them to be normal and fully cooperating members of society. This does not imply that no one ever suffers from illness or accident; such misfortunes are to be expected in the ordinary course of human life; and provision for these contingencies must be made. But for our purposes here I leave aside permanent physical disabilities or mental disorders so severe as to prevent persons from being normal and fully cooperating members of society in the usual sense.

Now the conception of persons as having the two moral powers, and therefore as free and equal, is also a basic intuitive idea assumed to be implicit in the public culture of a democratic society. Note, however, that it is formed by idealizing and simplifying in various ways. This is done to achieve a clear and uncluttered view of what for us is the fundamental question of political justice: namely, what is the most appropriate conception of justice for specifying the terms of social cooperation between citizens regarded as free and equal persons, and as normal and fully cooperating members of society over a complete life. It is this question that has been the focus of the liberal critique of aristocracy, of the socialist critique of liberal constitutional democracy, and of the conflict between liberals and conservatives at the present time over the claims of private property and the legitimacy (in contrast to the effectiveness) of social policies associated with the so-called welfare state.

IV

I now take up the idea of the original position.[17] This idea is introduced in order to work out which traditional conception of justice, or which variant of one of those conceptions, specifies the most appropriate principles for realizing liberty and equality once society is viewed as a system of cooperation between free and equal persons. Assuming we had this purpose in mind, let's see why we would introduce the idea of the original position and how it serves its purpose.

Consider again the idea of social cooperation. Let's ask: how are the fair terms of cooperation to be determined? Are they simply laid down by some outside agency distinct from the persons cooperating? Are they, for example, laid down by God's law? Or are these terms to be recognized by these persons as fair by reference to their knowledge of a prior and independent moral order? For example, are they regarded as required by natural law, or by a realm of values known by rational intuition? Or are these terms to be established by an undertaking among these persons themselves in the light of what they regard as their mutual advantage? Depending on which answer we give, we get a different conception of cooperation.

Since justice as fairness recasts the doctrine of the social contract, it adopts a form of the last answer: the fair terms of social cooperation are conceived as agreed to by those engaged in it, that is, by free and equal persons as citizens who are born into the society in which they lead their lives. But their agreement, like any other valid agreement, must be entered into under appropriate conditions. In particular, these conditions must situate free and equal persons fairly and must not allow some persons greater bargaining advantages than others. Further, threats of force and coercion, deception and fraud, and so on, must be excluded.

So far so good. The foregoing considerations are familiar from everyday life. But agreements in everyday life are made in some more or less clearly specified situation embedded within the background institutions of the basic structure. Our task, however, is to extend the idea of agreement to this background framework itself. Here we face a difficulty for any political conception of justice that uses the idea of a contract, whether social or otherwise. The difficulty is this: we must find some point of view, removed from and not distorted by the particular features and circumstances of the all-encompassing background framework, from which a fair agreement between free and equal persons can be reached. The original position, with the feature I have called "the veil of ignorance," is this point of view.[18] And the reason why the original position must abstract from and not be affected by the contingencies of the social world is that the conditions for a fair agreement on the principles of political justice between free and equal persons must eliminate the bargaining advantages which inevitably arise within background institutions of any society as the result of cumulative social, historical, and natural tendencies. These contingent advantages and accidental influences from the past should not influence an agreement on the principles which are to regulate the institutions of the basic structure itself from the present into the future.

Here we seem to face a second difficulty, which is, however, only apparent. To explain: from what we have just said it is clear that the original position is to be seen as a device of representation and hence any agreement reached by the parties must be regarded as both hypothetical and nonhistorical. But if so, since hypothetical agreements cannot bind, what is the significance of the original position?[19] The answer is implicit in what has already been said: it is given by the role of the various features of the original position as a device of representation. Thus, that the parties are symmetrically situated is required if they are to be seen as representatives of free and equal citizens who are to reach an agreement under conditions that are fair. Moreover, one of our considered convictions, I assume, is this: the fact that we occupy a particular social position is not a good reason for us to accept, or to expect others to accept, a conception of justice that favors those in this position. To model this conviction in the original position the parties are not allowed to know their social position; and the same idea is extended to other cases. This is expressed figuratively by saying that the parties are behind a veil of ignorance. In sum, the original position is simply a device of representation: it describes the parties, each of whom are responsible for the essential interests of a free and equal person, as fairly situated and as reaching an agreement subject to appropriate restrictions on what are to count as good reasons.[20]

Both of the above mentioned difficulties, then, are overcome by viewing the original position as a device of representation: that is, this position models what we regard as fair conditions under which the representatives of free and equal persons are to specify the terms of social cooperation in the case of the basic structure of society; and since it also models what, for this case, we regard as acceptable restrictions on reasons available to the parties for favoring one agreement rather than another, the conception of justice the parties would adopt identifies the conception we regard—*here* and *now*—as fair and supported by the best reasons. We try to model restrictions on reasons in such a way that it is perfectly evident which agreement would be made by the parties in the original position as citizens' representatives. Even if there should be, as surely there will be, reasons for and against each conception of justice available, there may be an overall balance of reasons plainly favoring one conception over the rest. As a device of representation the idea of the original position serves as a means of public reflection and self-clarification. We can use it to help us work out what we now think, once we are able to take a clear and uncluttered view of what justice requires when society is conceived as a scheme of cooperation between free and equal persons over time from one generation to the next. The original position serves as a unifying idea by which our considered convictions at all levels of generality are brought to bear on one another so as to achieve greater mutual agreement and self-understanding.

To conclude: we introduce an idea like that of the original position because there is no better way to elaborate a political conception of justice for the basic structure from the fundamental intuitive idea of society as a fair system of cooperation between citizens as free and equal persons. There are, however, certain hazards. As a device of representation the original position is likely to seem somewhat abstract and hence open to misunderstanding. The description of the parties may seem to presuppose some metaphysical conception of the person, for example, that the essential nature of persons is independent of and prior to their contingent attributes, including their final ends and attachments, and indeed, their character as a whole. But this is an illusion caused by not seeing the original position as a device of representation. The veil of ignorance, to mention one prominent feature of that position, has no metaphysical implications concerning the nature of the self; it does not imply that the self is ontologically prior to the facts about persons that the parties are excluded from knowing. We can, as it were, enter this position any time simply by reasoning for principles of justice in accordance with the enumerated restrictions. When, in this way, we simulate being in this position, our reasoning no more commits us to a metaphysical doctrine about the nature of the self than our playing a game like Monopoly commits us to thinking that we are landlords engaged in a desperate rivalry, winner take all.[21] We must keep in mind that we are trying to show how the idea of society as a fair system of social cooperation can be unfolded so as to specify the most appropriate principles for realizing the institutions of liberty and equality when citizens are regarded as free and equal persons.

V

I just remarked that the idea of the original position and the description of the parties may tempt us to think that a metaphysical doctrine of the person is presupposed. While I said that this interpretation is mistaken, it is not enough simply to disavow reliance on metaphysical doctrines, for despite one's intent they may still be involved. To rebut claims of this nature requires discussing them in detail and showing that they have no foothold. I cannot do that here.[22]

I can, however, sketch a positive account of the political conception of the person, that is, the conception of the person as citizen (discussed in Section III), involved in the original position as a device of representation. To explain what is meant by describing a conception of the person as political, let's consider how citizens are represented in the original position as free persons. The representation of their freedom seems to be one source of the idea that some metaphysical doctrine is presupposed. I have said elsewhere that citizens view themselves as free in three respects, so let's survey each of these briefly and indicate the way in which the conception of the person used is political.[23]

First, citizens are free in that they conceive of themselves and of one another as having the moral power to have a conception of the good. This is not to say that, as part of their political conception of themselves, they view themselves as inevitably tied to the pursuit of the particular conception of the good which they affirm at any given time. Instead, as citizens, they are regarded as capable of revising and changing this conception on reasonable and rational grounds, and they may do this if they so desire. Thus, as free persons, citizens claim the right to view their persons as independent from and as not identified with any particular conception of the good, or scheme of final ends. Given their moral power to form, to revise, and rationally to pursue a conception of the good, their public identity as free persons is not affected by changes over time in their conception of the good. For example, when citizens convert from one religion to another, or no longer affirm an established religious faith, they do not cease to be, for questions of political justice, the same persons they were before. There is no loss of what we may call their public identity, their identity as a matter of basic law. In general, they still have the same basic rights and duties; they own the same property and can make the same claims as before, except insofar as these claims were connected with their previous religious affiliation. We can imagine a society (indeed, history offers numerous examples) in which basic rights and recognized claims depend on religious affiliation, social class, and so on. Such a society has a different political conception of the person. It may not have a conception of citizenship at all; for this conception, as we are using it, goes with the conception of society as a fair system of cooperation for mutual advantage between free and equal persons.

It is essential to stress that citizens in their personal affairs, or in the internal life of associations to which they belong, may regard their final ends and attachments in a way very different from the way the political conception involves. Citizens may have, and normally do have at any given time, affections, devotions, and loyalties that they believe they would not, and indeed could and should not, stand apart from and objectively evaluate from the point of view of their purely rational good. They may regard it as simply unthinkable to view themselves apart from certain religious, philosophical, and moral convictions, or from certain enduring attachments and loyalties. These convictions and attachments are part of what we may call their "nonpublic identity." These convictions and attachments help to organize and give shape to a person's way of life, what one sees onself as doing and trying to accomplish in one's social world. We think that if we were suddenly without these particular convictions and attachments we would be disoriented and unable to carry on. In fact, there would be, we might think, no point in carrying on. But our conceptions of the good may and often do change over time, usually slowly but sometimes rather suddenly. When these changes are sudden, we are particularly likely to say that we are no longer the same person. We know what this means: we refer to a profound and pervasive shift, or reversal, in our final ends and character; we refer to our different nonpublic, and possibly moral or religious, identity. On the road to Damascus Saul of Tarsus becomes Paul the Apostle. There is no change in our public or political identity, nor in our personal identity as this concept is understood by some writers in the philosophy of mind.[24]

The second respect in which citizens view themselves as free is that they regard themselves as self-originating sources of valid claims. They think their claims have weight apart from being derived from duties or obligations specified by the political conception of justice, for example, from duties and obligations owed to society. Claims that citizens regard as founded on duties and obligations based on their conception of the good and the moral doctrine they affirm in their own life are also, for our purposes here, to be counted as self-originating. Doing this is reasonable in a political conception of justice for a constitutional democracy; for provided the conceptions of the good and the moral doctrines citizens affirm are compatible with the public conception of justice, these duties and obligations are self-originating from the political point of view.

When we describe a way in which citizens regard themselves as free, we are describing how citizens actually think of themselves in a democratic society should questions of justice arise. In our conception of a constitutional regime, this is an aspect of how citizens regard themselves. That this aspect of their freedom belongs to a particular political conception is clear from the contrast with a different political conception in which the members of society are not viewed as self-originating sources of valid claims. Rather, their claims have no weight except insofar as they can be derived from their duties and obligations owed to society, or from their ascribed roles in the social hierarchy justified by religious or aristocratic values. Or to take an extreme case, slaves are human beings who are not counted as sources of claims, not even claims based on social duties or obligations, for slaves are not counted as capable of having duties or obligations. Laws that prohibit the abuse and maltreatment of slaves are not founded on claims made by slaves on their own behalf, but on claims originating either from slaveholders, or from the general interests of society (which does not include the interests of slaves). Slaves are, so to speak, socially dead: they are not publicly recognized as persons at all.[25] Thus, the contrast with a political conception which allows slavery makes clear why conceiving of citizens as free persons in virtue of their moral powers and their having a conception of the good, goes with a particular political conception of the person. This conception of persons fits into a political conception of justice founded on the idea of society as a system of cooperation between its members conceived as free and equal.

The third respect in which citizens are regarded as free is that they are regarded as capable of taking responsibility for their ends and this affects how their various claims are assessed.[26] Very roughly, the idea is that, given just background institutions and given for each person a fair index of primary goods (as required by the principles of justice), citizens are thought to be capable of adjusting their aims and aspirations in the light of what they can reasonably expect to provide for. Moreover, they are regarded as capable of restricting their claims in matters of justice to the kinds of things the principles of justice allow. Thus, citizens are to recognize that the weight of their claims is not given by the strength and psychological intensity of their wants and desires (as opposed to their needs and requirements as citizens), even when their wants and desires are rational from their point of view. I cannot pursue these matters here. But the procedure is the same as before: we start with the basic intuitive idea of society as a system of social cooperation. When this idea is developed into a conception of political justice, it implies that, viewing ourselves as persons who can engage in social cooperation over a complete life, we can also take responsibility for our ends, that is, that we can adjust our ends so that they can be pursued by the means we can reasonably expect to acquire given our prospects and situation in society. The idea of responsibility for ends is implicit in the public political culture and discernible in its practices. A political conception of the person articulates this idea and fits it into the idea of society as a system of social cooperation over a complete life.

To sum up, I recapitulate three main points of this and the preceding two sections:

First, in Section III persons were regarded as free and equal in virtue of their possessing to the requisite degree the two powers of moral personality (and the powers of reason, thought, and judgment connected with these powers), namely, the capacity for a sense of justice and the capacity for a conception of the good. These powers we associated with two main elements of the idea of cooperation, the idea of fair terms of cooperation and the idea of each participant's rational advantage, or good.

Second, in this section (Section V), we have briefly surveyed three respects in which persons are regarded as free, and we have noted that in the public political culture of a constitutional democratic regime citizens conceive of themselves as free in these respects.

Third, since the question of which conception of political justice is most appropriate for realizing in basic institutions the values of liberty and equality has long been deeply controversial within the very democratic tradition in which citizens are regarded as free and equal persons, the aim of justice as fairness is to try to resolve this question by starting from the basic intuitive idea of society as a fair system of social cooperation in which the fair terms of cooperation are agreed upon by citizens themselves so conceived. In Section IV, we saw why this approach leads to the idea of the original position as a device of representation.

VI

I now take up a point essential to thinking of justice as fairness as a liberal view. Although this conception is a moral conception, it is not, as I have said, intended as a comprehensive moral doctrine. The conception of the citizen as a free and equal person is not a moral ideal to govern all of life, but is rather an ideal belonging to a conception of political justice which is to apply to the basic structure. I emphasize this point because to think otherwise would be incompatible with liberalism as a political doctrine. Recall that as such a doctrine, liberalism assumes that in a constitutional democratic state under modern conditions there are bound to exist conflicting and incommensurable conceptions of the good. This feature characterizes modern culture since the Reformation. Any viable political conception of justice that is not to rely on the autocratic use of state power must recognize this fundamental social fact. This does not mean, of course, that such a conception cannot impose constraints on individuals and associations, but that when it does so, these constraints are accounted for, directly or indirectly, by the requirements of political justice for the basic structure.[27]

Given this fact, we adopt a conception of the person framed as part of, and restricted to, an explicitly political conception of justice. In this sense, the conception of the person is a political one. As I stressed in the previous section, persons can accept this conception of themselves as citizens and use it when discussing questions of political justice without being committed in other parts of their life to comprehensive moral ideals often associated with liberalism, for example, the ideals of autonomy and individuality. The absence of commitment to these ideals, and indeed to any particular comprehensive ideal, is essential to liberalism as a political doctrine. The reason is that any such ideal, when pursued as a comprehensive ideal, is incompatible with other conceptions of the good, with forms of personal, moral, and religious life consistent with justice and which, therefore, have a proper place in a democratic society. As comprehensive moral ideals, autonomy and individuality are unsuited for a political conception of justice. As found in Kant and J. S. Mill, these comprehensive ideals, despite their very great importance in liberal thought, are extended too far when presented as the only appropriate foundation for a constitutional regime.[28] So understood, liberalism becomes but another sectarian doctrine.

This conclusion requires comment: it does not mean, of course, that the liberalisms of Kant and Mill are not appropriate moral conceptions from which we can be led to affirm democratic institutions. But they are only two such conceptions among others, and so but two of the philosophical doctrines likely to persist and gain adherents in a reasonably just democratic regime. In such a regime the comprehensive moral views which support its basic institutions may include the liberalisms of individuality and autonomy; and possibly these liberalisms are among the more prominent doctrines in an overlapping consensus, that is, in a consensus in which, as noted earlier, different and even conflicting doctrines affirm the publicly shared basis of political arrangements. The liberalisms of Kant and Mill have a certain historical preeminence as among the first and most important philosophical views to espouse modern constitutional democracy and to develop its underlying ideas in an influential way; and it may even turn out that societies in which the ideals of autonomy and individuality are widely accepted are among the most well-governed and harmonious.[29]

By contrast with liberalism as a comprehensive moral doctrine, justice as fairness tries to present a conception of political justice rooted in the basic intuitive ideas found in the public culture of a constitutional democracy. We conjecture that these ideas are likely to be affirmed by each of the opposing comprehensive moral doctrines influential in a reasonably just democratic society. Thus justice as fairness seeks to identify the kernel of an overlapping consensus, that is, the shared intuitive ideas which when worked up into a political conception of justice turn out to be sufficient to underwrite a just constitutional regime. This is the most we can expect, nor do we need more.[30] We must note, however, that when justice as fairness is fully realized in a well-ordered society, the value of full autonomy is likewise realized. In this way justice as fairness is indeed similar to the liberalisms of Kant and Mill; but in contrast with them, the value of full autonomy is here specified by a political conception of justice, and not by a comprehensive moral doctrine.

It may appear that, so understood, the public acceptance of justice as fairness is no more than prudential; that is, that those who affirm this conception do so simply as a *modus vivendi* which allows the groups in the overlapping consensus to pursue their own good subject to certain constraints which each thinks to be for its advantage given existing circumstances. The idea of an overlapping consensus may seem essentially Hobbesian. But against this, two remarks: first, justice as fairness is a moral conception: it has conceptions of person and society, and concepts of right and fairness, as well as principles of justice with their complement of the virtues through which those principles are embodied in human character and regulate political and social life. This conception of justice provides an account of the cooperative virtues suitable for a political doctrine in view of the conditions and requirements of a constitutional regime. It is no less a moral conception because it is restricted to the basic structure of society, since this restriction is what enables it to serve as a political conception of justice given our present circumstances. Thus, in an overlapping consensus (as understood here), the conception of justice as fairness is not regarded merely as a *modus vivendi.*

Second, in such a consensus each of the comprehensive philosophical, religious, and moral doctrines accepts justice as fairness in its own way; that is, each comprehensive doctrine, from within its own point of view, is led to accept the public reasons of justice specified by justice as fairness. We might say that they recognize its concepts, principles, and virtues as theorems, as it were, at which their several views coincide. But this does not make these points of coincidence any less moral or reduce them to mere means. For, in general, these concepts, principles, and virtues are accepted by each as belonging to a more comprehensive philosophical, religious, or moral doctrine. Some may even affirm justice as fairness as a natural moral conception that can stand on its own feet. They accept this conception of justice as a reasonable basis for political and social cooperation, and hold that it is as natural and fundamental as the concepts and principles of honesty and mutual trust, and the virtues of cooperation in everyday life. The doctrines in an overlapping consensus differ in how far they maintain a further foundation is necessary and on what that further foundation should be. These differences, however, are compatible with a consensus on justice as fairness as a political conception of justice.

VII

I shall conclude by considering the way in which social unity and stability may be understood by liberalism as a political doctrine (as opposed to a comprehensive moral conception).[31]

One of the deepest distinctions between political conceptions of justice is between those that allow for a plurality of opposing and even incomensurable conceptions of the good and those that hold that there is but one conception of the good which is to be recognized by all persons, so far as they are fully rational. Conceptions of justice which fall on opposite sides of this divide are distinct in many fundamental ways. Plato and Aristole, and the Christian tradition as represented by Augustine and Aquinas, fall on the side of the one rational good. Such views tend to be teleological and to hold that institutions are just to the extent that they effectively promote this good. Indeed, since classical times the dominant tradition seems to have been that there is but one rational conception of the good, and that the aim of moral philosophy, together with theology and metaphysics, is to determine its nature. Classical utilitarianism belongs to this dominant tradition. By contrast, liberalism as a political doctrine supposes that there are many conflicting and incommensurable conceptions of the good, each compatible with the full rationality of human persons, so far as we can ascertain within a workable political conception of justice. As a consequence of this supposition, liberalism assumes that it is a characteristic feature of a free democratic culture that a plurality of conflicting and incommensurable conceptions of the good are affirmed by its citizens. Liberalism as a political doctrine holds that the question the dominant tradition has tried to answer has no practicable answer; that is, it has no answer suitable for a political conception of justice for a democratic society. In such a society a teleological political conception is out of the question: public agreement on the requisite conception of the good cannot be obtained.

As I have remarked, the historical origin of this liberal supposition is the Reformation and its consequences. Until the Wars of Religion in the sixteenth and seventeenth centuries, the fair terms of social cooperation were narrowly drawn: social cooperation on the basis of mutual respect was regarded as impossible with persons of a different faith; or (in the terminology I have used) with persons who affirm a fundamentally different conception of the good. Thus one of the historical roots of liberalism was the development of various doctrines urging religious toleration. One theme in justice as fairness is to recognize the social conditions that give rise to these doctrines as among the so-called subjective circumstances of justice and then to spell out the implications of the principle of toleration.[32] As liberalism is stated by Constant, de Tocqueville, and Mill in the nineteenth century, it accepts the plurality of incommensurable conceptions of the good as a fact of modern democratic culture, provided, of course, these conceptions respect the limits specified by the appropriate principles of justice. One task of liberalism as a political doctrine is to answer the question: how is social unity to be understood, given that there can be no public agreement on the one rational good, and a plurality of opposing and incommensurable conceptions must be taken as given? And granted that social unity is conceivable in some definite way, under what conditions is it actually possible?

In justice as fairness, social unity is understood by starting with the conception of society as a system of cooperation between free and equal persons. Social unity and the allegiance of citizens to their common institutions are not founded on their all affirming the same conception of the good, but on their publicly accepting a political conception of justice to regulate the basic structure of society. The concept of justice is independent from and prior to the concept of goodness in the sense that its principles limit the conceptions of the good which are permissible. A just basic structure and its background institutions establish a framework within which permissible conceptions can be advanced. Elsewhere I have called this relation between a conception of justice and conceptions of the good the priority of right (since the just falls under the right). I believe this priority is characteristic of liberalism as a political doctrine and something like it seems essential to any conception of justice reasonable for a democratic state. Thus to understand how social unity is possible given the historical conditions of a democratic society, we start with our basic intuitive idea of social cooperation, an idea present in the public culture of a democratic society, and proceed from there to a public conception of justice as the basis of social unity in the way I have sketched.

As for the question of whether this unity is stable, this importantly depends on the content of the religious, philosophical, and moral doctrines available to constitute an overlapping consensus. For example, assuming the public political conception to be justice as fairness, imagine citizens to affirm one of three views: the first view affirms justice as fairness because its religious beliefs and understanding of faith lead to a principle of toleration and underwrite the fundamental idea of society as a scheme of social cooperation between free and equal persons; the second view affirms it as a consequence of a comprehensive liberal moral conception such as those of Kant and Mill; while the third affirms justice as fairness not as a consequence of any wider doctrine but as in itself sufficient to express values that normally outweigh whatever other values might oppose them, at least under reasonably favorable conditions. This overlapping consensus appears far more stable than one founded on views that express skepticism and indifference to religious, philosophical, and moral values, or that regard the acceptance of the principles of justice simply as a prudent *modus vivendi* given the existing balance of social forces. Of course, there are many other possibilities.

The strength of a conception like justice as fairness may prove to be that the more comprehensive doctrines that persist and gain adherents in a democratic society regulated by its principles are likely to cohere together into a more or less stable overlapping consensus. But obviously all this is highly speculative and raises questions which are little understood, since doctrines which persist and gain adherents depend in part on social conditions, and in particular, on these conditions when regulated by the public conception of justice. Thus we are forced to consider at some point the effects of the social conditions required by a conception of political justice on the acceptance of that conception itself. Other things equal, a conception will be more or less stable depending on how far the conditions to which it leads support comprehensive religious, philosophical, and moral doctrines which can constitute a stable overlapping consensus. These questions of stability I cannot discuss here.[33] It suffices to remark that in a society marked by deep divisions between opposing and incommensurable conceptions of the good justice as fairness enables us at least to conceive how social unity can be both possible and stable.

NOTES

1. Cambridge, MA: Harvard University Press, 1971.
2. A number of these changes, or shifts of emphasis, are evident evident in three lectures entitled "Kantian Constructivism in Moral Theory," *Journal of Philosophy* 77 (September 1980). For example, the account of what I have called "primary goods" is revised so that it clearly depends on a particular conception of persons and their higher-order interests; hence this account is not a purely psychological, sociological, or historical thesis. See pp. 526f. There is also throughout those lectures a more explicit emphasis on the role of a conception of the person as well as on the idea that the justification of a conception of justice is a practical social task rather than an epistemological or metaphysical problem. See pp. 518f. And in this connection the idea of "Kantian constructivism" is introduced, especially in the third lecture. It must be noted, however, that this idea is not proposed as Kant's idea: the adjective "Kantian" indicates analogy not identity, that is, resemblance in enough fundamental respects so that the adjective is appropriate. These fundamental respects are certain structural features of justice as fairness and elements of its content, such as the distinction between what may be called

the Reasonable and the Rational, the priority of right, and the role of the conception of the persons as free and equal, and capable of autonomy, and so on. Resemblances of structural features and content are not to be mistaken for resemblances with Kant's views on questions of epistemology and metaphysics. Finally, I should remark that the title of those lectures, "Kantian Constructivism in Moral Theory," was misleading; since the conception of justice discussed is a political conception, a better title would have been "Kantian Constructivism in Political Philosophy." Whether constructivism is reasonable for moral philosophy is a separate and more general question.

3. *Theory*, Sec. 2, and see the index; see also "The Basic Structure as Subject," in *Values and Morals*, eds. Alvin Goldman and Jaegwon Kim (Dordrecht: Reidel, 1978), pp. 47–71.

4. See "Basic Structure as Subject," ibid., pp. 48–50.

5. This idea was introduced in *Theory*, pp. 387f., as a way to weaken the conditions for the reasonableness of civil disobedience in a nearly just democratic society. Here and later in Secs. VI and VII it is used in a wider context.

6. *Theory*, Preface, p. viii.

7. Ibid., pp. 582f. On the role of a conception of justice in reducing the revergence of opinion, see pp. 44f., 53, 314, and 564. At various places the limited aims in developing a conception of justice are noted: see p. 364 on not expecting too much of an account of civil disobedience; pp. 200f. on the inevitable indeterminacy of a conception of justice in specifying a series of points of view from which questions of justice can be resolved; pp. 89f. on the social wisdom of recognizing that perhaps only a few moral problems (it would have been better to say: problems of political justice) can be satisfactorily settled, and thus of framing institutions so that intractable questions do not arise; on pp. 53, 87ff., 320f. the need to accept simplifications is emphasized. Regarding the last point, see also "Kantian Constructivism," pp. 560–64.

8. The statement of these principles differs from that given in *Theory* and follows the statement in "The Basic Liberties and Their Priority," *Tanner Lectures on Human Values*, Vol. III (Salt Lake City: University of Utah Press, 1982), p. 5. The reasons for the changes are discussed at pp. 46–55 of that lecture. They are important for the revisions made in the account of the basic liberties found in *Theory* in the attempt to answer the objections of H.L.A. Hart; but they need not concern us here.

9. ·The idea of the worth of these guarentees is discussed ibid., pp. 40f.

10. *Theory*, pp. 20f., 48–51, and 120f.

11. Ibid., pp. 580–83.

12. Ibid., pp. 214f.

13. On Kantian constructivism, see especially the third lecture referrerd to in footnote 2 above.

14. Although *Theory* uses this idea from the outset (it is introduced on p. 4), it does not emphasize, as I do here and in "Kantian Constructivism," that the basic ideas of justice as fairness are regarded as implicit or latent in the public culture of a democratic society.

15. It should be emphasized that a conception of the person, as I understand it here, is a normative conception, whether legal, political, or moral, or indeed also philosophical or religious, depending on the overall view to which it belongs. In this case the conception of the person is a moral conception, one that begins from our everyday conception of persons as the basic units of thought, deliberation and responsibility, and adapted to a political conception of justice and not to a comprehensive moral doctrine. It is in effect a political conception of the person, and given the aims of justice as fairness, a conception of citizens. Thus, a conception of the person is to be distinguished from an

account of human nature given by natural science or social theory. On this point, see "Kantian Constructivism," pp. 534f.

16. *Theory*, Sec. 77.

17. Ibid., Sec. 4, Ch. 3, and the index.

18. In the veil of ignorance, see ibid., Sec. 24, and the index.

19. This question is raised by Ronald Dworkin in the first part of his very illuminating, and to me highly instructive, essay "Justice and Rights" (1973), reprinted in *Taking Rights Seriously* (Cambridge, MA: Harvard University Press, 1977). Dworkin considers several ways of explaining the use of the original position in an account of justice that invokes the idea of the social contract. In the last part of the essay (pp. 173–83), after having surveyed some of the constructivist features of justice as fairness (pp. 159–68) and argued that it is a right-based and not a duty-based or a goal-based view (pp. 168–77), he proposes that the original position with the veil of ignorance be seen as modeling the force of the natural right that individuals have to equal concern and respect in the design of the political institutions that govern them (p. 180). He thinks that this natural right lies as the basis of justice as fairness and that the original position serves as a device for testing which principles of justice this right requires. This is an ingenious suggestion but I have not followed it in the text. I prefer not to think of justice as fairness as a right-based view; indeed, Dworkin's classification scheme of right-based, duty-based, and goal-based views (pp. 171f.) is too narrow and leaves out important possibilities. Thus, as explained in Sec. II above, I think of justice as fairness as working up into idealized conceptions certain fundamental intuitive ideas such as those of the person as free and equal, of a well-ordered society, and of the public role of a conception of political justice, and as connecting these fundamental intuitive ideas with the even more fundamental and comprehensive intuitive idea of society as a fair system of cooperation over time from one generation to the next. Rights, duties, and goals are but elements of such idealized conceptions. Thus, justice as fairness is a conception-based, or as Elizabeth Anderson has suggested to me, an ideal-based view, since these fundamental intuitive ideas reflect ideals implicit or latent in the public culture of a democratic society. In this context the original position is a device of representation that models the force, not of the natural right of equal concern and respect, but of the essential elements of these fundamental intuitive ideas as identified by the reasons for principles of justice that we accept on due reflection. As such a device, it serves first to combine and then to focus the resultant force of all these reasons in selecting the most appropriate principles of justice for a democratic society. (In doing this the force of the natural right of equal concern and respect will be covered in other ways.) This account of the use of the original position resembles in some respects an account Dworkin rejects in the first part of his essay, especially pp. 153f. In view of the ambiguity and obscurity of *Theory* on many of the points he considers, it is not my aim to criticize Dworkin's valuable discussion, but rather to indicate how my understanding of the original position differs from his. Others may prefer his account.

20. The original position models a basic feature of Kantian constructivism, namely, the distinction between the Reasonable and the Rational, with the Reasonable as prior to the Rational. (For an explanation of this distinction, see "Kantian Constructivism," pp. 528–32, and passim.) The relevance of this distinction here is that *Theory* more or less consistently speaks not of rational but of reasonable (or sometimes of fitting or appropriate) conditions as constraints on arguments for principles of justice (see pp. 18f., 20f., 120f., 130f., 138, 446, 516f., 578, 584f.). These constraints are modeled in the original position and thereby imposed on the parties: their deliberations are subject,

and subject absolutely, to the reasonable conditions the modeling of which makes the original position fair. The Reasonable, then, is prior to the Rational, and this gives the priority of right. Thus, it was an error in *Theory* (and a very misleading one) to describe a theory of justice as part of the theory of rational choice, as on pp. 16 and 583. What I should have said is that the conception of justice as fairness uses an account of rational choice subject to reasonable conditions to characterize the deliberations of the parties as representatives of free and equal persons; and all of this within a political conception of justice, which is, of course, a moral conception. There is no thought of trying to derive the content of justice within a framework that uses an idea of the rational as the sole normative idea. That thought is incompatible with any kind of Kantian view.

21. *Theory*, pp. 138f., 147. The parties in the original position are said (p. 147) to be theoretically defined individuals whose motivations are specified by the account of that position and not by a psychological view about how human beings are actually motivated. This is also part of what is meant by saying (p. 121) that the acceptance of the particular principles of justice is not conjectured as a psychological law or probability but rather follows from the full description of the original position. Although the aim cannot be perfectly achieved, we want the argument to be deductive, "a kind of moral geometry." In "Kantian Constructivism" (p. 532) the parties are described as merely artificial agents who inhabit a construction. Thus I think R. B. Brandt mistaken in objecting that the argument from the original position is based on defective psychology. See his *A Theory of the Good and the Right* (Oxford: Clarendon Press, 1979), pp. 239–42. Of course, one might object to the original position that it models the conception of the person and the deliberations of the parties in ways that are unsuitable for the purposes of a political conception of justice; but for these purposes psychological theory is not directly relevant. On the other hand, psychological theory is relevant for the account of the stability of a conception of justice, as discussed in *Theory*, Pt. III. See below, footnote 33. Similarly, I think Michael Sandel mistaken in supposing that the original position involves a conception of the self " . . .shorn of all its contingently-given attributes," a self that "assumes a kind of supra-empirical status, . . . and given prior to its ends, a pure subject of agency and possession, ultimately thin." See *Liberalism and the Limits of Justice* (Cambridge: Cambridge University Press, 1982), pp. 93–95. I cannot discuss these criticisms in any detail. The essential point (as suggested in the introductory remarks) is not whether certain passages in *Theory* call for such an interpretation (I doubt that they do), but whether the conception of justice as fairness presented therein can be understood in the light of the interpretation I sketch in this article and in the earlier lectures on constructivism, as I believe it can be.

22. Part of the difficulty is that there is no accepted understanding of what a metaphysical doctrine is. One might say, as Paul Hoffman has suggested to me, that to develop a political conception of justice without presupposing, or explicitly using, a metaphysical doctrine, for example, some particular metaphysical conception of the person, is already to presuppose a metaphysical thesis: namely, that no particular metaphysical doctrine is required for this purpose. One might also say that our everyday conception of persons as the basic units of deliberation and responsibility presupposes, or in some way involves, certain metaphysical theses about the nature of persons as moral or political agents. Following the method of avoidance, I should not want to deny these claims. What should be said is the following. If we look at the presentation of justice as fairness and note how it is set up, and note the ideas and conceptions it uses, no particular metaphysical doctrine about the nature of persons, distinctive and opposed to

other metaphysical doctrines, appears among its premises, or seems required by its argument. If metaphysical presuppositions are involved, perhaps they are so general that they would not distinguish between the distinctive metaphysical views—Cartesian, Leibnizian, or Kantia; realist, idealist, or materialist—with which philosophy traditionally has been concerned. In this case, they would not appear to be relevant for the structure and content of a political conception of justice one way or the other. I am grateful to Danial Brudney and Paul Hoffman for discussion of these matters.

23. For the first two respects, see "Kantian Constructivism," pp. 544f. (For the third respect, see footnote 26 below.) The account of the first two respects found in those lectures is further developed in the text above and I am more explicit on the distinction between what I call here our "public" versus our "nonpublic or moral identity." The point of the term "moral" in the latter phrase is to indicate that persons' conceptions of the (complete) good are normally an essential element in characterizing their nonpublic (or nonpolitical) identity, and these conceptions are understood as normally containing important moral elements, although they include other elements as well, philosophical and religious. The term "moral" should be thought of as a stand-in for all these possibilities. I am indebted to Elizabeth Anderson for discussion and clarification of this distinction.

24. Here I assume that an answer to the problem of personal identity tries to specify the various criteria (for example, psychological continuity of memories and physical continuity of body, or some part thereof) in accordance with which two different psychological states, or actions (or whatever), which occur at two different times may be said to be states or actions of the same person who endures over time; and it also tries to specify how this enduring person is to be conceived, whether as a Cartesian or a Leibnizian substance, or as a Kantian transcendental ego, or as a continuant of some other kind, for example, bodily or physical. See the collection of essays edited by John Perry, *Personal Identity* (Berkeley, CA: University of California Press, 1975), especially Perry's introduction, pp. 3–30; and Sydney Shoemaker's essay in *Personal Identity* (Oxford: Basil Blackwell, 1984), both of which consider a number of views. Sometimes in discussions of this problem, continuity of fundamental aims and aspirations is largely ignored, for example, in views like H. P. Grice's (included in Perry's collection) which emphasizes continuity of memory. Of course, once continuity of fundamental aims and aspirations is brought in, as in Derek Parfit's *Reasons and Persons* (Oxford: Clarendon Press, 1984), Pt. III, there is no sharp distinction between the problem of persons' nonpublic or moral identity and the problem of their personal identity. This latter problem raises profound questions on which past and current philosophical views widely differ, and surely will continue to differ. For this reason it is important to try to develop a political conception of justice which avoids this problem as far as possible.

25. For the idea of social death, see Orlando Patterson, *Slave and Social Death* (Cambridge, MA: Harvard University Press, 1982), esp. pp. 5–9, 38–45, 337. This idea is interestingly developed in this book and has a central place in the author's comparative study of slavery.

26. See "Social Unity and Primary Goods," in *Utilitarianism and Beyond*, eds. Amartya Sen and Bernard Williams (Cambridge: Cambridge University Press, 1982), Sec. IV, pp. 167–70.

27. For example, churches are constrained by the principle of equal liberty of conscience and must conform to the principle of toleration, universities by what may be required to maintain fair equality of opportunity, and the rights of parents by what is necessary to maintain their childrens' physical well-being and to assure the adequate develop-

ment of their intellectual and moral powers. Because churches, universities, and parents exercise their authority within the basic structure, they are to recognize the requirements this structure imposes to maintain background justice.

28. For Kant, see *The Foundations of the Metaphysics of Morals* and *The Critique of Practical Reason.* For Mill, see *On Liberty,* particularly Ch. 3, where the ideal of individuality is most fully discussed.

29. This point has been made with respect to the liberalisms of Kant and Mill, but for American culture one should mention the important conceptions of democratic individuality expressed in the works of Emerson, Thoreau, and Whitman. These are instructively discussed by George Kateb in his "Democratic Individuality and the Claims of Politics," *Political Theory* 12 (August 1984).

30. For the idea of the kernel of an overlapping consensus (mentioned above), see *Theory,* last par. of Sec. 35, pp. 220f. For the idea of full autonomy, see "Kantian Constructivism," pp. 528ff.

31. This account of social unity is found in "Social Unity and Primary Goods," referred to in footnote 27 above. See esp. pp. 160f., 170–73, 183f.

32. The distinction between the objective and the subjective circumstances of justice is made in *Theory,* pp. 126ff. The importance of the role of the subjective circumstances is emphasized in "Kantian Constructivism," pp. 540–42.

33. Part III of *Theory* has mainly three aims: first to give an account of goodness as rationality (Ch. 7) which is to provide the basis for identifying primary goods, those goods which, given the conception of persons, the parties are to assume are needed by the persons they represent (pp. 397, 433f.); second, to give an account of the stability of the stability of a conception of justice (Chs. 8–9), and of justice as fairness in particular, and to show that this conception is more stable than other traditional conceptions with which it is compared, as well as stable enough; and third, to give an account of the good of a well-ordered society, that is, of a just society in which justice as fairness is the publicly affirmed and effectively realized political conception of justice (Chs. 8–9 and culminating in Sec. 86). Among the faults of Part III, I now think, are these. The account of goodness as rationality often reads as an account of the complete good for a comprehensive moral conception: all it need do is to explain the list of primary goods and the basis of the various natural goods recognized by common sense and in particular, the fundamental significance of self-respect and self-esteem (which, as David Sachs and Laurence Thomas have pointed out to me, are not properly distinguished), and so of the social bases of self-respect as a primary good. Also, the account of the stability of justice as fairness was not extended, as it should have been, to the important case of overlapping consensus, as sketched in the text: instead, this account was limited to the simplest case where the public conception of justice is affirmed as in itself sufficient to express values that normally outweigh, given the political context of a constitutional regime, whatever values might oppose them (see the third view in the overlapping consensus indicated in the text). In view of the discussion in Secs. 32–35 of Ch. 4 of liberty of conscience, the extension to the case of overlapping consensus is essential. Finally, the relevance of the idea of a well-ordered society as a social unions of social unions to giving an account of the good of a just society was not explained fully enough. Throughout Part III too many connections are left for the reader to make, so that one may be left in doubt as to the point of much of Chs. 8 and 9.

COMMUNITARIANISM AND CULTURE

Liberalism identifies democracy with the constitutional state, due process, and the civil liberties enjoyed by the individual. But it ignores the substantive concerns of democracy in favor of its formal characteristics. Or, at least, such is the communitarian view. John Dewey provides a foundation for this argument in a seminal chapter, "The Search for the Great Community," from *The Public and Its Problems*. Government is, for Dewey, merely a mechanism for securing the effective operation of democracy, and bureaucracy often threatens its real purpose: participation.

Political activity presupposes a context, or a "community," and this is also the case for ideals such as equality and liberty. The great advocate of pragmatism, in fact, actually defines democracy as "the idea of community life itself." Equality comes to mean more than the "mechanical identity" of individuals within a community and liberty is, for him, purely abstract if it is defined in terms of autonomy from all social ties or as the simple affirmation of individualism. People are the socialized products of various group formations and must be recognized as such. For this reason, only in a community can the communication between different interests, through which the public can genuinely define its interests, take place.

But the ability to articulate those interests, and to reflect upon them, is precisely what modern life appears to undermine. As a consequence, according to Hannah Arendt, politics is in danger of losing its deeper meaning. The social character of modern life is threatening what previously were understood as the private and the public realm. This selection from her classic study, *The Human Condition,* analyzes a situation in which the private either defines the public or, in the case of authoritarian forms of collectivism, is invaded by it. Politics disappears along with any direct interchange among citizens concerned with existential and normative rather than purely instrumental issues. Alienation is the result of a world in which the bureaucratic state has supplanted the Greek *polis*.

"The Procedural Republic and the Unencumbered Self," by Michael Sandel, seeks to explore some of these themes for this moment in time. He identifies liberalism with the inalienable rights of the individual and the refusal to identify its regulative principles with any vision of the "good." Liberalism offers, in short, an impartial framework within which individuals can decide upon their own ends as well as those of the society within which they live. This presupposes a free and rational subject unencumbered by emotional attachments to any particular tradition or group; its commitment to freedom makes this vision attractive. But, according to Sandel, it fails to make sense of either everyday morality with its historically situated allegiances or political life wherein the interests of the community demand expression. Liberalism deprives the individual of his or her traditions even as it lacks the categories with which to make sense of history or a community. This is precisely what requires correction by the communitarians.

JOHN DEWEY

The Search
for the Great Community

We have had occasion to refer in passing to the distinction between democracy as a social idea and political democracy as a system of government. The two are, of course, connected. The idea remains barren and empty save as it is incarnated in human relationships. Yet in discussion they must be distinguished. The idea of democracy is a wider and fuller idea than can be exemplified in the state even at its best. To be realized it must affect all modes of human association, the family, the school, industry, religion. And even as far as political arrangements are concerned, governmental institutions are but a mechanism for securing to an idea channels of effective operation. It will hardly do to say that criticisms of the political machinery leave the believer in the idea untouched. For, as far as they are justified—and no candid believer can deny that many of them are only too well grounded—they arouse him to bestir himself in order that the idea may find a more adequate machinery through which to work. What the faithful insist upon, however, is that the idea and its external organs and structures are not to be identified. We object to the common supposition of the foes of existing democratic government that the accusations against it touch the social and moral aspirations and ideas which underlie the political forms. The old saying that the cure for the ills of democracy is more democracy is not apt if it means that the evils may be remedied by introducing more machinery of the same kind as that which already exists, or by refining and perfecting that machinery. But the phrase may also indicate the need of returning to the idea itself, of clarifying and deepening our apprehension of it, and of employing our sense of its meaning to criticize and re-make its political mainfestations.

Confining ourselves, for the moment, to political democracy, we must, in any case, renew our protest against the assumption that the idea has itself produced the governmental practices which obtain in democratic states: general suffrage, elected representatives, majority rule, and so on. The idea has influenced the concrete political movement, but it has not caused it. The transition from family and dynastic government supported by

the loyalties of tradition to popular government was the outcome primarily of technological discoveries and inventions working a change in the customs by which men had been
bound together. It was not due to the doctrines of doctrinaires. The forms to which we
are accustomed in democratic governments represent the cumulative effect of a multitude
of events, unpremeditated as far as political effects were concerned and having unpredictable consequences. There is no sanctity in universal suffrage, frequent elections, majority rule, congressional and cabinet government. These things are devices evolved in the
direction in which the current was moving, each wave of which involved at the time of its
impulsion a minimum of departure from antecedent custom and law. The devices served a
purpose; but the purpose was rather that of meeting existing needs which had become too
intense to be ignored, than that of forwarding the democratic idea. In spite of all defects,
they served their own purpose well.

Looking back, with the aid which *ex posto facto* experience can give, it would be hard
for the wisest to devise schemes which, under the circumstances, would have met the
needs better. In this retrospective glance, it is possible, however, to see how the doctrinal
formulations which accompanied them were inadequate, one-sided and positively erroneous. In fact they were hardly more than political war-cries adopted to help in carrying
on some immediate agitation or in justifying some particular practical polity struggling
for recognition, even though they were asserted to be absolute truths of human nature or
of morals. The doctrines served a particular local pragmatic need. But often their very
adaptation to immediate circumstances unfitted them, pragmatically, to meet more enduring and more extensive needs. They lived to cumber the political ground, obstructing
progress, all the more so because they were uttered and held not as hypotheses with which
to direct social experimentation but as final truths, dogmas. No wonder they call urgently
for revision and displacement.

Nevertheless the current has set steadily in one direction: toward democratic forms.
That government exists to serve its community, and that this purpose cannot be achieved
unless the community itself shares in selecting its governors and determining their policies, are a deposit of fact left, as far as we can see, permanently in the wake of doctrines and
forms, however transitory the latter. They are not the whole of the democratic idea, but
they express it in its political phase. Belief in this political aspect is not a mystic faith as if
in some overruling providence that cares for children, drunkards and others unable to help
themselves. It marks a well-attested conclusion from historic facts. We have every reason
to think that whatever changes may take place in existing democratic machinery, they will
be of a sort to make the interest of the public a more supreme guide and criterion of governmental activity, and to enable the public to form and manifest its purposes still more
authoritatively. In this sense the cure for the ailments of democracy is more democracy.
The prime difficulty, as we have seen, is that of discovering the means by which a scattered, mobile and manifold public may so recognize itself as to define and express its interests. This discovery is necessarily precedent to any fundamental change in the machinery.
We are not concerned therefore to set forth counsels as to advisable improvements in the
political forms of democracy. Many have been suggested. It is no derogation of their relative worth to say that consideration of these changes is not at present an affair of primary

importance. The problem lies deeper; it is in the first instance an intellectual problem: the search for conditions under which the Great Society may become the Great Community. When these conditions are brought into being they will make their own forms. Until they have come about, it is somewhat futile to consider what political machinery will suit them.

In a search for the conditions under which the inchoate public now extant may function democratically, we may proceed from a statement of the nature of the democratic idea in its generic social sense. From the standpoint of the individual, it consists in having a responsible share according to capacity in forming and directing the activities of the groups to which one belongs and in participating according to need in the values which the groups sustain. From the standpoint of the groups, it demands liberation of the potentialities of members of a group in harmony with the interests and goods which are common. Since every individual is a member of many groups, this specification cannot be fulfilled except when different groups interact flexibly and fully in connection with other groups. A member of a robber band may express his powers in a way consonant with belonging to that group and be directed by the interest common to its members. But he does so only at the cost of repression of those of his potentialities which can be realized only through membership in other groups. The robber band cannot interact flexibly with other groups; it can act only through isolating itself. It must prevent the operation of all interests save those which circumscribe it in its separateness. But a good citizen finds his conduct as a member of a political group enriching and enriched by his participation in family life, industry, scientific and artistic associations. There is a free give-and-take: fullness of integrated personality is therefore possible of achievement, since the pulls and responses of different groups reënforce one another and their values accord.

Regarded as an idea, democracy is not an alternative to other principles of associated life. It is the idea of community life itself. It is an ideal in the only intelligible sense of an ideal: namely, the tendency and movement of some thing which exists carried to its final limit, viewed as completed, perfected. Since things do not attain such fulfillment but are in actuality distracted and interfered with, democracy in this sense is not a fact and never will be. But neither in this sense is there or has there ever been anything which is a community in its full measure, a community unalloyed by alien elements. The idea or ideal of a community presents, however, actual phases of associated life as they are freed from restrictive and disturbing elements, and are contemplated as having attained their limit of development. Wherever there is conjoint activity whose consequences are appreciated as good by all singular persons who take part in it, and where the realization of the good is such as to effect an energetic desire and effort to sustain it in being just because a community. The clear consciousness of a communal life, in all its implications, constitutes the idea of democracy.

Only when we start from a community as a fact, grasp the fact in thought so as to clarify and enhance its constituent elements, can we reach an idea of democracy which is not utopian. The conceptions and shibboleths which are traditionally associated with the idea of democracy take on a veridical and directive meaning only when they are construed as marks and traits of an association which realizes the defining characteristics of a community. Fraternity, liberty and equality isolated from communal life are hopeless abstractions. Their separate assertion leads to mushy sentimentalism or else to extravagant and fanatical violence which in the end defeats its own aims. Equality then becomes a creed of mechanical identity which is false to facts and impossible of realization. Effort to attain it is divisive of the vital bonds which hold men together; as far as it puts forth issue, the outcome is a mediocrity in which good is common only in the sense of being average and vulgar. [Liberty is then thought of as independence of social ties, and ends in dissolution and anarchy.] It is more difficult to sever the idea of brotherhood from that of a community, and hence [it is either practically ignored in the movements which identify democracy with Individualism,] or else it is a sentimentally appended tag. In its just connection with communal experience, fraternity is another name for the consciously appreciated goods which accrue from an association in which all share, and which give direction to the conduct of each. Liberty is that secure release and fulfillment of personal potentialities which take place only in rich and manifold association with others: the power to be an individualized self making a distinctive contribution and enjoying in its own way the fruits of association. Equality denotes the unhampered share which each individual member of the community has in the consequences of associated action. It is equitable because it is measured only by need and capacity to utilize, not by extraneous factors which deprive one in order that another may take and have. A baby in the family is equal with others, not because of some antecedent and structural quality which is the same as that of others, but in so far as his needs for care and development are attended to without being sacrificed to the superior strength, possessions and matured abilities of others. Equality does not signify that kind of mathematical or physical equivalence in virtue of which any one element may be substituted for another. It denotes effective regard for whatever is distinctive and unique in each, irrespective of physical and psychological inequalities. It is not a natural possession but is a fruit of the community when its action is directed by its character as a community.

Associated or joint activity is a condition of the creation of a community. But association itself is physical and organic, while communal life is moral, that is emotionally, intellectually, consciously sustained. Human beings combine in behavior as directly and unconsciously as do atoms, stellar masses and cells; as directly and unknowingly as they divide and repel. They do so in virtue of their own structure, as man and woman unite, as the baby seeks the breast and the breast is there to supply its need. They do so from external circumstances, pressure from without, as atoms combine or separate in presence of an electric charge, or as sheep huddle together from the cold. Associated activity needs no explanation; things are made that way. But no amount of aggregated collective action of itself constitutes a community. For beings who observe and think, and whose ideas are absorbed by impulses and become sentiments and interests, "we" is as inevitable as "I." But "we" and "our" exist only when the consequences of combined action are perceived and become an object of desire and effort, just as "I" and "mine" appear on the scene only when a distinctive share in mutual action is consciously asserted or claimed. Human associations may be ever so organic in origin and firm in operation, but they develop into societies in a human sense only as their consequences, being known, are esteemed and sought for. Even if "society" were as much an organism as some writers have held, it would not on that account be society. Interactions, transactions, occur *de facto* and the results of interdependence follow. But participation in activities and sharing in results are additive concerns. They demand *communication* as a prerequisite.

HANNAH ARENDT

The Public and the Private Realm

THE SOCIAL AND THE PRIVATE

What we called earlier the rise of the social coincided historically with the transformation of the private care for private property into a public concern. Society, when it first entered the public realm, assumed the disguise of an organization of property-owners who, instead of claiming access to the public realm because of their wealth, demanded protection from it for the accumulation of more wealth. In the words of Bodin, government belonged to kings and property to subjects, so that it was the duty of the kings to rule in the interest of their subjects' property. "The common-wealth," as has recently been pointed out, "largely existed for the common *wealth*."[1]

When this common wealth, the result of activities formerly banished to the privacy of the households, was permitted to take over the public realm, private possessions—which are essentially much less permanent and much more vulnerable to the mortality of their owners than the common world, which always grows out of the past and is intended to last for future generations—began to undermine the durability of the world. It is true that wealth can be accumulated to a point where no individual life-span can use it up, so that the family rather than the individual becomes its owner. Yet wealth remains something to be used and consumed no matter how many individual life-spans it may sustain. Only when wealth became capital, whose chief function was to generate more capital, did private property equal or come close to the permanence inherent in the commonly shared world.[2] However, this permanence is of a different nature; it is the permanence of a process rather than the permanence of a stable structure. Without the process of accumulation, wealth would at once fall back into the opposite process of disintegration through use and consumption.

Common wealth, therefore, can never become common in the sense we speak of a common world; it remained, or rather was intended to remain, strictly private. Only the government, appointed to shield the private owners from each other in the competitive struggle for more wealth, was common. The obvious contradiction in this modern concept of government, where the only thing people have in common is their private interests, need no longer bother us at it still bothered Marx, since we know that the contradiction between private and public, typical of the initial stages of the modern age, has been a temporary phenomenon which introduced the utter extinction of the very difference between the private and public realms, the submersion of both in the sphere of the social. By the same token, we are in a far better position to realize the consequences for human existence when both the public and private spheres of life are gone, the public because it has become a function of the private and the private because it has become the only common concern left.

Seen from this viewpoint, the modern discovery of intimacy seems a flight from the whole outer world into the inner subjectivity of the individual, which formerly had been sheltered and protected by the private realm. The dissolution of this realm into the social may most conveniently be watched in the progressing transformation of immobile into mobile property until eventually the distinction between property and wealth, between the *fungibiles* and the *consumptibiles* of Roman law, loses all significance because every tangible, "fungible" thing has become an object of "consumption"; it lost its private use value which was determined by its location and acquired an exclusively social value determined through its ever-changing exchangeability whose fluctuation could itself be fixed only temporarily by relating it to the common denominator of money.[3] Closely connected with this social evaporation of the tangible was the most revolutionary modern contribution to the concept of property, according to which property was not a fixed and firmly located part of the world acquired by its owner in one way or another but, on the contrary, had its source in man himself, in his possession of a body and his indisputable ownership of the strength of this body, which Marx called "labor-power."

Thus modern property lost its wordly character and was located in the person himself, that is, in what an individual could lose only along with his life. Historically, Locke's assumption that the labor of one's body is the origin of property is more than doubtful; but in view of the fact that we already live under conditions where our only reliable property is our skill and our labor power, it is more than likely that it will become true. For wealth, after it became a public concern, has grown to such proportions that it is almost unmanageable by private ownership. It is as though the public realm had taken its revenge against those who tried to use it for their private interests. The greatest threat here, however, is not the abolition of private ownership of wealth but the abolition of private property in the sense of a tangible, worldly place of one's own.

In order to understand the danger to human existence from the elimination of the private realm, for which the intimate is not a very reliable substitute, it may be best to consider those non-privative traits of privacy which are older than, and independent of, the discovery of intimacy. The difference between what we have in common and what we own privately is first that our private possessions, which we use and consume daily, are much more urgently needed than any part of the common world; without property, as Locke pointed out, "the common is of no use."[4] The same necessity that, from the standpoint of the public realm, shows only its negative aspect as a deprivation of freedom possesses a driving force whose urgency is unmatched by the so-called higher desires and aspirations of man; not only will it always be the first among man's needs and worries, it will also prevent the apathy and disappearance of initiative which so obviously threatens all overly wealthy communities.[5] Necessity and life are so intimately related and connected that life itself is threatened where necessity is altogether eliminated. For the elimination of necessity, far from resulting automatically in the establishment of freedom, only blurs the distinguishing line between freedom and necessity. (Modern discussions of freedom, where freedom is never understood as an objective state of human existence but either presents an unsolvable problem of subjectivity, of an entirely undetermined or determined will, or develops out of necessity, all point to the fact that the objective, tangible difference between being free and being forced by necessity is no longer perceived.)

The second outstanding non-privative characteristic of privacy is that the four walls of one's private property offer the only reliable hiding place from the common public world, not only from everything that goes on in it but also from its very publicity, from being seen and being heard. A life spent entirely in public, in the presence of others, becomes, as we would say, shallow. While it retains its visibility, it loses the quality of rising into sight from some darker ground which must remain hidden if it is not to lose its depth in a very real, non-subjective sense. The only efficient way to guarantee the darkness of what needs to be hidden against the light of publicity is private property, a privately owned place to hide in.[6]

While it is only natural that the non-privative traits of privacy should appear most clearly when men are threatened with deprivation of it, the practical treatment of private property by premodern political bodies indicates clearly that men have always been conscious of their existence and importance. This, however, did not make them protect the activities in the private realm directly, but rather the boundaries separating the privately owned from other parts of the world, most of all from the common world itself. The distinguishing mark of modern political and economic theory, on the other hand, in so far as it regards private property as a crucial issue, has been its stress upon the private activities of property-owners and their need of government protection for the sake of accumulation of wealth at the expense of the tangible property itself. What is important to the public realm, however, is not the more or less enterprising spirit of private businessmen but the fences around the houses and gardens of citizens. The invasion of privacy by society, the "socialization of man" (Marx), is most efficiently carried through by means of expropriation, but this is not the only way. Here, as in other respects, the revolutionary measures of socialism or communism can very well be replaced by a slower and no less certain "withering away" of the private realm in general and of private property in particular.

The distinction between the private and public realms, seen from the viewpoint of privacy rather than of the body politic, equals the distinction between things that should be shown and things that should be hidden. Only the modern age, in its rebellion against society, has discovered how rich and manifold the realm of the hidden can be under the conditions of intimacy; but it is striking that from the beginning of history to our own time it has always been the bodily part of human existence that needed to be hidden in privacy, all things connected with the necessity of the life process itself, which prior to the modern age comprehended all activities serving the subsistence of the individual and the survival of the species. Hidden away were the laborers who "with their bodies minister to the [bodily] needs of life,"[7] and the women who with their bodies guarantee the physical survival of the species. Women and slaves belonged to the same category and were hidden away not only because they were somebody else's property but because their life was "laborious," devoted to bodily functions.[8] In the beginning of the modern age, when "free" labor had lost its hiding place in the privacy of the household, the laborers were hidden away and segregated from the community like criminals behind high walls and under constant supervision.[9] The fact that the modern age emancipated the working classes and the women at nearly the same historical moment must certainly be counted among the characteristics of an age which no longer believes that bodily functions and material concerns should be hidden. It is all the more symptomatic of the nature of these phenomena that the few remnants of strict privacy even in our own civilization relate to "necessities" in the original sense of being necessitated by having a body.

THE LOCATION OF HUMAN ACTIVITIES

Although the distinction between private and public coincides with the opposition of necessity and freedom, of futility and permanence, and, finally, of shame and honor, it is by no means true that only the necessary, the futile, and the shameful have their proper place in the private realm. The most elementary meaning of the two realms indicates that there are things that need to be hidden and others that need to be displayed publicly if they are to exist at all. If we look at these things, regardless of where we find them in any given civilization, we shall see that each human activity points to its proper location in the world. This is true for the chief activities of the *vita activa*, labor, work, and action; but there is one, admittedly extreme, example of this phenomenon, whose advantage for illustration is that it played a considerable role in political theory.

Goodness in an absolute sense, as distinguished from the "good-for" or the "excellent" in Greek and Roman antiquity, became known in our civilization only with the rise of Christianity. Since then, we know of good works as one important variety of possible human action. The well-known antagonism between early Christianity and the *res publica*, so admirably summed up in Tertullian's formula, *nec ulla magis res aliena quam publica* ("no matter is more alien to us than what matters publicly"),[10] is usually and rightly understood as a consequence of early eschatological expectations that lost their immediate significance only after experience had taught that even the downfall of the Roman Empire did not mean the end of the world.[11] Yet the otherworldliness of Christianity has still another root, perhaps even more intimately related to the teachings of Jesus of Nazareth, and at any rate so independent of the belief in the perishability of the world that one is tempted to see in it the true inner reason why Christian alienation from the world could so easily survive the obvious non-fulfilment of its eschatological hopes.

The one activity taught by Jesus in word and deed is the activity of goodness, and goodness obviously harbors a tendency to hide from being seen or heard. Christian hostility toward the public realm, the tendency at least of early Christians to lead a life as far removed from the public realm as possible, can also be understood as a self-evident consequence of devotion to good works, independent of all beliefs and expectations. For it is manifest that the moment a good work becomes known and public, it loses its specific character of goodness, of being done for nothing but goodness' sake. When goodness appears openly, it is no longer goodness, though it may still be useful as organized charity or an act of solidarity. Therefore: "Take heed that ye do not your alms before men, to be seen of them." Goodness can exist only when it is not perceived, not even by its author; whoever sees himself performing a good work is no longer good, but at best a useful member of society or a dutiful member of a church. Therefore: "Let not thy left hand know what thy right hand doeth."

It may be this curious negative quality of goodness, the lack of outward phenomenal manifestation, that makes Jesus of Nazareth's appearance in history such a profoundly paradoxical event; it certainly seems to be the reason why he thought and taught that no man can be good: "Why callest thou me good? none is good, save one, that is, God."[12] The same conviction finds its expression in the talmudic story of the thirty-six righteous men, for the sake of whom God saves the world and who also are known to nobody, least of all to themselves. We are reminded of Socrates' great insight that no man can be wise, out of which love for wisdom, or philosophy, was born; the whole life story of Jesus seems to testify how love for goodness arises out of the insight that no man can be good.

Love of wisdom and love of goodness, if they resolve themselves into the activities of philosophizing and doing good works, have in common that they come to an immediate end, cancel themselves, so to speak, whenever it is assumed that man can *be* wise or *be* good. Attempts to bring into being that which can never survive the fleeting moment of the deed itself have never been lacking and have always led into absurdity. The philosophers of late antiquity who demanded of themselves to *be* wise were absurd when they claimed to be happy when roasted alive in the famous Phaleric Bull. And no less absurd is the Christian demand to *be* good and to turn the other cheek, when not taken metaphorically but tried as a real way of life.

But the similarity between the activities springing from love of goodness and love of wisdom ends here. Both, it is true, stand in a certain opposition to the public realm, but the case of goodness is much more extreme in this respect and therefore of greater relevance in our context. Only goodness must go into absolute hiding and flee all appearance if it is not to be destroyed. The philosopher, even if he decides with Plato to leave the "cave" of human affairs, does not have to hide from himself; on the contrary, under the sky of ideas he not only finds the true essences of everything that is, but also himself, in the dialogue between "me and myself" (*eme emautō*) in which Plato apparently saw the essence of thought.[13] To be in solitude means to be with one's self, and thinking, therefore, though it may be the most solitary of all activities, is never altogether without a partner and without company.

The man, however, who is in love with goodness can never afford to lead a solitary life, and yet his living with others and for others must remain essentially without testimony and lacks first of all the company of himself. He is not solitary, but lonely; when living with others he must hide from them and cannot even trust himself to witness what he is doing. The philosopher can always rely upon his thoughts to keep him company, whereas good deeds can never keep anybody company; they must be forgotten the moment they are done, because even memory will destroy their quality of being "good." Moreover, thinking, because it can be remembered, can crystallize into thought, and thoughts, like all things that owe their existence to remembrance, can be transformed into tangible objects which, like the written page or the printed book, become part of the human artifice. Good works, because they must be forgotten instantly, can never become part of the world; they come and go, leaving no trace. They truly are not of this world.

It is this worldlessness inherent in good works that makes the lover of goodness an essentially religious figure and that makes goodness, like wisdom in antiquity, an essentially non-human, superhuman quality. And yet love of goodness, unlike love of wisdom, is not restricted to the experience of the few, just as loneliness, unlike solitude, is within the range of every man's experience. In a sense, therefore, goodness and loneliness are of much greater relevance to politics than wisdom and solitude; yet only solitude can become an authentic way of life in the figure of the philosopher, whereas the much more general experience of loneliness is so contradictory to the human condition of plurality that it is simply unbearable for any length of time and needs the company of God, the only imaginable witness of good works, if it is not to annihilate human existence altogether. The otherworldliness of religious experience, in so far as it is truly the experience of love in the sense of an activity, and not the much more frequent one of beholding passively a revealed truth, manifests itself within the world itself; this, like all other activities, does not leave the world, but must be performed within it. But this manifestation, though it appears in the space where other activities are performed and depends upon it, is of an actively negative nature; fleeing the world and hiding from its inhabitants, it negates the space the world offers to men, and most of all that public part of it where everything and everybody are seen and heard by others.

Goodness, therefore, as a consistent way of life, is not only impossible within the confines of the public realm, it is even destructive of it. Nobody perhaps has been more sharply aware of this ruinous quality of doing good than Machiavelli, who, in a famous passage, dared to teach men "how not to be good."[14] Needless to add, he did not say and did not mean that men must be taught how to be bad; the criminal act, though for other reasons, must also flee being seen and heard by others. Machiavelli's criterion for political action was glory, the same as in classical antiquity, and badness can no more shine in glory than goodness. Therefore all methods by which "one may indeed gain power, but not glory" are bad.[15] Badness that comes out of hiding is impudent and directly destroys the common world; goodness that comes out of hiding and assumes a public role is no longer good, but corrupt in its own terms and will carry its own corruption wherever it goes. Thus, for Machiavelli, the reason for the Church's becoming a corrupting influence in Italian politics was her participation in secular affairs as such and not the individual corruptness of bishops and prelates. To him, the alternative posed by the problem of religious rule over the secular realm was inescapably this: either the public corrupted the religious body and thereby became itself corrupt, or the religious body remained uncorrupt and destroyed the public realm altogether. A reformed Church therefore was even more dangerous in Machiavelli's eyes, and he looked with great respect but greater apprehension upon the religious revival of his time, the "new orders" which, by "saving religion from being destroyed by the licentiousness of the prelates and heads of the Church," teach people to be good and not "to resist evil"—with the result that "wicked rulers do as much evil as they please."[16]

We chose the admittedly extreme example of doing good works, extreme because this activity is not even at home in the realm of privacy, in order to indicate that the historical judgments of political communities, by which each determined which of the activities of the *vita activa* should be shown in public and which be hidden in privacy, may have their correspondence in the nature of these activities themselves. By raising this question, I do not intend to attempt an exhaustive analysis of the activities of the *vita activa*, whose articulations have been curiously neglected by a tradition which considered it chiefly from the standpoint of the *vita contemplativa*, but to try to determine with some measure of assurance their political significance.

NOTES

1. R. W. K. Hinton, "Was Charles I a Tyrant?" *Review of Politics*, Vol. XVIII (January, 1956).

2. For the history of the word "capital" deriving from the Latin *caput*, which in Roman law was employed for the principal of a debt, see W. J. Ashley, *op. cit.*, pp. 429 and 433, n. 183. Only eighteenth-century writers began to use the word in the modern sense as "wealth invested in such a way as to bring gain."

3. Medieval economic theory did not yet conceive of money as a common denominator and yardstick but counted it among the *consumptibiles*.

4. *Second Treatise of Civil Government*, sec. 27.

5. The relatively few instances of ancient authors praising labor and poverty are inspired by this danger (for references see G. Herzog-Hauser, *op. cit.*).

6. The Greek and Latin words for the interior of the house, *megaron* and *atrium,* have a strong connotation of darkness and blackness (see Mommsen, *op. cit.*, pp. 22 and 236).

7. Aristotle *Politics* 1254b25.

8. The life of a woman is called *ponetikos* by Aristotle, *On the Generation of Animals* 775a33. That women and slaves belonged and lived together, that no woman, not even the wife of the household head, lived among her equals—other free women—so that rank depended much less on birth than on "occupation" or function, is very well presented by Wallon (*op. cit.*, I, 77 ff.), who speaks of a "confusion des rangs, ce partage de toutes les fonctions domestiques": "Les femmes . . . se confondaient avec leurs esclaves dans les soins habituels de la vie intérieure. De quelque rang qu'elles fussent, le travail était leur apanage, comme aux hommes la guerre."

9. See Pierre Brizon, *Histoire du travail et des travailleurs* (4th ed.; 1926), p. 184, concerning the conditions of factory work in the seventeenth century.

10. Tertullian *op. cit.* 38.

11. This difference of experience may partly explain the difference between the great sanity of Augustine and the horrible concreteness of Tertullian's views on politics. Both were Romans and profoundly shaped by Roman political life.

12. Luke 8:19. The same thought occurs in Matt. 6:1–18, where Jesus warns against hypocrisy, against the open display of piety. Piety cannot "appear unto men" but only unto God, who "seeth in secret." God, it is true, "shall reward" man, but not, as the standard translation claims, "openly." The German word *Scheinheiligkeit* expresses this religious phenomenon, where mere appearance is already hypocrisy, quite adequately.

13. One finds this idiom *passim* in Plato (see esp. *Gorgias* 482).

14. *Prince*, ch. 15.

15. *Ibid.*, ch. 8.

16. *Discourses*, Book III, ch. 1.

Michael J. Sandel

The Procedural Republic
and the Unencumbered Self

Political philosophy seems often to reside at a distance from the world. Principles are one thing, politics another, and even our best efforts to "live up" to our ideals typically founder on the gap between theory and practice.[1]

But if political philosophy is unrealizable in one sense, it is unavoidable in another. This is the sense in which philosophy inhabits the world from the start; our practices and institutions are embodiments of theory. To engage in a political practice is already to stand in relation to theory.[2] For all our uncertainties about ultimate questions of political philosophy—of justice and value and the nature of the good life—the one thing we know is that we live *some* answer all the time.

In this essay I will try to explore the answer we live now, in contemporary America. What is the political philosophy implicit in our practices and institutions? How does it stand, as philosophy? And how do tensions in the philosophy find expression in our present political condition?

It may be objected that it is a mistake to look for a single philosophy, that we live no "answer," only answers. But a plurality of answers is itself a kind of answer. And the political theory that affirms this plurality is the theory I propose to explore.

THE RIGHT AND THE GOOD

We might begin by considering a certain moral and political vision. It is a liberal vision, and like most liberal visions gives pride of place to justice, fairness, and individual rights. Its core thesis is this: a just society seeks not to promote any particular ends, but enables its citizens to pursue their own ends, consistent with a similar liberty for all; it therefore must govern by principles that do not presuppose any particular conception of the good. What justifies these regulative principles above all is not that they maximize the general welfare, or cultivate virtue, or otherwise promote the good, but rather that they conform to the concept of *right*, a moral category given prior to the good, and independent of it.

This liberalism says, in other words, that what makes the just society just is not the *telos* or purpose or end at which it aims, but precisely its refusal to choose in advance among competing purposes and ends. In its constitution and its laws, the just society seeks to provide a framework within which its citizens can pursue their own values and ends, consistent with a similar liberty for others.

The ideal I've described might be summed up in the claim that the right is prior to the good, and in two senses: The priority of the right means first, that individual rights cannot be sacrificed for the sake of the general good (in this it opposes utilitarianism), and second, that the principles of justice that specify these rights cannot be premised on any particular vision of the good life. (In this it opposes teleological conceptions in general.)

This is the liberalism of much contemporary moral and political philosophy, most fully elaborated by Rawls, and indebted to Kant for its philosophical foundations.[3] But I am concerned here less with the lineage of this vision than with what seem to me three striking facts about it.

First, it has a deep and powerful philosophical appeal. Second, despite its philosophical force, the claim for the priority of the right over the good ultimately fails. And third, despite its philosophical failure, this liberal vision is the one by which we live. For us in late twentieth-century America, it is our vision, the theory most thoroughly embodied in the practices and institutions most central to our public life. And seeing how it goes wrong as philosophy may help us to diagnose our present political condition. So first, its philosophical power; second, its philosophical failure; and third, however briefly, its uneasy embodiment in the world.

But before taking up these three claims, it is worth pointing out a central theme that connects them. And that is a certain conception of the person, of what it is to be a moral agent. Like all political theories, the liberal theory I have described is something more than a set of regulative principles. It is also a view about the way the world is, and the way we move within it. At the heart of this ethic lies a vision of the person that both inspires and undoes it. As I will try to argue now, what make this ethic so compelling, but also, finally, vulnerable, are the promise and the failure of the unencumbered self.

KANTIAN FOUNDATIONS

The liberal ethic asserts the priority of right, and seeks principles of justice that do not presuppose any particular conception of the good.[4] This is what Kant means by the supremacy of the moral law, and what Rawls means when he writes that "justice is the first virtue of social institutions."[5] Justice is more than just another value. It provides the framework that *regulates* the play of competing values and ends; it must therefore have a sanction independent of those ends. But it is not obvious where such a sanction could be found.

Theories of justice, and for that matter, ethics, have typically founded their claims on one or another conception of human purposes and ends. Thus Aristotle said the measure of a *polis* is the good at which it aims, and even J. S. Mill, who in the nineteenth century called "justice the chief part, and incomparably the most binding part of all morality," made justice an instrument of utilitarian ends.[6]

This is the solution Kant's ethic rejects. Different persons typically have different desires and ends, and so any principle derived from them can only be contingent. But the moral law needs a *categorical* foundation, not a contingent one. Even so universal a desire as happiness will not do. People still differ in what happiness consists of, and to install any particular conception as regulative would impose on some the conceptions of others, and so deny at least to some the freedom to choose their *own* conceptions. In any case, to govern ourselves in conformity with desires and inclinations, given as they are by nature or circumstance, is not really to be *self*-governing at all. It is rather a refusal of freedom, a capitulation to determinations given outside us.

According to Kant, the right is "derived entirely from the concept of freedom in the external relationships of human beings, and has nothing to do with the end which all men have by nature [i.e., the aim of achieving happiness] or with the recognized means of attaining this end."[7] As such, it must have a basis prior to all empirical ends. Only when I am governed by principles that do not presuppose any particular ends am I free to pursue my own ends consistent with a similar freedom for all.

But this still leaves the question of what the basis of the right could possibly be. If it must be a basis prior to all purposes and ends, unconditioned even by what Kant calls "the special circumstances of human nature,"[8] where could such a basis conceivably be found? Given the stringent demands of the Kantian ethic, the moral law would seem almost to require a foundation in nothing, for any empirical procondition would undermine its priority. "Duty!" asks Kant at his most lyrical, "What origin is there worthy of thee, and where is to be found the root of thy noble descent which proudly rejects all kinship with the inclinations?"[9]

His answer is that the basis of the moral law is to be found in the *subject*, not the object of practical reason, a subject capable of an autonomous will. No empirical end, but rather "a subject of ends, namely a rational being himself, must be made the ground for all maxims of action."[10] Nothing other than what Kant calls "the subject of all possible ends himself" can give rise to the right, for only this subject is also the subject of an autonomous will. Only this subject could be that "something which elevates man above himself as part of the world of sense" and enables him to participate in an ideal, unconditioned realm wholly independent of our social and psychological inclinations. And only this thoroughgoing independence can afford us the detachment we need if we are ever freely to choose for ourselves, unconditioned by the vagaries of circumstance.[11]

Who or what exactly is this subject? It is, in a certain sense, *us*. The moral law, after all, is a law we give *ourselves*; we don't *find* it, we *will* it. That is how it (and we) escape the reign of nature and circumstance and merely empirical ends. But what is important to see is that the "we" who do the willing are not "we" qua particular persons, you and me, each for ourselves—the moral law is not up to us as individuals—but "we" qua participants in what Kant calls "pure practical reason," "we" qua participants in a transcendental subject.

Now what is to guarantee that I *am* a subject of this kind, capable of exercising pure practical reason? Well, strictly speaking, there *is* no guarantee; the transcendental subject is only a possibility. But it is a possibility I must *presuppose* if I am to think of myself as a free moral agent. Were I wholly an empirical being, I would not be capable of freedom, for every exercise of will would be conditioned by the desire for some object. All choice would be heteronomous choice, governed by the pursuit of some end. My will could never be a first cause, only the effect of some prior cause, the instrument of one or another impulse or inclination. "When we think of ourselves as free," writes Kant, "we transfer ourselves into the intelligible world as members and recognize the autonomy of the will."[12] And so the notion of a subject prior to and independent of experience, such as the Kantian ethic requires, appears not only possible but indispensible, a necessary presupposition of the possibility of freedom.

How does all of this come back to politics? As the subject is prior to its ends, so the right is prior to the good. Society is best arranged when it is governed by principles that do not presuppose any particular conception of the good, for any other arrangement would fail to respect persons as being capable of choice; it would treat them as objects rather than subjects, as means rather than ends in themselves.

We can see in this way how Kant's notion of the subject is bound up with the claim for the priority of right. But for those in the Anglo-American tradition, the transcendental subject will seem a strange foundation for a familiar ethic. Surely, one may think, we can take rights seriously and affirm the primacy of justice without embracing the *Critique of Pure Reason*. This, in any case, is the project of Rawls.

He wants to save the priority of right from the obscurity of the transcendental subject. Kant's idealist metaphysic, for all its moral and political advantage, cedes too much to the transcendent, and wins for justice its primacy only by denying it its human situation. "To develop a viable Kantian conception of justice," Rawls writes, "the force and content of Kant's doctrine must be detached from its background in transcendental idealism" and recast within the "canons of a reasonable empiricism."[13] And so Rawls' project is to preserve Kant's moral and political teaching by replacing Germanic obscurities with a domesticated metaphysic more congenial to the Anglo-American temper. This is the role of the original position.

FROM TRANSCENDENTAL SUBJECT TO UNENCUMBERED SELF

The original position tries to provide what Kant's transcendental argument cannot—a foundation for the right that is prior to the good, but still situated in the world. Sparing all but essentials, the original position works like this: It invites us to imagine the principles we would choose to govern our society if we were to choose them in advance, before we knew the particular persons we would be—whether rich or poor, strong or weak, lucky or unlucky—before we knew even our interests or aims or conceptions of the good. These principles—the ones we would choose in that imaginary situation—are the principles of justice. What is more, if it works, they are principles that do not presuppose any particular ends.

What they *do* presuppose is a certain picture of the person, of the way we must be if we are beings for whom justice is the first virtue. This is the picture of the unencumbered self, a self understood as prior to and independent of purposes and ends.

Now the unencumbered self describes first of all the way we stand toward the things we have, or want, or seek. It means there is always a distinction between the values I *have* and the person I *am*. To identify any characteristics as *my* aims, ambitions, desires, and so on, is always to imply some subject "me" standing behind them, at a certain distance, and the shape of this "me" must be given prior to any of the aims or attributes I bear. One consequence of this distance is to put the self *itself* beyond the reach of its experience, to secure its identity once and for all. Or to put the point another way, it rules out the possibility of what we might call *constitutive* ends. No role or commitment could define me so completely that I could not understand myself without it. No project could be so essential that turning away from it would call into question the person I am.

For the unencumbered self, what matters above all, what is most essential to our personhood, are not the ends we choose but our capacity to choose them. The original position sums up this central claim about us. "It is not our aims that primarily reveal our nature," writes Rawls, "but rather the principles that we would acknowledge to govern the background conditions under which these aims are to be formed . . . We should therefore reverse the relation between the right and the good proposed by teleological doctrines and view the right as prior."[14]

Only if the self is prior to its ends can the right be prior to the good. Only if my identity is never tied to the aims and interests I may have at any moment can I think of myself as a free and independent agent, capable of choice.

This notion of independence carries consequences for the kind of community of which we are capable. Understood as unencumbered selves, we are of course free to join in voluntary association with others, and so are capable of community in the cooperative sense. What is denied to the unencumbered self is the possibility of membership in any community bound by moral ties antecedent to choice; he cannot belong to any community where the self *itself* could be at stake. Such a community—call it constitutive as against merely cooperative—would engage the identity as well as the interests of the participants, and so implicate its members in a citizenship more thoroughgoing than the unencumbered self can know.

For justice to be primary, then, we must be creatures of a certain kind, related to human circumstance in a certain way. We must stand to our circumstance always at a certain distance, whether as transcendental subject in the case of Kant, or as unencumbered selves in the case of Rawls. Only in this way can we view ourselves as subjects as well as objects of experience, as agents and not just instruments of the purposes we pursue.

The unencumbered self and the ethic it inspires, taken together, hold out a liberating vision. Freed from the dicates of nature and the sanction of social roles, the human subject is installed as sovereign, cast as the author of the only moral meanings there are. As participants in pure practical reason, or as parties to the original position, we are free to construct principles of justice unconstrained by an order of value antecedently given. And as actual, individual selves, we are free to choose our purposes and ends unbound by such an order, or by custom or tradition or inherited status. So long as they are not unjust, our conceptions of the good carry weight, whatever they are, simply in virtue of our having chosen them. We are, in Rawls' words, "self-originating sources of valid claims."[15]

This is an exhilarating promise, and the liberalism it animates is perhaps the fullest expression of the Enlightenment's quest for the self-defining subject. But is it true? Can we make sense of our moral and political life by the light of the self-image it requires? I do not think we can, and I will try to show why not by arguing first within the liberal project, then beyond it.

JUSTICE AND COMMUNITY

We have focused so far on the foundations of the liberal vision, on the way it derives the principles it defends. Let us turn briefly now to the substance of those principles, using Rawls as our example. Sparing all but essentials once again, Rawls' two principles of justice are these: first, equal basic liberties for all, and second, only those social and economic inequalities that benefit the least-advantaged members of society (the difference principle).

In arguing for these principles, Rawls argues against two familiar alternatives—utilitarianism and libertarianism. He argues against utilitarianism that it fails to take seriously the distinction between persons. In seeking to maximize the general welfare, the utilitarian treats society as whole, as if it were a single person; it conflates our many, diverse desires into a single system of desires, and tries to maximize. It is indifferent to the distribution of satisfactions among persons, except insofar as this may affect the overall sum. But this fails to respect our plurality and distinctness. It uses some as means to the happiness of all, and so fails to respect each as an end in himself. While utilitarians may sometimes defend individual rights, their defense must rest on the calculation that respecting those rights will serve utility in the long run. But this calculation is contingent and uncertain. So long as utility is what Mill said it is, "the ultimate appeal on all ethical questions,"[16] individual rights can never be secure. To avoid the danger that their life prospects might one day be sacrificed for the greater good of others, the parties to the original position therefore insist on certain basic liberties for all, and make those liberties prior.

If utilitarians fail to take seriously the distinctness of persons, libertarians go wrong by failing to acknowledge the arbitariness of fortune. They define as just whatever distribution results from an efficient market economy, and oppose all redistribution on the grounds that people are entitled to whatever they get, so long as they do not cheat or steal or otherwise violate someone's rights in getting it. Rawls opposes this principle on the ground that the distribution of talents and assets and even efforts by which some get more and others get less is arbitary from moral point of view, a matter of good luck. To distribute the good things in life on the basis of these differences is not to do justice, but simply to carry over into human arrangements the arbitrariness of social and natural contingency. We deserve, as individuals, neither the talents our good fortune may have brought, nor the benefits that flow from them. We should therefore regard these talents as common assets, and regard one another as common beneficiaries of the rewards they bring. "Those who have been favored by nature, whoever they are, may gain from their good fortune only on terms that improve the situation of those who have lost out. . . . In justice as fairness, men agree to share one another's fate."[17]

This is the reasoning that leads to the difference principle. Notice how it reveals, in yet another guise, the logic of the unencumbered self. I cannot be said to deserve the benefits that flow from, say, my fine physique and good looks, because they are only accidental, not essential facts about me. They describe attributes I *have*, not the person I *am*, and so cannot give rise to a claim of desert. Being an unencumbered self, this is true of *everything* about me. And so I cannot, as an individual, deserve anything at all.

However jarring to our ordinary understandings this argument may be, the picture so far remains intact; the priority of right, the denial of desert, and the unencumbered self all hang impressively together.

But the difference principle requires more, and it is here that the argument comes undone. The difference principle begins with the thought, congenial to the unencumbered self, that the assets I have are only accidentally mine. But it ends by assuming that these assets are therefore *common* assets and that society has a prior claim on the fruits of their exercise. But this assumption is without warrant. Simply because I, as an individual, do not have a privileged claim on the assets accidentally residing "here," it does not follow that everyone in the world collectively does. For there is no reason to think that their location in society's province or, for that matter, within the province of humankind, is any *less* arbitrary from a moral point of view. And if their arbitrariness within *me* makes them ineligible to serve *my* ends, there seems no obvious reason why their arbitrariness within any particular society should not make them ineligible to serve that society's ends as well.

To put the point another way, the difference principle, like utilitarianism, is a principle of sharing. As such, it must presuppose some prior moral tie among those whose assets it would deploy and whose efforts it would enlist in a common endeavor. Otherwise, it is simply a formula for using some as means to others' ends, a formula this liberalism is committed to reject.

But on the cooperative vision of community alone, it is unclear what the moral basis for this sharing could be. Short of the constitutive conception, deploying an individual's assets for the sake of the common good would seem an offense against the "plurality and distinctness" of individuals this liberalism seeks above all to secure.

If those whose fate I am required to share really are, morally speaking, *others*, rather than fellow participants in a way of life with which my identity is bound, the difference principle falls prey to the same objections as utilitarianism. Its claim on me is not the claim of a constitutive community whose attachments I acknowledge, but rather the claim of a concatenated collectivity whose entanglements I confront.

What the difference principle requires, but cannot provide, is some way of identifying those *among* whom the assets I bear are properly regarded as common, some way of seeing ourselves as mutually indebted and morally engaged to begin with. But as we have seen, the constitutive aims and attachments that would save and situate the difference principle are precisely the ones denied to the liberal self; the moral encumbrances and antecedent obligations they imply would undercut the priority of right.

What, then, of those encumbrances? The point so far is that we cannot be persons for whom justice is primary, and also be persons for whom the difference principle is a principle of justice. But which must give way? Can we view ourselves as independent selves, independent in the sense that our identity is never tied to our aims and attachments?

I do not think we can, at least not without cost to those loyalties and convictions whose moral force consists partly in the fact that living by them is inseparable from understanding ourselves as the particular persons we are—as members of this family or community or nation or people, as bearers of that history, as citizens of this republic. Allegiances such as these are more than values I happen to have, and to hold, at a certain distance. They go beyond the obligations I voluntarily incur and the "natural duties" I owe to human beings as such. They allow that to some I owe more than justice requires or even permits, not by reason of agreements I have made but instead in virtue of those more or less enduring attachments and commitments that, taken together, partly define the person I am.

To imagine a person incapable of constitutive attachments such as these is not to conceive an ideally free and rational agent, but to imagine a person wholly without character, without moral depth. For to have character is to know that I move in a history I neither summon nor command, which carries consequences nonetheless for my choices and conduct. It draws me closer to some and more distant from others; it makes some aims more appropriate, others less so. As a self-interpreting being, I am able to reflect on my history and in this sense to distance myself from it, but the distance is always precarious and provisional, the point of reflection never finally secured outside the history itself. But the liberal ethic puts the self beyond the reach of its experience, beyond deliberation and reflection. Denied the expansive self-understandings that could shape a common life, the liberal self is left to lurch between detachment on the one hand, and entanglement on the other. Such is the fate of the unencumbered self, and its liberating promise.

THE PROCEDURAL REPUBLIC

But before my case can be complete, I need to consider one powerful reply. While it comes from a liberal direction, its spirit is more practical than philosophical. It says, in short, that I am asking too much. It is one thing to seek constitutive attachments in our private lives; among families and friends, and certain tightly knit groups, there may be found a common good that makes justice and rights less pressing. But with public life—at least today, and probably always—it is different. So long as the nation-state is the primary form of political association, talk of constitutive community too easily suggests a darker politics rather than a brighter one; amid echoes of the moral majority, the priority of right, for all its philosophical faults, still seems the safer hope.

This is a challenging rejoinder, and no account of political community in the twentieth century can fail to take it seriously. It is challenging not least because it calls into question the status of political philosophy and its relation to the world. For if my argument is correct, if the liberal vision we have considered is not morally self-sufficient but parasitic on a notion of community it officially rejects, then we should expect to find that the political practice that embodies this vision is not *practically* self-sufficient either—that it must draw on a sense of community it cannot supply and may even undermine. But is that so far from the circumstance we face today? Could it be that through the original position darkly, on the far side of the veil of ignorance, we may glimpse an intimation of our predicament, a refracted vision of ourselves?

How does the liberal vision—and its failure—help us make sense of our public life and its predicament? Consider, to begin, the following paradox in the citizen's relation to the modern welfare state. In many ways, we in the 1980s stand near the completion of a liberal project that has run its course from the New Deal through the Great Society and into the present. But notwithstanding the extension of the franchise and the expansion on individual rights and entitlements in recent decades, there is a widespread sense that, individually and collectively, our control over the forces that govern our lives is receding rather than increasing. This sense is deepened by what appear simultaneously as the power and the powerlessness of the nation-state. On the one hand, increasing numbers of citizens view the state as an overly intrusive presence, more likely to frustrate their purposes than advance them. And yet, despite its unprecedented role in the economy and society, the modern state seems itself disempowered, unable effectively to control the domestic economy, to respond to persisting social ills, or to work America's will in the world.

This is a paradox that has fed the appeals of recent politicians (including Carter and Reagan), even as it has frustrated their attempts to govern. To sort it out, we need to identify the public philosophy implicit in our political practice, and to reconstruct its arrival. We need to trace the advent of the procedural republic, by which I mean a public life animated by the liberal vision and self-image we've considered.

The story of the procedural republic goes back in some ways to the founding of the republic, but its central drama begins to unfold around the turn of the century. As national markets and large-scale enterprise displaced a decentralized economy, the decentralized political forms of the early republic became outmoded as well. If democracy was to survive, the concentration of economic power would have to be met by a similar concentration of political power. But the Progressives understood, or some of them did, that the success of democracy required more than the centralization of government; it also required the nationalization of politics. The primary form of political community had to be a recast on a national scale. For Herbert Croly, writing in 1909, the "nationalizing of American political, economic, and social life" was "an essentially formative and enlightening political transformation." We would become more of a democracy only as we became "more of a nation . . . in ideas, in institutions, and in sprit."[19]

This nationalizing project would be consummated in the New Deal, but for the democratic tradition in America, the embrace of the nation was a decisive departure. From Jefferson to the populists, the party of democracy in American political debate had been, roughly speaking, the party of the provinces, of decentralized power, of small-town and small-scale America. And against them had stood the party of the nation—first Federalists, then Whigs, then the Republicans of Lincoln—a party that spoke for the consolidation of the union. It was thus the historic achievement of the New Deal to unite, in a single party and political program, what Samuel Beer has called "liberalism and the national idea."[20]

What matters for our purpose is that, in the twentieth century, liberalism made its peace with concentrated power. But it was understood at the start that the terms of this peace required a strong sense of national community, morally and politically to underwrite the extended involvements of a modern industrial order. If a virtuous republic of small-scale, democratic communities was no longer a possibility, a national republic seemed democracy's next best hope. This was still, in principle at least, a politics of the common good. It looked to the nation, not as a neutral framework for the play of competing interests, but rather as a formative community, concerned to shape a common life suited to the scale of modern social and economic forms.

But this project failed. By the mid- or late twentieth century, the national republic had run its course. Except for extraordinary moments, such as war, the nation proved too vast a scale across which to cultivate the shared self-understandings necessary to community in the formative, or constitutive sense. And so the gradual shift, in our practices and institutions, from a public philosophy of common purposes to one of fair procedures, from a politics of good to a politics of right, from the national republic to the procedural republic.

OUR PRESENT PREDICAMENT

A full account of this transition would take a detailed look at the changing shape of political institutions, constitutional interpretation, and the terms of political discourse in the broadest sense. But I suspect we would find in the *practice* of the procedural republic two broad tendencies foreshadowed by its philosophy: first, a tendency to crowd out democratic possibilities; second, a tendency to undercut the kind of community on which it nonetheless depends.

Where liberty in the early republic was understood as a function of democratic institutions and dispersed power,[21] liberty in the procedural republic is defined in opposition to democracy, as an individual's guarantee against what the majority might will. I am free insofar as I am the bearer of rights, where rights are trumps.[22] Unlike the liberty of the early republic, the modern version permits—in fact even requires—concentrated power. This has to do with the universalizing logic of rights. Insofar as I have a right, whether to free speech or a minimum income, its provision cannot be left to the vagaries of local preferences but must be assured at the most comprehensive level of political association. It cannot be one thing in New York and another in Alabama. As rights and entitlements expand, politics is therefore displaced from smaller forms of association and relocated at the most universal form—in our case, the nation. And even as politics flows to the nation, power shifts away from democratic institutions (such as legislatures and political parties) and toward institutions designed to be insulated from democratic pressures, and hence better equipped to dispense and defend individual rights (notably the judiciary and bureaucracy).

These institutional developments may begin to account for the sense of powerlessness that the welfare state fails to address and in some ways doubtless deepens. But it seems to me a further clue to our condition recalls even more directly the predicament of the unencumbered self lurching, as we left it, between detachment on the one hand, the entanglement on the other. For it is a striking feature of the welfare state that it offers a powerful promise of individual rights, and also demands of its citizens a high measure of mutual engagement. But the self-image that attends the rights cannot sustain the engagement.

As bearers of rights, where rights are trumps, we think of ourselves as freely choosing, individual selves, unbound by obligations antecedent to rights, or to the agreements we make. And yet, as citizens of the procedural republic that secures these rights, we find ourselves implicated willy-nilly in a formidable array of dependencies and expectations we did not choose and increasingly reject.

In our public life, we are more entangled, but less attached, than ever before. It is as though the unencumbered self presupposed by the liberal ethic had begun to come true—less liberated than disempowered, entangled in a network of obligations and involvements unassociated with any act of will, and yet unmediated by those common identifications or expansive self-definitions that would make them tolerable. As the scale of social and political organization has become more comprehensive, the terms of our collective identity have become more fragmented, and the forms of political life have outrun the common purpose needed to sustain them.

Something like this, it seems to me, has been unfolding in America for the past half-century or so. I hope I have said at least enough to suggest the shape a fuller story might take. And I hope in any case to have conveyed a certain view about politics and philosophy and the relation between them—that our practices and institutions are themselves embodiments of theory, and to unravel their predicament is, at least in part, to seek after the self-image of the age.

NOTES

1. An excellent example of this view can be found in Samuel Huntington, *American Politics: The Promise of Disharmony* (Cambridge: Harvard University Press, 1981). See especially his discussion of the "ideals versus institutions" gap, pp. 10–12, 39–41, 61–84, 221–262.

2. See, for example, the conceptions of a "practice" advanced by Alasdair MacIntyre and Charles Taylor. MacIntyre, *After Virtue* (Notre Dame: University of Notre Dame Press, 1981), pp. 175–209. Taylor, "Interpretation and the Sciences of Man." *Review of Metaphysics* 25, (1971) pp. 3–51.

3. John Rawls, *A Theory of Justice*. (Oxford: Oxford University Press, 1971). Immanuel Kant, *Groundwork of the Metaphysics of Morals*, trans. H. J. Paton. (1785; New York: Harper and Row, 1956). Kant, *Critique of Pure Reason*, trans. Norman Kemp Smith (1781, 1787; London: Macmillan, 1929). Kant, *Critique of Practical Reason*, trans. I. W. Beck (1788; Indianapolis: Bobbs-Merrill, 1956). Kant, "On the Common Saying: This May Be True in Theory, But It Does Not Apply in Practice,'" in Hans Reiss, ed., *Kant's Political Writings*. (1793; Cambridge: Cambridge University Press, 1970). Other recent versions of the claim for the priority of the right over good can be found in Robert Norick, *Anarchy, State and Utopia* (New York: Basic Books, 1974); Ronald Dworkin, *Taking Rights Seriously* (London: Duckworth, 1977); Bruce Ackerman, *Social Justice in the Liberal State* (New Haven: Yale University Press, 1980).

4. This section, and the two that follow, summarize arguments developed more fully in Michael Sandel, *Liberalism and the Limits of Justice* (Cambridge: Cambridge University Press, 1982).

5. Rawls (1971), p. 3.

6. John Stuart Mill, *Utilitarianism*, in *The Utilitarians* (1893; Garden City: Doubleday, 1973), p. 465; Mill, *On Liberty* in *The Utilitarians*, p. 485 (Originally published 1849).

7. Kant (1793), p. 73.

8. Kant (1785), p. 92.

9. Kant (1788), p. 89.

10. Kant (1785), p. 105.

11. Kant (1788), p. 89.

12. Kant (1785), p. 121.

13. Rawls, "The Basic Structure as Subject," *American Philosophical Quarterly* (1977), p. 165.

14. Rawls (1971), p. 560.

15. Rawls, "Kantian Constructivism in Moral Theory," *Journal of Philosophy* 77 (1980), p. 543.

16. Mill (1849), p. 485.

17. Rawls (1971), pp. 101–102.

19. Croly. *The Promise of American Life* (Indianapolis: Bobbs-Merrill, 1965), pp. 270–273.

20. Beer, "Liberalism and the National Idea." *The Public Interest*. (Fall 1966), pp. 70–82.

21. See, for example, Laurence Tribe, *American Constitutional Law* (Mineola: The Foundation Press, 1978), pp. 2–3.

22. See Ronald Dworkin, "Liberalism," in Stuart Hampshire, ed., *Public and Private Morality* (Cambridge: Cambridge University Press, 1978), p. 136.

THE CONSERVATIVE DISPOSITION

Conservatism is often considered a simple reaction against either reform or revolution. But this is itself predicated on certain positive assumptions about politics. According to Michael Oakeshott, among the leading English thinkers since World War II, conservatism is based on a certain disposition for following a given form of conduct. His classic essay "On Being Conservative" initally notes the conservative's propensity to "prefer the familiar to the unknown"; the disposition is fundamentally cautious and predicated on "rational prudence." Innovations are greeted skeptically, and reformers have the onus of proof in showing how a proposed change will be beneficial. According to Oakeshott, "Every change is an emblem of extinction," and conservatives will logically seek to mitigate it and to assimilate the new as quickly and painlessly as possible.

The conservative disposition, arguably, involves a primarily cultural awareness of having something to lose from change. To conservatives, traditions and customs have value in their own right, and relativism is anathema. Leo Strauss, the German exile who had such a profound impact on political theory in the United States, abhorred the decline in liberal education and the increasing refusal to engage the authoritative voices of the Western political tradition. Such voices receive expression in the "great books" and the ongoing "conversation" over enduring issues whose incessant examination places the critic in opposition to the relativizing tendencies of mass culture. In this way, self-consciously, political theory strives to create an intellectual "aristocracy within mass society."

Opposition to this assault on tradition takes a somewhat different form in "The Adversary Culture and the New Class," by Norman Podhoretz, who, as editor of *Commentary*, provided intellectual sustenance to the neoconservative movement of the 1980s in the United States. Podhoretz is appalled by the "virulent hostility" of an intellectual minority from the 1960s toward the capitalistic ethos embraced by the majority of Americans. Their support for affirmative action and the welfare state militates against American individualism; their multiculturalism and sympathy for the Third World undermines inherited western values; and their leftism was directed against not only capitalism but the struggle against communist totalitarianism in the cold war. They are the enemy, not the "friend." Podhoretz has no use for the aristocratic pretensions of Strauss or Oakeschott. He stands in support of "middle-class values." Neoconservatives are, in this sense, the adversaries of the "adversary culture," and they have largely come to dominate the ideological agenda in the United States as the century draws to a close.

MICHAEL OAKESHOTT

On Being Conservative

The common belief that it is impossible (or, if not impossible, then so unpromising as to be not worthwhile attempting) to elicit explanatory general principles from what is recognized to be conservative conduct is not one that I share. It may be true that conservative conduct does not readily provoke articulation in the idiom of general ideas, and that consequently there has been a certain reluctance to undertake this kind of elucidation; but it is not to be presumed that conservative conduct is less eligible than any other for this sort of interpretation, for what it is worth. Nevertheless, this is not the enterprise I propose to engage in here. My theme is not a creed or a doctrine, but a disposition. To be conservative is to be disposed to think and behave in certain manners; it is to prefer certain kinds of conduct and certain conditions of human circumstances to others; it is to be disposed to make certain kinds of choices. And my design here is to construe this disposition as it appears in contemporary character, rather than to transpose it into the idiom of general principles.

The general characteristics of this disposition are not difficult to discern, although they have often been mistaken. They centre upon a propensity to use and to enjoy what is available rather than to wish for or to look for something else; to delight in what is present rather than what was or what may be. Reflection may bring to light an appropriate gratefulness for what is available, and consequently the acknowledgement of a gift or an inheritance from the past; but there is no mere idolizing of what is past and gone. What is esteemed is the present; and it is esteemed not on account of its connections with a remote antiquity, nor because it is recognized to be more admirable than any possible alternative, but on account of its familiarity: not, *Verweile doch, du bist so schön*, but, *Stay with me because I am attached to you.*

If the present is arid, offering little or nothing to be used or enjoyed, then this inclination will be weak or absent; if the present is remarkably unsettled, it will display itself in a search for a firmer foothold and consequently in a recourse to and an exploration of the past; but it asserts itself characteristically when there is much to be enjoyed, and it will be strongest when this is combined with evident risk of loss. In short, it is a disposition appropriate to a man who is acutely aware of having something to lose which he has learned to care for; a man in some degree rich in opportunities for enjoyment, but not so rich that he can afford to be indifferent to loss. It will appear more naturally in the old than in the young, not because the old are more sensitive to loss but because they are apt to be more fully aware of the resources of their world and therefore less likely to find them inadequate. In some people this disposition is weak merely because they are ignorant of what their world has to offer them: the present appears to them only as a residue of inopportunities.

To be conservative, then, is to prefer the familiar to the unknown, to prefer the tried to the untried, fact to mystery, the actual to the possible, the limited to the unbounded, the near to the distant, the sufficient to the superabundant, the convenient to the perfect, present laughter to utopian bliss. Familiar relationships and loyalties will be preferred to the allure of more profitable attachments; to acquire and to enlarge will be less important than to keep, to cultivate and to enjoy; the grief of loss will be more acute than the excitement of novelty or promise. It is to be equal to one's own fortune, to live at the level of one's own means, to be content with the want of greater perfection which belongs alike to oneself and one's circumstances. With some people this is itself a choice; in others it is a disposition which appears, frequently or less frequently, in their preferences and aversions, and is not itself chosen or specifically cultivated.

Now, all this is represented in a certain attitude towards change and innovation; change denoting alterations we have to suffer and innovation those we design and execute.

Changes are circumstances to which we have to accommodate ourselves, and the disposition to be conservative is both the emblem of our difficulty in doing so and our resort in the attempts we make to do so. Changes are without effect only upon those who notice nothing, who are ignorant of what they possess and apathetic to their circumstances; and they can be welcomed indiscriminately only by those who esteem nothing, whose attachments are fleeting and who are strangers to love and affection. The conservative disposition provokes neither of these conditions: the inclination to enjoy what is present and available is the opposite of ignorance and apathy and it breeds attachment and affection. Consequently, it is averse from change, which appears always, in the first place, as deprivation. A storm which sweeps away a copse and transforms a favourite view, the death of friends, the sleep of friendship, the desuetude of customs of behaviour, the retirement of a favourite clown, involuntary exile, reversals of fortune, the loss of abilities enjoyed and their replacement by others—these are changes, none perhaps without its compensations, which the man of conservative temperament unavoidably regrets. But he has difficulty in reconciling himself to them, not because what he has lost in them was intrinsically better than any alternative might have been or was incapable of improvement, nor because what he has lost was something he actually enjoyed and had learned how to enjoy and what takes its place is something to which he has acquired no attachment. Consequently, he will find small and slow changes more tolerable than large and sudden; and he will value highly every appearance of continuity. Some changes, indeed, will present no difficulty; but, again, this is not because they are manifest improvements but merely because they are easily assimilated: the changes of the seasons are mediated by their recurrence and the growing up of children by its continuousness. And, in general, he will accommodate himself more readily to changes which do not offend expectation than to the destruction of what seems to have no ground of dissolution within itself.

Moreover, to be conservative is not merely to be averse from change (which may be an idiosyncrasy); it is also a manner of accommodating ourselves to changes, an activity imposed upon all men. For, change is a threat to identity, and every change is an emblem of extinction. But a man's identity (or that of a community) is nothing more than an unbroken rehearsal of contingencies, each at the mercy of circumstance and each significant in proportion to its familiarity. It is not a fortress into which we may retire, and the only means we have of defending it (that is, ourselves) against the hostile forces of change is in the open field of our experience; by throwing our weight upon the foot which for the time being is most firmly placed, by cleaving to whatever familiarities are not immediately threatened and thus assimilating what is new without becoming unrecognizable to ourselves. The Masai, when they were moved from their old country to the present Masai reserve in Kenya, took with them the names of their hills and plains and rivers and gave them to the hills and plains and rivers of the new country. And it is by some such subterfuge of conservatism that every man or people compelled to suffer a notable change avoids the shame of extinction.

Changes, then, have to be suffered; and a man of conservative temperament (that is, one strongly disposed to preserve his identity) cannot be indifferent to them. In the main, he judges them by the disturbance they entail and, like everyone else, deploys his resources to meet them. The idea of innovation, on the other hand, is improvement. Nevertheless, a man of this temperament will not himself be an ardent innovator. In the first place, he is not inclined to think that nothing is happening unless great changes are afoot and therefore he is not worried by the absence of innovation: the use and enjoyment of things as they are occupies most of his attention. Further, he is aware that not all innovation is, in fact, improvement; and he will think that to innovate without improving is either designed or inadvertent folly. Moreover, even when an innovation commends itself as a convincing improvement, he will look twice at its claims before accepting them. From his point of view, because every improvement involves change, the disruption entailed has always to be set against the benefit anticipated. But when he has satisfied himself about this, there will be other considerations to be taken into the account. Innovating is always an equivocal enterprise, in which gain and loss (even excluding the loss of familiarity) are so closely interwoven that it is exceedingly difficult to forecast the final up-shot: there is no such thing as an unqualified improvement. For, innovating is an activity which generates not only the 'improvement' sought, but a new and complex situation of which this is only one of the components. The total change is always more extensive than the change designed; and the whole of what is entailed can neither be foreseen nor circumscribed. Thus, whenever there is innovation there is the certainty that the change will be greater than was intended, that there will be loss as well as gain and that the loss and the gain will not be equally distributed among the people affected; there is the chance that the benefits derived will be greater than those which were designed; and there is the risk that they will be off-set by changes for the worse.

From all this the man of conservative temperament draws some appropriate conclusions. First, innovation entails certain loss and possible gain, therefore, the onus of proof, to show that the proposed change may be expected to be on the whole beneficial, rests with the would-be innovator. Secondly, he believes that the more closely an innovation resembles growth (that is, the more clearly it is intimated in and not merely imposed upon the situation) the less likely it is to result in a preponderance of loss. Thirdly, he thinks that an innovation which is a response to some specific defect, one designed to redress some specific disequilibrium, is more desirable than one which springs from a notion of a generally improved condition of human circumstances, and is far more desirable than one generated by a vision of perfection. Consequently, he prefers small and limited innovations to large and indefinite. Fourthly, he favours a slow rather than a rapid pace, and pauses to observe current consequences and make appropriate adjustments. And lastly, he belives the occasion to be important; and, other things being equal, he considers the most favourable occasion for innovation to be when the projected change is most likely to be limited to what is intended and least likely to be corrupted by undesired and unmanageable consequences

The disposition to be conservative is, then, warm and positive in respect of enjoyment, and correspondingly cool and critical in respect of change and innovation: these two inclinations support and elucidate one another. The man of conservative temperament believes that a known good is not lightly to be surrendered for an unknown better. He is not in love with what is dangerous and difficult; he is unadventurous; he has no impulse to sail uncharted seas; for him there is no magic in being lost, bewildered or shipwrecked. If he is forced to navigate the unknown, he sees virtue in heaving the lead every inch of the way. What others plausibly identify as timidity, he recognizes in himself as rational prudence; what others interpret as inactivity, he recognizes as a disposition to enjoy rather than to exploit. He is cautious, and he is disposed to indicate his assent or dissent, not in absolute, but in graduated terms. He eyes the situation in terms of its propensity to disrupt the familiarity of the features of his world.

. . . How, then, are we to construe the disposition to be conservative in respect of politics? And in making this inquiry what I am interested in is not merely the intelligibility of this disposition in any set of circumstances, but its intelligibility in our own contemporary circumstances.

Writers who have considered this question commonly direct our attention to beliefs about the world in general, about human beings in general, about associations in general and even about the universe; and they tell us that a conservative disposition in politics can be correctly construed only when we understand it as a reflection of certain beliefs of these kinds. It is said, for example, that conservatism in politics is the appropriate counterpart of a generally conservative disposition in respect of human conduct: to be reformist in business, in morals or in religion and to be conservative in politics is represented as being inconsistent. It is said that the conservative in politics is so by virtue of holding certain religious beliefs; a belief, for example, in a natural law to be gathered from human experience, and in a providential order reflecting a divine purpose in nature and in human history to which it is the duty of mankind to conform its conduct and departure from which spells injustice and calamity. Further, it is said that a disposition to be conservative in politics reflects what is called an 'organic' theory of human society; that it is tied up with a belief in the absolute value of human personality, and with a belief in a primordial propensity of human beings to sin. And the 'conservatism' of an Englishman has even been connected with Royalism and Anglicanism.

Now, setting aside the minor complaints one might be moved to make about this account of the situation, it seems to me to suffer from one large defect. It is true that many of these beliefs have been held by people disposed to be conservative in political activity, and it may be true that these people have also believed their disposition to be in some way confirmed by them, or even to be founded upon them; but, as I understand it, a disposition to be conservative in politics does not entail either that we should hold these beliefs to be true or even that we should suppose them to be true. Indeed, I do not think it is necessarily connected with any particular beliefs about the universe, about the world in general or about human conduct in general. What it is tied to is certain beliefs about the activity of governing and the instruments of government, and it is in terms of beliefs on these topics, and not on others, that it can be made to appear intelligible. And, to state my view briefly before elaborating it, what makes a conservative disposition in politics intelligible is nothing to do with a natural law or a providential order, nothing to do with morals or religion; it is the observation of our current manner of living combined with the belief (which from our point of view need be regarded as no more than an hypothesis) that governing is a specific and limited activity, namely the provision and custody of general rules of conduct, which are understood, not as plans for imposing substantive activities, but as instruments enabling people to pursue the activities of their own choice with the minimum frustration, and therefore something which it is appropriate to be conservative about.

Let us begin at what I believe to be the proper starting-place; not in the empyrean, but with ourselves as we have come to be. I and my neighbours, my associates, my compatriots, my friends, my enemies and those who I am indifferent about, are people engaged in a great variety of activities. We are apt to entertain a multiplicity of opinions on every conceivable subject and are disposed to change these beliefs as we grow tired of them or as they prove unserviceable. Each of us is pursuing a course of his own; and there is no project so unlikely that somebody will not be found to engage in it, no enterprise so foolish that somebody will not undertake it. There are those who spend their lives trying to sell copies of the Anglican Catechism to the Jews. And one half of the world is engaged in trying to make the other half want what it has hitherto never felt the lack of. We are all inclined to be passionate about our own concerns, whether it is making things or selling them, whether it is business or sport, religion or learning, poetry, drink or drugs. Each of us has preferences of his own. For some, the opportunities of making choices (which are numerous) are invitations readily accepted; others welcome them less eagerly or even find them burdensome. Some dream dreams of new and better worlds: others are more inclined to move in familiar paths or even to be idle. Some are apt to deplore the rapidity of change, others delight in it; all recognize it. At times we grow tired and fall asleep: it is a blessed relief to gaze in a shop window and see nothing we want; we are grateful for ugliness merely because it repels attention. But, for the most part, we pursue happiness by seeking the satisfaction of desires which spring from one another inexhaustably. We enter into relationships of interest and of emotion, of competition, partnership, guardianship, love, friendship, jealousy and hatred, some of which are more durable than others. We make agreements with one another; we have expectations about one another's conduct; we approve, we are indifferent and we disapprove. This multiplicity of activity and variety of opinion is apt to produce collisions: We pursue courses which cut across those of others, and we do not all approve the same sort of conduct. But, in the main, we get along with one another, sometimes by giving way, sometimes by standing fast, sometimes in a compromise. Our conduct consists of activity assimilated to that of others in small, and for the most part unconsidered and unobtrusive, adjustments.

Why all this should be so, does not matter. It is not necessarily so. A different condition of human circumstance can easily be imagined, and we know that elsewhere and at other times activity is, or has been, far less multifarious and changeful and opinion far less diverse and far less likely to provoke collision; but, by and large, we recognize this to be our condition. It is an acquired condition, though nobody designed or specifically chose it in preference to all others. It is the product, not of 'human nature' let loose, but of human beings impelled by an acquired love of making choices for themselves. And we know as little and as much about where it is leading us as we know about the fashion in hats of twenty years' time or the design of motor-cars.

Surveying the scene, some people are provoked by the absence of order and coherence which appears to them to be its dominant feature; its wastefulness, its frustration, its dissipation of human energy, its lack not merely of a premediatated destination but even of any discernible direction of movement. It provides an excitement similar to that of a stock-car race; but it has none of the satisfaction of a well-conducted business enterprise. Such people are apt to exaggerate the current disorder; the absence of plan is so conspicuous that the small adjustments, and even the more massive arrangements, which restrain the chaos seem to them nugatory; they have no feeling for the warmth of untidiness but only for its inconvenience. But what is significant is not the limitations of their powers of observation, but the turn of their thoughts. They feel that there ought to be something that ought to be done to convert this so-called chaos into order, for this is no way for rational human beings to be spending their lives. Like Apollo when he saw Daphne with her hair hung carelessly about her neck, they sigh and say to themselves: 'What if it were properly arranged.' Moreover, they tell us that they have seen in a dream the glorious, collisionless manner of living proper to all mankind, and this dream they understand as their warrant for seeking to remove the diversities and occasions of conflict which distinguish our current manner of living. Of course, their dreams are not all exactly alike; but they have this in common: each is a vision of a condition of human circumstance from which the occasion of conflict has been removed, a vision of human activity co-ordinated and set going in a single direction and of every resource being used to the full. And such people appropriately understand the office of government to be the imposition upon its subjects of the condition of human circumstances of their dream. To govern is to turn a private dream into a public and compulsory manner of living. Thus, politics becomes an encounter of dreams and the activity in which government is held to this understanding of its office and provided with the appropriate instruments.

I do not propose to criticize this jump to glory style of politics in which governing is understood as a perpetual take-over bid for the purchase of the resources of human energy in order to concentrate them in a single direction; it is not at all unintelligible, and there is much in our circumstances to provoke it. My purpose is merely to point out that there is another quite different understanding of government, and that it is no less intelligible and in some respects perhaps more appropriate to our circumstances.

The spring of this other disposition in respect of governing and the instruments of government—a conservative disposition—is to be found in the acceptance of the current condition of human circumstances as I have described it: the propensity to make our own choices with passion, the diversity of beliefs each held with the conviction of its exclusive truth; the inventiveness, the changefulness and the absence of any large design; the excess, the over-activity and the informal compromise. And the office of government is not to impose other beliefs and activities upon its subjects, not to tutor or to educate them, not to make them better or happier in another way, not to direct them, to galvanize them into action, to lead them or to coordinate their activities so that no occasion of conflict shall occur; the office of government is merely to rule. This is a specific and limited activity, easily corrupted when it is combined with any other, and, in the circumstances, indispensable. The image of the ruler is the umpire whose business is to administer the rules of the game, or the chairman who governs the debate according to known rules but does not himself participate in it.

Now people of this disposition commonly defend their belief that the proper attitude of government towards the current condition of human circumstance is one of acceptance by appealing to certain general ideas. They contend that there is absolute value in the free play of human choice, that private property (the emblem of choice) is a natural right, that it is only in the enjoyment of diversity of opinion and activity that true belief and good conduct can be expected to disclose themselves. But I do not think that this disposition requires these or any similar beliefs in order to make it intelligible. Something much smaller and less pretentious will do: the observation that this condition of human circumstance is, in fact, current, and that we have learned to enjoy it and how to manage it; that we are not children *in statu pupillari* but adults who do not consider themselves under any obligation to justify their preference for making their own choices; and that it is beyond human experience to suppose that those who rule are endowed with a superior wisdom which discloses to them a better range of beliefs and activities and which gives them authority to impose upon their subjects a quite different manner of life. In short, if the man of this disposition is asked: Why ought governments to accept the current diversity of opinion and activity in preference to imposing upon their subjects a dream of their own? it is enough for him to reply: Why not? Their dreams are no different from those of anyone else; and if it is boring to have to listen to dreams of others being recounted, it is insufferable to be forced to re-enact them. We tolerate monomaniacs, it is our habit to do so; but why should we be *ruled* by them? Is it not (the man of conservative disposition asks) an intelligible task for a government to protect its subjects against the nuisance of those who spend their energy and their wealth in the service of some pet indignation, endeavouring to impose it upon everybody, not by suppressing their activities in favour of others of a similar kind, but by setting a limit to the amount of noise anyone may emit?

Nevertheless, if this acceptance is the spring of the conservative's disposition in respect of government, he does not suppose that the office of government is to do nothing. As he understands it, there is work to be done which can be done only in virtue of a genuine acceptance of current beliefs simply because they are current and current activities simply because they are afoot. And, briefly, the office he attributes to government is to resolve some of the collisions which this variety of beliefs and activities generates; to preserve peace, not by placing an interdict upon choice and upon the diversity that springs from the exercise of preference, not by imposing substantive uniformity, but by enforcing general rules of procedure upon all subjects alike.

Government, then, as the conservative in this matter understands it, does not begin with a vision of another, different and better world, but with the observation of the self-government practised even by men of passion in the conduct of their enterprises; it begins in the informal adjustments of interests to one another which are designed to release those who are apt to collide from the mutual frustration of a collision. Sometimes these adjustments are no more than agreements between two parties to keep out of each other's way; sometimes they are of wider application and more durable character, such as the International Rules for the prevention of collisions at sea. In short, the intimations of government are to be found in ritual, not in religion or philosophy; in the enjoyment of orderly and peaceable behaviour, not in the search for truth or perfection.

But the self-government of men of passionate belie and enterprise is apt to break down when it is most needed. It often suffices to resolve minor collisions of interest, but beyond these it is not to be relied upon. A more precise and a less easily corrupted ritual is required to resolve the massive collisions which our manner of living is apt to generate and to release us from the massive frustrations in which we are apt to become locked. The custodian of this ritual is 'the government', and the rules it imposes are 'the law'. One may imagine a government engaged in the activity of an arbiter in cases of collisions of interest but doing its business without the aid of laws, just as one may imagine a game without rules and an umpire who was appealed to in cases of dispute and who on each occasion merely used his judgement to devise *ad hoc* a way of releasing the disputants from their mutual frustration. But the diseconomy of such an arrangement is so obvious that it could only be expected to occur to those inclined to believe the ruler to be supernaturally inspired and to those disposed to attribute to him a quite different office—that of leader, or tutor, or manager. At all events the disposition to be conservative in respect of government is rooted in the belief that where government rests upon the acceptance of the current activities and beliefs of its subjects, the only appropriate manner of ruling is by making and enforcing rules of conduct. In short, to be conservative about government is a reflection of the conservatism we have recognized to be appropriate in respect of rules of conduct.

To govern, then, as the conservative understands it, is to provide a *vinculum juris* for those manners of conduct which, in the circumstances, are least likely to result in a frustrating collision of interests; to provide redress and means of compensation for those who suffer from others behaving in a contrary manner; sometimes to provide punishment for those who pursue their own interests regardless of the rules; and, of course, to provide a sufficient force to maintain the authority of an arbiter of this kind. Thus, governing is recognized as a specific and limited activity; not the management of an enterprise, but the rule of those engaged in a great diversity of self-chosen enterprises. It is not concerned with concrete persons, but with activities; and with activities only in respect of their propensity to collide with one another. It is not concerned with moral right and wrong; it is not designed to make men good or even better; it is not indispensable on account of 'the natural depravity of mankind' but merely because of their current disposition to be extravagant; its business is to keep its subjects at peace with one another in the activities in which they have chosen to seek their happiness. And if there is any general idea entailed in this view, it is, perhaps, that a government which does not sustain the loyalty of its subjects is worthless; and that while one which (in the old puritan phrase) 'commands for truth' is incapable of doing so (because some of its subjects will believe its 'truth' to be error), one which is indifferent to 'truth' and 'error' alike, and merely pursues peace, presents no obstacle to the necessary loyalty.

Now, it is intelligible enough that any man who thinks in this manner about government should be averse from innovation: government is providing rules of conduct, and familiarity is a supremely important virtue in a rule. Nevertheless, he has room for other thoughts. The current condition of human circumstances is one in which new activities (often springing from new inventions) are constantly appearing and rapidly extend themselves, and in which beliefs are perpetually being modified or discarded; and for the rules to be inappropriate to the current activities and beliefs is as unprofitable as for them to be unfamiliar. For example, a variety of inventions and considerable changes in the conduct of business, seem now to have made the current law of copyright inadequate. And it may be thought that neither the newspaper nor the motor-car nor the aeroplane have yet received proper recognition in the law of England; they have all created nuisances that call out to be abated. Or again, at the end of the last century our governments engaged in an extensive codification of large parts of our law and in this manner both brought it into closer relationship with current beliefs and manners of activity and insulted if from the small adjustment to circumstances which are characteristic of the operation of our common law. But many of these Statutes are now hopelessly out of date. And there are older Acts of Parliament (such as the Merchant Shipping Act), governing large and important departments of activity, which are even more inappropriate to current circumstances. Innovation, then, is called for if the rules are to remain appropriate to the activities they govern. But, as the conservative understands it, modification of the rules should always reflect, and never impose, a change in the activities and beliefs of those who are subject to them, and should never on any occasion be so great as to destroy the *ensemble*. Consequently, the conservative will have nothing to do with innovations designed to meet merely hypothetical situations; he will prefer to enforce a rule he has got rather than invent a new one; he will think it appropriate to delay a modification of the rules until it is clear that the change of circumstance it is designed to reflect has come to stay for a while; he will be suspicious of proposals for change in excess of what the situation calls for, of rulers who demand extra-ordinary powers in order to make great changes and whose utterances are tied to generalities like 'the public good' or 'social justice', and of Saviours of Society who buckle on armour and seek dragons to slay; he will think it proper to consider the occasion of the innovation with care; in short, he will be disposed to regard politics as an activity in which a valuable set of tools is renovated from time to time and kept in trim rather than as an opportunity for perpetual re-equipment.

All this may help to make intelligible the disposition to be conservative in respect of government; and the detail might be elaborated to show, for example, how a man of this disposition understands the other great business of a government, the conduct of a foreign policy; to show why he places so high a value upon the complicated set of arrangements we call 'the institution of private property'; to show the appropriateness of his rejection of the view that politics is a shadow thrown by economics; to show why he believes that the main (perhaps the only) specifically economic activity appropriate to government is the maintenance of a stable currency. But, on this occasion, I think there is something else to be said.

To some people, 'government' appears as a vast reservoir of power which inspires them to dream of what use might be made of it. They have favourite projects, of various dimensions, which they sincerely believe are for the benefit of mankind, and to capture this source of power, if necessary to increase it, and to use it for imposing their favourite projects upon their fellows is what they understand as the adventure of governing men. They are, thus, disposed to recognize government as an instrument of passion; the art of politics is to inflame and direct desire. In short, governing is understood to be just like any other activity—making and selling a brand of soap, exploiting the resources of a locality, or developing a housing estate—only the power here is (for the most part) already mobilized, and the enterprise is remarkable only because it aims at monopoly and because of its promise of success once the source of power has been captured. Of course a private enterprise politician of this sort would get nowhere in these days unless there were people with wants so vague that they can be prompted to ask for what he has to offer, or with wants so servile that they prefer the promise of a provided abundance to the opportunity of choice and activity on their own account. And it is not all as plain sailing as it might appear: often a politician of this sort misjudges the situation; and then, briefly, even in democratic politics, we become aware of what the camel thinks of the camel driver.

Now, the disposition to be conservative in respect of politics reflects a quite different view of the activity of governing. The man of this disposition understands it to be the business of a government not to inflame passion and give it new objects to feed upon, but to inject into the activities of already too passionate men an ingredient of moderation; to restrain, to deflate, to pacify and to reconcile; not to stoke the fires of desire, but to damp them down. And all this, not because passion is vice and moderation virtue, but because moderation is indispensable if passionate men are to escape being locked in an encounter of mutual frustration. A government of this sort does not need to be regarded as the agent of a benign providence, as the custodian of a moral law, or as the emblem of a divine order. What it provides is something that its subjects (if they are such people as we are) can easily recognize to be valuable; indeed, it is something that, to some extent, they do for themselves in the ordinary course of business or pleasure. They scarcely need to be reminded of its indispensability, as Sextus Empiricus tells us the ancient Persians were accustomed periodically to remind themselves by setting aside all laws for five hair-raising days on the death of a king. Generally speaking, they are not averse from paying the modest cost of this service; and they recognize that the appropriate attitude to a government of this sort is loyalty (sometimes a confident loyalty, at others perhaps the heavy-hearted loyalty of Sidney Godolphin), respect and some suspicion, not love or devotion or affection. Thus, governing is understood to be a secondary activity; but it is recognized also to be a specific activity, not easily to be combined with any other, because all other activities (except the mere contemplation of the scene) entail taking sides and the surrender of the indifference appropriate (on this view of things) not only to the judge but also to the legislator, who is understood to occupy a judicial office. The subjects of such a government require that it shall be strong, alert, resolute, economical and neither capricious nor overactive: they have no use for a referee who does not govern the game according to the rules, who takes sides, who plays a game of his own, or who is always blowing his whistle; after all, the game's the thing, and in playing the game we neither need to be, nor at present are disposed to be, conservative.

But there is something more to be observed in this style of governing than merely the restraint imposed by familiar and appropriate rules. Of course, it will not countenance government by suggestion or cajolery or by any other means than by law; an avuncular Home Secretary or a threatening Chancellor of the Exchequer. But the spectacle of its indifference to the beliefs and substantive activities of its subjects may itself be expected to provoke a habit of restraint. Into the heat of our engagements, into the passionate clash of beliefs, into our enthusiasm for saving the souls of our neighbours or of all mankind, a government of this sort injects an ingredient, not of reason (how should we expect that?) but of the irony that is prepared to counteract one vice by another, of the raillery that deflates extravagance without itself pretending to wisdom, of the mockery that disperses tension, of inertia and of scepticism; indeed, it might be said that we keep a government of this sort to do for us the scepticism we have neither the time nor the inclination to do for ourselves. It is like the cool touch of the mountain that one feels in the plain even on the hottest summer day. Or, to leave metaphor behind, it is like the 'governor' which, by controlling the speed at which its parts move, keeps an engine from racketing itself to pieces.

It is not, then, mere stupid prejudice which disposes a conservative to take this view of the activity of governing; nor are any highfalutin metaphysical beliefs necessary to provoke it or make it intelligible. It is connected merely with the observation that where activity is bent upon enterprise the indispensable counterpart is another order of activity, bent upon restraint, which is unavoidably corrupted (indeed, altogether abrogated) when the power assigned to it is used for advancing favourite projects. An 'umpire' who at the same time is one of the players is no umpire; 'rules' about which we are not disposed to be conservative are not rules but incitements to disorder; the conjunction of dreaming and ruling generates tyranny.

Political conservatism is, then, not at all unintelligible in a people disposed to be adventurous and enterprising, a people in love with change and apt to rationalize their affections in terms of 'progress'.[1] And one does not need to think that the belief in 'progress' is the most cruel and unprofitable of all beliefs, arousing cupidity without satisfying it, in order to think it inappropriate for a government to be conspicuously 'progressive'. Indeed, a disposition to be conservative in respect of government would seem to be pre-eminently appropriate to men who have something to do and something to think about on their own account, who have a skill to practise or an intellectual fortune to make, to people whose passions do not need to be inflamed, whose desires do not need to be provoked and whose dreams of a better world need no prompting. Such people know the value of a rule which imposes orderliness without directing enterprise, a rule which concentrates duty so that room is left for delight. They might even be prepared to suffer a legally established ecclesiastical order; but it would not be because they believed it to represent some unassailable religious truth, but merely because it restrained the indecent competition of sects and (as Hume said) moderated 'the plague of a too diligent clergy'.

Now, whether or not these beliefs recommend themselves as reasonable and appropriate to our circumstances and to the abilities we are likely to find in those who rule us, they and their like are in my view what make intelligible a conservative disposition in respect of politics. What would be the appropriateness of this disposition in circumstances other than our own, whether to be conservative in respect of government would have the same relevance in the circumstances of an unadventurous, a slothful or a spiritless people, is a question we need not try to answer: we are concerned with ourselves as we are. I myself think that it would occupy an important place in any set of circumstances. But what I hope I have made clear is that it is not at all inconsistent to be conservative in respect of government and radical in respect of almost every other activity. And, in my opinion, there is more to be learnt about this disposition from Montaigne, Pascal, Hobbes and Hume than from Burke or Bentham.

Of the many entailments of this view of things that might be pointed to, I will notice one, namely, that politics is an activity unsuited to the young, not on account of their vices but on account of what I at least consider to be their virtues.

Nobody pretends that it is easy to acquire or to sustain the mood of indifference which this manner of politics calls for. To rein in one's own beliefs and desires, to acknowledge the current shape of things, to feel the balance of things in one's hand, to tolerate what is abominable, to distinguish between crime and sin, to respect formality even when it appears to be leading to error, these are difficult achievements; and they are achievements not to be looked for in the young.

Everybody's young days are a dream, a delightful insanity, a sweet solipsism. Nothing in them has a fixed shape, nothing a fixed price; everything is a possibility, and we live happily on credit. There are no obligations to be observed; there are no accounts to be kept. Nothing is specified in advance; everything is what can be made of it. The world is a mirror in which we seek the reflection of our own desires. The allure of violent emotions is irresistible. When we are young we are not disposed to make concessions to the world; we never feel the balance of a thing in our hands—unless it be a cricket bat. We are not apt to distinguish between our liking and our esteem; urgency is our criterion of importance; and we do not easily understand that what is humdrum need not be despicable. We are impatient of restraint; and we readily believe, like Shelley, that to have contracted a habit is to have failed. These, in my opinion, are among our virtues when we are young; but how remote they are from the disposition appropriate for participating in the style of goverment I have been describing. Since life is a dream, we argue (with plausible but erroneous logic) that politics must be an encounter of dreams, in which we hope to impose our own. Some unfortunate people, like Pitt (laughably called 'the Younger'), are born old, and are eligible to engage in politics almost in their cradles; others, perhaps more fortunate, belie the saying that one is young only once, they never grow up. But these are exceptions. For most there is what Conrad called the 'shadow line' which, when we pass it, discloses a solid world of things, each with its fixed shape, each with its own point of balance, each with its price; a world of fact, not poetic image, in which what we have spent on one thing we cannot spend on another; a world inhabited by others besides ourselves who cannot be reduced to mere reflections of our own emotions. And coming to be at home in this commonplace world qualifies us (as no knowledge of 'political science' can ever qualify us), if we are so inclined and have nothing better to think about, to engage in what the man of conservative disposition understands to be political activity.

NOTE

1. I have forgotten to ask myself the question: Why, then, have we so neglected what is appropriate to our circumstances as to make the activist dreamer the stereotype of the modern politician? And I have tried to answer it elsewhere.

LEO STRAUSS

What Is Liberal Education?

Liberal education is education in culture or toward culture. The finished product of a liberal education is a cultured human being. "Culture" (*cultura*) means primarily agriculture: the cultivation of the soil and its products, taking care of the soil, improving the soil in accordance with its nature. "Culture" means derivatively and today chiefly the cultivation of the mind, the taking care and improving of the native faculties of the mind in accordance with the nature of the mind. Just as the soil needs cultivators of the soil, the mind needs teachers. But teachers are not as easy to come by as farmers. The teachers themselves are pupils and must be pupils. But there cannot be an infinite regress: ultimately there must be teachers who are not in turn pupils. Those teachers who are not in turn pupils are the great minds or, in order to avoid any ambiguity in a matter of such importance, the greatest minds. Such men are extremely rare. We are not likely to meet any of them in any classroom. We are not likely to meet any of them anywhere. It is a piece of good luck if there is a single one alive in one's time. For all practical purposes, pupils, of whatever degree of proficiency, have access to the teachers who are not in turn pupils, to the greatest minds, only through the great books. Liberal education will then consist in studying with the proper care the great books which the greatest minds have left behind—a study in which the more experienced pupils assist the less experienced pupils, including the beginners.

This is not an easy task, as would appear if we were to consider the formula which I have just mentioned. That formula requires a long commentary. Many lives have been spent and may still be spent in writing such commentaries. For instance, what is meant by the remark that the great books should be studied "with the proper care"? At present I mention only one difficulty which is obvious to everyone among you: the greatest minds do not all tell us the same things regarding the most important themes; the community of the greatest minds is rent by discord and even by various kinds of discord. Whatever further consequences this may entail, it certainly entails the consequence that liberal education cannot be simply indoctrination. I mention yet another difficulty. "Liberal education is education in culture." In what culture? Our answer is: culture in the sense of the Western tradition. Yet Western culture is only one among many cultures. By limiting ourselves to Western culture, do we not condemn liberal education to a kind of parochialism, and is not parochialism incompatible with the liberalism, the generosity, the openmindedness, of liberal education? Our notion of liberal education does not seem to fit an age which is aware of the fact that there is not *the* culture of *the* human mind, but a variety of cultures. Obviously, culture if susceptible of being used in the plural is not quite the same thing as culture which is a *singulare tantum*, which can be used only in the singular. Culture is now no longer, as people say, an absolute, but has become relative. It is not easy to say what culture susceptible of being used in the plural means. As a consequence of this obscurity people have suggested, explicitly or implicitly, that culture is any pattern of conduct common to any human group. Hence we do not hesitate to speak of the culture of suburbia or of the cultures of juvenile gangs, both nondelinquent and delinquent. In other words, every human being outside of lunatic asylums is a cultured human being, for he participates in a culture. At the frontiers of research there arises the question as to whether there are not cultures also of inmates of lunatic asylums. If we contrast the present-day usage of "culture" with the original meaning, it is as if someone would say that the cultivation of a garden may consist of the garden's being littered with empty tin cans and whisky bottles and used papers of various descriptions thrown around the garden at random. Having arrived at this point, we realize that we have lost our way somehow. Let us then make a fresh start by raising the question: what can liberal education mean here and now?

Liberal education is literate education of a certain kind: some sort of education in letters or through letters. There is no need to make a case for literacy; every voter knows that modern democracy stands or falls by literacy. In order to understand this need we must reflect on modern democracy. What is modern democracy? It was once said that democracy is the regime that stands or falls by virtue: a democracy is a regime in which all or most adults are men of virtue, and since virtue seems to require wisdom, a regime in which all or most adults are virtuous and wise, or the society in which all or most adults have developed their reason to a high degree, or *the* rational society. Democracy, in a word, is meant to be an aristocracy which has broadened into a universal aristocracy. Prior to the emergency of modern democracy some doubts were felt whether democracy thus understood is possible. As one of the two greatest minds among the theorists of democracy put it, "If there were a people consisting of gods, it would rule itself democratically. A government of such perfection is not suitable for human beings." This still and small voice has by now become a high-powered loud-speaker.

There exists a whole science—the science which I among thousands profess to teach, political science—which so to speak has no other theme than the contrast between the original conception of democracy, or what one may call the ideal of democracy, and democracy as it is. According to an extreme view, which is the predominant view in the profession, the ideal of democracy was a sheer delusion, and the only thing which matters is the behavior of democracies and the behavior of men in democracies. Modern democracy, so far from being universal aristocracy, would be mass rule were it not for the fact that the mass cannot rule, but is ruled by elites, that is, groupings of men who for whatever reason are on top or have a fair chance to arrive at the top; one of the most important virtues required for the smooth working of democracy, as far as the mass is concerned, is said to be electoral apathy, viz., lack of public spirit; not indeed the salt of the earth, but the salt of modern democracy are those citizens who read nothing except the sports page and the comic section. Democracy is then not indeed mass rule, but mass culture. A mass culture is a culture which can be appropriated by the meanest capacities without any intellectual and moral effort whatsoever and at a very low monetary price. But even a mass culture and precisely a mass culture requires a constant supply of what are called new ideas, which are the products of what are called creative minds: even singing commercials lose their appeal if they are not varied from time to time. But democracy, even if it is only regarded as the hard shell which protects the soft mass culture, requires in the long run qualities of an entirely different kind: qualities of dedication, of concentration, of breadth, and of depth. Thus we understand most easily what liberal education means here and now. Liberal education is the counterpoison to mass culture, to the corroding effects of mass culture, to its inherent tendency to produce nothing but "specialists without spirit or vision and voluptuaries without heart." Liberal education is the ladder by which we try to ascend from mass democracy to democracy as originally meant. Liberal education is the necessary endeavor to found an aristocracy within democratic mass society. Liberal education reminds those members of a mass democracy who have ears to hear, of human greatness.

Someone might say that this notion of liberal education is merely political, that it dogmatically assumes the goodness of modern democracy. Can we not turn our backs on modern society? Can we not return to nature, to the life of preliterate tribes? Are we not crushed, nauseated, degraded by the mass of printed material, the graveyards of so many beautiful and majestic forests? It is not sufficient to say that this is mere romanticism, that we today cannot return to nature: may not coming generations, after a man-wrought cataclysm, be compelled to live in illiterate tribes? Will our thoughts concerning thermonuclear wars not be affected by such prospects? Certain it is that the horrors of mass culture (which include guided tours to integer nature) render intelligible the longing for a return to nature. An illiterate society at its best is ruled by age-old ancestral custom which it traces to original founders, gods, or sons of gods or pupils of gods; since there are no letters in such a society, the late heirs cannot be in direct contact with the original founders; they cannot know whether the fathers or grandfathers have not deviated from what the original founders meant, or have not defaced the divine message by merely human additions or subtractions; hence an illiterate society cannot consistently act on its principle that the best is the oldest. Only letters which have come down from the founders can make it possible for the founders to speak directly to the latest heirs. It is then self-contradictory to wish to return to illiteracy. We are compelled to live with books. But life is too short to live with any but the greatest books. In this respect as well as in some others, we do well to take as our model that one among the greatest minds who because of his common sense is *the* mediator between us and the greatest minds. Socrates never wrote a book, but he read books. Let me quote a statement of Socrates which says almost everything that has to be said on our subject, with the noble simplicity and quiet greatness of the ancients.

"Just as others are pleased by a good horse or dog or bird, I myself am pleased to an even higher degree by good friends. . . . And the treasures of the wise men of old which they left behind by writing them in books, I unfold and go through them together with my friends, and if we see something good, we pick it out and regard it as a great gain if we thus become useful to one another." The man who reports this utterance adds the remark: "When I heard this, it seemed to me both that Socrates was blessed and that he was leading those listening to him toward perfect gentlemanship." This report is defective since it does not tell us anything as to what Socrates did regarding those passages in the books of the wise men of old of which he did not know whether they were good. From another report we learn that Euripides once gave Socrates the writing of Heraclitus and then asked him for his opinion about that writing. Socrates said: "What I have understood is great and noble; I believe this is also true of what I have not understood; but one surely needs for understanding that writing some special sort of a diver."

Education to perfect gentlemanship, to human excellence, liberal education consists in reminding oneself of human excellence, of human greatness. In what way, by what means does liberal education remind us of human greatness? We cannot think highly enough of what liberal education is meant to be. We have heard Plato's suggestion that education in the highest sense is philosophy. Philosophy is the quest for wisdom or quest for knowledge regarding the most important, the highest, or the most comprehensive things; such knowledge, he suggested, is virtue and is happiness. But wisdom is inaccessible to man, and hence virtue and happiness will always be imperfect. In spite of this, the philosopher, who, as such, is not simply wise, is declared to be the only true king; he is declared to possess all the excellences of which man's mind is capable, to the highest degree. From this we must draw the conclusion that we cannot be philosophers—that we cannot acquire the highest form of education. We must not be deceived by the fact that we meet many people who say that they are philosophers. For those people employ a loose expression which is perhaps necessitated by administrative convenience. Often they mean merely that they are members of philosophy departments. And it is as absurd to expect members of philosophy departments to be philosophers as it is to expect members of art departments to be artists. We cannot be philosophers, but we can love philosophy; we can try to philosophize. This philosophizing consists at any rate primarily and in a way chiefly in listening to the conversation between the great philosophers or, more generally and more cautiously, between the greatest most philosophers or, more generally and more cautiously, between the great minds, and therefore in studying the great books. The greatest minds to whom we ought to listen are by no means exclusively the greatest minds of the West. It is merely an unfortunate necessity which prevents us from listening to the greatest minds of India and of China: we do not understand their languages, and we cannot learn all languages.

To repeat: liberal education consists in listening to the conversation among the greatest minds. But here we are confronted with the overwhelming difficulty that this conversation does not take place without our help—that in fact we must bring about that conversation. The greatest minds utter monologues. We must transform their monologues into a dialogue, their "side by side" into a "together." The greatest minds utter monologues even when they write dialogues. When we look at the Platonic dialogues, we observe that there is never a dialogue among minds of the highest order: all Platonic dialogues are dialogues between a superior man and men inferior to him. Plato apparently felt that one could not write a dialogue between two men of the highest order. We must then do something which the greatest minds were unable to do. Let us face this difficulty—a difficulty so great that it seems to condemn liberal education as an absurdity. Since the greatest minds contradict one another regarding the most important matters, they compel us to judge of their monologues; we cannot take on trust what any one of them says. On the other hand, we cannot but notice that we are not competent to be judges.

This state of things is concealed from us by a number of facile delusions. We somehow believe that our point of view is superior, higher than those of the greatest minds—either because our point of view is that of our time, and our time, being later than the time of the greatest minds, can be presumed to be superior to their times; or else because we believe that each of the greatest minds was right from his point of view but not, as he claims, simply right: we know that there cannot be *the* simply true substantive view, but only a simply true formal view; that formal view consists in the insight that every comprehensive view is relative to a specific perspective, or that all comprehensive views are mutually exclusive and none can be simply true. The facile delusions which conceal from us our true situation all amount to this: that we are, or can be, wiser than the wisest men of the past. We are thus induced to play the part, not of attentive and docile listeners, but of impresarios or lion-tamers. Yet we must face our awesome situation, created by the necessity that we try to be more than attentive and docile listeners, namely, judges, and yet we are not competent to be judges. As it seems to me, the cause of this situation is that we have lost all simply authoritative traditions in which we could trust, the *nomos* which gave us authoritative guidance, because our immediate teachers and teachers' teachers believed in the possibility of a simply rational society. Each of us here is compelled to find his bearings by his own powers, however defective they may be.

We have no comfort other than that inherent in this activity. Philosophy, we have learned, must be on its guard against the wish to be edifying—philosophy can only be intrinsically edifying. We cannot exert our understanding without from time to time understanding something of importance; and this act of understanding may be accompanied by the awareness of our understanding, by the understanding of understanding, by *noesis noeseos*, and this is so high, so pure, so noble an experience that Aristotle could ascribe it to his God. This experience is entirely independent of whether what we understand primarily is pleasing or displeasing, fair or ugly. It leads us to realize that all evils are in a sense necessary if there is to be understanding. It enables us to accept all evils which befall us and which may well break our hearts in the spirit of good citizens of the city of God. By becoming aware of the dignity of the mind, we realize the true ground of the dignity of man and therewith the goodness of the world, whether we understand it as created or as uncreated, which is the home of man because it is the home of the human mind.

Liberal education, which consists in the constant intercourse with the greatest minds, is a training in the highest form of modesty, not to say of humility. It is at the same time a training in boldness: it demands from us the complete break with the noise, the rush, the thoughtlessness, the cheapness of the Vanity Fair of the intellectuals as well as of their enemies. It demands from us the boldness implied in the resolve to regard the accepted views as mere opinions, or to regard the average opinions as extreme opinions which are at least as likely to be wrong as the most strange or the least popular opinions. Liberal education is liberation from vulgarity. The Greeks had a beautiful word for "vulgarity"; they called it *apeirokalia*, lack of experience in things beautiful. Liberal education supplies us with experience in things beautiful.

NORMAN PODHORETZ

The Adversary Culture and the New Class

Among the many puzzles thrown up by the disruptions of the 1960s in the United States, none seemed more perplexing than the virulent hostility toward their own country which was evidently felt by some of the most privileged elements of American society. That blacks should resent or even be enraged by American society seemed entirely understandable and, indeed, proper. Having been victimized for so long by discrimination, poverty, and lack of opportunity, they had good reason to protest, to demonstrate, to disrupt. But what reason did undergraduates at Berkeley, Columbia, and Harvard have for feeling the same way and engaging in the same kind of behavior? Why should young people from prosperous families who had been given—as the saying used to go—"every advantage," who were enjoying what to all outward appearances was a life of luxury, indulgence, and ease, and who could look forward with relative one year ahead, characterize themselves as "niggers"? ("The Student as Nigger" was actually the title of a widely circulated manifesto of the period). In what intelligible sense could these young scions of the American upper classes be compared to a group at the bottom of the American heap?

Such talk of "the student as nigger" might have been dismissed as a particularly flamboyant form of adolescent self-dramatization if not for another perplexing fact: that it was ratified by very large numbers of people in the adult world, including, as it sometimes seemed, the entire membership of the academic and journalistic professions. Far from ridiculing the idea that the prosperous and privileged young of America in reality constituted an oppressed and downtrodden minority, sociologists and editorialists, foundation executives and columnists were busily at work generating arguments to prove that the contention was sound. These adult apologists, who kept telling us what the young people were "trying to tell us" (though their services in this respect often struck one as supererogatory), were, moreover, a privileged group themselves, occupying for the most part extremely well-paid positions to which great influence and considerable prestige were attached. Why should they be as hostile to America as the words they kept putting into the mouths of the "young" so clearly suggested they were?

Throughout the years roughly bounded by the end of the Civil War and the beginning of the Second World War, no one would have been surprised to find intellectuals and expiring intellectuals expressing hostility toward American society. With the rapid industrial expansion of the country in the decades after the Civil War, America more and more became the quintessential "business civilization"—a society in which tremendous power of every kind was vested in the business class. But as this power grew, and as the abuses flowing so abundantly from its exercise accumulated, resistance to it also developed. Antitrust laws, progressive income taxes, regulatory legislation, electoral reform, and the rise of organized labor—all were directed at diminishing or at least controlling the rampant economic and political power of the "robber barons," of "Wall Street," of the trusts and the monopolies. Efforts of this nature were supported by rival economic groups— farmers, small-town merchants, independent professionals, and manual workers—whose interests were threatened and often trampled upon by big business, and who attacked the new order of things in the name of values like free competition and equality of opportunity, which big business itself, of course, also honored (if more in the breach than in the observance).

At the same time, however, a more radical assault on the new order was also being mounted, which in the long run perhaps proved more decisive. It was an assault directed against the spiritual and cultural power of business—that is, against the very values that the populists and the Progressives and the labor movement shared with big business and to which they appealed in their own struggle for a greater share of political and economic power. In this cultural battle, the weapons used were not political, and progress was not measured in legislative victories. The relevant weapons were ideas and the object was to persuade and influence. Nor was the point to expose the injustices flowing from a business civilization (or a capitalist system, as some Americans later learned to call it); the emphasis here fell on spiritual rather than material considerations. Of course, separating the spiritual from the material was not always possible or desirable. Nevertheless, there did develop a critique of capitalist America which centered independently on what in our own day is known as the "quality of life." Indeed, so vivid an autonomous existence did this critique achieve that it retained its plausibility even at a time when the strictly economic arguments against the system (the Marxist ones, among others) seemed to have been refuted by the spread of affluence to unprecedentedly large numbers of people.

This cultural critique consisted essentially of three related elements. First of all, it was said that a society in which business was the leading species of enterprise put a premium on selfishness while doing everything it could to dampen the altruistic potentialities of human nature. People were rewarded for being selfish and penalized for caring about others; they were encouraged to compete instead of to cooperate. The result was an erosion of communal attachments and loyalties, and the creation of a harsh, brutal, heartless society of isolated individuals connected one to the other by a "cash nexus" and nothing more lasting or binding.

In addition to encouraging the worst kind of "rugged individualism," a business civilization, it was charged, stimulated the basest of human passions—material greed. The lust for money and for the things money could buy became so ferocious that more elevated tastes were forced to go begging for satisfaction. People grew narrow and gross, incapable of appreciating anything whose value could not be counted in dollars. The arts were thus meaningless to them, or at least a showy adornment pressed into the service of an ostentatios vulgarity. And just as individuals living under such circumstances were related only by a "cash nexus," so their only religion was worship (in William James's phrase) of "the bitch-goddess SUCCESS."

These attacks on the individualism, materialism, and philistinism of a business civilization were rooted in Christianity and derived a good part of their effectiveness from the continuing strength, sometimes latent, sometimes active, of Christian belief in the United States. But there was a third element of the critique which was rooted in secular and even anti-Christian sources, and this was the attack on the puritanism of "bourgeois" or "middle-class" society. Such a society, it was said, while rewarding the lust for money, penalized all the healthier appetites. The only pleasures it sanctioned were whatever pleasures might be connected with work, ambition, the sense of having "made it" or won out in a brutal competitive struggle. All other pleasures, whether of the mind or of the body, were frowned upon as wicked or as debilitating or as a waste of precious time. A life lived under the rule of these values was stern, joyless, desiccated, prissy, provincial, repressed.

In elaborating this critique, intellectuals—and especially intellectuals primarily interested in the arts—quite naturally played the leading role. For the very act of becoming an intellectual or an artist in America[1] came to mean that one was in effect joining the party of opposition—placing oneself (to use the term made famous by Lionel Trilling in *Beyond Culture*) in an "adversary" relation to the business civilization and all its works. To be sure, some of these "works" that were opposed (though there were such prominent exceptions as William Faulkner) included values like religious piety, patriotism, and the martial virtues that derived not from capitalism but from precapitalist roots: the ethos of the rural community and the small town. But as was evident from the term "booboisie" invented by H. L. Mencken to suggest an identification between the "hick" of the hinterland and the businessman (wherever he might live and however large or small his business), the two tended to flow together in the adversary American mind into a single enemy.

Nor did membership in the adversary culture merely involve subscribing to abstract doctrines critical of bourgeois society; it also involved matters of style and sensibility. Thus the "modernist" movement which began sweeping through all the arts around the turn of the century and which was characterized above all else by an unremitting impulse toward formal experimentation—Ezra Pound's "make it new!" was the great slogan—represented something more than an effort to escape from played-out aesthetic conventions and to find fresher forms of expression and interpretation. There was in this movement a powerful will to *épater le bourgeois*, to provoke and outrage the middle-class audience by upsetting its normal expectations and offending its sense of intelligibility, fitness, and order. While very often attacking or ridiculing the bourgeois world in substantive terms (through, for example, unflattering portraits and characterization), the modernist movement was simultaneously mounting an assault on the very structure of its sensibility. Indeed, Edmund Wilson in his book on the Symbolists, *Axel's Castle*, went so far as to suggest that the modernist revolution in the arts was analogous both in purpose and significance to the Russian Revolution: as the one represented a challenge to the rule of the bourgeoisie in the world of politics, the other represented a challenge to its rule in the world of imagination and ideas.

That modernist or avant-garde artists and their critical partisans should stand in an adversary relation to bourgeois society was to be expected almost by definition. But in America even artists and intellectuals like Theodore Dreiser or Van Wyck Brooks who were opposed on aesthetic grounds to modernism shared fully in its attitude toward the business civilization. Until, that, is, the Second World War and its aftermath. While business as such continued to be treated with contempt throughout the 1940s and 1950s— this was the period of books like *The Organization Man* and *The Man in the Gray Flannel Suit* which amounted to nothing more than updated and popularized versions of the cultural critique—a new and more positive attitude toward American society itself, and even toward the capitalist system, began to emerge among artists and intellectuals. Those who participated in and applauded this surprising phenomenon said that as compared with the alternatives of Nazi Germany on the one side and Soviet Russia on the other, America looked very good to them—especially since "countervailing forces," as John Kenneth Galbraith called them, had by now cut into the power of big business and made for a more pluralistic cultural climate and one more hospitable to values other than those of commerce. Those who deplored this development said that the intellectuals were simply "selling out" for good jobs and a better social position, and that we were faced with the onset of a new "age of conformity."

Such worries, as we now know, were misplaced. The first postwar decade turned out to be not the beginning of a new "age of conformity"—that is, of amity between the intellectuals and American society—but a temporary aberration, destined to be corrected, and with a vengeance, in the decade ahead. To journalists and popular sociologists with short historical memories, this correction looked like a novel development. It was not; it was a return to the traditional stance of the intellectual community in relation to American society.

There was, however, one truly novel element in the situation of the sixties: the vastly enlarged numbers of people who now either belonged to the intellectual community or were under its direct influence. In the past intellectuals had constituted a tiny minority of the population, but with the tremendous expansion of higher education in the period after World War II, millions upon millions of young people began to be exposed to—one might even say indoctrinated in—the adversary culture of the intellectuals. To be sure, very few of these young people actually became intellectuals in any real sense, but a great many were deeply influenced by ideas which had once been confined pretty much to the intellectual community itself. Thus what had formerly been the attitudes of a minuscule group on the margins of American society now began assuming the proportions of a veritable mass movement. And since so many of these young people eventually wound up working in the mass media, such attitudes acquired a new ability to penetrate into previously inaccessible areas of American culture. . . .

The reason, then, that the adversary culture was not killed by kindness is that it was encouraged by kindness. Tocqueville points out that the French Revolution—the revolution of the bourgeoisie against the aristocracy—erupted out of an improving rather than a worsening situation. As the power and confidence of the middle class increased, so did its appetite and hence also its animosity toward the *ancien régime*. Is it too fanciful to apply the same analysis to the intellectual class in America in the 1960s? Certainly it did not seem too fanciful to many of the intellectuals themselves. During the sixties, a theory began to circulate to the effect that a "New Class" was maturing in America made up of persons whose "capital" consisted not of money or property but of education, brains, and technical expertise—intellectuals, in the broadest sense—and that in an advanced stage of capitalist development such as the United States was now reaching, this New Class would eventually replace the old owners and entrepreneurs—that is, the bourgeoisie—as the ruling elite.

In this "liberal" variant of the theory (propounded by writers as diverse as Daniel Bell, David T. Bazelon, and John Kenneth Galbraith) the intellectuals were seen as the beneficiaries of an orderly transfer of power destined to take place as the byproduct of structural changes in the economic organization of the system. But there was another variant—a radical or neo-Marxist one (whose most prominent proponent was probably C. Wright Mills). In that version the intellectuals were seen as the agents of revolution, replacing the proletariat, the class that Marx had cast in this role but that had evidently traded its historic birthright for a mess of affluent pottage.

Whether in its liberal or its neo-Marxist version, the dream of power seems to have acted upon the intellectuals as Tocqueville says the same dream acted upon the bourgeoisie in prerevolutioary France: it sharpened the appetite and exacerbated hostility to the tottering and doddering ruling class of the old regime which so stubbornly insisted on postponing the inevitable with one stratagem after another. Thus if in an earlier period bourgeois society was hated because it ignored and despised the intellectuals, now it was hated because, despite all the concessions it had made, it still refused to be *ruled* by the intellectuals. . . .

What the properous young intellectuals who compared themselves to "niggers" were really "trying to tell us" was that they were being denied their "fair share," not of the middle-class security and comfort with which they were already so obviously and plentifully supplied, but of the political power which they believed should rightly be theirs. (Naturally, they never doubted for a moment that they would exercise it in the best interests of all, and especially the downtrodden.) This is why the issue of "participating in the decisions which affect our lives" became so important to the radicals of the sixties and later to their milder liberal progeny.

Within the radical New Left it was believed that power would have to be wrested by force, and it was also believed—*sincerely* believed—that this was possible because the United States was in a "revolutionary situation." As in the depression, the failures of the system—its inability to eradicate poverty and racism—were providing revolutionary fuel. But now, in contrast to the depression, even the successes of the system—the spread of affluence to the greatest majority of the populace—were creating radical discontent. The "best" of the young were refusing to join the "establishment"; they were dropping out and developing a "counterculture" of their own based on the rejection of the "Puritan ethic" and indeed of all middle-class values: work, ambition, discipline, monogramy, and the family. Clearly, then, the system was no longer viable; clearly it was being destroyed by "internal contradictions" which, if not precisely those foreseen by Marx (for the working class was being subjected to embourgeoisement rather than pauperization and could therefore no longer be depended upon to serve as the vanguard of the revolution), were nevertheless deep enough to tear everything apart and bring the entire structure down.

This analysis was developed long before American combat troops were sent to Vietnam and long before the first riot broke out in the black ghettos of the North. But it obviously gained in credibility as the war became a more and more burning issue, especially on the campuses, and as the civil-rights movement, with its tactics of litigation and nonviolence, gave way to a "Black Power" movement based on violence and threats of violence. For with every collapse of the authorities in the face of an aggressive challenge—violent demonstrations, the seizure and occupation of buildings, "nonnegotiable demands"—more and more evidence was provided for the idea that the system was falling apart and that a revolution was about to break out.

The sixties ended, however, not with a revolution but with the election of Richard Nixon: Richard Nixon, who better than any single figure in American public life seemed to epitomize everything in opposition to which the adversary culture had always defined itself. But the response to this defeat was not a new withdrawal. It was, on the contrary, a new determination to mount an effective political challenge, this time "working within the system" to get rid of the usurper who had seized the throne and to place political power at long last into the proper hands. This effort, which called itself the New Politics, sought to forge a coalition of two disparate elements: those who were, or felt themselves to be, deprived of the full benefits of middle-class comfort and security (the blacks and the poor) and those who were, or felt themselves to be, deprived of the full benefits of political power (the New Class). Operating through the candidacy of George McGovern for President, the New Politics came infinitely closer to actual power than any political movement associated with the adversary culture had ever done before, and though it suffered a humiliating defeat at the hands of Richard Nixon in 1972, it participated centrally in the successful campaign to drive him from the White House in 1974. Two years later, the presidential candidate backed by the New Politics, Morris Udall, lost out to an ambiguous figure named Jimmy Carter who then went on as President to staff his administration with veterans of the New Politics and more recent converts to its point of view. Full political power, then, had not been achieved, but obviously great progress had been made.

Yet, so far as the adversary culture in particular was concerned, much greater progress had been made in the world of ideas and attitudes than in the political realm. By the end of the 1960s the values of the business class were no longer dominant in America—or even, it sometimes seemed from the readiness with which it assented to attacks on its own position, within the business class itself. In one sense, for example, individualism had grown rampant in America, but not at all in the sense once prized by the business world. The ascendant ethic preached in the public schools, in the mass media, and even in comic books and pornographic magazines now seemed to be that nothing—not wives, not husbands, not children, and certainly not the state—must stand in the way of the individual's right to self-fulfillment and self-expression in the realm of morals, sex, and personal relations (which was, of course, the adversary culture's traditional version of individualism as well as its answer to middle-class or bourgeois values). But where economic enterprise was concerned, the opposite view prevailed: there every obstacle must be put in the way of "rugged individualism" and the more state control the better. And a similar fate had overtaken the old materialism of the business class. Profits were now "obscene"; economic growth was now a "threat to the environment"; prosperity was now "waste" and the criminal squandering of putatively scarce natural resources.

Obviously, the progress of the adversary culture in the war of ideas served the political interests of the New Class. For the more the economic life of the country shifted from private to state controlled enterprise, the less power would accrue to businessmen and the more power would accrue to the professional and technical intelligentsia. But toward the end of the 1960s, a new and complicating element began to enter the picture. Repelled by the sight that the sixties had vouchsafed of what the adversary culture looked like in action, and therefore of what it might look like in power, a group of dissident intellectuals, mostly, but not exclusively, associated with magazines like *Commentary* and the *Public Interest*, appeared on the scene to defend middle-class values, and even capitalism itself, as the indispensable basis of liberty, democracy, widespread material prosperity, and a whole range of private human decencies. One member of the group, Hilton Kramer, harking back to Joseph Schumpeter (who influenced other members of the group as well), even argued that the adversary culture itself owed its existence to these values, both in the sense that they had provided it with the freedom to develop—a freedom the "socialist" countries had never been willing to grant—and in the deeper sense that its commitment to experimentation and novelty was a reflection in aesthetic terms of the general bourgeois commitment to constant technological innovation and continuous social change.

These intellectual adversaries of the adversary culture were often called "neoconservatives," a designation happily accepted by some (like Irving Kristol) but rejected at first by most others, who continued to think of themselves as liberals. "Neoliberal" would perhaps have been a more accurate label for the entire group than neoconservative, but this label was destined to be claimed a little later by a different group of dissident liberals (themselves influenced by the neoconservatives).[2] In any case, the liberalism of the neoconservatives was old and not new—that is, it derived from the New Deal and not from the New Politics. The New Politics liberalism of the sixties and seventies, in the judgment of the neoconservatives, was not entitled to be called liberal at all, and was indeed antiliberal in many crucial respects. Thus, for example, the new "liberals," in direct violation of traditional liberal principles, supported quota systems rather than individual merit—or equality of result rather than equality of opportunity—as the road to social justice. But this brand of egalitarianism was not simply antiliberal; it also contributed to the undermining of middle-class values by making rewards contingent upon membership in a group favored for one reason or another by the government, rather than upon individual effort and achievement. It could be understood, then, as an extension into concrete social policy of the adversary culture's assault on the "Protestant ethic."[3]

In thus challenging the adversary culture, the neoconservative dissidents did not go quite so far as William F. Buckley, Jr., on their Right, who once said that he would rather be ruled by the first two thousand names in the Boston telephone book than by the combined faculties of Harvard and MIT. But the neoconservatives (several of whom were themselves distinguished Harvard professors) went far enough in expressing doubt over the desirability of a society ruled by their own kind to suggest the possibility of a deepening schism within the intellectual community.

Certainly these intellectual adversaries of the adversary culture were exerting a marked influence by the mid-1970s. Their writings were being read and discussed in many circles, and the election of Ronald Reagan in 1980 could be, and was, seen as a mark of their spreading influence.

To be sure, they still represented a minority within the intellectual community, but no smaller perhaps than the adversary culture itself had once been within the world out of which it had dialectically emerged exactly a hundred years before. The effect the neoconservative dissidents might have on the future course of events was difficult to predict. But as the first century of business domination in America drew to a close, the very existence of a significant party of intellectuals to whom the defense of middle-class values seemed necessary to the preservation of liberty, democracy, and even civilization itself was already casting an anxious shadow over the otherwise cheerful prospects of the adversary culture in the realm of ideas and attitudes, and of the New Class in the arena of economic and political power.

NOTES

1. This is not to imply that the attitudes of the adversary culture were indigenous or peculiar to America. Similar stories could be told of all the industrial countries. But there were important differences between Europe and America in the rising as in so many other areas. For example, in Europe opposition to the rising power of industrial capitalism came (at least until 1945) from the Right as well as the Left, taking the form of fascism and of literally reactionary political movements which advocated the restoration of monarchy or of an essentially feudal social organization. Although major American writers living in Europe like T. S. Eliot and Ezra Pound were among the sympathizers of these movements, nothing really comparable materialized in the United States, possibly because this country had no feudal past.

2. If, as Kristol has said, a neoconservative is a "liberal who has been mugged by reality," a neoliberal, according to John Podhoretz, is a "liberal who has been mugged by a neoconservative."

3. Of course there was a conflict between radical egalitarianism and the idea of a society run by intellectuals. But destroying middle-class values was more important for the moment than worrying about how the values that would replace them could be squared with those in the name of which the revolution was being fought. Needless to say, the New Class was not the first insurgent class in history to have faced this problem, and if its dreams of political rule were ever to come true, it would no doubt resolve the contradiction in the manner of all past revolutionaries: through ideological fiat backed by the coercive power of the state.

ANARCHISM AND FREEDOM

Anarchism was originally understood as projecting a society without government. Therein lies its allure. Individuals are seen as capable of governing themselves and exercising their responsibility to the community without reference to the disfiguring influence of bureaucracy or private property. Augustin Souchy, a "student of revolution" whose activities on behalf of the anarchist movement spanned much of this century, reflects upon these notions as well as upon his life in the conclusion to his autobiography. Where once he believed in the absolute character of the revolution, he now recognizes its limits. But Souchy is proud of the experiments undertaken by the anarchists in Spain and the *kibbutzim* in Israel as well as the way in which many anarchist demands have found their way into contemporary discourse. Indeed, there is a sense in which the goal has become less important than the striving to achieve it.

An ethical perspective also informs the thinking of Martin Buber; a leading figure in the Zionist movement and a major philosopher of existentialism. This selection from *Paths to Utopia* highlights his concern over the way in which society is being assimilated by the state and authentically human interconnections between people are being lost. Even representative democracy cannot overcome the increasing passivity of people and the felt need for a community unified by spiritual and moral bonds. Thus, the vision of Martin Buber ultimately projects a rebirth of the commune or the kibbutz.

In Defense of Anarchism, by Robert Paul Wolff, underscores the tension between the moral autonomy of the individual and the legitimate authority of the state. Choosing one or the other is impractical. Either autonomy is surrendered, in which case subordination of the individual to any form of government is possible, or all governments must be considered illegitimate institutions whose commands must be judged and evaluated before they are obeyed. But, insofar as the state is itself a social construct, Wolff believes it *must* be possible for rational people to set private interest aside, pursue the common good, and create an association that maximizes their autonomy: reason can once again join with freedom. But until then, anarchism, in keeping with its tradition, will continue to project the possibility for a new order beyond the confines of the real.

AUGUSTIN SOUCHY

Conclusion to *Beware Anarchist!*: A Life for Freedom

It always seemed to me that the way of endeavor is preferable to what has actually been attained. In summing up my life I did not hesitate to compress my life's work into the lapidary sentence: "Great ambition, little achievement." When I was young I believed in the chiliastic realm of "liberty, equality and fraternity." Today, I believe in a continuous evolutionary process more than in an imaginary world.

At the end of World War I we, the radicals of the left, hoped that the Russian Revolution was the beginning of a new era, similar to that of the French Revolution of 1789. However, the Bolshevik dictatorship, which suppressed not only the followers of czarism but also dissident revolutionaries, was a bitter disappointment.

I was called a "student of revolution." This is correct insofar as participation in the revolutions of this century was the greater part of my life's work. When I was fifteen years old I heard from my father the fairy tale of dialectical materialsm, according to which it is a law of nature that capitalism must be in time replaced by socialism. I abandoned this superstition later in my life. I never became a professional revolutionary because I did not want to make a living on the basis of revolutionary activities. I do not see revolution as a goal but only as an accelerated phase of development. Trotsky's thesis of the "permanent revolution" is a propaganda slogan. The expression is attributed to Karl Marx; a state of lasting revolution never existed in history. Revolutions break out when unbearable economic and political, social or national situations trigger revolt. They end with the dying down of collective energies. This was the case with the last revolution in Portugal. The depth, duration, content and significance of revolutions cannot be foreseen. At first I believed in the might of the revolution but later I was well aware of its limitations. Two phases can be seen in revolutionary developments: at first overthrow of the old rulers and then establishment of a new revolutionary power. The process is violent and rarely without bloodshed. The revolutions of the twentieth century had—with few exceptions—two faces: one showing the liberating revolt and the other the oppressive dictatorship. It was like this from Russia to Cuba. In 1921 had the sailors of Kronstadt, together with the Left Social Revolutionaries, the Maximalists, syndicalists and anarchists, been victorious, Soviet Russia would be today an authentic socialist republic with autonomous collectives and political freedoms, without the shame of prisons, work and concentrations camps and mental institutions for political opponents. I have learned three lessons from my experiences:

1. Individual force is not a means towards establishment of a free society. Collective force is inevitable during revolutions but its effects are limited. It contributes to the overthrow of a dictatorship or oppressive government. However, liberty is again endangered when the leaders become dictators. The most outstanding examples in our century are Lenin, Stalin and Castro.

2. A victorious social revolution can succeed in distributing wealth between all in a grandiose manner but cannot guarantee well-being for all times.

3. Communism, established as party dictatorship, abolished all political freedom obtained in the past century but the economic equality so boastfully propagandized failed to materialize. Hence it is not in the interest of workers to support the power struggle of Communist parties.

I was often asked: Why could anarchism never prevail? Is this not attributable to its unrealistic utopian objectives? I answered: Every social objective has utopian features. Only its materialization shows what is unrealistic. Anarchism is by no means merely utopia; it has eminently practical traits. The most important libertarian social experiments of the twentieth century are the collective enterprises in Spain during the civil war and the kibbutzim in Israel. In both cases we have to do with the realization of an anarchist concept as outlined by Proudhon, Kroptkin and Gustav Landauer. The outgrowth of the initiative of the participants of the Spanish *collectividades* and the Israeli *kibbutzim* is built on fundamental social justice and personal freedom. They were and are still functioning effectively without outer compulsion and government interference. Social contrasts are nonexistent. The *collectividades* and *kibbutzim* are proof that free communities are possible in practice and that libertarian socialism is not a utopia. At closer look, the utopian feature of anarchism is nothing else but libertarian humanism. What today is believed to be an "unrealistic economic order" has been seen in the past century by anarchist theorists of the Marxist school of political science as a socialist federalist alternative. The demand of today's unions for co-determination and self-determination in factories was always the objective of the anarchists. The demand for general disarmament and international control of arms production, a slogan of anarchists of the past century, is today the request of all fighters for peace. On the new continent, especially in the U.S., there is no more anarchist-baiting. I was on a six weeks lecture tour in the U.S. and Canada during the summer of 1976. On July 18 the Rev. Bruce Southworth gave a Sunday sermon on "Anarchism and Politics" in the Community Church of New York, which was also broadcast. The next day I spoke in the same church about the anarchist way to socialism. In Philadelphia, Minneapolis and New Orleans I was given the opportunity to speak in churches. Above the pulpit was the picture of a Spanish militia man. Radio stations of several cities invited me to speak about anarchism. In a dozen cities I was the house guest of sympathetic professors, students, workers and intellectuals. Thus I came to know another America, the America of the idealists who want to transform society. In these circles I encountered fighting spirit combined with practical, altruistic solidarity. The Americans, descendants of daring immigrants, will fight without western European help to maintain freedom and achieve social justice.

A last word: The social problems of today are not the same as those of the beginning of this century. Power relations have shifted, and the conditions of life changes. With technical and industrial progress enormous as they are we can expect—barring an apocalyptic catastrophe—that by the end of the twenty-first century mass misery will have disappeared and the social contrasts minimized. Then we will see that the bread and butter question is not the social problem. New problems, unknown today, will arise. One example: half a century ago the word and concept of "ecology" was familiar only to experts; today, however, it is commonplace. Around 1900 the working people were fighting for bread but in the 1960s students revolted against authoritarian establishments. In the year 2000 will freedom-loving men and women have to fight again to overthrow dictatorships and authoritarian regimes? An old social problem will certainly remain also in the future. That is the antagonism between authority and freedom. As in the past the pendulum of history will also swing between the opposite poles: authority as opposed to freedom.

When socio-economic problems are resolved, socio-psychic complications will arise. Complete conformism will never be attained, even in a classless society. In the past political and social contrasts between those exercising authority (mostly belonging to the other generations) and the youth outside the establishment institutions have led to violent outbreaks. This has not changed even today but it does not mean that it will always be the same. It is not utopian to propagate the solution of all social contradiction by peaceful means. The nonviolent contrast between generations of social, economic and ethnically different groups is spiritually fruitful, creative and progressive.

The objectives of anarchists have always been and are today: prosperity for all, freedom for everybody and respect for the dignity of man—unfortunately only theoretically recognized by governments—and, I might add, universal peace. But as long as power systems exist, nothing will change. My goal is the establishment of a social order free of force to replace organized compulsion and violence.

MARTIN BUBER

In the Midst of Crisis

For the last three decades we have felt that we were living in the initial phases of the greatest crisis humanity has ever known. It grows increasingly clear to us that the tremendous happenings of the past years, too, can be understood only as symptoms of this crisis. It is not merely the crisis of one economic and social system being superseded by another, more or less ready to take its place; rather all systems, old and new, are equally involved in the crisis. What is in question, therefore, is nothing less than man's whole existence in the world.

Ages ago, far beyond our calculation, this creature "Man" set out on his journey; from the point of view of Nature a well-nigh incomprehensible anomaly; from the point of view of the spirit an incarnation hardly less incomprehensible, perhaps unique; from the point of view of both a being whose very essence it was to be threatened with disaster every instant, both from within and without, exposed to deeper and deeper crises. During the ages of his earthly journey man has multiplied what he likes to call his "power over Nature" in increasingly rapid tempo, and he has borne what he likes to call the "creations of his spirit" from triumph to triumph. But at the same time he has felt more and more profoundly, as one crisis succeeded another, how fragile all his glories are; and in moments of clairvoyance he has come to realize that in spite of everything he likes to call "progress" he is not travelling along the high-road at all, but is picking his precarious way along a narrow ledge between two abysses. The graver the crisis becomes the more earnest and consciously responsible is the knowledge demanded of us; for although what is demanded is a deed, only that deed which is born of knowledge will help to overcome the crisis. In a time of great crisis it is not enough to look back to the immediate past in order to bring the enigma of the present nearer to solution: we have to bring the stage of the journey we have now reached face to face with its beginnings, so far as we can picture them.

The essential thing among all those things which once helped man to emerge from Nature and, notwithstanding his feebleness as a natural being, to assert himself—more essential even than the making of a "technical" world out of things expressly formed for the purpose—was this: that he banded together with his own kind for protection and hunting, food gathering and work; and did so in such a way that from the very beginning and thereafter to an increasing degree he faced the others as more or less independent entities and communicated with them as such, addressing and being addressed by them in that manner. This creation of a "social" world out of persons at once mutually dependent and independent differed in kind from all similar undertakings on the part of animals, just as the technical work of man differed in kind from all the animals' works. Apes, too, make use of some stick they happen to have found, as a lever, a digging-tool or a weapon; but that is an affair of chance only: they cannot conceive and produce a tool as an object constituted so and not otherwise and having an existence of its own. And again, many of the insects live in societies built up on a strict division of labour; but it is just this division of labour that governs absolutely their relations with one another; they are all as it were tools; only, their own society is the thing that makes use of them for its "instinctive" purposes; there is no improvisation, no degree, however modest, of mutual independence, no possibility of "free" regard for one another, and thus no person-to-person relationship. Just as the specific technical creations of man mean the conferring of independence on things, so his specific social creation means the conferring of independence on beings of his own kind. It is in the light of this specifically human idiosyncrasy that we have to interpret man's journey with all its ups and downs, and so also the point we have reached on this journey, our great and particular crisis.

In the evolution of mankind hitherto this, then, is the line that predominates: the forming and re-forming of communities on the basis of growing personal independence, their mutual recognition and collaboration on that basis. The two most important steps that the man of early times took on the road to human society can be established with some certainty. The first is that inside the individual clan each individual, through an extremely primitive form of division of labour, was recognized and utilized in his special capacity, so that the clan increasingly took on the character of an ever-renewed association of persons each the vehicle of a different function. The second is that different clans would, under certain conditions, band together in quest of food and for campaigns, and consolidated their mutual help as customs and laws that took firmer and firmer root; so that as once between individuals, so now between communities people discerned and acknowledged differences of nature and function. Wherever genuine human society has since developed it has always been on this same basis of functional autonomy, mutual recognition and mutual responsibility, whether individual or collective. Power-centres of various kinds have split off, organizing and guaranteeing the common order and security of all; but to the political sphere in the stricter sense, the State with its police-system and its bureaucracy, there was always opposed the organic, functionally organized society as such, a great society built up of various societies, the great society in which men lived and worked completed with one another and helped one another; and in each of the big and little societies composing it, in each of these communes and communities the individual human being, despite all the difficulties and conflicts, felt himself at home as once in the clan, felt himself approved and affirmed in his functional independence and responsibility.

All this changed more and more as the centralistic political principle subordinated the de-centralistic social principle. The crucial thing here was not that the State, particularly in its more or less totalitarian forms, weakened and gradually displaced the free associations, but that the political principle with all its centralistic features percolated into the associations themselves, modifying their structure and their whole inner life, and thus politicized society to an ever-increasing extent. Society's assimilation in the State was accelerated by the fact that, as a result of modern industrial development and its ordered chaos, involving the struggle of all against all for access to raw materials and for a larger share of the world-market, there grew up, in place of the old struggles between States, struggles between whole societies. The individual society, feeling itself threatened not only by its neighbours' lust for aggression but also by things in general, knew no way of salvation save in complete submission to the principle of centralized power; and, in the democratic forms of society no less than in its totalitarian forms, it made this its guiding principle. Everywhere the only thing of importance was the minute organization of power, the unquestioning observance of slogans, the saturation of the whole of society with the renal or supposed interests of the State. Concurrently with this there is an internal development. In the monstrous confusion of modern life, only thinly disguised by the reliable functioning of the economic and State-apparatus, the individual clings desperately to the collective. The little society in which he was embedded cannot help him; only the great collectivities, so he thinks, can do that, and he is all too willing to let himself be deprived of personal responsibility: he only wants to obey. And the most valuable of all goods—the life between man and man—gets lost in the process; the autonomous relationships become meaningless, personal relationships wither; and the very spirit of man hires itself out as a functionary. The personal human being ceases to be the living member of a social body and becomes a cog in the "collective" machine. Just as his degenerate technology is causing man to lose the feel of good work and proportion, so the degrading social life he leads is causing him to lose the feel of community—just when he is so full of the illusion of living in perfect devotion to his community.

A crisis of this kind cannot be overcome by struggling back to an earlier stage of the journey, but only by trying to master the problems as they are, without minimizing them. There is no going back for us, we have to go through with it. But we shall only get through if we know *where* we want to go.

We must begin, obviously, with the establishment of a vital peace which will deprive the political principle of its supremacy over the social principle. And this primary objective cannot in its turn be reached by any devices of political organization, but only by the resolute will of all peoples to cultivate the territories and raw materials of our planet and govern its inhabitants, *together*. At this point, however, we are threatened by a danger greater than all the previous ones: the danger of a gigantic centralization of power covering the whole planet and devouring all free community. Everything depends on not handing the work of planetary management over to the political principle.

Common management is only possible as socialistic management. But if the fatal question for contemporary man is: Can he or can he not decide in favour of, and educate himself up to, a common socialistic economy? then the propriety of the question lies in an inquiry into Socialism itself: what sort of Socialism is it to be, under whose aegis the common economy of man is to come about, if at all?

The ambiguity of the terms we are employing is greater here than anywhere else. People say, for instance, that Socialism is the passing of the control of the means of production out of the hands of the entrepreneurs into the hands of the collectivity; but again, it all depends on what you mean by "collectivity". If it is what we generally call the "State", that is to say, an institution in which a virtually unorganized mass allows its affairs to be conducted by "representation", as they call it, then the chief change in a socialistic society will be this: that the workers will feel themselves represented by the holders of power. But what is representation? Does not the worst defect of modern society lie precisely in everybody letting himself be represented *ad libitum*? And in a "socialistic" society will there not, on top of this passive political representation, be added a passive economic representation, so that, with everybody letting himself be represented by everybody else, we reach a state of practically unlimited representation and hence, ultimately, the reign of practically unlimited centralist accumulation of power? But the more a human group lets itself be represented in the management of its common affairs, and the more it lets itself be represented from outside, the less communal life there is in it and the more impoverished it becomes as a community. For community—not the primitive sort, but the sort possible and appropriate to modern man—declares itself primarily in the common and active management of what it has in common, and without this it cannot exist.

The primary aspiration of all history is a genuine community of human beings—genuine because it is *community all through*. A community that failed to base itself on the actual and communal life of big and little groups living and working together, and on their mutual relationships, would be fictitious and counterfeit. Hence everything depends on whether the collectivity into whose hands the control of the means of production passes will facilitate and promote in its very structure and in all its institutions the genuine common life of the various groups composing it—on whether, in fact, these groups themselves become proper foci of the productive process; therefore on whether the masses are so organized in their separate organizations (the various "communities") as to be as powerful as the common economy of man permits; therefore on whether centralist representation only goes as far as the new order of things absolutely demands. The fatal question does not take the form of a fundamental Either-Or: it is only a question of the right line of demarcation that has to be drawn ever anew—the thousandfold system of demarcation between the spheres which must of necessity be centralized and those which can operate in freedom; between the degree of government and the degree of autonomy; between the law of unity and the claims of community. The unwearying scrutiny of conditions in terms of the claims of community, as something continually exposed to the depredations of centralist power—the *custody of the true boundaries*, ever changing in accordance with changing historical circumstances: such would be the task of humanity's spiritual conscience, a Supreme Court unexampled in kind, the right true representation of a living idea. A new incarnation is waiting here for Plato's "custodians".

Representation of an idea, I say: not of a rigid principle but of a living form that wants to be shaped in the daily stuff of this earth. Community should not be made into a principle; it, too, should always satisfy a situation rather than an abstraction. The realization of community, like the realization of any idea, cannot occur once and for all time: always it must be the moment's answer to the moment's question, and nothing more.

In the interests of its vital meaning, therefore, the idea of community must be guarded against all contamination by sentimentality or emotionalism. Community is never a mere attitude of mind, and if it is *feeling* it is an inner disposition that is felt. Community is the inner disposition or constitution of a life in common, which knows and embraces in itself hard "calculation", adverse "chance", the sudden access of "anxiety". It is community of tribulation and only because of that community of spirit; community of toil and only because of that community of salvation. Even those communities which call the spirit their master and salvation their Promised Land, the "religious" communities, are community only if they serve their lord and master in the midst of simple, unexalted, unselected reality, a reality not so much chosen by them as sent to them just as it is; they are community only if they prepare the way to the Promised Land through the thickets of this pathless hour. True, it is not "works" that count, but the work of faith does. A community of faith truly exists only when it is a community of work.

The real essence of community is to be found in the fact—manifest or otherwise—that it has a centre. The real beginning of a community is when its members have a common relation to the centre overriding all other relations: the circle is described by the radii, not by the points along its circumference. And the originality of the centre cannot be discerned unless it is discerned as being transpicuous to the light of something divine. All this is true; but the more earthly, the more creaturely, the more attached the centre is, the truer and more transpicuous it will be. This is where the "social" element comes in. Not as something separate, but as the all-pervading realm where man stands the test; and it is here that the truth of the centre is proved. The early Christians were not content with the community that existed alongside or even above the world, and they went into the desert so as to have no more community save with God and no more disturbing world. But it was shown them that God does not wish man to be alone with him; and above the holy impotence of the hermit there rose the Brotherhood. Finally, going beyond St. Benedict, St. Francis entered into alliance with all creatures.

Yet a community need not be "founded". Wherever historical destiny had brought a group of men together in a common fold, there was room for the growth of a genuine community; and there was no need of an altar to the city deity in the midst when the citizens knew they were united round—and by—the Nameless. A living togetherness, constantly renewing itself, was already there, and all that needed strengthening was the immediacy of relationships. In the happiest instances common affairs were deliberated and decided not through representatives but in gatherings in the market-place; and the unity that was felt in public permeated all personal contacts. The danger of seclusion might hang over the community, but the communal spirit banished it; for here this spirit flourished as nowhere else and broke windows for itself in the narrow walls, with a large view of people, mankind and the world.

All this, I may be told, has gone irrevocably and for ever. The modern city has no agora and the modern man has no time for negotiations of which his elected representatives can very well relieve him. The pressure of numbers and the forms of organization have destroyed any real togetherness. Work forges other personal links than does leisure, sport again others than politics, the day is cleanly divided and the soul too. These links are material ones; though we follow our common interests and tendencies together, we have no use for "immediacy". The collectivity is not a warm, friendly gathering but a great link-up of economic and political forces inimical to the play of romantic fancies, only understandable in terms of quantity, expressing itself in actions and effects—a thing which the individual has to belong to with no intimacies of any kind but all the time conscious of his energetic contribution. Any "unions" that resist the inevitable trend of events must disappear. There is still the family, of course, which, as a domestic community, seems to demand and guarantee a modicum of communal life; but it too will either emerge from the crisis in which it is involved, as an association for a common purpose, or else it will perish.

Faced with this medley of correct premises and absurd conclusions I declare in favour of a rebirth of the commune. A rebirth—not a bringing back. It cannot in fact be brought back, although I sometimes think that every touch of helpful neighbourliness in the apartment-house, every wave of warmer comradeship in the lulls and "knock-offs" that occur even in the most perfectly "rationalized" factory, means an addition to the world's community-content; and although a rightly constituted village commune sometimes strikes me as being a more real thing than a parliament; but it cannot be brought back. Yet whether a rebirth of the commune will ensue from the "water and spirit" of the social transformation that is imminent—on this, it seems to me, hangs the whole fate of the human race. An organic commonwealth—and only such common-wealths can join together to form a shapely and articulated race of men—will never build itself up out of individuals but only out of small and ever smaller communities: a nation is a community to the degree that it is a community of communities. If the family does not emerge from the crisis which today has all the appearance of a disintegration, purified and renewed, then the State will be nothing more than a machine stoked with the bodies of generations of men. The community that would be capable of such a renewal exists only as a residue. If I speak of its rebirth I am not thinking of a permanent world-situation but an altered one. By the new communes—they might equally well be called the new Co-operatives—I mean the subjects of a changed economy: the collectives into whose hands the control of the means of production is to pass. Once again, everything depends on whether they will be ready.

Just how much economic and political autonomy—for they will of necessity be economic and political units at once—will have to be conceded to them is a technical question that must be asked and answered over and over again; but asked and answered beyond the technical level, in the knowledge that the internal authority of a community hangs together with its external authority. The relationship between centralism and decentralization is a problem which, as we have seen, cannot be approached in principle, but, like everything to do with the relationship between idea and reality, only with great spiritual tact, with the constant and tireless weighting and measuring of the right proportion between them. Centralization—but only so much as is indispensible in the given conditions of time and place. And if the authorities responsible for the drawing and re-drawing of lines of demarcation keep an alert conscience, the relations between the base and the apex of the power-pyramid will be very different from what they are now, even in States that call themselves Communist, i.e. struggling for community. There will have to be a system of representation, too, in the sort of social pattern I have in mind; but it will not, as now, be composed of the pseudo-representatives of amorphous masses of electors but of representatives well tested in the life and work of the communes. The represented will not, as they are today, be bound to their representatives by some windy abstraction, by the mere phraseology of a party-programme, but concretely, through common action and common experience.

The essential thing, however, is that the process of community-building shall run all through the relations of the communes with one another. Only a community of communities merits the title of Commonwealth.

The picture I have hastily sketched will doubtless be laid among the documents of "Utopian Socialism" until the storm turns them up again. Just as I do not believe in Marx's "gestation" of the new form, so I do not believe either in Bakunin's virgin-birth from the womb of Revolution. But I do believe in the meeting of idea and fate in the creative hour.

R O B E R T   P A U L   W O L F F

Beyond the Legitimate State

We have come to a dead end in our search for a viable form of political association which will harmonize the moral autonomy of the individual with the legitimate authority of the state. The one proposal which appears genuinely to resolve the conflict, namely unanimous direct democracy, is so restricted in its application that it offers no serious hope of ever being embodied in an actual state. Indeed, since it achieves its success only by ruling out precisely the conflicts of opinion which politics is designed to resolve, it may be viewed as the limiting case of a solution rather than as itself a true example of a legitimate state.

A contractual democracy is legitimate, to be sure, for it is founded upon the citizens' promise to obey its commands. Indeed, any state is legitimate which is founded upon such a promise. However, all such states achieve their legitimacy only by means of the citizens' forfeit of their autonomy, and hence are not solutions to the fundamental problem of political philosophy. Majoritarian democracy claims a deeper justification than merely an original promise. It presents itself as the only viable form of political community in which the citizenry rule themselves, and thus preserve their autonomy while collecting their individual authority into the authority of the state. Unfortunately, our examination of the various arguments in support of majority rule has revealed that this additional claim is unfounded. Whatever else may be said for a majoritarian democracy, it does not appear to be true that the minority remain free and self-ruled while submitting to the majority.

Our failure to discover a form of political association which could combine moral autonomy with legitimate authority is not a result of the imperfect rationality of men, nor of the passions and private interests which deflect men from the pursuit of justice and the general good. Many political philosophers have portrayed the state as a necessary evil forced upon men by their own inability to abide by the principles of morality, or as a tool of one class of men against the others in the never-ending struggle for personal advantage. Marx and Hobbes agree that in a community of men of good will, where the general good guided every citizen, the state would be unnecessary. They differ only in the degree of their hope that so happy a condition can ever be realized.

Nor does our dilemma grow out of the familiar limitations of intellect and knowledge which afflict all but the most extraordinary men. It may be that in a technologically complex world only a few men can hope to master the major political issues well enough to have genuinely personal convictions about them. By positing a society of rational men of good will, however, we have eliminated such well-known obstacles to the fully just state. The magnitude of our problem is indicated by our inability to solve the dilemma of autonomy and authority even for a utopian society! By and large, political philosophers have supposed that utopia was logically possible, however much they may have doubted that it was even marginally probable. But the arguments of this essay suggest that the just state must be consigned the category of the round square, the married bachelor, and the unsensed sense-datum.

If autonomy and authority are genuinely incompatible, only two courses are open to us. Either we must embrace philosophical anarchism and treat *all* governments as nonlegitimate bodies whose commands must be judged and evaluated in each instance before they are obeyed; or else, we must give up as quixotic the pursuit of autonomy in the political realm and submit ourselves (by an implicit promise) to whatever form of government appears most just and beneficent at the moment. (I cannot resist repeating yet again that if we take this course, *there is no universal or a priori reason for binding ourselves to a democratic government rather than to any other sort.* In some situations, it may be wiser to swear allegiance to a benevolent and efficient dictatorship than to a democracy which imposes a tyrannical majority on a defenseless minority. *And in those cases where we have sworn to obey the rule of the majority, no additional binding force will exist beyond what would be present had we promised our allegiance to a king!*)

It is out of the question to give up the commitment to moral autonomy. Men are no better than children if they not only accept the rule of others from force of necessity, but embrace it willingly and forfeit their duty unceasingly to weigh the merits of the actions which they perform. When I place myself in the hands of another, and permit him to determine the principles by which I shall guide my behavior, I repudiate the freedom and reason which give me dignity. I am then guilty of what Kant might have called the sin of willful heteronomy.

There would appear to be no alternative but to embrace the doctrine of anarchism and categorically deny *any* claim to legitimate authority by one man over another. Yet I confess myself unhappy with the conclusion that I must simply leave off the search for legitimate collective authority. Perhaps it might be worth saying something about the deeper philosophical reasons for this reluctance.

Man confronts a natural world which is irreducibly *other*, which stands over against him, independent of his will and indifferent to his desires. Only religious superstition or the folly of idealist metaphysics could encourage us to assume that nature will prove ultimately rational, or that the opposition between man and objects must in principle be surmountable. Man also confronts a social world which *appears* other, which *appears* to stand over against him, at least partially independent of his will and frequently capricious in its frustration of his desires. Is it also folly to suppose that this opposition can be overcome, and that man can so perfectly conquer society as to make it his tool rather than his master?

To answer this question, we must determine whether the appearance of the objectivity of society is also reality, or whether perhaps here, in the realm of institutions and interpersonal relationships, man's estrangement from the society which dominates him is accidental, adventitious, and ultimately eradicable.

Each individual is born into a social world which is already organized into regular patterns of behavior and expectation. At first, he is aware only of the few persons in his immediate physical environment and of their qualities and appearance. Very soon, the infant learns to expect repeated sequences of behavior from those around him. Later still, the child comes to see these significant persons as playing certain defined roles (mother, father, teacher, policeman) which are also played by other persons in different situations (other children also have mothers and fathers, etc.). The learning of language reinforces this awareness, for built into the word "father" is the notion that there may be many fathers to many children. The child matures and develops a personality by identifying with various role-bearers in his world and internalizing as his own the patterns of behavior and belief which constitute the roles. He *becomes* someone in this way, and also *discovers* who he is by reflecting on the alternatives which life offers him. Characteristically, the adolescent goes through a period of role definition during which he tentatively tries on a variety of roles, in order to test their appropriateness for him. (This is perhaps a description biased by contemporary Western experience. In some cultures, of course, the uncertainty over roles which produces an "identity crisis" never occurs since it is laid down by the society what set of roles the individual shall internalize and act out. For the purposes of this discussion, however, that point is not significant.)

Thus, the social world presents to each individual an objective reality with independently existing structures, just as the physical world does. The infant learns where his body ends and the objects around him begin. He distinguishes between what is within his control (various movements of his body) and what does not respond to his will. In exactly the same way, he learns to recognize the intractable realities of his social environment. When a boy is asked what he wants to be, he is really being asked which already existing social role he wishes to adopt as an adult. His answer—that he wants to be a fireman, or an engineer, or an explorer—indicates that he understands perfectly well the nature of the question. He may see himself, at least in a society like ours, as exercising some control over the roles which he shall adopt; but neither the questioner nor the boy would suppose that either of them has any control over the existence and nature of the roles themselves! Even the social rebel characteristically opts for an existing role, that of bohemian, or beatnik, or revolutionary. Like all role-players, such rebels wear the clothes, live in the quarters, and use the language appropriate to the role which they have chosen.

In any reasonably complex society, social roles are in turn organized into even more extensive patterns of behavior and belief, to which we apply the term "institutions." The church, the state, the army, the market are all such systems of roles. The characteristic interactions of the constituent roles of an institution are determined independently of particular individuals, just as the roles themselves are. At this level of complexity of organization, however, a new phenomenon appears which vastly increases the apparent objectivity of social reality, namely what has come to be known as the "paradox of unintended consequences." Each person in an institutional structure pursues goals and follows patterns at least partially laid down for him by the society—that is, already existing when he takes on the role and hence *given* to him. In his roles, however, he should be able to see the relationship between what he does and what results, even though he may not feel free to alter his goals or try new means. In the process of interaction with other individual role-players, more far-reaching results will be produced which may be neither anticipated nor particularly desired by any person in the system. These unintended consequences will therefore appear to the role-players as somehow not their doing, and hence objective in just the way that natural occurrences are objective. To cite a classic example, as each entrepreneur strives to increase his profit by cutting his price slightly, hoping thereby to seize a larger portion of the total market, the market price of his commodity falls steadily and everyone experiences a decline in profits. If he thinks about it at all, the entrepreneur will characteristically suppose himself to be caught in the grip of a "falling market," which is to say a natural or objective force over which he has no control. Even after he recognizes the causal relationship between his individual act of pricecutting and the drop in the market price, he is liable to think himself powerless to reverse the workings of the "laws of the marketplace." (Perhaps it is worth noting that, contrary to the assumptions of classical liberal economic theory, the entrepreneur is as much in the grip of social forces when he plays the role of capitalist as when he feels the pinch of the market. Even the most casual cross-cultural comparison reveals that "economic man" is a social role peculiar to certain cultures, and not at all the natural man who emerges when the distorting forces of tradition and superstition are lifted.)

The experience of the entrepreneur is reduplicated ending so that men come to imagine themselves more completely enslaved by society than they ever were by nature. Yet their conviction is fundamentally wrong, for while the natural world really does exist independently of man's beliefs or desires, and therefore exercises a constraint on his will which can at best be mitigated or combatted, the social world is nothing in itself, and consists merely of the totality of the habits, expectations, beliefs, and behavior patterns of all the individuals who live in it. To be sure, insofar as men are ignorant of the total structures of the institutions within which they play their several roles, they will be the victims of consequences unintended by anyone; and, of course, to the extent that men are set against one another by conflicting interests, those whose institutional roles give them advantages of power or knowledge in the social struggle will prevail over those who are relatively disadvantaged. But since each man's unfreedom is entirely a result either of ignorance or of a conflict of interests, it ought to be in principle possible for a society of rational men of good will to eliminate the domination of society and subdue it to their wills in a manner that is impossible in the case of nature.

Consider as an example the economic institutions of society. At first, men play their several economic roles (farmer, craftsman, trader, fisherman) in complete ignorance of the network of interactions which influence the success of their endeavors and guide them into sequences of decisions, for good or ill, whose structure and ultimate outcome they cannot see. These same men imagine themselves encapsulated in a set of unchanging economic roles whose patterns, rewards, and systematic relationships are quite independent of their wills. Slowly, as the systematic interconnections themselves become more complex and mutually dependent, man's understanding of the economy as a whole grows, so that, for example, entrepreneurs begin to realize that their profits depend upon the total quantity of goods produced by themselves and their fellow capitalists, and the accumulation of individual desires for those goods which, collectively, constitute the level of demand. The first stage in the mastery of the economy may consist simply in the discovery of such aggregate quantities as demand, supply, interest rate, profit level, and even market price. That is to say, men must *discover* that the interaction of many individual acts of buying and selling establishes a single market price, which reflects the relation of supply to demand of the commodity being marketed. After realizing that such a marketwide price exists, men can begin to understand how it is determined. Only then can they consider the possibility of making that price a direct object of decision, and thus finally free themselves from the tyranny of the market.

In addition to the ignorance which enslaves even those in positions of power in the economy (the capitalists in a laissez-faire system), the pursuit of private interest results in the exploitation and enslavement of those whose roles in the economy carry relatively little power. Hence even the farthest advance imaginable of social knowledge would not suffice to liberate all men from their social bonds unless it were accompanied by a transformation of private interest into a concern for the general good. But if so utopian a condition were achieved, then surely men could once and for all reconquer their common product, society, and at least within the human world, move from the realm of necessity into the realm of freedom. Death and taxes, it is said, are the only certainties in this life; a folk maxim which reflects the deep conviction that men cannot escape the tyranny of either nature or society. Death will always be with us, reminding us that we are creatures of nature. But taxes, along with all the other instruments of social action, are human products, and hence must in the end submit to the collective will of a society of rational men of good will.

It should now be clear why I am unwilling to accept as final the negative results of our search for a political order which harmonizes authority and autonomy. The state is a social institution, and therefore no more than the totality of the beliefs, expectations, habits, and interacting roles of its members and subjects. When rational men, in full knowledge of the proximate and distant consequences of their actions, determine to set private interest aside and pursue the general good it *must* be possible for them to create a form of association which accomplishes that end without depriving some of them of their moral autonomy. The state, in contrast to nature, cannot be ineradicably *other*.

Utopian Glimpses of a World without States

Through the exercise of *de facto* legitimate authority, states achieve what Max Weber calls the imperative coordination of masses of men and women. To some extent, of course, this coordination consists in the more-or-less voluntary submission by large numbers of people to institutional arrangements which are directly contrary to their interests. Threats of violence or economic sanction play a central role in holding the people in line, although as Weber very persuasively argues, the myth of legitimacy is also an important instrument of domination.

But even if there were no exploitation or domination in society, it would still be in men's interest to achieve a very high level of social coordination, for reasons both of economic efficiency and of public order. At our present extremely advanced stage of division of labor, relatively minor disruptions of social coordination can produce a breakdown of the flow of goods and services necessary to sustain life.

Consequently, it is worth asking whether a society of men who have been persuaded of the truth of anarchism—a society in which no one claims legitimate authority or would believe such a claim if it were made—could through alternative methods achieve an adequate level of social coordination.

There are, so far as I can see, three general sorts of purposes, other than the domination and exploitation of one segment of society by another, for which men might wish to achieve a high order of social coordination. First, there is the collective pursuit of some *external* national goal such as national defense, territorial expansion, or economic imperialism. Second, there is the collective pursuit of some *internal* goal wich requires the organization and coordination of the activities of large numbers of people, such as traffic safety, to cite a trivial example, or the reconstruction of our cities, to cite an example not so trivial. Finally, there is the maintenance of our industrial economy whose functional differentiation and integration—to use the sociologist's jargon—are advanced enough to sustain an adequately high level of production. Is there any way in which these ends could be served other than by commands enforced by coercion and by the myth of legitimacy?

I do not now have a complete and coherent answer to this question, which is in a way the truest test of the political philosophy of anarchism, but I shall make a few suggestions which may open up fruitful avenues of investigation.

With regard to matters of national defense and foreign adventure, it seems to me that there is much to be said for the adoption of a system of voluntary compliance with governmental directives. If we assume a society of anarchists—a society, that is to say, which has achieved a level of moral and intellectual development at which superstitious beliefs in legitimacy of authority have evaporated—then the citizenry would be perfectly capable of choosing freely whether to defend the nation and carry its purpose beyond the national borders. The army itself could be run on the basis of voluntary commitments and submission to orders. To be sure, the day might arrive when there were not enough volunteers to protect the freedom and security of the society. But if that were the case, then it would clearly be illegitimate to command the citizens to fight. Why should a nation continue to exist if its populace does not wish to defend it? One thinks here of the contrast between the Yugoslav partisans or Israeli soldiers, on the one hand, and the American forces in Vietnam on the other.

The idea of voluntary compliance with governmental directives is hardly new, but it inevitably provokes the shocked reaction that social chaos would result from any such procedure. My own opinion is that superstition rather than reason lies behind this reaction. I personally would feel quite safe in an America whose soldiers were free to choose when and for what they would fight.

Voluntary compliance would go far toward generating sufficient social coordination to permit collective pursuit of domestic goals as well. In addition, I believe that much could be done through the local, community-based development of a consensual or general will with regard to matters of collective rather than particular interest. In the concluding chapter of my book, *The Poverty of Liberalism*, I have offered a conceptual analysis of the several modes of community. I will simply add that achievement of the sorts of community I analyzed there would require a far-reaching decentralization of the American economy.

This last point brings me to the most difficult problem of all—namely, the maintenance of a level of social coordination sufficient for an advanced industrial economy. As Friedrich Hayek and a number of other classical liberal political economists have pointed out, the natural operation of the market is an extremely efficient way of coordinating human behavior on a large scale without coercion or appeal to authority. Nevertheless, reliance on the market is fundamentally irrational once men know how to control it in order to avoid its undesired consequences. The original laissez-faire liberals viewed the laws of the market as objective laws of a benevolent nature; modern laissez-faire liberals propose that we go on confusing nature and society, even though we have the knowledge to subordinate the market to our collective will and decision.

Only extreme economic decentralization could permit the sort of voluntary economic coordination consistent with the ideals of anarchism and affluence. At the present time, of course, such decentralization would produce economic chaos, but if we possessed a cheap, local source of power and an advanced technology of small-scale production, and if we were in addition willing to accept a high level of economic waste, we might be able to break the American economy down into regional and subregional units of manageable size. The exchanges between the units would be inefficient and costly—very large inventory levels, inelasticities of supply and demand, considerable waste, and so forth. But in return for this price, men would have increasing freedom to act autonomously. In effect, such a society would enable all men to be autonomous agents, whereas in our present society, the relatively few autonomous men are—as it were—parasitic upon the obedient, authority-respecting masses.

These remarks fall far short of a coherent projection of an anarchist society, but they may serve to make the ideal seem a bit less like a mere fantasy of utopian political philosophy.

Part II

CHANGING THE WORLD

DEMOCRATIC SOCIALISM

Socialism was the watchword of the international labor movement for most of the twentieth century. It generated numerous interpretations, fostered a diverse intellectual dialogue, and produced numerous political figures of the first rank. Socialism was traditionally understood in terms of its profound connection to democratic traditions, and this theme underlies the selections presented in this section.

It is logical to begin with "From the Rights of Man to Socialism" by Jean Jaurès, the undisputed moral leader of French socialism for over twenty years, whose assassination in 1914 abolished the last great hope of resistance to the imperialist ambitions of the "great powers." The speech included here finds the modern roots of socialism in the bourgeois notion of "right" and also provides a sense of the diverse intellectual development of the socialist idea in France. Jaurès never identified socialism with a centralized bureaucracy. He insisted instead on its pluralistic character and its connection with an emancipated world in which "the splendor of wealth will make manifest the victory of right, and joy will be the radiance of justice."

Rosa Luxemburg illuminates precisely what socialism is *not* in her prophetic critique of the Russian Revolution. Written while in jail for opposing World War I, just before her tragic death during the German Revolution of 1919, it decries the dictatorship of a clique and identifies a genuine "dictatorship of the proletariat" with the radical application of democracy, the abolition of all class privileges, and the creation of a new and invigorated public sphere. The working class must participate directly in building a new society; only in this way can it realize what Rosa Luxemburg always believed, that "freedom is only and exclusively freedom for the one who thinks differently."

According to Carlo Rosselli, however, such a stance necessarily calls for making explicit the connection between liberalism and socialism. This obviously means rejecting the increasingly rigid forms of orthodox Marxism advocated in the Soviet Union during the 1920s and 1930s. A guiding force of Italian social democracy, Rosselli fought for the loyalist cause during the Spanish Civil War and was assassinated by Mussolini's henchmen in France in 1936. Rosselli emphasized the importance of parliamentarism and valued the "classless society" only as an ethical ideal. For, in his view, the future demanded something different: a socialism willing to embrace the formal virtues of liberalism fused with a liberalism committed to economic equality.

For all these thinkers, socialism is both an idea and a movement of the masses. Its success has been enormous. But, for Henry Pachter, the price has been high. Socialism has largely been robbed of its critical and ethical purpose. Pachter, a communist during the 1920s and then a social democrat, who participated in the European struggle against fascism, saw the value of the socialist idea in its willingness to resist all forms of class domination and every attempt to transform human beings into a "cost of production." Socialism is not equivalent with a set of institutions, policies, or systematic principles. It is a quest for freedom, and for this reason Henry Pachter could write: "One cannot have socialism. One is a socialist."

JEAN JAURÈS

From the Rights of Man to Socialism

Only socialism will give the Declaration of the Rights of Man its entire meaning. Revolutionary bourgeois law has, indeed, freed the human personality from any shackles. But it forces new generations to pay a duty on the capital accumulated by their predecessors, and, by granting to a minority the right to collect that duty, it imposes upon human personality as a whole a kind of mortgage in favor of the past and the advantage of a single class.

We, on the contrary, claim that all the means of production and wealth accumulated by humanity must be put at the disposal of all human activities and help to make them free. We hold that every man has, from now onward, a right to all the means of development created by humanity. Man does not come into the world weak and naked, exposed to all kinds of oppressions and exploitations. He comes into it as a person vested with a right, who can claim for his entire development the free use of the work tools accumulated by the effort of humanity. Every individual has a right to demand of humanity everything that will aid his effort: he has the right to work, to produce, to create, and no category of men may draw usury from this work or put it under its yoke. And, since the community can assure the right of the individual only by putting the means of production at his disposal, the community must be vested with the sovereign right of property over these means. . . .

The Declaration of the Rights of Man was also an affirmation of life, an appeal to life. The French Revolution proclaimed in it the rights of living man. It did not grant to past humanity the right to bind present humanity. It did not grant to the past services of kings and nobles the right to weigh upon present and living humanity and check its growth. On the contrary, living humanity seized all the live forces bequeathed by the past and put them to its use. French unity, created by the kings, became the decisive weapon against the kings. Similarly, the big forces of production accumulated by the bourgeoisie will become the decisive weapon of human liberation against capitalist privilege.

Life does not abolish the past; it subdues it. The Revolution is not a break; it is a conquest. And when the proletariat achieves that conquest, when socialism is established, all the human effort accumulated through the centuries will be like a rich and benevolent nature receiving all persons from their birth and assuring them a full development.

This is why there is a root of socialism even in bourgeois revolutionary law, in the Declaration of the Rights of Man. But this internal logic of the idea of right and humanity would have remained dormant and ineffective without the vigorous external action of the proletariat. It intervened in the Revolution from its first days. It does not listen to the absurd class advice of those who like Marat tell it: "What are you doing? And why do you march to take the Bastille, which never locked up proletarians?" The proletariat marched; it attacked; it decided the success of the great days; it went to the frontiers; it saved the Revolution at home and abroad; it became a necessary force and picked up, on the way, the prize of its unceasing action. In three years, from 1789 to 1792, it turned a semibourgeois, semidemocratic regime into a pure democracy, in which proletarian action is sometimes dominant. By deploying its force, the proletariat becomes self-confident; it ended by saying, with Baboeuf, that, having created a common power, that of the nation, it must use it to achieve the common welfare.

Thus socialism ceased to be a vague philosophical speculation and became a living force. Socialism arose from the French Revolution by the combined action of two forces: the force of the idea of right, and the force of the nascent proletarian action. So it is not an abstract utopia. It surges from the most boiling and effervescent hot springs of modern life.

After many trials, partial victories, and failures, the new bourgeois order developed through a variety of political regimes. Under the Empire, during the Restoration, the economic system of the bourgeoisie, founded upon unlimited competition, began to produce its effects: an undoubted increase of wealth, but also immorality, cunning, perpetual struggle, disorder, and oppression. The genius of Fourier consisted in realizing that it was possible to remedy the disorder and to cleanse and order the social system, not only without lowering the production of wealth, but actually increasing it. It was not an ascetic ideal, but rather a free scope for all talents, for all instincts. The same association that will abolish crises will multiply wealth by coordinating and combining efforts. The touch of asceticism, with which the Revolution darkened socialism, was now mingled with the great current of modern production and affluence. Through Fourier, through Saint-Simon, socialism appeared as a force able not only to repel capitalism, but to overtake it.

In the new order glimpsed by these men of genius, justice will not be bought at the price of the joys of life. On the contrary, the just organization of human forces will increase their productive power. The splendor of wealth will make manifest the victory of right, and joy will be the radiance of justice. Baboeuf's idea had not been the negation of the Revolution, but rather its boldest throb. In the same way, Fourierism and Saint-Simonism are not the negation or restriction of modern life, but rather its passionate enlargement. Always and everywhere, socialism is a living force, moving with the ardent current of life.

To these great dreams of harmony and wealth for all, to these grand constructive designs of Fourier and Saint-Simon, the bourgeoisie of Louis-Philippe replied with an increased class exploitation, with an intensive and exhausting utilization of the strength of the workers, and with an orgy of government concessions, monopolies, dividends, and premiums. It would have been naive, to say the least, to fight this daring exploitation for any length of time with idyllic dreams. Proudhon replied with a bitter criticism of property, rent, and profit; here, too, what had to be said was said from the bitter inspiration and at the actual dictation of life.

But how can this work of criticism be completed by a work of organization? How can all the social elements menaced or oppressed by the powers of banks, monopolies, and capitalism group themselves into a vast fighting unit? Proudhon quickly saw that the army of social democracy was heterogeneous, composed of a factory proletariat still insufficient in numbers and strength, a merchant and industrial petty bourgeoisie, and craftsmen doomed but not yet abolished by capitalist concentration and absorption. Hence the hesitations and contradictions of the positive part of Proudhon's work; hence a strange mixture of reaction and revolution as he tries to save by factitious combinations the credit of the petty bourgeoisie while he foresees the coming of the working class as the revolutionary force. Proudhon would have liked to suspend the course of history, to adjourn the revolutionary crisis of 1848 to give economic revolution time to clarify its outline and give human minds a better orientation. These hesitations, these scruples, these contradictory efforts could come only from the contact of sincere socialist thought with a complex and still uncertain reality.

In 1848, the grand, decisive, and substantial force manifested and organized itself. The growth of big industry stimulated the rise of a proletariat, ever more numerous, more coherent, more conscious. Those who, with Marx, hailed the coming of this decisive power, those who understood that it will transform the world, could exaggerate the speed of economic process. Less prudent than Proudhon, less aware than he of the powers of resistance and change of small industry, they could simplify the problem unduly and magnify the absorptive strength of concentrated capital.

But, with all the reservations and restrictions produced by the study of an ever-complex and multiplied reality, it remains true that the purely proletarian class is growing in numbers, that it represents an ever growing proportion of human societies, that it is grouped in ever vaster centers of production. And it remains true that this proletarian clan is prepared to conceive, through large-scale production, a large-scale property, whose limit is social property.

With Baboeuf, socialism had been the most ardent shiver of the democratic Revolution; with Fourier and Saint-Simon, the most magnificent enlargement of the promises of wealth and power that daring capitalism lavished upon the world; with Proudhon, the sharpest warning to the societies devoured by the bourgeoisie. Now socialism is, with and in the proletariat, the strongest of social powers. . . .

Socialism is not an arbitrary and utopian conception; it moves and develops in full reality; it is a great force of life, blended into the whole of life, and soon capable of directing life. To the incomplete application of justice and human rights by the bourgeois and democratic Revolution, it has opposed the full and decisive interpretation of the Rights of Man. To the incomplete, narrow, and chaotic organization of wealth attempted by capitalism, it has opposed a magnificent conception of harmonious wealth, where the effort of each individual is strengthened by the mutual effort of all. To the aridity of bourgeois arrogance and egotism, shrunken by monopolist and elitist exploitation, it has opposed a revolutionary bitterness, an avenging and provoking irony, a deadly analysis that dissolves lies. Finally, to the social primacy of capital, it has opposed organization on ever-stronger class lines of a growing proletariat. . . .

While the real, substantial forces of socialism grow, the technical means of putting it into practice appear ever more definite. The nation is becoming more united and more sovereign; it is forced to take over more and more economic functions—a rough prelude to social property. In the great urban and industrial communities, democracy is becoming more and more involved in problems of property and administration of collective domains through questions of public hygiene, housing, lighting, education, and food supply. Cooperatives of all kinds, of consumers and of producers, are multiplying. Labor and professional organizations are growing and becoming more subtle and diversified. . . .

It is henceforth certain that capitalist privilege will not be replaced by the ponderous monopoly of a central bureaucracy. Rather, the nation, sovereign of property and guardian of the social right, will have innumerable organs—communes, cooperatives, unions— which will give social property the freest and subtlest of movements and harmonize with the infinite mobility and variety of individual forces. There exists a technical as well as a social and intellectual preparation for socialism. Those who, excited by the work already accomplished, believe that a socialist world can be created at once by decree, by a proletarian fiat lux (let there be light), are like children. But those who cannot see that an irrestible force of evolution spells the doom of the class system and of the reign of the bourgeoisie are mad.

ROSA LUXEMBURG

Democracy and Dictatorship

Lenin says: the bourgeois state is an instrument of oppression of the working class; the socialist state, of the bourgeoisie. To a certain extent, he says, it is only the capitalist state stood on its head. This simplified view misses the most essential thing: bourgeois class rule has no need of the political training and education of the entire mass of the people, at least not beyond certain narrow limits. But for the proletarian dictatorship that is the life element, the very air without which it is not able to exist.

"Thanks to the open and direct struggle for governmental power," writes Trotsky, "the laboring masses accumulate in the shortest time a considerable amount of political experience and advance quickly from one stage to another of their development."

Here Trotsky refutes himself and his own friends. Just because this is so, they have blocked up the fountain of political experience and the source of this rising development by their suppresion of public life! Or else we would have to assume that experience and development were necessary up to the seizure of power by the Bolsheviks, and then, having reached their highest peak, became superfluous thereafter. (Lenin's speech: Russia is won for socialism!!!)

In reality, the opposite is true! It is the very giant tasks which the Bolsheviks have undertaken with courage and determination that demand the most intensive political training of the masses and the accumulation of experience.

Freedom only for the supporters of the government, only for the members of one party—however numerous they may be—is no freedom at all. Freedom is always and exclusively freedom for the one who thinks differently. Not because of any fanatical concept of "justice" but because all that is instructive, wholesome and purifying in political freedom depends on this essential characteristic, and its effectiveness vanishes when "freedom" becomes a special privilege.

The Bolsheviks themselves will not want, with hand on heart, to deny that, step by step, they have to feel out the ground, try out, experiment, test now one way, now another, and that a good many of their measures do not represent priceless pearls of wisdom. Thus it must and will be with all of us when we get to the same point—even if the same difficult circumstances may not prevail everywhere.

The tacit assumption underlying the Lenin-Trotsky theory of the dictatorship is this: that the socialist transformation is something for which a ready-made formula lies completed in the pocket of the revolutionary party, which needs only to be carried out energetically in practice. This is, unfortunately—or perhaps fortunately—not the case. Far from being a sum of ready-made prescriptions which have only to be applied, the practical realization of socialism as an economic, social and juridical system is something which lies completely hidden in the mists of the future. What we possess in our program is nothing but a few main signposts which indicate the general direction in which to look for the necessary measures, and the indications are mainly negative in character at that. Thus we know more or less what we must eliminate at the outset in order to free the road for a socialist economy. But when it comes to the nature of the thousand concrete, practical measures, large and small, necessary to introduce socialist principles into economy, law and all social relationship, there is no key in any socialist party program or textbook. That is not a shortcoming but rather the very thing that makes scientific socialism superior to the utopian varieties.

The socialist system of society should only be, and can only be, a historical product, born out of the school of its own experiences, born in the course of its realization, as a result of the developments of living history, which—just like organic nature of which, in the last analysis, it forms a part—has the fine habit of always producing along with any real social need the means to its satisfaction, along with the task simultaneously the solution. However, if such is the case, then it is clear that socialism by its very nature cannot be decreed or introduced by *ukase* [proclamation]. It has as its prerequisite a number of measures of force—against property, etc. The negative, the tearing down, can be decreed; the building up, the positive, cannot. New territory. A thousand problems. Only experience is capable of correcting and opening new ways. Only unobstructed, effervescing life falls into a thousand new forms and improvisations, brings to light creative force, itself corrects all mistaken attempts. The public life of countries with limited freedom is so poverty-stricken, so miserable, so rigid, so unfruitful, precisely because, through the exclusion of democracy, it cuts off the living sources of all spiritual riches and progress. There it was political in character; the same thing applies to economic and social life also. The whole mass of the people must take part in it. Otherwise, socialism will be decreed from behind a few official desks by a dozen intellectuals.

Public control is indispensably necessary. Otherwise the exchange of experiences remains only with the closed circle of the officials of the new regime. Corruption becomes inevitable. Socialism in life demands a complete spiritual transformation in the masses degraded by centuries of bourgeois class rule. Social instincts in place of egotistical ones, mass initiative in place of inertia, idealism which conquers all suffering, etc. No one knows this better, describes it more penetratingly; repeats it more stubbornly than Lenin. But he is completely mistaken in the means he employs. Decree, dictatorial force of the factory overseer, Draconic penalties, rule by terror—all these things are but palliatives. The only way to a rebirth is the school of public life itself, the most unlimited, the broadest democracy and public opinion. It is rule by terror which demoralizes.

When all this is eliminated, what really remains? In place of the representative bodies created by general popular elections, Lenin and Trotsky have laid down the soviets as the only true representation of the laboring masses. But with the repression of political life in the land as a whole, life in the soviets must also become more and more crippled. Without general elections, without unrestricted freedom of press and assembly, without a free struggle of opinion, life dies out in every public institution, becomes a mere semblance of life, in which only the bureaucracy remains as the active element. Public life gradually falls asleep, a few dozen party leaders of inexhaustible energy and boundless experience direct and rule. Among them, in reality only a dozen outstanding heads do the leading and an elite of the working class is invited from time to time to meetings where they are to applaud the speeches of the leaders, and to approve proposed resolutions unanimously—at bottom, then, a clique affair—a dictatorship, to be sure, not the dictatorship of the proletariat, however, but only the dictatorship of a handful of politicians, that is a dictatorship in the bourgeois sense, in the sense of the rule of the Jacobins. Yes, we can go even further; such conditions must inevitably cause a brutalization of public life: attempted assassinations, shooting of hostages, etc. . . .

The basic error of the Lenin-Trotsky theory is that they too, just like Kautsky, oppose dictatorship to democracy. "Dictatorship or democracy" is the way the question is put by Bolsheviks and Kautsky alike. The latter naturally decides in favor of "democracy," that is, of bourgeois democracy, precisely because he opposes it to the alternative of the socialist revolution. Lenin and Trotsky, on the other hand, decide in favor of dictatorship in contradistinction to democracy, and thereby, in favor of the dictatorship of a handful of persons, that is, in favor of dictatorship on the bourgeois model. They are two opposite poles, both alike being far removed from a genuine socialist policy. The proletariat, when it seizes power, can never follow the good advice of Kautsky, given on the pretext of the "unripeness of the country," the advice being to renounce the socialist revolution and devote itself to democracy. It cannot follow this advice without betraying thereby itself, the International, and the revolution. It should and must at once undertake socialist measures in the most energetic, unyielding and unhesitant fashion, in other words, exercise a dictatorship, but a dictatorship of the *class*, not of a party or of a clique—dictatorship of the class, that means in the broadest public form on the basis of the most active, unlimited participation of the mass of the people, of unlimited democracy.

"As Marxists," writes Trotsky, "we have never been idol worshippers of formal democracy." Surely, we have never been idol worshippers of formal democracy. Nor have we ever been idol worshippers of socialism or Marxism either. Does it follow from this that we may also throw socialism on the scrap-heap, a la Cunow, Lensch and Parvus, if it becomes uncomfortable for us? Trotsky and Lenin are the living refutation of this answer.

"We have never been idol worshippers of formal democracy." All that that really means is: We have always distinguished the social kernel from the political form of *bourgeois* democracy; we have always revealed the hard kernel of social inequality and lack of freedom hidden under the sweet shell of formal equality and freedom—not in order to reject the latter but to spur the working class into not being satisfied with the shell, but rather, by conquering political power, to create a socialist democracy to replace bourgeois democracy—not to eliminate democracy altogether.

But socialist democracy is not something which begins only in the promised land after the foundations of socialist economy are created; it does not come as some sort of Christmas present for the worthy people who, in the interim, have loyally supported a handful of socialist dictators. Socialist democracy begins simultaneously with the beginnings of the destruction of class rule and of the construction of socialism. It begins at the very moment of the seizure of power by the socialist party. It is the same thing as the dictatorship of the proletariat.

Yes, dictatorship! But this dictatorship consists in the *manner of applying democracy*, not in its *elimination*, in energetic, resolute attacks upon the well-entrenched rights and economic relationships of bourgeois society, without which a socialist transformation cannot be accomplished. But this dictatorship must be the work of the *class* and not of a little leading minority in the name of the class—that is, it must proceed step by step out of the active participation of the masses; it must be under their direct influence, subjected to the control of complete public activity; it must arise out of the growing political training of the mass of the people.

Doubtless the Bolsheviks would have proceeded in this very way were it not that they suffered under the frightful compulsion of the World War, the German occupation and all the abnormal difficulties connected therewith, things which were inevitably bound to distort any socialist policy, however imbued it might be with the best intentions and the finest principles.

A crude proof of this is provided by the use of terror to so wide an extent by the Soviet government, especially in the most recent period just before the collapse of German imperialism, and just after the attempt on the life of the German ambassador. The commonplace to the effect that revolutions are not pink teas is in itself pretty inadequate.

Everything that happens in Russia is comprehensible and represents an inevitable chain of causes and effects, the starting point and end term of which are: the failure of the German proletariat and the occupation of Russia by German imperialism. It would be demanding something superhuman from Lenin and his comrades if we should expect of them that under such circumstances they should conjure forth the finest democracy, the most exemplary dictatorship of the proletariat and a flourishing socialist economy. By their determined revolutionary stand, their exemplary strength in action, and their unbreakable loyalty to international socialism, they have contributed whatever could possibly be contributed under such devilishly hard conditions. The danger begins only when they make a virtue of necessity and want to freeze into a complete theoretical system all the tactics forced upon them by these fatal circumstances, and want to recommend them to the international proletariat as a model of socialist tactics. When they get in their own light in this way, and hide their genuine, unquestionable historical service under the bushel of false steps forced upon them by necessity, they render a poor service to international socialism for the sake of which they have fought and suffered; for they want to place in its store-house as new discoveries all the distortions presribed in Russia by necessity and compulsion—in the last analysis only by-products of the bankruptcy of international socialism in the present world war.

Let the German government socialists cry that the rule of the Bolsheviks in Russia is a distorted expression of the dictatorship of the proletariat. If it was or is such, that is only because it is a product of the behavior of the German proletariat, in itself a distorted expression of the socialist class struggle. All of us are subject to the laws of history, and it is only internationally that the socialist order of society can be realized. The Bolsheviks have shown that they are capable of everything that a genuine revolutionary party can contribute within the limits of the historical possibilities. They are not supposed to perform miracles. For a model and faultless proletarian revolution in an isolated land, exhausted by world war, strangled by imperialism, betrayed by the international proletariat, would be a miracle.

What is in order is to distinguish the essential from the non-essential, the kernel from the accidental excrescences in the policies of the Bolsheviks. In the present period, when we face decisive final struggles in all the world, the most important problem of socialism was and is the burning question of our time. It is not a matter of this or that secondary question of tactics, but of the capacity for action of the proletariat, the strength to act, the will to power of socialism as such. In this, Lenin and Trotsky and their friends were the *first*, those who went ahead as an example to the proletariat of the world; they are still the *only ones* up to now who can cry with Hutten: "I have dared!"

This is the essential and *enduring* in Bolshevik policy. In *this* sense theirs is the immortal historical service of having marched at the head of the international proletariat with the conquest of political power and the practical placing of the problem of the realization of socialism, and of having advanced mightily the settlement of the score between capital and labor in the entire world. In Russia the problem could only be posed. It could not be solved in Russia. And in *this* sense, the future everywhere belongs to "bolshevism."

CARLO ROSSELLI

Liberal Socialism

The slow but inevitable erosion of Marxist socialism has not been accompanied, unfortunately, by a vigorous effort at reconstruction. The old faith is shaken, but the new one has not yet appeared. Socialism slowly went adrift, and when the time came to take fresh bearings, the majority of socialists shrank back, appalled at how far they had come. The old guard sank its dialectical claws into the sacred texts and held on tight, while the young oscillated between a mortifying dogmatism and the most painful uncertainty. The monopoly Marxism enjoyed for almost half a century meant that too many people lost the habit of thinking for themselves, in full independence of judgment, about the problems of socialism. As a result, the forced emancipation now taking place makes them dizzy.

Once again it proves easier to criticize than to reconstruct. But of what use is a critique if it is not accompanied by an attempt, at least, to rebuild? Here we are not in the realm of pure science. The socialist movement *exists*, prior to and independently of any theory and any theoretical justification. Twenty-five million human beings have organized under the banners of socialism and are struggling in the name of socialism for their own emancipation. Denial will not do; it is necessary always to keep in mind this immense factual reality. To put it briefly: until we figure out how to replace the old, worn-out Marxist view with a new one that satisfies to the same extent, though with the necessary modifications, the fundamental demands of the working masses, our work, if not completely futile, will certainly be of very little interest.

Now this fresher, more fruitful, and up-to-date view does not have to be created out of cerebral introspection. It already lives potentially in revisionist criticism and is gradually being realized through the workers' movement. Rather, the problem consists in making explicit what is implicit and getting rid of the residue that still clings to its ideology, in having the courage to call things by their real names. Revisionist neo-Marxism and workers' praxis are respectively the theoretical face and the practical face of a new liberal socialist conception in which the problems of social justice and living together can and should be put on the same level as those of liberty and individual life. Socialism must tend to become liberal, and liberalism to take on the substance of the proletarian struggle. It is not possible to be liberal without joining actively in the cause of the workers, and there is no way to serve the cause of labor efficiently without coming to grips with the philosophy of the modern world, a philosophy founded on the idea of development through oppositions eternally overcome; here lies the core of the liberal point of view.

All of European, and not just European, social democracy is moving toward a form of renewed liberalism that is absorbing into itself elements from movements that would seem to be opposed (bourgeois enlightenment and proletarian socalism). It is fighting everywhere for individual freedoms, political freedoms, freedom to vote, and freedom of conscience. The messianic and teleological aspects are receding into the background while problems of the concrete movement to emancipate the workers are coming to the fore. The ideal of a perfect society of free and equal persons, with no classes, no struggle, and no state, is being transformed more and more every day into a limiting ideal that in itself is worthless but that serves as a stimulus and a focus for the spirit. The new faith nourishes itself on the proletarian struggle and the proletarian ascent, on the effort of the entire society to supersede the narrow and unjust terms dictated by bourgeois society, on the eternal thirst for justice and urge for freedom. And more generally—rising to a detached contemplation of the social movement—it feeds on a vision of life as an inexhaustible clash of forces and ideologies that overcome themselves through mutual negation in order to accede to higher forms of social structure and spiritual activity.

The phrase "liberal socialism" has a strange sound to many who are accustomed to current political terminology. The word "liberalism" unfortunately has been used to smuggle so many different kinds of merchandise and has been so much the preserve of the bourgeoisie in the past, that today a socialist has difficulty bringing himself to use it. But I do not wish to propose a new party terminology here. I wish only to bring the socialist movement back to its first principles, to its historical and psychological origins, and to demonstrate that socialism, in the last analysis, is a philosophy of liberty.

In any case, the time when bourgeois politics and liberal, free-market politics were one and the same has passed. All over the world the bourgeoisies no longer defend free markets and are no longer necessarily liberal. The more the proletarian movement takes hold and an active sense of liberty gains strength among the masses, the more the bourgeoisie, in its most backward sectors, tries to escape from the discipline and pattern of liberty. Even the new directions that modern production—rationalized, mechanized, technocratic—is taking as it sacrifices the human personality of the worker are forcing socialists to assume a liberal function in the quite traditional sense of the term. The day will come when this word, this attribute, will be claimed with proud self-awareness by the socialist: that will be the day of his maturity, the day when he wins emancipation, at least in the domain of the spiritual.

Liberalism in its most straightforward sense can be defined as the political theory that takes the inner freedom of the human spirit as a given and adopts liberty as the ultimate goal, but also the ultimate means, the ultimate rule, of shared human life. The goal is to arrive at a condition of social life in which each individual is certain of being able to develop his own personality fully. Liberty is also the means in the sense that the final stage cannot be bestowed or imposed; it has to be earned through hard personal struggle, as the generations succeed one another in time. Liberalism conceives of liberty not as a fact of nature, but as becoming, as development. One is not born free; one becomes free. And one stays free by retaining an active and vigilant sense of one's autonomy, by constantly exercising one's freedoms.

Faith in liberty is at the same time a declaration of faith in man, in his unlimited perfectibility, in his capacity for self-determination, in his innate sense of justice. A true liberal is anything but a skeptic; he is a believer, even though he opposes all dogmatic pronouncements, and an optimist, even though his conception of life is virile and dramatic.

In the abstract, this is how matters stand. In historical terms, the question becomes more complicated because liberalism has both a conceptual history and a practical one, and in the course of its unfolding it has produced an extraordinary harvest of practical experience and successive degrees of conceptualization. It was born of modern critical thought and made its first mark on history at the time of the Reformation. The subsequent ferocity of the wars of religion, in which men slaughtered one another in the name of opposing faiths and opposing dogmas, was the matrix of the notion of liberty of religious conscience, which blossomed as a flower does amid ruins. Catholics and Protestants, incapable of exterminating each other, agreed to a truce and acknowledged the right of all individuals to profess the cult that each preferred. Liberty as a principle then spread to the sphere of cultural life in the seventeenth and eighteenth centuries through the influence of scientific progress and as a result of the economic and intellectual ascendancy of the bourgeoisie. The latter reached a high point with the publication of the *Encyclopédie* and finally achieved its political triumph with the revolution of 1789 and the accompanying Declaration of the Rights of Man. In our age the liberal idea has revealed its tendency to structure every aspect and every part of social life, especially the economic sphere. The result is that liberty, from being a notionally universal prerogative that in fact corresponded to the interests of a minority, is truly becoming the patrimony of all.

Socialism is nothing more than the logical development, taken to its extreme consequences, of the principle of liberty. Socialism, when understood in its fundamental sense and judged by its results—as the concrete movement for the emancipation of the proletariat—is liberalism in action; it means that liberty comes into the life of poor people. Socialism says: the abstract recognition of liberty of conscience and political freedoms for all, though it may represent an essential moment in the development of political theory, is a thing of very limited value when the majority of men, forced to live as a result of circumstances of birth and environment in moral and material poverty, are left without the possibility of appreciating its significance and taking any actual advantage of it. Liberty without the accompaniment and support of a minimum of economic autonomy, without emancipation from the grip of pressing material necessity, does not exist for the individual; it is a mere phantasm. In these circumstances the individual is enslaved by poverty, humiliated by his own subjection; and life presents only one aspect to him, gives him only one illusion to pursue: material satisfaction. Free in law, he is in fact a slave. And the sense of servitude is sharpened by bitterness and irony the moment the virtual slave becomes aware of his legal liberty and of the obstacles that society places in the way of his actually gaining it. Now the socialist contends that when socialism was born, modern society was full of individuals in this situation; and individuals in this situation still compose a large segment of the working class in the capitalist world today, deprived as they are of any control over the tools with which they work, of any share in the process of decision making that guides production, of any sense of dignity and responsibility in the workplace—dignity and responsibility, the first steps on the ladder leading from slavery to liberty.

In the name of liberty, and for the purpose of ensuring its effective possession by all men and not just a privileged minority, socialists postulate the end of bourgeois privilege and the effective extension of the liberties of the bourgeoisie privilege to all. In the name of liberty they ask for a more equal distribution of wealth and the automatic guarantee for every person of a life worth living. In the name of liberty they speak of socialization, the abolition, that is, of private ownership of the means of production and exchange. They want social life to be guided not by the egoistic criterion of personal utility, but by the social criterion, the criterion of the collective good. If the choice is between an intermediate grade of liberty that applies to the whole collectivity and an unbounded liberty furnished to a few at the expense of the many, an intermediate liberty is better, a hundred times better. Ethics, economics, and right all lead to this conclusion.

The socialist movement is, in consequence, the objective heir of liberalism: it carries this dynamic idea of liberty forward through the vicissitudes of history toward its actualization. Liberalism and socialism, rather than opposing one another in the manner depicted in out-dated polemics, are connected by an inner bond. Liberalism is the ideal force of inspiration, and socialism is the practice force of realization.

The bourgeoisie was, at one time, the standard-bearer of this idea of liberty; the liberal function was in its hands when it broke open the rigid, frozen order of the feudal world and sowed the seeds of fecund life. In its battle against the dogmatism of the church and monarchical absolutism, against the privileges of the nobility and clergy, against the dead realm of static, forced production, the bourgeoisie embodied, over a long sequence of centuries, the progressive impetus of the whole society. That is no longer true. The bourgeoisie has won; it has captured the dominating heights, but as it triumps, its revolutionary function and its progressive ferment fade away. It is no longer driven by a restless urge for liberty and progress to surpass the gains it has already made; it is no longer abetted by a universal ideal that transcends its class interests, as in 1789. Bourgeois liberalism, so called, has forged a closed and rigid system propped up by the array of economic, juridical and social principles that are synthesized in the expression "capitalist bourgeois state." It still harks back to the old principles of the French Revolution, but those principles have the appearance of being crystallized, embalmed, bereft of their inner significance; they now seem to be in contraindication to the spirit that inspired those who proclaimed these very principles in a rush of generous enthusiasm.

Bourgeois liberalism attempts to halt the historical process at its present stage, to perpetuate its own commanding position, to transform into a privilege what was once a right deriving from its undeniable pioneering work; it obstructs the entry of militant new social forces onto the stage of history. With its dogmatic attachment to the principles of economic libertarianism (private property, rights of inheritance, full freedom of initiative in every field, with the state as the organ responsible for internal policing and external defense), it has managed to shackle the dynamic spirit of liberalism to the transitory pattern of a particular social system. The truth is that liberalism is by definition historicist and relativistic; it sees history as a perpetual flux, an eternal becoming and overcoming, and nothing is more contrary to its essence than stasis, immobility, categorical certainty, and faith in the possession of absolute, definitive truths, of the kind that now characterize the bourgeois liberals.

Bourgeois liberalism is powerless to understand the problem posed by the socialist movement; in other words, it does not understand that political and social liberty by themselves are incapable of bringing about liberalism's true goal. It arbitrarily extends its historical experience to the proletariat and makes the absurd claim that the problem of liberty presents itself in the same terms for all social classes. It is clear, for example, that while the conquest of political liberty constituted for the bourgeoisie the sublimation and fulfillment of its own power, which had already come to dominate the economic and cultural sectors, the demand by the proletariat for political liberty and the achievement of it signified no more than the commencement of the struggle for economic emancipation, since it still had no real influence on the control centers of economic life. The process in the latter case is inverted, and this is probably one of the principal reasons for the crisis tormenting the socialist movements of Europe, especially since the war—the terrible disproportion between their economic force, technical capacity, and cultural level on one hand and their political power on the other. The proletariat came to possess a formidable political weapon, to which there did not correspond then (and does not correspond now) the sort of linkage needed to make it work.

Only a few components of the bourgeoisie still exercise a useful, in fact a practically indispensable, progressive function. Which ones? The ones that, quite apart from their privileges of birth, are doing creative work in the spheres of pure intellectual endeavor and managerial technique: the intellectuals, the scientists, the least corrupt and most active sector of the industrial and agrarian bourgeoisie, and also those imposing figures of the modern world, the entrepreneurs, the great captains of industry, those who play the same role in the economy that active politicians do in politics. No matter what the economic system, such persons will still have the task of coordinating the various factors of production and making sure that the rhythm of economic progress does not lag.

The proof of the liberal function that a few sections of the bourgeoisie still carry out is the existence, in all modern democracies, of democratic bourgeois parties that are not insensitive to the pressure of progress and that offer a hand, however cautiously and hesitantly, to the rising working class. But the bourgeoisie in the sense of social class (though it is really more a social and mental category than a class) that obtains the largest part of its income from accumulated capital and privileges, or at any rate that defends this system of privilege as being the one most fitted to preserve its dominance and most favorable to the development of social life, is no longer liberal and can no longer be liberal.

For the bourgeoisie still to be able to make any plausible claim to perform a liberal role, it and the economic system that conforms to its interests would have to show themselves capable, through the sheer innate virtue of basic principle, of meeting the demands of the new class, the Fourth Estate. The bourgeoisie would have to show that, for the sake of remaining faithful to its great historical tradition, it was capable of sacrificing the position of wealth and power it had won and of giving in voluntarily to the demands of the new social forces. But this amounts to asking for a superhuman act of disinterestedness and heroism! An appetite for self-immolation of this kind might be found in one or two exceptional and superior souls so divorced from the fate of their own social class as to attain the serene objectivity of the philosopher, or better still to embrace the cause of the oppressed, but certainly not in an entire class, holding on tightly to its possessions, its privileges, its power.

Where then is liberalism alive, where is it being implemented? In all the active, revolutionary (in the full sense of the word) force of history; in all the social forces that—without perhaps fully realizing it themselves—exercise an innovative function, in all the forces that aim to transcend the present condition of society and to open up ever new domains and new horizons for liberty and progress.

The poor, the oppressed, those unable to adapt themselves to the present state of affairs because they are suffering under it and feel limited and mutilated and are conscious of their mutilation: the new armies of liberalism will be these. The working class in modern capitalist society is the only class that, as a class, *can* be revolutionary. The socialism that conveys their demands, that fights against the actual state of affairs in the name of the needs of the greatest number and of a higher principle of liberty and justice, that awakens the masses from their ancient servitude and gives them a new consciousness of the inferior position they find themselves in, is the truly liberal and liberating political movement.

In the words of Saragat, one of the most thoughtful representatives of the new Italian socialism, "The proletariat is not trying to remake history from its inception; on the contrary it is doing no more than bring to completion an age-old task that was begun at the beginning of human society. . . . The idea of liberty is not born with the proletariat but with mankind, with the first ray of spiritual self-awareness in man. The task of the proletariat is to bear higher and farther the torch that was passed on to it, in the dramatic turmoil of history, by the classes that came before."

HENRY M. PACHTER

Aphorisms on Socialism

Ideas change but their formulas remain. Two people a thousand years apart may be of the same mind despite their differences. To be sure, no bore is more boring than the disciple who quotes what I said twenty years ago. Yet I love him—not for the doctrine he continues to profess but because once in our lives we hated and loved the same things, sang the same hymns, and were clubbed by the same police. By the same token, I would have loved the man who said, twenty-five hundred years ago, "Good government is one of which the people know it exists; not quite as good is the one which they praise"; or the man who said, "The meek shall inherit the earth." I suppose I would have recognized their voices before I appreciated their ideas. So it is with other saintly fools or with my old fellow militants. Marching together made us into a movement. The idea was a flag, and some sacrificed themselves for the flag—I always thought they were dying for me, not for the flag. Solidarity was from each to all for one another—not from all to the flag.

Sometimes we were wrong—maybe more often than we knew or would care to admit; perhaps we are wrong even now. Yet, were we given a chance to live our lives over again, we probably would make the same mistakes, fight the same enemies, hold sacred the same illusions—or similar ones that also are based on the same assumption: that Man is good. We were wrong most of the time when we tried to realize doctrines or when we followed a course of action that seemed to follow from the Scriptures. We were never wrong when we acted in solidarity with people who tried to shape their own destinies. How could we be wrong so long as we asserted our faith in Man? Even defeat could not disprove us; it only made our faith stronger. "Man is good." That is a proposition which is neither true nor untrue; it can be validated by the strong who believe in it militantly, or invalidated by the fainthearted.

Our real defeats were not the occasions when we were beaten; they came when we were told we had succeeded. Our ideas, let's face it, had a tremendous success; everybody stole them and "realized" them. The Nazis took May Day, the very name of socialism, and the pageantry of revolution. The Bolsheviks appropriated the doctrine of a planned economy. The Republicans have adopted the progressive income tax and the Democrats the welfare state. Nasser and King Saud nationalized large industries. Socialism has been hyphenated with nationalism, its mortal enemy, with anticlerical radicalism, and with clerical Christianity. It has been perverted into a totalitarian state philosophy and into the ideology of conservative labor parties. There is no cowardice that has not been justified by "socialist" consciences; no bold crime that has not been committed in the name of socialist efficiency.

They stole every part of the system, every single goal, and every doctrine; they claimed to have realized every socialist demand. Except one. They never stole the basic assumption that Man is good. Some will go so far as to admit that Man is perfectible, and they will proceed to educate him accordingly, by their own or even by our lights; but they will never let him educate himself. They will do everything for the people and eventually provide them with the most perfect socialist economy; but they will not allow these same people to act in their own behalf, make their own mistakes, and assert their own solidarity.

Socialism has become a doubtful word—not because it has been betrayed so often by its leaders, not because it has been diverted so often into strange channels, but because it has been institutionalized, taken over, and managed. Socialism is being *used!* Dare we protest? Dare we say that we never thought of Progress in terms of abstract achievements: so much planning, so much welfare, so much nationalization? Dare we return to the original meaning of socialism—*socii*, the fellows—as that which people have in common?

Many traits of "socialism" simply appeared when certain trends of modern industrialism were extrapolated. They call a socialist someone who admits that free enterprise can no longer handle today's problems. Atomic energy must be kept under safety rules by the government; communications must be supervised by the state; great hydraulic works must be undertaken by national planning boards; weak industries such as farming must be subsidized. Worse: an efficient defense industry, a crash rocket program can be planned by despotism better than by free agents; the interests of nationalism point toward a "socialized" economy, with more integration, more interventionism, more welfare and planning, more compulsory arbitration. A moderately progressive kind of welfare economy has been "creeping" rather far and fast lately, and the more intelligent business executives know—or even admit—that it is here to stay. Outside congressional and Fourth-of-July oratory, classical free enterprise is deader than a doornail, and socialists who continue to fight against its ghosts are museum pieces themselves.

It is about time for socialists to admit the facts: there is more "socialism" in the world today than capitalism or any other system. Although we don't like the kind of socialism that is being realized, we cannot simply repudiate or ignore it. Governments in most new countries are now in complete command of the national resources, either through ownership of the most important enterprises or by virtue of various control devices. Feudalistic and capitalistic forms of ownership are successfully checked by political means; the various underdeveloped economies are being developed according to plans that may satisfy the desires of their elites and will certainly flatter their national ambitions. Even in the advanced countries, older capitalistic traditions yield to "mixed economies" that are largely regulated; production goals and distributive aims are formulated through political infighting and the influence of pluralistic pressure groups. Staunch defenders of free enterprise now acknowledge that elements of "socialist" economic thinking have become part of their system, while orthodox disciples of the "economic" view of history now admit that wage, price, and related disputes have become "political."

Some socialists—the true ones, I think—do not agree that socialism is an extrapolation of present trends in the capitalist economy. The term socialism should have been saved from confusion with state capitalism or even state collectivist systems. Indeed, it should not be identified with any, not even the most perfect system; for originally socialism was a movement of protest against all systems. Its history in modern times begins with the Jacqueries and Martin Luther's indictment of the "Companies Monopolia"; it includes a sequence of anarchist, apocalyptic, and chiliastic rebellions against the domination and exploitation of man by man, against industrialism and the modern state, against commercialism and militarism. At times, these movements could merge in common hatred of an overriding symbol; capitalism provided the common denominator for all exploitation and domination. At all times, however, anticapitalism has had these two components: resistance to domination by an upper class, and resistance to an "inexorable law" which claims that exploitation of human "factors" is the necessary prerequisite of economic progress.

This democratic and humanistic root of socialism has flowered in conceptions like "industrial democracy" and "workers' control," in the "council" movements that recently sprang up in Poland and Hungary, in the American shop-steward law, and even in the German "codetermination" law. In a still more perverted form, it arises when workers repudiate socialist parties that (however ineffectively) try to defend their living standards, and follow the Communists who merely assert their freedom to protest. A minority of French Communists favors dictatorship and admires Bolshevik terror; most of them think they are defending democracy. In their propaganda speeches the Russians aptly refer to the "ruling circles" of the West; this target, which evokes memories of the "Elders of Zion" and other world conspiracies of the upper class, most effectively rallies pseudodemocratic and pseudosocialist instincts of anticapitalist defense.

It was the merit of Marx to focus opposition on the specific "system" of capitalism and the "economic laws." He also attacked the social class that benefits from this system and is interested in its preservation. But for him this was only one aspect of a two-faced phenomenon. The more capitalism develops, the less some parasitic beneficiary—the private owner of capital—is the villain of the piece. This villain's gradual disappearance or submission under the abstract law of profitability merely confirms what should have been clear to readers of *Capital* from the beginning: that class situations are not properly described by the symbols "rich" and "poor" but by economic function, and that authority is derived not from property but from the right to use it. The managers of large corporations are not exploiting people; they merely translate the equation of rational efficiency into "personnel relations." Likewise, the managers of Soviet state trusts administer the law of growth of industrial enterprises. Socialism is a human reaction against both forms of command over man. Though not hostile to industralism, socialism is not its fulfillment. Any society may use technological achievements without surrendering its own values. The Japanese militarists knew how to use industrialism; the Russian Bolsheviks abandoned themselves to its spirit. In the democracies the fight is still raging: will modern industry breed the perfect robot—or liberate man from drudgery and servitude? These alternatives require some reflection on the question of what socialism means today.

We are learning better to know our enemy. Marx still wrote against capitalism; today all of society is under indictment. Marx still could say confidently that at the end of capitalist development nothing would be left to do except to "expropriate the few owners of already socialized factories"; today we are frightened at the sight of the "already socialized minds." After the owners of the communications networks had been expropriated, their function still would be "socialized"—maybe without minds.

Many socialists today are fighting the spread of what has been called mass culture. None of this has been new since Huxley's *Brave New World*; but today it is a problem for socialists. Huxley still believed that he was satirizing the trend of capitalism (he said specifically that the entire, weird arrangement of his world had been engineered for the sole purpose of ensuring maximum consumption of surplus production), and he still implied that socialism would break this fatal trend. In the meantime, the collectivist heaven has developed traits that are worse than the capitalist hell. Capitalism brought oppression from outside, but left the inner man largely intact—so much so that he was able to rebel. Collectivism captures a person totally; consent is being "engineered" or given "freely." People are "reasonable" because they no longer see alternative choices. Capitalism crippled people's sensibilities, to be sure; collectivism demands that these sensibilities wither away.

No doubt most socialists are horrified by the picture of "socialism" that has unfolded over the past forty years, and they will insist that this is not what they had fought for. Certainly they are right. But liberals and democrats could have protested, a hundred years ago, against the way liberal and democratic ideals were being realized. They had to take the responsibility because at least one thing could not be denied: liberalism was run largely by liberals. Socialism, on the contrary, is being run by everybody but socialists. Sometimes it can hardly be distinguished from its worst enemies—state capitalism, fascism, and nationalism.

We may vainly protest that the most important characteristics of socialism are missing in all these mixed, adulterated, and perverted conceptions; that a socialist system run by nonsocialists is simply unthinkable; and that socialism is an integrated whole from which no single feature can be omitted or integrated into another system. All this is beside the point—or rather, this is just the point: that the enemy has infiltrated the fortress and the socialists are not in command of their own house. It is simply impossible to ignore the language of the common man and to insist that the name of socialism should be reserved for an esoteric notion of an esoteric sect; it is even less possible if the missing element in all these pseudosocialist systems is ill-defined. Socialists themselves have not agreed on its nature, nor have they warned others of the impending confusion. Moreover, the definition of pure or strict socialism, too, seems to be hyphenated. The moment I say "democratic socialism" I admit that there are other kinds, at least potentially, and that, to satisfy me, I have to add to the definition of socialism a foreign ingredient taken from another source. This attempt at evading the issue, therefore, defeats the claim that socialism is an organic whole.

Can socialism be an organic whole? There really should be but one such whole: Man. No institution, not the most perfect one, can or should be an end. Whoever thinks that social-ism or any other system is the end of history stops thinking as a socialist.

I shall confide a sad truth to you. Those who want a perfect socialism are not socialists. They substitute a system for the fullness of humanity. They perfect institutions instead of making them fit the needs of people. Beware lest they ultimately fit people to institutions. There can never be peace between man and man's works. But it is true that there never was less peace between them than now.

Our society cripples people and inflicts on them the disease that decimates "personality": A man is appreciated not for what he is but for what he usefully contributes; he is cleft down the middle into a public and a private being. The first is his material usefulness, and it includes every one of the qualities that make him replaceable; the other is hidden away, though it holds the unique qualities of his humanity. Our society deprives itself, and him, of what is the essential part of the personality.

In industrial-commercial relations, togetherness is neither freely granted out of the fullness of sympathy and generosity, nor is it ever allowed to bring out essential human impulses. It is a means to achieve productivity. Man himself is a means, not only for other men but for production goals. Wherever we see people together, their togetherness is either perverted or it turns away from society. Society, which does not need love, circum-scribed it within a sphere of regulated and permissible behavior—just as the Church, unable to cope with man's totality, found a niche for pardonable sin. In this process society immunizes itself against feeling: it prevents the most human needs from affecting human relations. The totality of Man is never present in society; the best of him remains private.

Capitalism does not impede creativity; it misdirects it by capturing its specific virtue. On the whole, capitalism has promoted progress. But it has done something to the inventor. He no longer considers himself an artist or creates out of the fullness of his life in the com-munity. The complaint that capitalism stifles creativity is ridiculous; we hear nothing but exaltations of so-called creativity. "Creative" of what? That is the question. The word makes no sense apart from any specific creation.

Productivity has been insulated; it has become an end in itself. This system also has permitted the advances of Soviet science. The price: science has been taken out of its polit-ical and philosophical context.

Lately, another flow of noble feelings has been isolated from its wellsprings of human gen-erosity and perverted into useful techniques of management. Business today is all for social welfare, for planning, for greater equality, and, *horrible dictu*, for "solidarity," "together-ness," and "group thinking." After taking over most of the institutions and the material aims, the enemy is availing himself of a mock-version of the socialist spirit. To make the perversion complete, some socialist thinkers now have been moved to join the chorus of protest against "mass culture." When this clarion was first sounded, by Le Bon and Ortega y Gasset, it was the war cry of declared antisocialists; with the exception of Hendrik de Man, no socialist at the time protested against these aspects of the new socialism.

Such an analysis might be rejected on the following grounds: the present mass cul-ture is characteristic of a capitalistic economy that still is being run by capitalists, and is working for their benefit; classes have not been abolished, and even where state capitalism prevails, its functionaries clearly constitute a new class of exploiters. If all this is true, socialists were even more mistaken than they seemed to be; they fought the wrong enemy on a false front. They laid all evils at the door of private capitalists or "bosses" instead of an institution that seems to be embracing considerably more territory than just private enter-prise; we have called it modern industrialism, and its characteristics are a particular ratio-nality and accounting mentality, a necessary division of labor, and a functional hierarchy.

Not private capital is the enemy but the capitalist calculability which defines man's worth by what he can contribute to the creation of value. Private capitalists are more or less needless costs in a modern industrial system and will be eliminated almost automati-cally, though slowly, should they prove to be too costly. Socialists still have to fight those who hold the levers of economic and political control, under whatever title; but on the ideological level these functionaries are better armed than the old capitalists. The capital-ist had to justify himself in terms of his usefulness to the promotion of progress; often he could not show cause but was unmasked as a mere parasite. The functionary barely faces this difficulty. He clearly fulfills a function determined by calculations of a electronic brain; he can show that in terms of these calculations he is just as useful as anybody else; he merely executes the equations of the perfect plan. His wages are those of an adminis-trator, and he has earned his share. Arcadij Gurland observed that the anticapitalist pro-tect, from its very beginnings, was "political": under the conditions of a strict European class society, it was a protest against the owners of a monopoly. Opposition against the "manager," hence, can be aroused in the name of democracy only.

If socialism is the functionally most streamlined system of production and distribu-tion, as provided by the most perfect electronic brains according to the economic equa-tions, then the argument that the manager has earned his share is unanswerable. The little fat which the bureaucrats may skim off the national soup really does not matter if other-wise they give their citizens good service. Socialists then cannot quarrel with the account-ing system either, because some accounting must be there to avoid unnecessary waste.

On technological grounds, a socialist expert of planning and accounting might not find too much to criticize in the budget of a pseudosocialist economy. Even so, a principled socialist opposition would be called into being whenever the definition of "national wel-fare" was at stake, i.e., if and only if the aims and goals of planning were subject to con-troversy. The government will always be able to show, figures in hand, that output and expenses should be increased, preferably in those places where greater customer satisfaction will eventually result in better production. Socialists may argue that they value leisure and easy production schedules more highly than national power and large production facilities, and that consumption allowances should be increased first for the aged and for retired people.

Here the human element in the argument disrupts the planners' calculations; the conflict between man and machine, or man and the organization, or man and the rationality of economic reckoning, has not changed, whether the executor of the abstract command of the figures is a private capitalist, a trust manager, or a bureaucrat. The socialist's function in this fight is still the same, whether the enemy be capitalism or socialism. The socialist represents humanity. To that extent, Marx's analysis of industrial labor is still correct: what he called "constant" costs still are the ones given by objective factors, and labor is the only "variable" cost. But he did not surmise that this criticism would still be valid under socialist conditions of production.

A graver drawback of recent advances toward socialism has been uncovered by Gunnar Myrdal. Planning, he says, is necessarily national planning first, and that means erecting protective barriers against the disruptive fluctuations that, periodically or constantly, are transmitted from the world markets to the national economies. Isolationism serves the interest of socialist planners; but it deprives the country's workers and consumers of all the checks on misplanning that normally control a national economy through the countervailing influence of foreign exchanges. Moreover, the closed economy leaves the government free to use foreign commerce for its particular political aims. For instance, the foreign transactions of the Soviet government are probably the single part of the world economy carried out with the least regard to cost; by that token, this operation might be called the "least capitalistic," but it is so conducted only for reasons of foreign policy. Any benefit to the people that might accrue from it is strictly accidental.

Socialism is not capitalism minus capitalists, nor the most advanced, streamlined system of industrial accountability; it cannot even be defined as a democratic system of such rational industrial relations properly institutionalized. On the contrary, socialists enter the picture precisely at the point where such a system breaks down and people refuse to obey the abstract law of efficiency. Socialists, at their best, always will represent the human protest against any system, and that is even more true when the system is more rational and more efficient and when the "human factor" is being managed more "scientifically." The human sense of dignity revolts against the dependence upon command powers, whether economic or political.

Our aim was to deprive people of the power to use other people as means to an end, however worthy the increase of productivity or the national welfare. This must remain the attitude of socialists under all systems. However, theoretical considerations and the evidence of recent history suggest that this conflict between man and things, or freedom and necessity, cannot be resolved. The aim then is to check the command powers through the countervailing powers of labor and other organizations.

The pluralistic system which this implies cannot be justified on the ground that it is more efficient than straight capitalism or straight despotism. It is not, and either of these systems will normally be more efficient. But it gives people a chance to wreck plans that were made without their consent, to assert their will, and to make their own mistakes. System-builders are so well-intentioned as to prevent people from making wrong decisions. They will do everything for the people except allow them to do anything for themselves. Even some enthusiasts of countervailing powers envisage those powers as a system, i.e., they assume that various powers sooner or later will become institutionalized and freeze into a well-organized system where, for example, wage conflicts will be superseded completely by a pyramid of negotiation and arbitration machinery which in the end will figure out what part of the national product each population group should get. Eventually this can be done by a special computer. Socialists may find a pluralistic arrangement more suitable for their purposes, but they must attempt to prevent its freezing into a system. They must be very flexible in promoting and checking the countervailing powers at the right times.

Philosophy has not found a solution to the problem of conflict, nor does historical evidence suggest any avenue of escape. The famous "leap into the realm of freedom" has not been defined as the *conquest* of Necessity but as the *insight* into its pattern or a choice between alternative aims. Reactionaries have seized upon this truth, in asking the silly (because incomplete) question, Freedom for what? Choice, the essence of freedom, is always a choice between possibilities; hence freedom is "for what" only to the extent that it is "from what." To conceal this dichotomy is a sleight-of-hand by which freedom is made to disappear. There is no genuine freedom when the choice is limited within a system. Freedom must always remain the liberty of refusing cooperation, of debating "necessity" and of disregarding "instrumental reason." Since necessity and instrumental reason will always be the specific patterns of the existing society, freedom can exist only if alternative frames of reference are offered by competing powers. Hence the system of countervailing powers should be as widely open as possible, the aim being not only to check the command powers of the ruling hierarchy but to establish the pattern of choices itself. With regard to labor, socialists do not represent the human "factor" in the production equation; they represent the human element in society. That is to say, they break every equation. They are not interested in establishing a system with a better equation (though they often pretend they are doing so), but in saving man from being a factor in an equation. What matters to them is the point where the equation breaks down and man emerges, not where a new equation is formed and man is again integrated into a new system. Socialism, so understood as the action of socialists, is not a social and economic system; it is motion. Proudly expressing the essence of labor at its best, Bernstein said: "The ultimate goal is nothing to me, the movement is everything." Marx's healthy contempt for wielders of "programs" is too well known to need quoting here, and even the great utopians used their programs only to realize their secret aim: to set people in motion. This is not to cite the Church Fathers as authorities but to answer the question of whether we can still call ourselves socialists in the same sense that they did. I think we can; socialism in this sense will be the slogan when in Poland, Yugoslavia, and elsewhere people present their demands for more self-determination and participation in deciding their own and their country's fate. Oppressed socialists under "socialism" are in the same position as Christians who uphold Christ against the churches.

Socialism first of all means movement; it is a freely organized movement. When the goal is reached, however, the movement may cease; "socialism" then dies for want of a cause. Nationalization, welfare, and planning—desirable as such—no longer symbolize man's aspiration to master his own destiny; they may well become the symbols of his inability to make responsible choices.

Socialism is not a thing to have; it cannot be abstractly defined. Suppose each worker owns his house and his car, and suppose the new techniques of economic control make it possible for capitalism to improve living standards, to give people economic security, and to narrow class differences: do we then still need socialism? I say yes, because it is a matter of attitudes. It is freedom, or the refusal to submit to commands. It is solidarity, or the refusal to forget people over the demands of technique.

One cannot have socialism. One is a socialist.

COMMUNISM AND REVOLUTION

Communist theory and practice places primacy on the political party above all. Lenin already made this clear in his classic text of 1902: *What Is To Be Done?* Composed of "professional revolutionary intellectuals," capable of preserving the vision of a revolution from the temptations posed by reform, this "vanguard party" will bring an understanding of their political mission to workers from "outside" their ranks. Organized in military style, along the principles of "democratic centralism," criticism can only occur within the confines of the party. It must be ready for action at any moment. Lenin indeed explicitly rejects any connection between liberalism and marxism and, implicitly, between the development of capitalism and socialism.

Antonio Gramsci draws the implication by viewing 1917 as a revolution "against *Das Kapital*." Among the founders of the Italian Communist Party, and the author of the legendary *Prison Notebooks* while incarcerated by Mussolini, he saw the Bolsheviks as denying the economic determinism traditionally associated with Marx and his rigid view of historical stages, in which only with a fully developed capitalism, and a substantial working-class majority, can a revolution occur. Gramsci did not foresee the dangers in this new form of historical voluntarism through which socialism would ultimately become identified with industrialization, and whereby it would fall upon the Bolsheviks to "create the conditions needed for the total achievement of their goal."

Arbitrariness was generated by the communist commitment to revolutionary voluntarism. The "dictatorship of the proletariat" itself becomes a case in point, which Josef Stalin himself readily admits in his important lecture of 1924, insofar as the state must remain "unrestricted by law and based in force." There are, in short, no checks upon the power of the state and no protection for minority views. The break between socialism and liberalism now becomes complete. Its purpose is to crush the resistance of enemies to the new order and consolidate the gains of the—authoritarian—communist revolution. The dictatorship, which Marx originally considered a "transitional state," will thus remain in place. Political practice, however, can always use an underpinning in theory. This was supplied by Mao Tse-tung in his important article of 1957 entitled "On the Correct Handling of Contradictions."

New forms of conflict demand the attention of the state. The issue is no longer merely one between classes. Mao makes clear how contradictions between "ourselves and the enemy and those among the people themselves," which manifest themselves as "antagonistic and non-antagonistic," call for different solutions by the state with respect to the use of coercion against persuasion. Agitated by the specter of the Hungarian uprising of 1956, however, the Chinese Communist leader immediately noted that the one form of contradiction can turn into another.

The validity of the terminology is not the issue. It is rather that Mao never supplies any viable criteria for distinguishing between these two forms of contradiction. The decision regarding when a contradiction is antagonistic or non-antagonistic—like all decisions—ultimately falls upon the party. And there is no possibility of appeal.

V. I. LENIN

What Is To Be Done?

It is no secret that two trends have taken shape in the present-day international Social-Democracy. The fight between these trends now flares up in a bright flame, and now dies down and smoulders under the ashes of imposing "truce resolutions." What this "new" trend, which adopts a "critical" attitude towards "obsolete dogmatic" Marxism, represents has with sufficient precision been *stated* by Bernstein, and *demonstrated* by Millerand.

Social-Democracy must change from a party of the social revolution into a democratic party of social reforms. Bernstein has surrounded this political demand with a whole battery of symmetrically arranged "new" arguments and reasonings. The possibility of putting Socialism on a scientific basis and of proving from the point of view of the materialist conception of history that it is necessary and inevitable was denied, as was also the growing impoverishment, proletarianization and the intensification of capitalist contradictions. The very conception, "*ultimate aim*," was declared to be unsound, and the idea of the dictatorship of the proletariat was absolutely rejected. It was denied that there is any counterdistinction in principle between liberalism and Socialism. *The theory of the class struggle* was rejected on the grounds that it could not be applied to a strictly democratic society, governed according to the will of the majority, etc.

Thus, the demand for a resolute turn from revolutionary Social-Democracy to bourgeois Social-reformism was accompanied by a no less resolute turn towards bourgeois criticism of all the fundamental ideas of Marxism. . . .

He who does not deliberately close his eyes cannot fail to see that the new "critical" trend in Socialism is nothing more nor less than a new variety of *opportunism*. And if we judge people not by the brilliant uniforms they don, not by the high-sounding appellations they give themselves, but by their actions, and by what they actually advocate, it will be clear that "freedom of criticism" means freedom for an opportunistic trend in Social-Democracy, the freedom to convert Social-Democracy into a democratic party of reform, the freedom to introduce bourgeois ideas and bourgeois elements into Socialism. . . .

Without a revolutionary theory there can be no revolutionary movement. This though cannot be insisted upon too strongly at a time when the fashionable preaching of opportunism goes hand in hand with an infatuation for the narrowest forms of practical activity. . . . Our Party is only in process of formation, its features are only just becoming outlined, and it is yet far from having settled accounts with other trends of revolutionary thought, which threaten to divert the movement from the correct path. . . . The national tasks of Russian Social-Democracy are such as have never confronted any other socialist party in the world. . . . The *role of vanguard fighter can be fulfilled only by a party that is guided by the most advanced theory.* . . .

. . . The strikes of the nineties represented the class struggle in embryo, but only in embryo. Taken by themselves, these strikes were simply trade union struggles, but not yet Social-Democratic struggles. They testified to the awakening antagonisms between workers and employers, but the workers were not, and could not be, conscious of the irreconcilable antagonism of their interests to the whole of the modern political and social system, i.e., theirs was not yet Social-Democratic consciousness. In this sense, the strikes of the nineties, in spite of the enormous progress they represented as compared with the "riots," remained a purely spontaneous movement.

We have said that *there could not yet be* Social-Democratic consciousness among the workers. It could only be brought to them from without. The history of all countries shows that the working class, exclusively by its own effort, is able to develop only trade union consciousness, i.e., the conviction that it is necessary to combine in unions, fight the employers and strive to compel the government to pass necessary labour legislation, etc. The theory of Socialism, however, grew out of the philosophic, historical and economic theories that were elaborated by the educated representatives of the propertied classes, the intellectuals. According to their social status, the founders of modern scientific Socialism, Marx and Engels, themselves belonged to the bourgeois intelligentisa. In the very same way, in Russia, the theoretical doctrine of Social-Democracy arose quite independently of the spontaneous growth of the working-class movement, it arose as a natural and inevitable outcome of the development of ideas among the revolutionary socialist intelligentsia. At the time of which we are speaking, i.e., the middle of the nineties, this doctrine not only represented the completely formulated program of the Emancipation of Labour group, but had already won over to its side the majority of the revolutionary youth in Russia.

Hence, we had both the spontaneous awakening of the masses of the workers, the awakening to conscious life and conscious struggle, and a revolutionary youth, armed with the Social-Democratic theory, eager to come into contact with the workers. In this connection it is particularly important to state the oft-forgotten (and comparatively little-known) fact that the *early* Social-Democrats of that period *zealously carried on economic agitation* (being guided in this by the really useful instructions contained in the pamphlet *On Agitation* that was still in manuscript), but they did not regard this as their sole task. On the contrary, *right from the very beginning* they advanced the widest historical tasks of Russian Social-Democracy in general, and the task of overthrowing the autocracy in particular. . . . The adherents of the "pure" working-class movement, the worshippers of the closest "organic" . . . contacts with the proletarian struggle, the opponents of any non-worker intelligentsia (even if it be a socialist intelligentsia) are compelled, in order to defend their positions, to resort to the arguments of the *bourgeois* "pure" trade union-ists. . . . This shows . . . that *all* worship of the spontaneity of the working-class move-ment, all belittling of the role of "the conscious element," of the role of Social-Democracy, *means, quite irrespective of whether the belittler wants to or not, strengthening the influence of the bourgeois ideology over the workers.* All those who talk about "overrating the importance of ideology," about exaggerating the role of the conscious element, etc., imagine that the pure working-class movement can work out, and will work out, an independent ideology for itself, if only the workers "wrest their fate from the hands of the leaders." But this is a profound mistake. . . .

Since there can be no talk of an independent ideology being developed by the masses of the workers themselves in the process of their movement the *only* choice is: either the bourgeois or the socialist ideology. There is no middle course (for humanity has not cre-ated a "third" ideology, and, moreover, in a society torn by class antagonisms there can never be a non-class or above-class ideology). Hence, to belittle the socialist ideology *in any way, to turn away from it in the slightest degree* means to strengthen bourgeois ideology. There is a lot of talk about spontaneity, but the *spontaneous* development of the working-class movement leads to its becoming subordinated to the bourgeois ideology, *leads to its developing according to the program* of the *Credo*,[2] for the spontaneous working-class move-ment is trade unionism, and trade unionism means the ideological enslavement of the workers by the bourgeoisie. Hence, our task, the task of Social-Democracy, is to *combat spontaneity*, to *divert* the working-class movement from this spontaneous, trade-unionist striving to come under the wing of the bourgeoisie, and to bring it under the wing of rev-olutionary Social-Democracy. The phrase employed by the authors of the "economic" let-ter in the *Iskra*, No. 12, about the efforts of the most inspired ideologists not being able to divert the working-class movement from the path that is determined by the interaction of the material elements and the material environment, *is absolutely tantamount therefore to the abandonment of Socialism.* . . .

We have seen that the conduct of the broadest political agitation, and consequently the organization of comprehensive political exposures, is an absolutely necessary, and the *most urgently* necessary, task of activity, that is, if that activity is to be truly Social-Democ-ratic. . . . *However much we may try* to "lend the economic struggle itself a political charac-ter" *we shall never be able* to develop the political consciousness of the workers (to the level of Social-Democratic political consciousness) by keeping within the framework of the eco-nomic struggle, for *that framework is too narrow.* . . . .

Class political consciousness can be brought to the workers *only from without*, that is, only from outside of the economic struggle, from outside of the sphere of relations between workers and employers. The sphere from which alone it is possible to obtain this knowledge is the sphere of relationships between *all* the classes and strata and the state and the government, the sphere of the interrelations between *all* the classes. For that rea-son, the reply to the question: what must be done in order to bring political knowledge to the workers? cannot be merely the one which, in the majority of cases, the practical [party] workers, especially those who are inclined towards Economism, mostly content themselves with, i.e., "go among the workers." To bring political knowledge to the *workers* the Social-Democrats must *go among all classes of the population*, must dispatch units of their army *in all directions*. . . .

. . . The political struggle of Social-Democracy is far more extensive and complex than the economic struggle of the workers against the employers and the government. Similarly (and indeed for that reason), the organization of a revolutionary Social-Democratic party must inevitably be of a *different* kind than the organizations of the workers designed for this struggle. A workers' organization must in the first place be a trade organization; secondly, it must be as broad as possible; and thirdly, it must be as little clandestine as possible (here, and further on, of course, I have only autocratic Russia in mind). On the other hand, the organizations of revolutionaries must consist first, foremost and mainly of people who make revolutionary activity their profession (that is why I speak of organizations of *revolutionaries*, meaning revolutionary Social-Democrats). In view of this common feature of the members of such an organization, *all distinctions as between workers and intellectuals*, and certainly distinctions of trade and profession, must be *utterly obliterated*. Such an organization must of necessity be not too extensive and as secret as possible. . . .

The workers' organizations for the economic struggle should be trade union organizations. Every Social-Democratic worker should as far as possible assist and actively work in these organizations. That is true. But it is not at all to our interest to demand that only Social-Democrats should be eligible for membership in the "trade" unions: that would only narrow down our influence over the masses. Let every worker who understands the need to unite for the struggle against the employers and the government join the trade unions. The very aim of the trade unions would be unattainable if they failed to unite all who have attained at least this elementary degree of understanding, and if they were not very *wide* organizations. And the wider these organizations are, the wider our influence over them will be—an influence due not only to the "spontaneous" development of the economic struggle but also to the direct and conscious effort of the socialist trade union members to influence their comrades. . . .

. . . A small, compact core of the most reliable, experienced and hardened workers, with responsible representatives in the principal districts and connected by all the rules of strict secrecy with the organization of revolutionaries, can, with the widest support of the masses and without any formal organization, perform *all* the functions of a trade union organization, and perform them, moreover, in a manner desirable to Social-Democracy. Only in this way can we secure the *consolidation* and development of a *Social-Democratic* trade union movement, in spite of all the gendarmes.

. . . I assert: 1) that no revolutionary movement can endure without a stable organization of leaders that maintains continuity; 2) that the wider the masses spontaneously drawn into the struggle, forming the basis of the movement and participating in it, the more urgent the need of such an organization, and the more solid this organization must be (for it is much easier for demagogues to sidetrack the more backward sections of the masses); 3) that such an organization must consist chiefly of people professionally engaged in revolutionary activity; 4) that in autocratic state, the more we *confine* the membership of such an organization to people who are professionally engaged in revolutionary activity and who have been professionally trained in the art of combatting the political police, the more difficult will it be to wipe out such as organization, and 5) the *greater* will be the number of people of the working class and of the other classes of society who will be able to join the movement and perform active work in it.

. . . The centralization of the most secret functions in an organization of revolutionaries will not diminish, but rather increase the extent and quality of the activity of a large number of other organizations which are intended for a broad public and are therefore as loose and as non-secret as possible, such as workers' trade unions, workers' self-education circles and circles for reading illegal literature, socialist and also democratic circles among *all* other sections of the population, etc., etc. We must have such circles, trade unions and organizations everywhere in *as large a number as possible* and with the widest variety of functions; but it would be absurd and dangerous to *confuse* them with the organization of *revolutionaries*, to obliterate the border line between them, to dim still more the masses' already incredibly hazy appreciation of the fact that in order to "serve" the mass movement we must have people who will devote themselves exclusively to Social-Democratic activities, and that such people must *train* themselves patiently and steadfastly to be professional revolutionaries.

Yes, this appreciation has become incredibly dim. Our chief sin with regard to organization is that by *our amateurishness we have lowered the prestige of revolutionaries in Russia.* A person who is flabby and shaky in questions of theory, who has a narrow outlook, who pleads the spontaneity of the masses as an excuse for his own sluggishness, who resembles a trade union secretary more than a people's tribune, who is unable to conceive of a broad and bold plan that would command the respect even of opponents, and who is inexperienced and clumsy in his own professional art—the art of combating the political police— why, such a man is not a revolutionary but a wretched amateur!

Let no active worker take offence at these frank remarks, for as far as insufficient training is concerned, I apply them first and foremost to myself. I used to work in a circle that set itself very wide, all-embracing tasks; and all of us, members of that circle, suffered painfully, acutely from the realization that we were proving ourselves to be amatuers at a moment in history when we might have been able to say, paraphrasing a well-known epigram: "Give us an organization of revolutionaries, and we shall overturn Russia!" And the more I recall the burning sense of shame I then experienced, the more bitter are my feelings towards those pseudo Social-Democrats whose teachings "bring disgrace on the calling of a revolutionary," who fail to understand that our task is not to champion the degrading of the revolutionary to the level of an amateur, but to *raise* the amateurs to the level of revolutionaries. . . .

ANTONIO GRAMSCI

The Revolution against *Capital*

The Bolshevik Revolution is now definitively part of the general revolution of the Russian people. The maximalists up until two months ago were the active agents needed to ensure that events should not stagnate, that the drive to the future should not come to a halt and allow a final settlement—a bourgeois settlement—to be reached. Now these maximalists have seized power and established their dictatorship, and are creating the socialist framework within which the revolution will have to settle down if it is to continue to develop harmoniously, without head-on confrontations, on the basis of the immense gains which have already been made.

The Bolshevik Revolution consists more of ideologies than of events. (And hence, at bottom, we do not really need to know more than we do.) This is the revolution against Karl Marx's *Capital*. In Russia, Marx's *Capital* was more the book of the bourgeoisie than of the proletariat. It stood as the critical demonstration of how events should follow a predetermined course: how in Russia a bourgeoisie had to develop, and a capitalist era had to open, with the setting-up of a Western-type civilization, before the proletariat could even think in terms of its own revolt, its own class demands, its own revolution. But events have overcome ideologies. Events have exploded the critical schema determining how the history of Russia would unfold according to the canons of historical materialism. The Bolsheviks reject Karl Marx, and their explicit actions and conquests bear witness that the canons of historical materialism are not so rigid as might have been and has been thought.

And yet there is a fatality even in these events, and if the Bolsheviks reject some of the statements in *Capital*, they do not reject its invigorating, immanent thought. These people are not "Marxists", that is all; they have not used the works of the Master to compile a rigid doctrine of dogmatic utterances never to be questioned. They live Marxist thought—that thought which is eternal, which represents the continuation of German and Italian idealism, and which in the case of Marx was contaminated by positivist and naturalist encrustations. This thought sees as the dominant factor in history, not raw economic facts, but man, men in societies, men in relation to one another, reaching agreements with one another, developing through these contacts (civilization) a collective, social will; men coming to understand economic facts, judging them and adapting them to their will until this becomes the driving force of the economy and moulds objective reality, which lives and moves and comes to resemble a current of volcanic lava that can be channelled wherever and in whatever way men's will determines.

Marx foresaw the foreseeable. But he could not foresee the European war, or rather he could not foresee that the war would last as long as it has or have the effects it has had. He could not foresee that in the space of three years of unspeakable suffering and miseries, this war would have aroused in Russia the collective popular will that it has aroused. *In normal times* a lengthy process of gradual diffusion through society is needed for such a collective will to form; a wide range of class experience is needed. Men are lazy, they need to be organized, first externally into corporations and leagues, then internally, within their thought and their will [. . .] need a ceaseless continuity and multiplicity of external stimuli. This is why, *under normal conditions*, the canons of Marxist historical criticism grasp reality, capture and clarify it. *Under normal conditions* the two classes of the capitalist world create history through an ever more intensified class struggle. The proletariat is sharply aware of its poverty and its ever-present discomfort and puts pressure on the bourgeoisie to improve its living standards. It enters into struggle, and forces the bourgeoisie to improve the techniques of production and make it more adapted to meeting the urgent needs of the proletariat. The result is a headlong drive for improvement, an acceleration of the rhythm of production, and a continually increasing output of goods useful to society. And in this drive many fall by the wayside, so making the needs of those who are left more urgent; the masses are forever in a state of turmoil, and out of this chaos they develop some order in their thoughts, and become ever more conscious of their own potential, of their own capacity to shoulder social responsibility and become the arbiters of their own destiny.

This is what happens under normal conditions. When events are repeated with a certain regularity. When history develops through stages which, though ever more complex and richer in significance and value, are nevertheless similar. But in Russia the war galvanized the people's will. As a result of the sufferings accumulated over three years, their will became as one almost overnight. Famine was imminent, and hunger, death from hunger could claim anyone, could crush tens of millions of men at one stroke. Mechanically at first, then actively and consciously after the first revolution, the people's will became as one.

Socialist propaganda put the Russian people in contact with the experience of other proletariats. Socialist propaganda could bring the history of the proletariat dramatically to life in a moment: its struggles against capitalism, the lengthy series of efforts required to emancipate it completely from the chains of servility that made it so abject and to allow it to forge a new consciousness and become a testimony today to a world yet to come. It was socialist propaganda that forged the will of the Russian people. Why should they wait for the history of England to be repeated in Russia, for the bourgeoisie to arise, for the class struggle to begin, so that class consciousness may be formed and the final catastrophe of the capitalist world eventually hit them? The Russian people—or at least a minority of the Russian people—has already passed through these experiences in thought. It has gone beyond them. It will make use of them now to assert itself just as it will make use of Western capitalist experience to bring itself rapidly to the same level of production as the Western world. In capitalist terms, North America is more advanced than England, because the Anglo-Saxons in North America took off at once from the level England had reached only after long evolution. Now the Russian proletariat, socialistically educated, will begin its history at the highest level England has reached today. Since it has to start from scratch, it will start from what has been perfected elsewhere, and hence will be driven to achieve that level of economic maturity which Marx considered to be a necessary condition for collectivism. The revolutionaries themselves will create the conditions needed for the total achievement of their goal. And they will create them faster than capitalism could have done. The criticisms that socialists have made of the bourgeois system, to emphasize its imperfections and its squandering of wealth, can now be applied by the revolutionaries to do better, to avoid the squandering and not fall prey to the imperfections. It will at first be a collectivism of poverty and suffering. But a bourgeois régime would have inherited the same conditions of poverty and suffering. Capitalism could do no more *immediately* than collectivism in Russia. In fact today it would do a lot less, since it would be faced *immediately* by a discontented and turbulent proletariat, a proletariat no longer able to support on behalf of others the suffering and privation that economic dislocation would bring in its wake. So even in absolute, human terms, socialism *now* can be justified in Russia. The hardships that await them after the peace will be bearable only if the proletarians feel they have things under their own control and know that by their efforts they can reduce these hardships in the shortest possible time.

One has the impression that the maximalists at this moment are the spontaneous expression of a *biological* necessity—that they *had* to take power if the Russian people were not to fall prey to a horrible calamity; if the Russian people, throwing themselves into the colossal labours needed for their own regeneration, were to feel less sharply the fangs of the starving wolf; if Russia were not to become a vast shambles of savage beasts tearing each other to pieces.

JOSEF STALIN

The Dictatorship of the Proletariat

From this theme I take the three main questions: (1) the dictatorship of the proletariat as the instrument of the proletarian revolution; (2) the dictatorship of the proletariat as the domination of the proletariat over the bourgeoisie; (3) the Soviet power as the state form of the dictatorship of the proletariat.

1. THE DICTATORSHIP OF THE PROLETARIAT AS THE INSTRUMENT OF THE PROLETARIAN REVOLUTION

The question of the proletarian dictatorship is above all a question of the main content of the proletarian revolution. The proletarian revolution, its movement, its scope and its achievements acquire flesh and blood only through the dictatorship of the proletariat. The dictatorship of the proletariat is the instrument of the proletarian revolution, its organ, its most important mainstay, brought into being for the purpose of, firstly, crushing the resistance of the overthrown exploiters and consolidating the achievements of the proletarian revolution, and, secondly, carrying the proletarian revolution to its completion, carrying the revolution to the complete victory of socialism. The revolution can vanquish the bourgeoisie, can overthrow its power, without the dictatorship of the proletariat. But the revolution will be unable to crush the resistance of the bourgeoisie, to maintain its victory and to push forward to the final victory of socialism unless, at a certain stage in its development, it creates a special organ in the form of the dictatorship of the proletariat as its principal mainstay.

"The fundamental question of revolution is the question of power." (*Lenin.*) Does this mean that all that is required is to assume power, to seize it? No, it does not mean that. The seizure of power is only the beginning. For many reasons the bourgeosie that is overthrown in one country remains for a long time stronger than the proletariat which has overthrown it. Therefore, the whole point is to retain power, to consolidate it, to make it invincible. What is needed to attain this? To attain this it is necessary to carry out at least the three main tasks that confront the dictatorship of the proletariat "on the morrow" of victory:

(a) to break the resistance of the landlords and capitalists who have been overthrown and expropriated by the revolution, to liquidate every attempt on their part to restore the power of capital;

(b) to organize construction in such a way as to rally all the labouring people around the proletariat, and to carry on this work along the lines of preparing for the liquidation, the abolition of classes;

(c) to arm the revolution, to organize the army of the revolution for the struggle against foreign enemies, for the struggle against imperialism.

The dictatorship of the proletariat is needed to carry out, to fulfill these tasks. . . .

It need hardly be proved that there is not the slightest possibility of carrying out these tasks in a short period, of doing all this in a few years. Therefore, the dictatorship of the proletariat, the transition from capitalism to communism, must not be regarded as a fleeting period of "super-revolutionary" acts and decrees, but as an entire historical era, replete with civil wars and external conflicts, with persistent organizational work and economic construction, with advances and retreats, victories and defeats. This historical era is needed not only to create the economic and cultural prerequisites for the complete victory of socialism, but also to enable the proletariat, first, to educate itself and become steeled as a force capable of governing the country, and, secondly, to re-educate and remould the petty-bourgeois strata along such lines as will assure the organization of socialist production.

2. THE DICTATORSHIP OF THE PROLETARIAT AS THE DOMINATION OF THE PROLETARIAT OVER THE BOURGEOISIE

The dictatorship of the proletariat arises not on the basis of the bourgeois order, but in the process of the breaking up of this order after the overthrow of the bourgeoisie, in the process of the expropriation of the landlords and capitalists, in the process of the socialization of the principal instruments and means of production, in the process of violent proletarian revolution. The dictatorship of the proletariat is a revolutionary power based on the use of force against the bourgeoisie.

The state is a machine in the hands of the ruling class for suppressing the resistance of its class enemies. *In this respect* the dictatorship of the proletariat does not differ essentially from the dictatorship of any other class, for the proletarian state is a machine for the suppression of the bourgeoisie. But there is one *substantial* difference. This difference consists in the fact that all hitherto existing class states have been dictatorships of an exploiting minority over the exploited majority, whereas the dictatorship of the proletariat is the dictatorship of the exploited majority over the exploiting minority.

Briefly: *the dictatorship of the proletariat is the rule—unrestricted by law and based on force— of the proletariat over the bourgeoisie, a rule enjoying the sympathy and support of the labouring and exploited masses. (The State and Revolution).* . . .

[The talk] about "pure" democracy, about "perfect" democracy, and the like, is but a bourgeois screen to conceal the indubitable fact that equality between exploited and exploiters is impossible. The theory of "pure" democracy is the theory of the upper stratum of the working class, which has been broken in and is being fed by the imperialist robbers. It was brought into being for the purpose of concealing the ulcers of capitalism, of touching up imperialism and lending it moral strength in the struggle against the exploited masses. Under capitalism there are no real "liberties" for the exploited, nor can there be, if for no other reason than that the premises, printing plants, paper supplies, etc., indispensable for the actual enjoyment of "liberties" are the privilege of the exploiters. Under capitalism the exploited masses do not, nor can they, really participate in the administration of the country, if for no other reason than that, even under the most democratic regime, governments, under the conditions of capitalism, are not set up by the people but by the Rothschilds and Stinnesses, the Rockefellers and Morgans. Democracy under capitalism is *capitalist* democracy, the democracy of the exploiting minority, based on the restriction of the rights of the exploited majority and directed against this majority. Only under the dictatorship of the proletariat the real "liberties" for the exploited and real participation in the administration of the country by the proletarians and peasants possible. Under the dictatorship of the proletariat, democracy is *proletarian* democracy, the democracy of the exploited majority, based upon the restriction of the rights of the exploiting minority and directed against this minority.

Second conclusion: The dictatorship of the proletariat cannot arise as the result of the peaceful development of bourgeois society and of bourgeois democracy; it can arise only as the result of the smashing of the bourgeois state machine, the bourgeois army, the bourgeois bureaucratic machine, the bourgeois police. . . .

3. THE SOVIET POWER AS THE STATE FORM OF THE DICTATORSHIP OF THE PROLETARIAT

The victory of the dictatorship of the proletariat signifies the suppression of the bourgeoisie, the smashing of the bourgeois state machine, and the substitution of proletarian democracy for bourgeois democracy. That is clear. But by means of what organizations can this colossal task be carried out? The old forms of organization of the proletariat, which grew up on the basis of bourgeois parliamentarism, are inadequate for this task—of that there can hardly be any doubt. What then, are the new forms of organization of the proletariat that are capable of serving as the gravediggers of the bourgeois state machine, that are capable not only of smashing this machine, not only of substituting proletarian democracy for bourgeois democracy, but also of becoming the foundation of the proletarian state power?

This new form of organization of the proletariat is the Soviets.

Wherein lies the strength of the Soviets as compared with the old forms of organization?

In that the Soviets are the most *all-embracing* mass organizations of the proletariat, for they and they alone embrace all workers without exception.

In that the Soviets are the *only* mass organizations which embrace all the oppressed and exploited, workers and peasants, soldiers and sailors, and in which the vanguard of the masses, the proletariat, can, for this reason, most easily and most completely exercise its political leadership of the mass struggle.

In that the Soviets are the *most powerful organs* of the revolutionary struggle of the masses, of the political actions of the masses, of the insurrection of the masses—organs capable of breaking the omnipotence of finance capital and of its political appendages.

In that the Soviets are the *immediate* organizations of the masses themselves, *i.e.,* they are *the most democratic* and therefore the most authoritative organizations of the masses, which facilitate to the utmost their participation in the work of building up the new state and in its administration, and which bring into full play the revolutionary energy, initiative and creative abilities of the masses in the struggle for the destruction of the old order, in the struggle for the new, proletarian order.

The Soviet power is the amalgamation and formation of the local Soviets into one common state organization, into the state organization of the proletariat as the vanguard of the oppressed and exploited masses and as the ruling class—their amalgamation into the republic of Soviets.

The essence of the Soviet power is contained in the fact that these organizations of a most pronounced mass character, these most revolutionary organizations of precisely those classes that were oppressed by the capitalists and landlords are now the *"permanent and sole* basis of the whole power of the state, of the whole state apparatus"; that

> "precisely those masses which even in the most democratic bourgeois republics, while being equal in law, have in fact been prevented by thousands of tricks and devices from taking part in political life and from enjoying democratic rights and liberties, are now drawn unfailingly into *constant* and, moreover, *decisive* participation in the democratic administration of the state." (Lenin, *Selected Works*, Vol. VII, p. 231.)

This is why the Soviet power is a *new form* of state organization, different in principle from the old bourgeois-democratic and parliamentary form, a *new type* of state, adapted not to the task of exploiting and oppressing the labouring masses, but to the task of completely emancipating them from all oppression and exploitation, to the tasks facing the dictatorship of the proletariat.

Lenin rightly says that with the appearance of the Soviet power "the era of bourgeois-democratic parliamentarism has come to an end, and a new chapter in world history—the era of proletarian dictatorship—has commenced."

What are the characteristic features of the Soviet power?

The Soviet power has a most pronounced mass character and is the most democratic state organization of all possible state organizations while classes continue to exist; for, being the arena of the bond and collaboration between the workers and the exploited peasants in their struggle against the exploiters, and basing itself in its work on this bond and on this collaboration, it represents, by virtue of this, the power of the majority of the population over the minority, it is the state of the majority, the expression of its dictatorship.

The Soviet power is the most internationalist of all state organizations in class society, for, since it destroys every kind of national oppression and rests on the collaboration of the labouring masses of the various nationalities, it facilitates, by virtue of this, the amalgamation of these masses into a single state union.

The Soviet power, by its very structure, facilitates the task of leading the oppressed and exploited masses for the vanguard of these masses—for the proletariat, as the most consolidated and most class-conscious core of the Soviets.

"The experience of all revolutions and of all movements of the oppressed classes, the experience of the world socialist movement teaches," says Lenin, "that the proletariat alone is able to unite and lead the scattered and backward stata of the toiling and exploited population." (*Selected Works*, Vol. VII, p. 232.)

The structure of the Soviet power facilitates the practical application of the lessons drawn from this experience.

The Soviet power, by combining the legislative and executive functions in a single state body and replacing territorial electoral constituencies by industrial units, factories and mills, thereby directly links the workers and the labouring masses in general with the apparatus of state administration, teaches them how to administer the country.

The Soviet power alone is capable of releasing the army from its subordination to bourgeois command and of converting it from the instrument of oppression of the people, which it is under the bourgeois order, into an instrument for the liberation of the people from the yoke of the bourgeoisie, both native and foreign.

"The Soviet organization of the state alone is capable of immediately and effectively smashing and finally destroying the old, *i.e.*, the bourgeois, bureaucratic and judicial apparatus." (*Ibid.*)

The Soviet form of state alone, by drawing the mass organizations of the toilers and exploited into constant and unrestricted participation in state administration, is capable of preparing the ground for the withering away of the state, which is one of the basic elements of the future stateless communist society.

The republic of Soviets is thus the political form, so long sought and finally discovered, within the framework of which the economic emancipation of the proletariat, the complete victory of socialism, is to be accomplished.

The Paris Commune was the embryo of this form; the Soviet power is its development and culmination.

That is why Lenin says:

"The republic of Soviets of Workers' Soldiers', and Peasants' Deputies is not only the form of a higher type of democratic institution . . . but is the *only form* capable of securing the most painless transition to socialism." (*Selected Works*, Vol. VI, p. 447)

MAO TSE-TUNG

On the Correct Handling of Contradictions among the People

TWO DIFFERENT TYPES OF CONTRADICTIONS

Never before has our country been as united as it is today. The victories of the bourgeois-democratic revolution and the socialist revolution and our achievements in socialist construction have rapidly changed the face of old China. A still brighter future for our motherland lies ahead. The days of national disunity and chaos which the people detested have gone, never to return. Led by the working class and the Communist Party, our six hundred million people, united as one, are engaged in the great task of building socialism. The unification of our country, the unity of our people and the unity of our various nationalities—these are the basic guarantees of the sure triumph of our cause. However, this does not mean that contradictions no longer exist in our society. To imagine that none exist is a naive idea which is at variance with objective reality. We are confronted by two types of social contradictions—those between ourselves and the enemy and those among the people themselves. The two are totally different in their nature.

To understand these two different types of contradictions correctly, we must first be clear on what is meant by "the people" and what is meant by "the enemy". The concept of "the people" varies in content in different countries and in different periods of history in the same country. Take our own country for example. During the War of Resistance Against Japan, all those classes, strata and social groups opposing Japanese aggression came within the category of the people, while the Japanese imperialists, the Chinese traitors and the pro-Japanese elements were all enemies of the people. During the War of Liberation, the U.S. imperialists and their running dogs—the bureaucrat-capitalists, the landlords and the Kuomintang reactionaries who represented these two classes—were the enemies of the people, while the other classes, strata and social groups, which opposed these enemies, all came within the category of the people. At the present stage, the period of building socialism, the classes, strata and social groups which favour, support and work for the cause of socialist construction all come within the category of the people, while the social forces and groups which resist the socialist revolution and are hostile to or sabotage socialist construction are all enemies of the people.

The contradictions between ourselves and the enemy are antagonistic contradictions. Within the ranks of the people, the contradictions among the working people are non-antagonistic, while those between the exploited and the exploiting classes have a non-antagonistic aspect in addition to an antagonistic aspect. There have always been contradictions among the people, but their content differs in each period of the revolution and in the period of socialist construction. In the conditions prevailing in China today, the contradictions among the people comprise the contradictions within the working class, the contradictions within the peasantry, the contradictions within the intelligentsia, the con-tradictions between the working class and the peasantry, the contradictions between the workers and peasants on the one hand and the intellectuals on the other, the contradictions between the working class and other sections of the working people on the one hand and the national bourgeoisie on the other, the contradictions within the national bourgeoisie; and so on. Our People's Government is one that genuinely represents the people's interests; it is a government that serves the people. Nevertheless, there are still certain contradictions between the government and the people. These include contradictions among the interests of the state, the interests of the collective and the interests of the individual; between democracy and centralism; between the leadership and the led; and the contradiction aris-ing from the bureaucratic style of work of certain government workers in their relations with the masses. All these are also contradictions among the people. Generally speaking, the people's basic identity of interests underlies the contradictions among the people.

In our country, the contradiction between the working class and the national bour-geoisie belongs to the category of contradictions among the people. By and large, the class struggle between the two is a class struggle within the ranks of the people, because the Chinese national bourgeoisie has a dual character. In the period of the bourgeois-democra-tic revolution, it had both a revolutionary and a conciliationist side to its character. In the period of the socialist revolution, exploitation of the working class for profit constitutes one side of the character of the national bourgeoisie, while its support of the Constitution and its willingness to accept socialist transformation constitute the other. The national bourgeoisie differs from the imperialists, the landlords and the bureaucrat-capitalists. The contradiction between the national bourgeoisie and the working class is one between the exploiter and the exploited, and is by nature antagonistic. But in the concrete conditions of China, this antagonistic class contradiction can, if properly handled, be transformed into a non-antagonistic one and be resolved by peaceful methods. However, it will change into a contradiction between ourselves and the enemy if we do not handle it properly and do not follow the policy of uniting with, criticizing and educating the national bour-geoisie, or if the national bourgeoisie does not accept this policy of ours.

Since they are different in nature, the contradictions between ourselves and the enemy and the contradictions among the people must be resolved by different methods. To put it briefly, the former are a matter of drawing a clear distinction between ourselves and the enemy, and the latter a matter of drawing a clear distinction between right and wrong. It is, of course, true that the distinction between ourselves and the enemy is also a matter of right and wrong. For example, the question of who is in the right, we or the domestic and foreign reactionaries, the imperialists, the feudalists and bureaucrat-capitalists, is also a matter of right and wrong, but it is in a different category from questions of right and wrong among the people.

Our state is a people's democratic dictatorship led by the working class and based on the worker-peasant alliance. What is this dictatorship for? Its first function is to suppress the reactionary classes and elements and those exploiters in our country who resist the socialist revolution, to suppress those who try to wreck our socialist construction, or in other words, to resolve the internal contradictions between ourselves and the enemy. For instance, to arrest, try and sentence certain counter-revolutionaries, and to deprive land-lords and bureaucrat-capitalists of their right to vote and their freedom of speech for a specified period of time—all this comes within the scope of our dictatorship. To maintain public order and safeguard the interests of the people, it is likewise necessary to exercise dictatorship over embezzlers, swindlers, arsonists, murderers, criminal gangs and other scoundrels who seriously disrupt public order. The second function of this dictatorship is to protect our country from subversion and possible aggression by external enemies. In that event, it is the task of this dictatorship to resolve the external contradiction between ourselves and the enemy. The aim of this dictatorship is to protect all our people so that they can devote themselves to peaceful labour and build China into a socialist country with a modern industry, agriculture, science and culture. Who is to exercise this dicata-torship? Naturally, the working class and the entire people under its leadership. Dictator-ship does not apply within the ranks of the people. The people cannot exercise dictatorship over themselves, nor must one section of the people oppress another. Law-breaking ele-ments among the people will be punished according to law, but this is different in princi-ple from the exercise of dictatorship to suppress enemies of the people. What applies among the people is democratic centralism. Our Constitution lays it down that citizens of the People's Republic of China enjoy freedom of speech, of the press, assembly, associa-tion, procession, demonstration, religious belief, and so on. Our Constitution also pro-vides that the organs of state must practise democratic centralism, that they must rely on the masses and that their personnel must serve the people. Our socialist democracy is democracy in the broadest sense such as is not to be found in any capitalist country. Our dictatorship is the people's democratic dictatorship led by the working class and based on the worker-peasant alliance. That is to say, democracy operates within the ranks of the peo-ple, while the working class, uniting with all others enjoying civil rights, and in the first place with the peasantry, enforces dictatorship over the reactionary classes and elements and all those who resist socialist transformation and oppose socialist construction. By civil rights, we mean, politically, the rights of freedom and democracy.

But this freedom is freedom with leadership and this democracy is democracy under centralized guidance, not anarchy. Anarchy does not accord with the interests or wishes of the people.

Certain people in our country were delighted by the events in Hungary. They hoped that something similar would happen in China, that thousands upon thousands of people would demonstrate in the streets against the People's Government. Their hopes ran counter to the interests of the masses and therefore could not possibly win their support. Deceived by domestic and foreign counter-revolutionaries, a section of the people in Hungary made the mistake of resorting to acts of violence against the People's Government, with the result that both the state and the people suffered. The damage done to the country's economy in a few weeks of rioting will take a long time to repair. There are other people in our country who wavered on the question of the Hungarian events because they were ignorant of the real state of affairs in the world. They think that there is too little freedom under our people's democracy and that there is more freedom under Western parliamentary democracy. They ask for a two-party system as in the West, with one party in office and the other out of office. But this so-called two-party system is nothing but a device for maintaining the dictatorship of the bourgeoisie; it can never guarantee freedom to the working people. As a matter of fact, freedom and democracy do not exist in the abstract, only in the concrete. In a society rent by class struggle, if there is freedom for the exploiting classes to exploit the working people, there is no freedom for the working people not to be exploited, and if there is democracy for the bourgeoisie, there is no democracy for the proletariat and other working people. The legal existence of the Communist Party is tolerated in some capitalist countries, but only to the extent that it does not endanger the fundamental interests of the bourgeoisie; it is not tolerated beyond that. Those who demand freedom and democracy in the abstract regard democracy as an end and not a means. Democracy sometimes seems to be an end, but it is in fact only a means. Marxism teaches us that democracy is part of the superstructure and belongs to the category of politics. That is to say, in the last analysis, it serves the economic base. The same is true of freedom. Both democracy and freedom are relative, not absolute, and they come into being and develop in specific historical conditions. Within the ranks of the people, democracy is correlative with centralism and freedom with discipline. They are the two opposites of a single entity, contradictory as well as united, and we should not one-sidedly emphasize one to the denial of the other. Within the ranks of the people, we cannot do without freedom, nor can we do without discipline; we cannot do without democracy, nor can we do without centralism. This unity of democracy and centralism, of freedom and discipline, constitutes our democratic centralism. Under this system, the people enjoy extensive democracy and freedom, but at the same time they have to keep within the bounds of socialist discipline. All this is well understood by the broad masses of the people.

In advocating freedom with leadership and democracy under centralized guidance, we in no way mean that coercive measures should be taken to settle ideological questions or questions involving the distinction between right and wrong among the people. All attempts to use administrative orders or coercive measures to settle ideological questions or questions of right and wrong are not only ineffective but harmful. We cannot abolish religion by administrative decree or force people not to believe in it. We cannot compel people to give up idealism, any more than we can force them to believe in Marxism. The only way to settle questions of an ideological nature or controversial issues among the people is by the democratic method, the method of discussion, of criticism, of persuasion and education, and not by the method of coercion or repression. To be able to carry on their production and studies effectively and to arrange their lives properly, the people want their government and those in charge of production and of cultural and educational organizations to issue appropriate orders of an obligatory nature. It is common sense that the maintenance of public order would be impossible without such administrative regulations. Administrative orders and the method of persuasion and education complement each other in resolving contradictions among the people. Even administrative regulations for the maintenance of public order must be accompanied by persuasion and education, for in many cases regulations alone will not work.

This democratic method of resolving contradictions among the people was epitomized in 1942 in the formula "unity, criticism, unity". To elaborate, it means starting from the desire for unity, resolving contradictions through criticism or struggle and arriving at a new unity on a new basis. In our experience this is the correct method of resolving contradictions among the people. In 1942 we used it to resolve contradictions inside the Communist Party, namely, the contradictions between the dogmatists and the great majority of the membership, and between dogmatism and Marxism. The "Left" dogmatists had restored to the method of "ruthless struggle and merciless blows" in inner-Party struggle. This method was incorrect. In criticizing "Left" dogmatism, we discarded this old method and adopted a new one, that is, one of starting from the desire for unity, distinguishing between right and wrong through criticism or struggle and arriving at a new unity on a new basis. This was the method used in the rectification movement of 1942. Thus within a few years, by the time the Chinese Communist Party held its Seventh National Congress in 1945, unity was achieved throughout the Party, and as a consequence the great victory of the people's revolution was won. The essential thing is to start from the desire for unity. For without this desire for unity, the struggle is certain to get out of hand. Wouldn't this be the same as "ruthless struggle and merciless blows"? And what Party unity would there be left? It was this very experience that led us to the formula: "unity, criticism, unity". Or, in other words, "learn from past mistakes to avoid future ones and cure the sickness to save the patient". We extended this method beyond our Party. We applied it with great success in the anti-Japanese base areas in dealing with the relations between the leadership and the masses, between the army and the people, between officers and men, between the different units of the army, and between the different groups of cadres. The use of this method can be traced back to still earlier times in our Party's history. It has been used ever since the building of our revolutionary armed forces and base areas in the south in 1927 to deal with the relations between the Party and the masses, between the army and the people, between officers and men, and other relations among the people. The only difference is that during the anti-Japanese war, we employed this method with much greater consciousness of purpose. And since the liberation of the whole country, we have employed this same method of "unity, criticism, unity" in our relations with the democratic parties and with industrial and commercial circles. Our task now is to continue to extend and make still better use of this method throughout the ranks of the people; we want all our factories, co-operatives, business establishments, schools, government offices and public organizations, in a word, all our six hundred million people, to use it in resolving contradictions among ourselves.

In ordinary circumstances, contradictions among the people are not antagonistic. But if they are not handled properly, or if we relax our vigilance and lower our guard, antagonism may arise. In a socialist country, a development of this kind is usually only a localized and temporary phenomenon. The reason is that the system of exploitation of man by man has been abolished and the interests of the people are basically the same. The antagonistic actions which took place on a fairly wide scale during the Hungarian events were the result of the operations of both domestic and foreign counter-revolutionary elements. This was a special as well as temporary phenomenon. It was a case of reactionaries inside a socialist country, in league with the imperialists, attempting to achieve their conspiratorial aims by taking advantage of contradictions among the people to foment dissension and stir up disorder. This lesson of the Hungarian events merits attention. . . .

Quite a few people fail to make a clear distinction between these two different types of contradictions—those between ourselves and the enemy and those among the people—and are prone to confuse the two. It must be admitted that it is sometimes quite easy to do so. We have had instances of such confusion in our work in the past. In the course of suppressing counter-revolutionaries, good people were sometimes mistaken for bad, and such things still happen today. We are able to keep our mistakes within bounds because it has been our policy to draw a sharp line between ourselves and the enemy and to rectify mistakes whenever discovered.

Marxist philosophy holds that the law of the unity of opposites is the fundamental law of the universe. This law operates universally, whether in the natural world, in human society, or in man's thinking. Between the opposites in a contradiction there is at once unity and struggle, and it is this that impels things to move and change. Contradictions exist everywhere, but they differ in accordance with the different nature of different things. In any given phenomenon or thing, the unity of opposites is conditional, temporary and transitory, and hence relative, whereas the struggle of opposites is absolute. Lenin gave a very clear exposition of this law. In our country, a growing number of people have come to understand it. For many people, however, acceptance of this law is one thing, and its application in examining and dealing with problems is quite another. Many dare not openly admit that contradictions still exist among the people of our country, although it is these very contradictions that are pushing our society forward. Many do not admit that contradictions continue to exist in a socialist society, with the result that they are handicapped and passive when confronted with social contradictions; they do not understand that socialist society will grow more united and consolidated through the ceaseless process of the correct handling and resolving of contradictions. For this reason, we need to explain things to our people, and to our cadres in the first place, in order to help them understand the contradictions in a socialist society and learn to use correct methods for handling these contradictions.

Contradictions in a socialist society are fundamentally different from those in the old societies, such as capitalist society. In capitalist society contradictions find expression in acute antagonisms and conflicts, in sharp class struggle; they cannot be resolved by the capitalist system itself and can only be resolved by socialist revolution. On the contrary, the case is different with contradictions in socialist society, where they are not antagonistic and can be resolved one after another by the socialist system itself. . . .

But our socialist system has only just been set up; it is not yet fully established or fully consolidated. In joint state-private industrial and commercial enterprises, capitalists still receive a fixed rate of interest on their capital, that is to say, exploitation still exists. So far as ownership is concerned, these enterprises are not yet completely socialist in character. Some of our agricultural and handicraft producers' co-operatives are still semi-socialist, while even in the fully socialist co-operatives certain problems of ownership remain to be solved. Relations between production and exchange in accordance with socialist principles are still being gradually established in various departments of our economy, and more and more appropriate forms are being sought. To decide the proper ratio between accumulation and consumption within each of the two sectors of socialist economy—that in which the means of production are owned by the whole people and that in which the means of production are collectively owned—and also between the two sectors themselves is a complicated problem for which it is not easy to work out a perfectly rational solution all at once. To sum up, socialist relations of production have been established and are in harmony with the growth of the productive forces, but they are still far from perfect, and this imperfection stands in contradiction to the growth of the productive forces. Apart from harmony as well as contradiction between the relations of production and the developing productive forces, there and the economic base. The superstructure consisting of the state system and laws of the people's democratic dictatorship and the socialist ideology guided by Marxism-Leninism plays a positive role in facilitating the victory of socialist transformation and the establishment of the socialist organization of labour; it is suited to the socialist economic base, that is, to socialist relations of production. But survivals of bourgeois ideology, certain bureaucratic ways of doing things in our state organs and defects in certain links in our state institutions are in contradiction with the socialist economic base. We must continue to resolve all such contradictions in the light of our specific conditions. Of course, new problems will emerge as these contradictions are resolved. And further efforts will be required to resolve the new contradictions. For instance, a constant process of readjustment through state planning is needed to deal with the contradiction between production and the needs of society, which will long remain as an objective reality. Every year our country draws up an economic plan in order to establish a proper ratio between accumulation and consumption and achieve a balance between production and needs. Balance is nothing but a temporary, relative unity of opposites. By the end of each year, this balance, taken as a whole, is upset by the struggle of opposites; the unity undergoes a change, balance becomes imbalance, unity becomes disunity, and once again it is necessary to work out a balance and unity for the next year. Herein lies the superiority of our planned economy. As a matter of fact, this balance, this unity, is partially upset every month or every quarter, and partial readjustments are called for. Sometimes, contradictions arise and the balance is upset because our subjective arrangements do not correspond to objective reality; this is what we call making a mistake. The ceaseless emergence and ceaseless resolution of contradictions is the dialectical law of the development of things.

Today, matters stand as follows. The large-scale and turbulent class struggles of the masses characteristic of the previous revolutionary periods have in the main ended, but class struggle is by no means entirely over. While welcoming the new system, the broad masses of the people are not yet quite accustomed to it. Government workers are not sufficiently experienced and have to undertake further study and exploration of specific policies. In other words, time is needed for our socialist system to become established and consolidated, for the masses to become accustomed to the new system, and for the government workers to learn and acquire experience. It is therefore imperative at this juncture that we should raise the question of distinguishing contradictions among the people from those between ourselves and the enemy, as well as the question of the correct handling of contradictions among the people, so as to unite the people of all nationalities in our country for a new battle, the battle against nature, to develop our economy and culture, to help the whole nation to traverse this period of transition fairly smoothly, to consolidate our new system and build up our new state.

THE FASCIST WORLDVIEW

Fascism initially rests on a certain national chauvinism combined with a contempt for rationalist preoccupations with universalism and individualism. Its moral relativism and intuitionism become clear in the section here from "Scenes and Doctrines of Nationalism" by Maurice Barrès. It is intended as a response to the belief in civil liberties and a universalist notion of justice by cosmopolitan "intellectuals" and left-wing supporters of Alfred Dreyfus, the Jewish captain falsely accused of treason in a sensational trial, who would come to symbolize the effects of anti-semitism and the arbitrary exercise of judicial authority. In 1901, Barrès himself helped form the *Action Francaise*, which would serve as the mainstay of French Fascism until its defeat in 1944, and theoretically legitimated the need for a state to act as it must in the name of the unique and integral values of the nation.

Benito Mussolini held that the state creates the nation by "conferring volition" and making people aware of their "moral unity." The state is active and incarnates the will of the people. It is all-embracing, and, according to Mussolini, "outside of it no human or spiritual values can exist." If only for this reason, loyalty must prove unconditional. The interests of the nation transcend those of political parties and private persons, and thus need a different form of expression. They require a leader, who is accountable only to his own will.

Jose Antonio Primo de Rivera, leader of the *Falange*, the Spanish form of fascism, believed that its philosophy speaks to the "deeper liberty of man" and the emotional bond tying together the people of a nation. Membership in the *Patria* or the *Vaterland*, or whatever, is a matter of blood and sensibility. Fascism declines to offer a program or concrete solutions to concrete problems; its partisans are ready to "suffer death and carry out hard missions" precisely for aims in which they have "no interest at all." Struggle assumes an independent value. The romantic quality of fascism is undeniable; it speaks of sacrifice for an indefinable goal, renunciation of the self, and the liberating experience of violence.

All these qualities are necessary, according to Adolf Hitler in his autobiographical *Mein Kampf*, because the time is drawing near for resolving the most profound of all historical conflicts: the battle between Aryan and Jew. Hitler presents a Manichean worldview upon which he develops a philosophy of history, a sociology, and a political theory. All economic conflicts between classes, all social tensions, all forms of political competition, are the result of behind-the-scenes manipulation by Jews aimed at burying the founders of culture: the Aryans. A conspiracy of such immense proportions—demands a resolute response. The retribution he seeks can indulge neither the sentiment of pity nor restraint, and it didn't.

MAURICE BARRÈS

Scenes and Doctrines of Nationalism

NATIONALISM AND DETERMINISM

For some people, the supernatural is dead. Their piety is not directed towards some object in the heavens. I have redirected my piety from the heavens to the earth, the earth that contains my dead.

My *intelligence* is tempted on all sides; everything interests me, stimulates me and amuses me. But there is, at the very bottom of our souls, a fixed point, a delicate nerve; if it is probed the result is a total reaction which I cannot mistrust, a movement of my whole being. It is not the awakening of the sensibilities of a mere individual; what frightens me is the awakening of my whole race.

... Sweet Antigone, a maid of twenty, you wanted to hide, to survive and to marry. But the Antigone who was as old as the illustrious race of the Labdaciades had to make her stand.

Creon was both master and stranger. He said: 'I know the laws of this country and I will apply them.' He judges with his intelligence; the intelligence, that insignificant thing which is only the surface of ourselves!

How different he is from Antigone, who brings the depths of her heredity to the same question, whose inspiration comes from those regions of the unconscious where respect, love and fear unite in a single, magnificent drive towards veneration.

She can do no other, and it is through the affirmation of that drive towards veneration that the city is shaken to the roots and is reconciled to itself through Antigone.

And so Creon himself, moved more by sorrow than by reason, falls to his knees.

So *the best line of argument* and the most complete demonstrations are not enough to convince me. My heart has to be filled spontaneously with a great respect and a great love. It is in these moments of total emotion that my heart tells me which things I must put beyond the test of reason.

After the long, hard work of foraging, after a subtle and profound search, I found the gushing source in my little garden. It comes from the vast ice-sheet which supplies all the fountains in my city.

How do those who never gain access to those subterranen reservoirs, who never know themselves with respect, with love and with fear as the continuation of their ancestors, ever find their way in life?

It is my sense of descent which provides me with the axis around which my total, self-contained idea of life revolves.

As long as I stay there, neither my descendants nor my benefactors will crumble into dust. And I am sure that I will be sheltered myself by some of those whom I awaken when I can no longer look after myself.

Thus I have my fixed points, my own landmarks both in the past and in posterity. If I read them again, I become conscious of one of the great traditions of French classicism. How could I not be prepared to make all the sacrifices necessary for the protection of that classicism which is my backbone.

When I say *backbone*, it is not a metaphor but the most powerful analogy. A long series of intellectual exercises multiplied over the preceding centuries has educated our reflexes.

Even thought is not free. I can live only in relation to my dead. They, and the earth of my country, command me to a particular way of life.

Terrified of my dependence, powerless to make myself what I want myself to be, I still want to see the powers that govern me face to face. I want to live with these my masters, to share fully in their strength by working out a self-conscious cult for them.

Others lose their sense of the unity of things when they analyse them; it is through analysis that I regain my sense of unity and reach what for me is the truth.

What is truth? Truth is not something to be known intellectually. Truth is finding a particular point, the only point, that one and no other, from which everything appears to us in its proper perspective.

Let us be more precise. How I like the saying of a certain painter: 'Sit in the right place and get the perspective correct.'

I must settle myself at that point which my eyes take as their own so that it is the past centuries which form my vision; that point from which everything is seen through the eyes of a Frenchman. The totality of these proper relationships between given objects and a given subject, the Frenchman, that is French truth and French justice; French reason is the discovery of these relationships. And pure nationalism is simply the discovery of that point, searching for it, and when it is found, holding fast to it and receiving from it our art, our politics and the manner of living our life . . .

BENITO MUSSOLINI

Fundamental Ideas

Like all sound political conceptions, Fascism is action and it is thought; action in which doctrine is immanent, and doctrine arising from a given system of historical forces in which it is inserted, and working on them from within (1). It has therefore a form correlated to contingencies of time and space; but it has also an ideal content which makes it an expression of truth in the higher region of the history of thought (2). There is no way of exercising a spiritual influence in the world as a human will dominating the will of others, unless one has a conception both of the transient and the specific reality on which that action is to be exercised, and of the permanent and universal reality in which the transient dwells and has its being. To know men one must know man; and to know man one must be acquainted with reality and its laws. There can be no conception of the State which is not fundamentally a conception of life: philosophy or intuition, system of ideas evolving within the framework of logic or concentrated in a vision or a faith, but always, at least potentially, an organic conception of the world.

Thus many of the practical expressions of Fascism—such as party organisation, system of education, discipline—can only be understood when considered in relation to its general attitude toward life. A spiritual attitude (3). Fascism sees in the world not only those superficial, material aspects in which man appears as an individual, standing by himself, self-centred, subject to natural law which instinctively urges him toward a life of selfish momentary pleasure; it sees not only the individual but the nation and the country; individuals and generations bound together by a moral law, with common traditions and a mission which suppressing the instinct for life closed in a brief circle of pleasure, builds up a higher life, founded on duty, a life free from the limitations of time and space, in which the individual, by self-sacrifice, the renunciation of self-interest, by death itself, can achieve that purely spiritual existence in which his value as a man consists.

The conception is therefore a spiritual one, arising from the general reaction of the century against the fiacid, materialistic positivism of the XIXth century. Anti-positivistic but positive; neither sceptical nor agnostic; neither pessimistic nor supinely optimistic as are, generally speaking, the doctrines (all negative) which place the centre of life outside man; whereas, by the exercise of his free will, man can and must create his own world.

Fascism wants man to be active and to engage in action with all his energies; it wants him to be manfully aware of the difficulties besetting him and ready to face them. It conceives of life as a struggle in which it behooves a man to win for himself a really worthy place, first of all by fitting himself (physically, morally, intellectually) to become the implement required for winning it. As for the individual, so for the nation, and so for mankind (4). Hence the high value of culture in all its forms (artistic, religious, scientific) (5), and the outstanding importance of education. Hence also the essential value of work, by which man subjugates nature and creates the human world (economic, political, ethical, intellectual).

This positive conception of life is obviously an ethical one. It invests the whole field of reality as well as the human activities which master it. No action is exempt from moral judgement; no activity can be despoiled of the value which a moral purpose confers on all things. Therefore life, as conceived of by the Fascist, is serious, austere, religious; all its manifestations are poised in a world sustained by moral forces and subject to spiritual responsabilities. The Fascist disdains an "easy" life (6).

The Fascist conception of life is a religious one (7), in which man is viewed in his immanent relation to a higher law, endowed with an objective will transcending the individual and raising him to conscious membership of a spiritual society. Those who perceive nothing beyond opportunistic considerations in the religious policy of the Fascist regime fail to realise that Fascism is not only a system of government but also and above all a system of thought.

In the Fascist conception of history, man is man only by virtue of the spiritual process to which he contributes as a member of the family, the social group, the nation, and in function of history to which all nations bring their contribution. Hence the great value of tradition in records, in language, in customs, in the rules of social life (8). Outside history man is a nonentity. Fascism is therefore opposed to all individualistic abstractions based on eighteenth-century materialism; and it is opposed to all Jacobinistic utopias and innovations. It does not believe in the possibility of "happiness" on earth as conceived by the economistic literature of the XVIIIth century, and it therefore rejects the teleological notion that at some future time the human family will secure a final settlement of all its difficulties. This notion runs counter to experience which teaches that life is in continual flux and in process of evolution. In politics Fascism aims at realism; in practice it desires to deal only with those problems which are the spontaneous product of historic conditions and which find or suggest their own solutions (9). Only by entering in to the process of reality and taking possession of the forces at work within it, can man act on man and on nature (10).

Anti-individualistic, the Fascist conception of life stresses the importance of the State and accepts the individual only in so far as his interests coincide with those of the State, which stands for the conscience and the universal will of man as a historic entity (11). It is opposed to classical liberalism which arose as a reaction to absolutism and exhausted its historical function when the State became the expression of the conscience and will of the people. Liberalism denied the State in the name of the individual; Fascism reasserts the rights of the State as expressing the real essence of the individual (12). And if liberty is to be the attribute of living men and not of abstract dummies invented by individualistic liberalism, then Fascism stands for liberty, and for the only liberty worth having, the liberty of the State and of the individual within the State (13). The Fascist conception of the State is all-embracing; outside of it no human or spiritual values can exist, much less have value. Thus understood, Fascism is totalitarian, and the Fascist State—a synthesis and a unit inclusive of all values—interprets, develops, and potentiates the whole life of a people (14).

No individuals or groups (political parties, cultural associations, economic unions, social classes) outside the State (15). Fascism is therefore opposed to Socialism to which unity within the State (which amalgamates classes into a single economic and ethical reality) is unknown, and which sees in history nothing but the class struggle. Fascism is likewise opposed to trade-unionism as a class weapon. But when brought within the orbit of the State, Fascism recognises the real needs which gave rise to socialism and trade-unionism, giving them due weight in the guild or corporative system in which divergent interests are coordinated and harmonised in the unity of the State (16).

Grouped according to their several interests, individuals form classes; they form trade-unions when organised according to their several economic activities; but first and foremost they form the State, which is no mere matter of numbers, the sum of the individuals forming the majority. Fascism is therefore opposed to that form of democracy which equates a nation to the majority, lowering it to the level of the largest number (17); but it is the purest form of democracy if the nation be considered—as it should be—from the point of view of quality rather than quantity, as an idea, the mightiest because the most ethical, the most coherent, the truest, expressing itself in a people as the conscience and will of the few, if not, indeed, of one, and ending to express itself in the conscience and the will of the mass, of the whole group ethnically moulded by natural and historical conditions into a nation, advancing, as one conscience and one will, along the self-same line of development and spiritual formation (18). Not a race, nor a geographically defined region, but a people, historically perpetuating itself; a multitude unified by an idea and imbued with the will to live, the will to power, self-consciousness, personality (19).

In so far as it is embodied in a State, this higher personality becomes a nation. It is not the nation which generates the State; that is an antiquated naturalistic concept which afforded a basis for XIXth century publicity in favor of national governments. Rather is it the State which creates the nation, conferring volition and therefore real life on a people made aware of their moral unity.

The right to national independence does not arise from any merely literary and idealistic form of self-consciousness; still less from a more or less passive and unconscious *de facto* situation, but from an active, self-conscious, political will expressing itself in action and ready to prove its rights. It arises, in short, from the existence, at least *in fieri*, of a State. Indeed, it is the State which, as the expression of a universal ethical will, creates the right to national independence (20).

A nation, as expressed in the State, is a living, ethical entity only in so far as it is progressive. Inactivity is death. Therefore the State is not only Authority which governs and confers legal form and spiritual value on individual wills, but it is also Power which makes its will felt and respected beyond its own frontiers, thus affording practical proof of the universal character of the decisions necessary to ensure its development. This implies organisation and expansion, potential if not actual. Thus the State equates itself to the will of man, whose development cannot be checked by obstacles and which, by achieving self-expression, demonstrates its own infinity (21).

The Fascist State, as a higher and more powerful expression of personality, is a force, but a spiritual one. It sums up all the manifestations of the moral and intellecutal life of man. Its functions cannot therefore be limited to those of enforcing order and keeping the peace, as the liberal doctrine had it. It is no mere mechanical device for defining the sphere within which the individual may duly exercise his supposed rights. The Fascist State is an inwardly accepted standard and rule of conduct, a discipline of the whole person; it permeates the will no less than the intellect. It stands for a principle which becomes the central motive of man as a member of civilised society, sinking deep down into his personality; it dwells in the heart of the man of action and of the thinker, of the artist and of the man of science: soul of the soul (22).

Fascism, in short, is not only a law-giver and a founder of institutions, but an educator and a promoter of spiritual life. It aims at refashioning not only the forms of life but their content—man, his character, and his faith. To achieve this purpose it enforces discipline and uses authority, entering into the soul and ruling with undisputed sway. Therefore it has chosen as its emblem the Lictor's rods, the symbol of unity, strength, and justice.

JOSE ANTONIO PRIMO DE RIVERA

What the Falange Wants

The Patria is a total unity, in which all individuals and classes are integrated; the Patria cannot be in the hands of the strongest class or of the best organized party. The Patria is a transcendent synthesis, an indivisible synthesis, with its own goals to fulfill; and we want this movement of today, and the state which it creates, to be an efficient, authoritarian instrument at the services of an indisputable unity, of that permanent unity, of that irrevocable unity that is the Patria.

And we already have the principle for our future acts and our present conduct, for we would be just another party if we came to announce a program of concrete solutions. Such programs have the advantage of never being fulfilled.

Here is what is required by our total sense of the Patria and the state which is to serve it:

That all the people of Spain, however diverse they may be, feel in harmony with an irrevocable unity of destiny.

That the political parties disappear. No one was ever born a member of a political party; on the other hand, we are all born members of a family; we are all neighbors in a municipality; we all labor in the exercise of a profession . . . . We want less liberal word-mongering and more respect for the deeper liberty of man. For one respects the liberty of man when he is esteemed, as we esteem him, the bearer of eternal values; when he is esteemed as the corporal substance of a soul capable of being damned and of being saved. Only when man is considered thus can it truly be said that his liberty is respected, and more especially if that liberty is joined, as we aspire to join it, to a system of authority, of hierarchy, and of order. . . .

Finally, we desire that if on some occasion this must be achieved by violence, there be no shrinking from violence. Because who has said—while speaking of "everything save violence"—that the supreme value in the hierarchy of values is amiability? Who has said that when our sentiments are insulted we are obliged to be accommodating instead of reacting like men? It is very correct indeed that dialectic is the first instrument of communication. But no other dialectic is admissible save the dialectic of fists and pistols when justice or the Patria is offended. . . .

But our movement would not be understood at all if it were believed to be only a manner of thinking. It is not a manner of thinking; it is a manner of being. We ought not merely to propose to ourselves a formal construction, a political architecture. Before life in its entirety, in each one of our acts, we must adopt a complete, profound, and human attitude. This attitude is the spirit of sacrifice and service, the ascetic and military sense of life. Henceforth let no one think that we recruit men in order to offer rewards; let no one imagine that we join together in the defense of privileges. I should like to have this microphone before me carry my voice into every last working-class home to say: Yes, we wear a tie; yes, you may say of us that we are *señoritos*. But we urge a spirit of struggle for things that cannot concern us as *señoritos*; we come to fight so that hard and just sacrifices may be imposed on many of our own class, and we come to struggle for a totalitarian state that can reach the humble as well as the powerful with its benefits. We are thus, for so always in our history have been the *señores*, because in distant lands, and in our very Patria, they have learned to suffer death and carry out hard missions for reasons in which, as *señoritos,* they had no interest at all.

I believe the banner is raised. Now we are going to defend it gaily, poetically. There are some who think that in order to unite men's wills against the march of the revolution it is proper to offer superficially gratifying solutions; they think it is necessary to hide everything in their propaganda which could awaken an emotion or signify energetic or extreme action. What equivocation! The peoples have never been moved by anyone save the poets, and woe to him who, before the poetry which destroys, does not know how to raise the poetry which promises!

In a poetic movement we shall raise this fervent feeling for Spain; we shall sacrifice ourselves; we shall renounce ourselves, and the triumph will be ours, a triumph—why need I say it?—that we are not going to win in the next elections. In those elections vote for whoever seems to you least undesirable. But our Spain will not emerge from [*the Cortes*], nor is our goal there. The atmosphere there is tired and murky, like a tavern at the end of a night of dissipation. That is not our place. Yes, I know that I am a candidate; but I am one without faith and without respect. I say this now, when it can mean that I lose votes. That matters not at all. We are not going to argue with habitués over the disordered remains of a dirty banquet. Our place is outside, though we may occasionally have to pass a few transient minutes within. Our place is in the fresh air, under the cloudless heavens, weapons in our hands, with the stars above us. Let the others go on with their merrymaking. We outside, in tense, fervent, and certain vigilance, already feel the dawn breaking in the joy of our hearts.

ADOLF HITLER

Nation and Race

There are numberless examples in history, showing with terrible clarity how each time Aryan blood has become mixed with that of inferior peoples the result has been an end of the culture-sustaining race. North America, the population of which consists for the most part of Germanic elements, which mixed very little with inferior coloured nations, displays humanity and culture very different from that of Central and South America, in which the settlers, mainly Latin in origin, mingled their blood very freely with that of the aborigines. Taking the above as an example, we clearly recognize the effects of racial intermixture. The man of Germanic race on the continent of America having kept himself pure and unmixed, has risen to be its master; and he will remain master so long as he does not fall into the shame of mixing the blood.

Perhaps the pacifist-humane idea is quite a good one in cases where the man at the top has first thoroughly conquered and subdued the world to the extent of making himself sole master of it. Then the principle when applied in practice, will not affect the mass of the people injuriously. Thus first the struggle and then pacifism. Otherwise, it means that humanity has passed the highest point in its development, and the end is not domination by any ethical idea, but barbarism, and chaos to follow. Some will naturally laugh at this, but this planet travelled through the ether for millions of years devoid of humanity, and it can only do so again if men forget that they owe their higher existence, not to the ideas of a mad ideologue, but to understanding and ruthless application of age-old natural laws.

All that we admire on this earth—science, art, technical skill and invention—is the creative product of only a small number of nations, and originally, perhaps, of one single race. All this culture depends on them for its very existence. If they are ruined, they carry with them all the beauty of this earth into the grave.

If we divide the human race into three categories—founders, maintainers, and destroyers of culture—the Aryan stock alone can be considered as representing the first category.

The Aryan races—often in absurdly small numbers—overthrow alien nations, and, favoured by the numbers of people of lower grade who are at their disposal to aid them, they proceed to develop, according to the special conditions for life in the acquired territories—fertility, climate, etc.—the qualities of intellect and organization which are dormant in them. In the course of a few centuries they create cultures, originally stamped with their own characteristics alone, and develop them to suit the special character of the land and the people which they have conquered. As time goes on, however, the conquerors sin against the principle of keeping the blood pure (a principle which they adhered to at first), and begin to blend with the original inhabitants whom they have subjugated, and end their own existence as a peculiar people; for the sin committed in Paradise was inevitably followed by expulsion.

From all time creative nations have been creative through and through, whether superficial observers do or do not realize it. Nothing but completed accomplishment is recognized by such people, for most men in this world are incapable of perceiving genius in itself, and see only the outward signs of it in the form of inventions, discoveries, buildings, paintings, etc. Even then it takes a long time before they arrive at comprehending it. Just as individual genius strives, under the spur of special inducements, to work out expression of itself in practical ways, so, in the life of nations, actual application of the creative forces which are in them is not produced except at the call of certain definite circumstances. We see this most clearly in the race which was and is the carrier of human cultural development—the Aryan.

For the development of the higher culture it was necessary that men of lower civilization should have existed, for none but they could be a substitute for the technical instruments, without which higher development was inconceivable. In its beginnings human culture certainly depended less on the tamed beast and more on employment of inferior human material.

It was not until the conquered races had been enslaved that a like fate fell on the animal world; the contrary was not the case, as many would like to believe. For it was the slave who first drew the plough, and after him the horse. None but pacifist fools can look on this as yet another token of human deprivity; others must see clearly that this development was bound to happen in order to arrive at a state of things in which those apostles are able to loose their foolish talk on the world.

Human progress is like ascending an endless ladder; a man cannot climb higher unless he has first mounted the lowest rung. Thus the Aryan had to follow the road leading him to realization, and not the one which exists in the dreams of a modern pacifist.

But the road which the Aryan had to tread was clearly marked out. As a conqueror he overthrew inferior men, and their work was done under his control, according to his will and for his purposes. But while extracting useful, if hard, work out of his subjects, he not only protected their lives, but also perhaps gave them an existence better than their former so-called freedom. So long as he continued to look on himself as the overlord, he not only maintained his mastery, but he was also the upholder and fosterer of culture. But as soon as the subjects began to raise themselves and—probably—to assimilate their language with that of the conqueror, the sharp barrier between lord and servant fell. The Aryan renounced purity of his own blood, and with it his right to stay in the Eden which he had created for himself. He sank, overwhelmed in the mixing of races, and by degrees lost forever his capacity for civilization until he began to resemble the subjected aboriginal race more than his fathers, both in mind and body. For a time he could still enjoy the blessings of civilization, but first indifference set in, and finally oblivion. This is how civilizations and empires break up, to make room for new creations.

Blood-mixture, with the lowering of the racial level which accompanies it, is the one and only reason that old civilizations disappear. It is not lost wars which ruin mankind, but loss of the powers of resistance, which belong to pure blood alone.

There is in our German language a word which is finely descriptive—readiness to obey the call of duty (*Pflichterfüllung*)—service in the general interest. The idea underlying such an attitude we call 'idealism,' in contradistinction to 'egoism'; and by it we understand the capacity for self-sacrifice in the individual for the community, for his fellow-men.

It is at times when ideals are threatening to disappear that we are able to observe an immediate diminution of that strength which is the essence of the community and a necessary condition of culture. Then selfishness becomes the governing force in a nation, and in the hunt after happiness the ties of order are loosened and men fall out of heaven straight into hell.

The exact opposite of the Aryan is the Jew. In hardly any nation in the world is the instinct of self-preservation more strongly developed than in the 'chosen people.' The best proof of this is the fact that the race still continues to exist. Where is there a people which for the last two thousand years has shown so little change in internal characteristics as the Jewish race? What race, in fact, has been involved in greater revolutionary changes than that one, and yet has survived intact after the most terrific catastrophes? How their determined will to live and to maintain the type is expressed by these facts!

The Jew's intellectual qualities were developed in the course of centuries. Today we think him 'cunning,' and in a certain sense it was the same at every epoch. But his intellectual capacity is not the result of personal development, but of education by foreigners.

Thus, since the Jew never possessed a culture of his own, the bases of his intellectual activity have always been supplied by others. His intellect has in all periods been developed by contact with surrounding civilizations. Never the opposite.

It is utterly incorrect to point to the fact that the Jews hold together in struggling with their fellow-men—or rather in plundering them—and conclude from it that they have a certain ideal of self-sacrifice.

Even in this the Jew guided by nothing more nor less than pure self-seeking; and that is why the Jewish State—which is supposed to be the living organism for maintaining and increasing a race—is entirely without frontiers. For the conception of a State with definite boundaries always implies the idealistic sentiment of a race within the State, also a proper conception of the meaning of work as an idea. For want of this conception, ambition is lacking to form or even maintain a State with definite boundaries. There is thus no basis on which a culture may be built up.

Thus the Jewish nation, with all its obvious intellectual qualities, has no real culture—certainly none peculiar to itself. For whatever culture the Jew appears to possess today is in the main the property of other peoples, which has become corrupted under his manipulation.

Originally the Aryan was probably a nomad and them, as time went on, he became settled; this, if nothing else, proves that he was never a Jew! No, the Jew is not a nomad, for even the nomad had already a definite attitude towards the conception 'work,' destined to serve as a basis for further development, so far as he possessed the necessary intellectual qualifications. But he did possess the power of forming ideals, if in a very rarefied form, so that his conception of life may have been alien, but not unsympathetic, to the Aryan races. In the Jew, however, that conception has no place; he was never a nomad, but was ever a parasite in the bodies of other nations. His having on occasion deserted his former sphere of life was not on all fours with his intentions, but was the consequence of his being at various periods ejected by the nations whose hospitality he had abused. His propagation of himself throughout the world is a typical phenomenon with all parasites; he is always looking for fresh feeding ground for his race.

His life within other nations can be kept up in perpetuity only if he succeeds in convincing the world that with him it is not a question of a race, but of a 'religious bond,' one however peculiar to himself. This is the first great lie!

In order to continue existing as a parasite within the nation, the Jew must set to work to deny his real inner nature. The more intelligent the individual Jew is, the better will he succeed in his deception—to the extent of making large sections of the population seriously believe that the Jew genuinely is a Frenchman or an Englishman, a German or an Italian, though of a different religion.

The present vast economic development is leading to a change in the social stratification of the nation. The small industries are gradually dying out, making it rarer for the worker to be able to secure a decent existence and visibly driving him to become one of the proletarian class. The outcome of all this is the 'factory worker,' whose essential distinguishing mark is that he is practically unable in later life to maintain his dignity and individuality. In the truest sense of the word he is possessionless; old age means suffering to him and can hardly be called life at all.

There was once at an earlier period a similar situation which was urgently in need of solution; a solution was discovered. Beside farmers and artisans was appearing a new State, whose officials were servants of the State and possessionless in the truest sense of the word. The State found a way out of that unhealthy condition of things; it assumed responsibility for the welfare of its servant who was unable himself to provide for his old age, and instituted the pension on retirement. Thus a whole class, left without possessions, was skilfully delivered from social misery and incorporated in the body of the nation.

Of late years the State has had to face the same question on a far larger scale. Fresh masses of people, amounting to millions, have been constantly removing from the villages to the large towns, to earn a living as factory workers in the new industries.

Thus a new class has actually come into being to which but little attention has been paid, and a day will come when one will have to ask whether the nation has the strength by its own efforts once more to incorporate the new class in the general community or whether the distinction of class and class is to broaden into a rift.

While the bourgeoisie has been ignoring this most difficult question and letting things happen as they please, the Jew has been considering the boundless possibilities which present themselves as regards the future. On the one hand he is making use of his capitalistic methods for exploiting humanity to the very fullest, and on the other he is getting ready to sacrifice his sway and very soon will come out as their leader in the fight against himself. 'Against himself' is, of course, only a figurative expression, for the great master of lies knows very well how to emerge with apparently clean hands and burden others with the blame. Since he has the impudence to lead the masses in person, it never occurs to the latter that it is the most infamous betrayal of all time.

The Jew's procedure is as follows: He addresses himself to the workers, pretends to have pity for their lot or indignation at their misery and poverty in order to gain their confidence. He takes trouble to study the real or imaginary hardness of their lives and to arouse a longing for a change of existence. With untold cleverness he intensifies the demand for social justice dormant in all men of Aryan stock and so stamps the struggle for removal of social evils with a quite definite character of universal world importance. He founds the doctrine of Marxism.

By mingling it inextricably with a whole mass of demands which are socially justifiable, he ensures the popularity of the doctrine, while on the other hand he causes decent people to be unwilling to support demands which, being presented in such a form, appear wrong from the start, nay, impossible of realization. For under the cloak of purely social ideas there lie hidden truly devilish intentions, and these are brought into the open with impudent downrightness and frankness. By categorically denying the importance of personality, and so of the nation and its racial significance, they destroy the elementary principles of all human culture.

The Jew divides the organization of his world-teaching into two categories, which, though apparently separate, really form an inseparable whole; the political and the labour movements.

The trades-union movement is the more wooing one. It offers the workman help and protection in his hard fight for existence, for which he has to thank the greed or short-sightedness of many an employer, and also the possibility of wresting better living conditions. If the worker shrinks from entrusting the blind caprice of men, often heartless and with but little sense of responsibility, with the defence of his right to live as a man, at a time when the State—i.e., the organized community—is paying practically no attention to him, he will have to protect his interests himself. Now that the so-called national bourgeoisie, blinded by money interest, is setting every obstacle in the way of this struggle for a living, and is not only opposing, but universally and actively working against all attempts to shorten the inhumanly long hours of work, put an end to child labour, protect the women, and produce healthy conditions in factories and dwellings—the cleverer Jew is identifying himself with the under-dog. He is gradually assuming leadership of the trades-union movement—all the easier because what matters to him is not so much genuine removal of social evils as the formation of a blindly obedient fighting force in industry for the purpose of destroying national economic independence.

The Jew forcibly drives all competitors off the field. Helped by his innate greedy brutality, he sets the trades-union movement on a footing of brute force. Anyone with intelligence enough to resist the Jewish lure is broken by intimidation, however determined and intelligent he may be. These methods are vastly successful.

By means of the trades-union, which might have been the saving of the nation, the Jew actually destroys the bases of the nation's economics.

The political organization proceeds on parallel lines with the foregoing. It works in with the trades-union movement, since the latter prepares the masses for the political organization, and in fact drives them forcibly into it. It is, moreover, the constant money source out of which the political organization feeds its vast machine. It is the organ of control for the political work and acts as whipper-in for all great demonstrations, political in character. Finally it loses it economic character altogether, serving the political idea with its chief weapon, the general strike.

By creating a press, which is on the intellectual level of the least educated, the political and labour organization obtains means of compulsion, enabling it to make the lowest strata of the nation ready for the most hazardous enterprises.

It is the Jewish press which, in an absolutely fanatical campaign of calumny, tears down all which may be regarded as the prop of a nation's independence, its civilization, and its economic autonomy. It roars especially against those who have strength of character enough not to bow to Jewish domination or whose intellectual capacity appears to the Jew in the light of a menace to himself.

The ignorance displayed by the mass of the people as to the true nature of the Jews and the lack of instinctive perception of our upper class make the people easy dupes of this Jewish campaign of lies. While the natural timidity of the upper class makes it turn away from a man who is being thus attacked by the Jews with lies and calumny, the stupidity or simple-mindedness of the masses causes them to believe all they hear. The State authorities either cower in silence or—more frequently still—in order to put an end to the Jews' press campaign, they persecute those who are being unjustly attacked, and this, in the eyes of such Jacks-in-office, stands for vindication of State authority and maintenance of peace and order.

Thus, if we review all the causes of the German collapse, the final and decisive one is seen to be the failure to realize the racial problem and, more especially, the Jewish menace.

The defeats on the field of battle of August, 1918, might have been borne with the utmost ease. It was not they which overthrew us; what overthrew us was the force which prepared for those defeats by robbing the nation of all political and moral instinct and strength, by schemes which had been under way for many decades. In ignoring the question of maintaining the racial basis of our nationality, the old Empire disregarded the one and only law which makes life possible on this earth.

The loss of racial purity ruins the fortunes of a race forever; it continues to sink lower and lower and its consequences can never be expelled again from body and mind.

Thus all attempts at reform, and all social work, all political efforts, every increase of economic prosperity, and every apparent addition to scientific knowledge went for nothing. The nation and the organism which made life possible for it on this earth—i.e., the

State—did not grow sounder, but waned visibly more and more. The brillance of the old Empire failed to conceal the inner weakness, and all attempts to add strength to the Reich came to nothing each time, because they persisted in ignoring the most essential questions of all.

That is why in August, 1914, a nation did not rush full of determination into the battle; it was merely the last flicker of a national instinct of self-preservation face to face with the advancing forces of Marxism and pacifism, crippling the body of our nation. But since in those fateful days no one realized the domestic foe, resistance was all in vain, and Providence chose not to reward the victorious sword, but followed the law of eternal retribution.

Part III

THE RADICAL IMAGINATION

CRITICAL THEORY

Upon being named director of the Institute for Social Research in 1930, Max Horkheimer shifted its interest from political economy and the labor movement to a new, interdisciplinary form of research. His inaugural lecture, included here, contests the dominance of idealism and positivism. It emphasizes the importance of empirical research guided by the norms of freedom. It wishes to make philosophy deal with the unrealized happiness of the individual. It introduces, in short, a new way of thinking whose representatives would become known as "the Frankfurt School."

On its margins stood Walter Benjamin. A relatively unheralded literary critic during his lifetime, Benjamin was primarily influenced by the Marxism of Bertolt Brecht and the study of Jewish mysticism fostered by Gershom Scholem. He died in 1940 while fleeing the Nazis. Just before his death, however, he finished what would become known as his "Theses on the Philosophy of History." Here, his new way of historical thinking takes particularly radical form. Benjamin calls into question the understanding of progress in teleological terms, whether unilinear or dialectical, and argues that we must instead consider history as a construct with a normative content. If genuine progress is to occur, we must look back in order to move forward; the moment for reconstructing history always exists, just as the possibility for redeeming its lost emancipatory moments always exists. Such is the meaning behind the famous phrase that every moment is "the strait gate through which the Messiah might pass."

Walter Benjamin called upon radicals to "brush history against the grain," and his fellow Institute member Herbert Marcuse attempted to make good on this appeal. His understanding of critical theory was extremely popular among the intellectual radicals of the 1960s. His most influential work was surely *One-Dimensional Man*, and the selection included here, "Liberation from the Affluent Society," summarizes many of its most important themes. Extraordinary technological possibilities are turned towards regressive ends. The radical proletariat of the past has now been integrated. The culture industry is lowering the lowest common denominator in order to assure the greatest profits for its profits. Radical ideas are losing their genuinely emancipatory content in the very process of making them popular. Alternatives are becoming integrated into the status quo, the ability to engage in critical reflection is diminishing, and a drop is occuring in what Marx termed the "material level of culture." All this is what Marcuse hopes to resist by reaffirming the classical commitment of political theory to an unrealized vision of freedom.

MAX HORKHEIMER

The State of Contemporary Social Philosophy and the Tasks of an Institute for Social Research

Although social philosophy is the focus of general philosophical concern, it is in no better shape today than most philosophical, indeed most fundamentally intellectual, efforts. One is unable to find a substantive conception of social philosophy that could be considered everywhere as binding. Given the present situation in the sciences, in which the traditional boundaries between disciplines are in question and we do not yet know where they might be drawn in the future, the attempt to give ultimate definitions for academic domains seems rather untimely. Nevertheless, one can reduce the general views of social philosophy to one brief idea. According to it, the final goal of social philosophy is the philosophical interpretation of human fate—insofar as humans are not mere individuals but members of a community. Social philosophy must therefore primarily concern itself with those phenomena that can be interpreted only in the context of the social existence of humans, such as the state, law, economy, religion: in short, with all of the material and spiritual culture of humanity as such.

Social philosophy, thus understood, became in the history of classical German Idealism the decisive philosophical task. Its most brilliant achievements are in turn the most powerful aspects of Hegel's system. To be sure, even before Hegel, philosophy attempted to understand socio-philosophical phenomena: Kant's main works contain the philosophical theories of science, law, art, and religion. But this kind of social philosophy was grounded in a philosophy of the individual: those realms of being were to be seen as the designs of the autonomous individual. Kant made the total unity of the rational subject into the sole source of all constitutive principles for each cultural sphere. The being and the structure of culture were to be derived solely from the dynamic of the individual, from the basic activities of a spontaneous ego. In terms of Kant's philosophy, we certainly should not equate the autonomous subject with an empirical human being. Nevertheless, we certainly are able to investigate all aspects of cultural creativity in the temperament of each individual rational being. All-encompassing structures of being that belong to a supra-personal whole, and are only discoverable within a social totality to which we would have to subject ourselves, do not exist; their assertion would be dogmatic, and any action directed towards them would have to be grounded heteronomically. The moral individual as seen in the *Metaphysical Foundations of Jurisprudence* is thus an individual "subjected to no other laws than those that it has (either alone or at least together with others) established for itself."[1]

The German Idealism connected with Kant developed the interconnection between autonomous reason and empirical being. The tension between a finite human being and the ego as infinite obligation can, however, still be discerned—in Fichte's first philosophy of the self-reflecting mind. The eternal ought, the instruction to satisfy our human destiny, flows from the depths of subjectivity. The medium of philosophy is here still self-reflection. But Hegel has freed this self-reflection from the chains of introspection, and referred the question of our own being, the question of the autonomous culture-creating subject, to the labor of history—through which it gives itself objective form.

For Hegel, the structure of objective spirit [*Geist*], which realizes in history the cultural artifacts of the absolute spirit (i.e., art, religion, philosophy), is not discerned any longer from a critical analysis of personality [*Persönlichkeit*], but rather from universal dialectical logic. The development and the works of the objective spirit are not arrived at by the free decisions of a subject, but by the spirit of the dominant peoples that succeed each other on the battlefields of history. The destiny of the particular fulfills itself in the fate of the universal. The essence, the substantial content, of the individual is not revealed in personal actions but in the life of the totality to which it belongs. Thus, Hegel's Idealism has become in its constitutive parts social philosophy: the philosophical understanding of the collective whole, in which we live and which serves as the foundation for all creations of absolute culture, is now simultaneously knowledge of the meaning of our own being, its true worth and contents.

Let me remain for a moment with this Hegelian conception! From its dissolution and the impossibility of recreating it in thought without falling behind the present state of knowledge, one is in principle able to explicate the present state of social philosophy. Hegel assigned the realization of the goal of Reason to the objective spirit, in the last instance to the world-spirit. The development of this spirit is shown in the conflict of the "concrete ideas," the "spirit of the peoples," out of which "as signs and ornaments of its grandeur" the world-historical kingdoms emerge in necessary sequence.[2] This development happens regardless of whether individuals in their historical actions know of it and will it; the development has its own law. Nevertheless, as with the French Enlightenment and English liberalism, Hegel does accept the drives and passions of human beings as real motive powers. Even the great men are driven to their actions by their own ends. They "have formed purposes to satisfy themselves, not others."[3] Yet they are in their world "its clear-sighted ones; *their* deeds, *their* words are the best of that time."[4] Nothing, however, has happened in history without "interest on the part of the actors."[5] The interests of the great men as well as those of the masses are of course used "cunningly" by the rational law of development to its own end. And as Hegel explains past history only indirectly with that law, but directly with competing interests, so does he explain the life-process of modern society. While himself referring to the liberal economists Smith, Say, and Ricardo, he shows how out of the "medley of arbitrariness,"[6] which is created by the striving of individuals to satisfy their needs and wants, the totality is maintained. "In bourgeois society," he writes in the *Philosophy of Right*, "each member is his own end, everything else is nothing to him. But except in contact with others he cannot attain the whole compass of his ends, and therefore these others are means to the end of the particular member. A particular end, however, assumes the form of universality through this relation to other people, and it is attained in the simultaneous attainment of the welfare of others."[7] Thus, and only thus, can the state exist according to Hegel: it is directly determined by the conflict of interest in society.

But if history and the state are created eternally out of the "medley of arbitrariness," if therefore the historian has to deal with a chain of pain and death, of stupidity and baseness, and if finite being perishes in indescribable agony and history can be seen in Hegel's term as the "slaughter-bench at which the happiness of peoples, the wisdom of states, and the virtue of individuals are being sacrificed,"[8] then philosophy transcends the viewpoint of the empirical observer. Because "what is called reality," he teaches in the *Philosophy of History*, "is seen by philosophy only as something rotten, which seems to exist but is not real in and for itself. This insight, one might say, is consolation against the conception of absolute disaster, the madness of all that which has come to pass. Consolation, however, is only a substitute for the misfortune that should never have happened, and makes its home in the finite world. Philosophy is therefore not a consolation; it is more: it reconciles, it transfigures, a reality that appears to be unjust, making it appear rational. It exhibits it as such, shows it to be grounded in the idea itself, as that with which reason is supposed to be satisfied."[9] The "transfiguration" of which Hegel speaks is precisely attained by that theory according to which the true essence of human beings does not exist in mere inwardness and the actual fate of finite individuals, but asserts itself in the lives of peoples and is realized in the state. With the thought that the material essence, the idea, is preserved in world history, the destruction of the individual seems to carry no philosophical weight. In this regard, the philosopher is able to declare: "The particular is for the most part of too trifling value as compared with the general: individuals are sacrificed and abandoned. The idea pays the price of existence and of transitoriness, not from itself, but from the passions of individuals."[10] Only insofar as the individual partakes in the totality as a living being—or better, only insofar as the totality lives within the individual—is the individual endowed with reality. For the life of the totality is the life of the spirit. The totality at its most determined is the state. It "does not exist for its citizens; one might say it is the end and they are its means."[11]

According to Hegel, the finite individual being can attain the conceptual consciousness of its freedom within the state only through idealist speculative thinking. He essentially saw in this mediating function the achievement of his philosophy, and thus of philosphy as such. Philosophy is to him identical with the transfiguration of the real "that appears unjust." When the esteem of his system had waned in Germany around the middle of the last century, a future-oriented, individualistic society believing in progress replaced the metaphysics of the objective spirit with an unmediated belief in the prestabilized harmony of individual interests. It seemed as if what was needed to mediate between the empirical existence of the individual and the consciousness of its freedom in the social totality was not philosophy, but steady progress in the positive sciences, technology, and industry. But as the disappointment in that belief grew, a scorned metaphysics took its revenge. Deserted by the philosophical conviction that the divine idea existing within the totality is its true reality, the individual experienced the world as "medley of arbitrariness" and itself as the mere "price of existence and transitoriness." The sober glance directed towards the particular and the immediate was no longer capable of discerning "the cunning of Reason" behind the surface of warring individual wills, perpetual need, the indignities of the everyday world, and the terror of history. And so Hegel's greatest enemy, Schopenhauer, saw the dawn of his antihistorical, pessimistic, and consolatory philosophy.

The conviction that each and every one by virtue of his association with a historical unity and its own characteristic laws, which forms the dialectic of world history, partakes of the eternal life of the spirit—this notion ensuring the salvation of the individual from the infamous chain of becoming and perishing—disappeared with objective idealism. The suffering and the death of individuals threatened to appear in their naked meaning-less-ness—the last fact of an age enthralled by facts. With the deepening of the contradiction in the principle of individualistic life-form (that is, the contradiction between the unbroken progress of the happiness of the individuals within a given social context on the one hand, and the prospects of their actual situation on the other), philosophy, and especially social philosophy, was called more and more urgently to play again the role that Hegel had assigned to it. And social philosophy has heeded that call.

The cautious theory of Marburg neo-Kantianism states that a human being is not just an individual, but a being that stands "in various pluralities . . . in rank and file" and that "only in unit" can fulfill "the circles of its being,"[12] while the philosophical teachings of the present maintain that the meaning of existence, as in Hegel, fulfills itself only within metapersonal units of history such as class, state, or nation. From Hermann Cohen to Othmar Spann, philosophy has brought forth varying shades of socio-philosophical systems in the last few years. Even recent attempts at grounding moral and legal philosophy anew, in contradistinction to positivism, virtually have only one point in common, namely, the striving to find above and beyond the ground of actual incidents a higher realm of being or, at least, a higher realm of norms or ethics with its own characteristic laws in which finite human beings partake, but which cannot itself be reduced to natural incidences. Indeed, they too form a transition to a new philosophy of an objective spirit. While even Kelsen's individualistic and relativistic theory of law carries these features, one can find them in a higher degree in the formalistic value philosophy of the southwestern neo-Kantian school (as well as in Adolf Reinach's phenomenological theory): the essence of the structures of law—for example, the essence of private property, the essence of promise, the essence of the legal claim—can each be seen in its own "objective manifestation." Scheler's material ethics of value, his teaching of the being-in-itself of values, has made recently in the work of its most important representative, Nicolai Hartmann, the conscious connection to the philosophy of the objective spirit. The theory of the spirit of peoples had again been proclaimed by Scheler himself even before the publication of Hartmann's ethics.[13]

All of these projects of contemporary social philosophy seem to provide individual human beings with access into a supra-personal sphere that is more invested with being, more meaningful, more substantial than their own existence. They therefore accomplish the task of transfiguration prescribed by Hegel. Further, in Heidegger's *Sein und Zeit*—the only modern philosophical work that radically rejects social philosophy and that discovers real being only in the interior of individually existing human beings—care [*Sorge*] is the focal point. This philosophy of individual human existence is in its simple contents not transfiguration in Hegel's sense. Human existence is in it only a being-unto-death, a sheer finitude. It is a melancholy philosophy. If it is acceptable at this point to put the matter bluntly, one might say that today social philosophy meets the desire of a life hindered in its own individual pursuit of happiness with a new statement of meaning. Social philosophy appears to be part of the philosophical and religious efforts to plant the hopeless individual existence back into the womb, or to put it, in Sombart's term, in the "golden ground" of meaningful totalities.

But, ladies and gentlemen, having confronted this situation of social philosophy, let us now turn to delineate its deficiency. Social philosophy today, as we have seen, has taken a generally polemical stand against positivism. Positivism, it is charged, sees only the particular and in the realm of society thus sees only the individual and the relations between individuals; all is exhausted by facts. That there are facts that can be ascertained by means of analytical science, philosophy does not dispute. But philosophy posits against these facts more or less constructively, more or less in its own philosophizing, ideas, essences, totalities, independent spheres of objective spirit, units of meaning, spirit of peoples that it considers to be "more original" or even "genuine" elements of being. The discovery of certain unprovable metaphysical presuppositions within positivism is taken by philosophy as constituting lawful ground for raising the metaphysical stakes. So it happens that against the school of Vilfredo Pareto, for example—a school that, because of its positivist understanding of reality, has to deny the existence of class, nation, humanity—various standpoints, from which these entities are posited, are offered as a "different world view," a "different metaphysics," or a "different consciousness," without ever making a binding commitment possible. There are, one might say, different conceptions of reality, which make it possible to investigate what kind of genesis they had, to which sensibility of life and to which social group they belong, without providing an objectively grounded priority.

It is precisely in this dilemma of social philosophy, which speaks of its subject, the cultural life of humanity, in terms of professions of faith, and which sees the differences between the social theories of Auguste Comte, Karl Marx, Max Weber, and Max Scheler as different acts of faith, rather than distinguishing them in terms of true/false or, as of now, problematic theories—precisely in this dilemma do we perceive the deficiency that has to be overcome. To be sure, the simultaneous existence and validity of varying conceptions of reality signify the contemporary intellectual situation at large, but this variety addresses a plethora of scientific areas and spheres of life; it does not concern one and the same conceptual field. The constitutive categories of philology and those of physics might thus diverge so far that it seems difficult to harmonize them; but within physics, indeed within the sciences of inorganic nature in general, there is no such tendency to construct non-compatible concepts of reality: the opposite is rather the case. Here, the concrete scientific investigation of the empirical subject matter proves to be a corrective.

At this point one might interject the view that social philosophy is not a scientific discipline, that it is materialist sociology whose subject matter involves distinct forms of socialization. As a discipline it investigates the various concrete ways in which people live together, all forms of associations: from the family to economic groups, and from political associations to the state and to humanity. In it, one might find objective determinations on the same level as in political economy. But sociology has nothing to say either about the degree of reality or about the value of those phenomena. All that is the province of social philosophy; and for these essential questions as it deals with them there are final pronouncements, but no universally binding, true statements which are an integral part of large-scale investigations.

This view presupposes a conception of philosophy that is no longer tenable. However one might want to draw the boundaries between the particular disciplines of sociology and social philosophy, which, I believe, would necessitate a high degree of arbitrariness, one thing is certain: If socio-philosophical thought about the relationship of the individual to society, the meaning of culture, the formation of communities, or the overall status of social life—in short, about the great, principal questions—should be left behind as the sediment in the reservoir of social scientific problems after those problems that can be advanced in concrete investigations have been drained off, then social philosophy can still perform a social function (e.g., that of transfiguration), but its intellectual fruitfulness would be destroyed. The relationship between the philosophical and the empirical disciplines should not be conceptualized as if it were philosophy that treated the essential problems, constructing theories that cannot be attacked by the empirical sciences, its own conceptions of reality and systems embracing the totality, while in contrast empirical science comes out of its long, boring studies fragmented into a thousand individual questions, in order only to end up in the chaos of specialization. This view, according to which the empirical scientist has to regard philosophy as a beautiful yet scientifically fruitless enterprise, and the philosopher in contrast emancipates himself from the empirical scientist because the former assumes that he cannot wait for the latter in his far-reaching quest, is presently being superseded by the thought of an ongoing dialectical permeation and evolution of philosophical theory and empirical-scientific praxis. In this regard, the relations between the philosophy of nature and the natural sciences present us with good examples. Chaotic specialization is not being superseded by bad syntheses of specialized research results, nor is the impartiality of empirical research secured through the attempt to eliminate the theoretical elements with it. Rather, chaotic specialization is overcome by the fact that philosophy is able to inject spiritual impulses into empirical research through its own theoretical intention towards the whole, the essential, while being open enough to be itself influenced and transformed by the developments in concrete research.

The correction of the deficiency in the situation of social philosophy hinted at above seems to us to lie neither in a profession of faith of a more or less constructive interpretation of cultural life, nor in positing a new meaning for society, state, law, and what have you. Today, on the contrary, and I am surely not alone in this opinion, all depends on organizing research around current philosophical problematics which, in turn, philosophers, sociologists, political economists, historians, and psychologists engage by joining enduring research groups in order to do together what in other areas one is able to do alone in the laboratory and what all true scientists have always done: namely, to pursue their philosophical questions directed at the big picture with the finest scientific methods, to transform and to make more precise these questions as the work progresses, to find new methods, and yet never lose sight of the whole. In this way, no positive or negative answers to philosophical questions can be given. Instead, the philosophical questions themselves are dialectically integrated into the empirical scientific process; that is to say, their answers are to be found in the progress of substantive knowledge which also effects the form. This approach to the science of society cannot be mastered by one person alone—given the vast subject matter as well as the variety of indispensable scientific methods whose assistance is called for. Despite the gigantic effort on his part, even Max Scheler has failed in this regard.

Given this situation, one has to view the transformation of the chair of this university for the directorship of the Institute for Social Research into a chair for social philosophy and its relocation to the Department of Philosophy as highly legitimate. Carl Grünberg held this chair as a lecturer in political economy in the Department of Political Science. With the new, difficult, and decisive task of employing a grand empirical scientific apparatus in the service of social philosophy, with my appointment I have felt the immeasurable gap separating a great scientist whose name is mentioned with great respect and thankfulness all over the world wherever work in his discipline is being done, from the young, unknown man who was designated as his successor. His long illness belongs to those senseless facts in the life of individuals that put philosophical transfiguration to shame. According to his own deeply rooted and precisely defined interests, as determined by the historical school of political economy, he emphasized first and foremost the history of the labor movement. In doing so, his all-encompassing knowledge of the relevant sources in the world has made possible the acquisition of archival material and especially of a unique special library now containing approximately fifty thousand volumes; this library is now being put to good use, not just by students at our university, but also by many scholars in and outside of Germany. The series of writings from the Institute, edited by him, contains only works that have been recognized by relevant authorities of diverse political viewpoints as exceptional scientific achievements.

Having set myself the task of directing the work of the Institute towards a new goal following the prolonged illness of its director, I am able to draw not only on the experience of its associates and its collected library treasures, but on the Institute's charter, defined in an important way by its director. According to this charter, the director, designated by the minister, is independent "with respect both to the educational administration and the founders" to the point where there exists, as Grünberg used to say, in place of a council charter "the dictatorship of the director." Because of it, it will be possible for me to use what has been created by him in order to erect with my colleagues, at least on a small scale, a dictatorship of the planned work over the coexistence of philosophical construction and empirical research in the theory of society. As a philosopher in the sense of my teacher, Hans Cornelius, I accepted the call to direct this research institute in order to pursue this possibility, which is equally important to philosophy and empirical science, and not to make factual research into the auxiliary of philosophy.

But now some of you would like to know details about how these conceptions could be implemented, how one might conceive of their working in practice. Within the time allotted to me, I cannot address this issue adequately enough to give you an example of how it is possible to implement what has been said. It is not an example picked at random, fancied for this particular occasion, but one that gives the stated methodological conviction a concrete problematic which will become, in a short while, the trajectory of the collective work in the Institute.

There is one question around which the discussion of society has started to crystallize itself ever more clearly, in social philosophy, narrowly understood, as well as in the circles of sociology. It is not just a fashionable question, but one which presents an actualized version of some of the most ancient and important philosophical problems: the question of the connection between the economic life of society, the psychological development of its individuals and the changes within specific areas of culture to which belong not only the intellectual legacy of the sciences, art and religion, but also law, customs, fashion, public opinion, sports, entertainments, lifestyles, and so on. The intention to study these three processes presents merely an updated version by way of contemporary methodologies and the present state of our knowledge, of the ancient question as to the relation of particular existence and universal reason, of the real and the idea, of life and spirit—adapted to a new problematic.

Mostly, however, one reflects either metaphysically on the above theme, as in Scheler's "Sociology of Knowledge," or one states, more or less dogmatically, some general thesis on it; that is to say, one usually picks one of the theses advanced in history in a simplified fashion and, remaining dogmatically abstract, battles it out with all the other theses. Thus, one can find the following pronouncement: that economy and spirit are the respective expressions of one and the same essence: this amounts to a bad Spinozism. Or one can find the following: ideas, "spiritual" contents, force themselves into history and determine the actions of humans, so that they become primary while material life remains merely derivative; world and history have their source in the spirit: this would amount to an abstract, badly understood Hegel. Or one finds the contrary belief: the economy, material being, is the only true reality; the human psyche as well as law, art, and philosophy are purely derivative and mere reflections of it; this would be an abstract and therefore badly understood Marx. Besides the fact that these theses naively posit an uncritical, outdated separation of spirit and reality, a separation that is not dialectically sublated, those kinds of statements, if they are taken seriously in their abstractness, are ultimately devoid of any type of verification procedures: all can indiscriminately claim for themselves to present the truth. These dogmatic convictions are spared the scientific difficulties of the problem, if only because they consciously or unconsciously take the total identity of ideational and material processes for granted—not caring for, or even ignoring, the complex role of the psychic mediations.

The issue is seen quite differently if we pose the question more precisely in the following manner: In a definite time frame and in some particular countries, what relations can we delineate between a particular social group and the role of this group in the economy, the changes in the psychical structure of its members, and the thoughts and institutions created by it which influence it as a whole through the social totality? Then the possibility of real research projects that will be conducted in the Institute can come into view. At first, we would like to direct them towards a very important and particular social group in Germany, skilled labor and white-collar employees, and continue after that with the corresponding segments in the other highly developed European countries.

There is little time left to give a necessarily summary and insufficient overview of the most important paths that the full members of the Institute will have to follow in close-knit fashion to initially gather the empirical material with which the relations in question can be studied. At the top of the list is obviously the interpretation of the published statistics, the reports of organizations and political associations, the material of public corporations, and so on. This can happen only in connection with the ongoing analysis of the overall economic situation. Furthermore, it is necessary to investigate sociologically and psychologically the press and literature for the value of their pronouncements on the situation of the groups in question, but also because of literature's categorical structure, which enables it to influence the members of these groups. Especially important is then the development of a variety of survey methods. Questionnaires, amongst others, can be integrated into our research in manifold ways and can be of good service, if one always keeps in mind that inductive conclusions derived through them alone are always prematurely drawn. The essential purpose of questionnaires in our case is twofold: first, they should stimulate the research and keep it in touch with reality; second, they can be used to check knowledge gained by other means and thereby preempt errors. For the design of these questionnaires American social research has done important preliminary work which we will assimilate and advance for our own purposes. Also, we will have to use expert opinions on a grander scale. Where it is possible to advance particular aspects of problems by as yet unrecorded experiences of competent evaluators, one should try to include them wherever one might find them. Most times that will mean using the experience of practitioners for the sciences. A special task, moreover, is the collection and interpretation of documents that cannot be found in books. To that end, namely to employ scientifically the extremely rich sociological archives of the International Labor Bureau in Geneva, we will create a branch of the Institute there. Mr. Albert Thomas, the director of the International Labor Organization, has welcomed our plan and assured us, in a most pleasant manner, of his support. One has to add to all these paths, naturally, the methodological study of all published and forthcoming scientific treatises on the subject.

Each of these methods alone is completely insufficient, but perhaps all together, through years of patient and extended research, they might bear fruit for the general problematic. This can only be the case, in turn, if the members of the Institute constantly refer to the material and form their opinions not according to their own preferences, but according to the demands of the subject; if they refrain from all terms of transfiguration—and, finally, if we can preserve the unified intention to oppose both dogmatic ossification and descent into the technical-empirical.

I conclude. It has only been possible for me to delineate from all the tasks of the Institute the collective research work whose implementation will be the focus of the years to come. Besides that, the independent research of the individual members in the areas of theoretical economics, economic history, and the history of the labor movement should equally be borne in mind. The Institute will follow its mandate as a teaching institute within the university by holding regular programs such as lectures, lessons, and talks. These shall be considered additions to the regular university teaching since they will introduce the work of the Institute, report the newest developments in its research, and advance an education that meets the challenge of a philosophically oriented social science as explained above.

I could only hint at all these special tasks. On the other hand, it seems to me as if even this short report about the specifics has weakened our ability to remember the fundamentals. Indeed, this lecture has become almost a symbol for the strange difficulty of social philosophy—that the universal and the particular, the theoretical conceptualization and individual experience, penetrate each other. I am convinced that my explication in this regard has been insufficient. Allowing myself to hope that you have followed this lecture with forbearance, I ask for your good wishes and trust for the work itself. Carl Grunberg talked at the opening of the Institute about the fact that everyone is led in his/her scientific work by the impulse of a worldview. May the guiding impulse of this Institute be the unchangeable will to unflinchingly serve the truth!

NOTES

1. Kant, *Sämtliche Werke*, Akademie-Ausgabe, vol. 6.
2. Hegel, *Philosophy of Right*, trans. T. R. Knox (London, 1952), par. 352. Translator's note: While I have followed standard English translations of Hegel, I have modified the translation according to the German original and Horkheimer's use of it.
3. Hegel, *Philosophy of History*, trans. J. Sibree (New York, 1956), p. 30.
4. Ibid.
5. Ibid., p. 23.
6. Hegel, *Philosophy of Right*, Par. 189 Addition.
7. Ibid., Par. 182 Addition.
8. Hegel, *Philosophy of History*, p. 21.
9. Hegel, *Philosophie der Weltgeschichte*, ed. G. Lasson Leipsig, 1920), vol. 1. p. 55.
10. Hegel, *Philosophy of History*, p. 33.
11. Hegel, *Philosophie der Weltgeschichte*, p. 91.
12. Hermann Cohen, *Ethik des reinen Willens (Ethics of Pure Will*, 3d ed., Berlin, 1921), p. 8.
13. Max Scheler, "Probleme einer Soziologie des Wissens," in Scheler, ed., *Versuche zu einer Soziologie des Wissens* (Munich and Leipzig, 1924), p. 13.

WALTER BENJAMIN

Theses on the Philosophy of History

The story is told of an automaton constructed in such a way that it could play a winning game of chess, answering each move of an opponent with a countermove. A puppet in Turkish attire and with a hookah in its mouth sat before a chessboard placed on a large table. A system of mirrors created the illusion that this table was transparent from all sides. Actually, a little hunchback who was an expert chess player sat inside and guided the puppet's hand by means of strings. One can imagine a philosophical counterpart to this device. The puppet called "historical materialism" is to win all the time. It can easily be a match for anyone if it enlists the services of theology, which today, as we know, is wizened and has to keep out of sight.

"One of the most remarkable characteristics of human nature," writes Lotze, "is, alongside so much selfishness in specific instances, the freedom from envy which the present displays toward the future." Reflection shows us that our image of happiness is thoroughly colored by the time to which the course of our own existence has assigned us. The kind of happiness that could arouse envy in us exists only in the air we have breathed, among people we could have talked to, women who could have given themselves to us. In other words, our image of happiness is undissolubly bound up with the image of redemption. The same applies to our view of the past, which is the concern of history. The past carries with it a temporal index by which it is referred to redemption. There is a secret agreement between past generations and the present one. Our coming was expected on earth. Like every generation that preceded us, we have been endowed with a *weak* Messianic power, a power to which the past has a claim. That claim cannot be settled cheaply. Historical materialists are aware of that.

A chronicler who recites events without distinguishing between major and minor ones acts in accordance with the following truth: nothing that has ever happened should be regarded as lost for history. To be sure, only a redeemed mankind receives the fullness of its past—which is to say, only for a redeemed mankind has its past become citable in all its moments. Each moment it has lived becomes a *citation á l'ordre du jour*—and that day is Judgment Day.

> Seek for food and clothing first, then the Kingdom of God shall be added unto you. —
> Hegel, 1807.

The class struggle, which is always present to a historian influenced by Marx, is a fight for the crude and material things without which no refined and spiritual things could exist. Nevertheless, it is not in the form of the spoils which fall to the victor that the latter make their presence felt in the class struggle. They manifest themselves in this struggle as courage, humor, cunning, and fortitude. They have retroactive force and will constantly call in question every victory, past and present, of the rulers. As flowers turn toward the sun, by dint of a secret heliotropism the past strives to turn toward that sun which is rising in the sky of history. A historical materialist must be aware of this most inconspicuous of all transformations.

The true picture of the past flits by. The past can be seized only as an image which flashes up at the instant when it can be recognized and is never seen again. "The truth will not run away from us": in the historical outlook of historicism these words of Gottfried Keller mark the exact point where historical materialism cuts through historicism. For every image of the past that is not recognized by the present as one of its own concerns threatens to disappear irretrievably. (The good tidings which the historian of the past brings with throbbing heart may be lost in a void the very moment he opens his mouth.)

To articulate the past historically does not mean to recognize it "the way it really was" (Ranke). It means to seize hold of a memory as it flashes up at a moment of danger. Historical materialism wishes to retain that image of the past which unexpectedly appears to man singled out by history at a moment of danger. The danger affects both the content of the tradition and its receivers. The same threat hangs over both: that of becoming a tool of the ruling classes. In every era the attempt must be made anew to wrest tradition away from a conformism that is about to overpower it. The Messiah comes not only as the redeemer, he comes as the subduer of Antichrist. Only that historian will have the gift of fanning the spark of hope in the past who is firmly convinced that *even the dead* will not be safe from the enemy if he wins. And this enemy has not ceased to be victorious.

> Consider the darkness and the great cold
> In this vale which resounds with misery.
> —Brecht, *The Threepenny Opera*

To historians who wish to relive an era, Fustel de Coulanges recommends that they blot out everything they know about the later course of history. There is no better way of characterizing the method with which historical materialism has broken. It is a process of empathy whose origin is the indolence of the heart, *acedia*, which despairs of grasping and holding the genuine historical image as it flares up briefly. Among medieval theologians it was regarded as the root cause of sadness. Flaubert, who was familiar with it, wrote, "Few will be able to guess how sad one had to be in order to resuscitate Carthage." The nature of this sadness stands out more clearly if one asks with whom the adherents of historicism actually empathize. The answer is inevitable: with the victor. And all rulers are the heirs of those who conquered before them. Hence, empathy with the victor invariably benefits the rulers. Historical materialists know what that means. Whoever has emerged victorious participates to this day in the triumphal procession in which the present rulers step over those who are lying prostrate. According to traditional practice, the spoils are carried along in the procession. They are called cultural treasures, and a historical materialist views them with cautious detachment. For without exception the cultural treasures he surveys have an origin which he cannot contemplate without horror. They owe their existence not only to the efforts of the great minds and talents who have created them, but also to the anonymous toil of their contemporaries. There is no document of civilization which is not at the same time a document of barbarism. And just as such a document is not free of barbarism, barbarism taints also the manner in which it was transmitted from one owner to another. A historical materialist therefore dissociates himself from it as far as possible. He regards it as his task to brush history against the grain.

The tradition of the oppressed teaches us that the "state of emergency" in which we live is not the exception but the rule. We must attain to a conception of history that is in keeping with this insight. Then we shall clearly realize that it is our task to bring about a real state of emergency, and this will improve our position in the struggle against fascism. One reason why fascism has a chance is that in the name of progress its opponents treat it as a historical norm. The current amazement that the things we are experiencing are "still" possible in the twentieth century is not philosophical. This amazement is not the beginning of knowledge—unless it is the knowledge that the view of history which gives rise to it is untenable.

> My wing is ready for flight,
> I would like to turn back,
> If I stayed timeless time,
> I would have little luck.
> —Gerhard Scholem, "Gruss vom Angelus"

A Klee painting named *Angelus Novus* shows an angel looking as though he is about to move away from something he is fixedly contemplating. His eyes are staring, his mouth is open, his wings are spread. This is how one pictures the angel of history. His face is turned toward the past. Where we perceive a chain of events, he sees one single catastrophe which keeps piling wreckage upon wreckage and hurls it in front of his feet. The angel would like to stay, awaken the dead, and make whole what has been smashed. But a storm is blowing from Paradise; it has got caught in his wings with such violence that the angel can no longer close them. This storm irresistibly propels him into the future to which his back is turned, while the pile of debris before him grows skyward. This storm is what we call progress.

The themes which monastic discipline assigned to friars for meditation were designed to turn them away from the world and its affairs. The thoughts which we are developing here originate from similar considerations. At a moment when the politicians in whom the opponents of fascism had placed their hopes are prostrate and confirm their defeat by betraying their own cause, these observations are intended to disentangle the political worldlings from the snares in which the traitors have entrapped them. Our consideration proceeds from the insight that the politicians' stubborn faith in progress, their confidence in their "mass basis," and, finally, their servile integration in an uncontrollable apparatus have been three aspects of the same thing. It seeks to convey an idea of the high price our accustomed thinking will have to pay for a conception of history that avoids any complicity with the thinking to which these politicians continue to adhere.

The conformism which has been part and parcel of Social Democracy from the beginning attaches not only to its political tactics but to its economic views as well. It is one reason for its later breakdown. Nothing has corrupted the German working class so much as the notion that it was moving with the current. It regarded technological developments as the fall of the stream with which it thought it was moving. From there is was but a step to the illusion that the factory work which was supposed to tend toward technological progress constituted a political achievement. The old Protestant ethic of work was resurrected among German workers in secularized form. The Gotha Program already bears traces of this confusion, defining labor as "the source of all wealth and all culture." Smelling a rat, Marx countered that "the man who possesses no other property than his labor power" must of necessity become "the slave of other men who have made themselves the owners." However, the confusion spread, and soon thereafter Josef Dietzgen proclaimed: "The savior of modern times is called work. The . . . improvement . . . of labor constitutes the wealth which is now able to accomplish what no redeemer has ever been able to do." This vulgar-Marxist conception of the nature of labor bypasses the question of how its products might benefit the workers while still not being at their disposal. It recognizes only the progress in the mastery of nature, not the retrogression of society; it already displays the technocratic features later encountered in fascism. Among these is a conception of nature which differs ominously from the one in the socialist utopias before the 1848 revolution. The new conception of labor amounts to the exploitation of the proletariat. Compared with this positivistic conception, Fourier's fantasies, which have so often been ridiculed, prove to be surprisingly sound. According to Fourier, as a result of efficient cooperative labor, four moons would illuminate the earthly night, the ice would recede from the poles, sea water would no longer taste salty, and beasts of prey would do man's bidding. All this illustrates a kind of labor which, far from exploiting nature, is capable of delivering her of the creations which lie dormant in her womb as potentials. Nature, which, as Dietzgen puts it, "exists gratis," is a complement to the corrupted conception of labor.

We need history, but not the way a spoiled loafer in the garden of knowledge needs it.
—Nietzsche, *Of the Use and Abuse of History*

Not man or men but the struggling, oppressed class itself is the depository of historical knowledge. In Marx it appears as the last enslaved class, as the avenger that completes the task of liberation in the name of generation of the downtrodden. This conviction, which had a brief resurgence in the Spartacist group, has always been objectionable to Social Democrats. Within three decades they managed virtually to erase the name of Blanqui, though it had been the rallying sound that had reverberated through the preceding century. Social Democracy thought fit to assign to the working class the role of the redeemer of future generations, in this way cutting the sinews of its greatest strength. This training made the working class forget both its hatred and its spirit of sacrifice, for both are nourished by the image of enslaved ancestors rather than that of liberated grandchildren.

> Every day our cause becomes clearer and people get smarter.
> —Wilhelm Dietzgen, *Die Religion der Sozialdemokratie*

Social Democratic theory, and even more its practice, have been formed by a conception of progress which did not adhere to reality but made dogmatic claims. Progress as pictured in the minds of Social Democrats was, first of all, the progress of mankind itself (and not just advances in men's ability and knowledge). Second, it was something boundless, in keeping with the infinite perfectibility of mankind. Third, progress was regarded as irresistible, something that automatically pursued a straight or spiral course. Each of these predicates is controversial and open to criticism. However, when the chips are down, criticisms must penetrate beyond these predicates and focus on something that they have in common. The concept of the historical progress of mankind cannot be sundered from the concept of its progression through a homogeneous, empty time. A critique of the concept of such a progression must be the basis of any criticism of the concept of progress itself.

> Origin is the goal.
> —Karl Kraus, *Worte in Versen*, vol. I

History is the subject of a structure whose site is not homogeneous, empty time, but time filled by the presence of the now [*Jetztzeit*]. Thus, to Robespierre ancient Rome was a past charged with the time of the now which he blasted out of the continuum of history. The French Revolution reviewed itself as Rome reincarnate. It evoked ancient Rome the way fashion evokes costumes of the past. Fashion has a flair for the topical, no matter where it stirs in the thickets of long ago; it is a tiger's leap into the past. This jump, however, takes place in an arena where the ruling class gives the commands. The same leap in the open air of history is the dialectical one, which is how Marx understood the revolution.

The awareness that they are about to make the continuum of history explode is characteristic of the revolutionary classes at the moment of their action. The great revolution introduced a new calendar. The initial day of a calendar serves as a historical time-lapse camera. And, basically, it is the same day that keeps recurring in the guise of holidays, which are days of remembrance. Thus, the calendars do not measure time as clocks do; they are monuments of a historical consciousness of which not the slightest trace has been apparent in Europe in the past hundred years. In the July Revolution an incident occurred which showed this consciousness still alive. On the first evening of fighting it turned out that the clocks in the towers were being fired on simultaneously and independently from several places in Paris. An eyewitness, who may have owed his insight to the rhyme, wrote as follows:

> Who would have believed it! We are told that New Joshuas at the
> foot of every tower, as though irritated with time itself, fired at the
> dials in order to stop the day.

A historical materialist cannot do without the notion of a present which is not a transition, but in which time stands still and has come to a stop. For this notion defines the present in which he himself is writing history. Historicism gives the "eternal" image of the past; historical materialism supplies a unique experience with the past. The historical materialist leaves it to others to be drained by the whore called "Once upon a time" in historicism's bordello. He remains in control of his powers, man enough to blast open the continuum of history.

Historicism rightly culminated in universal history. Materialistic historiography differs from it as to method more clearly than from any other kind. Universal history has no theoretical armature. Its method is additive; it musters a mass of data to fill the homogeneous, empty time. Materialistic historiography, on the other hand, is based on a constructive principle. Thinking involves not only the flow of thoughts, but their arrest as well. Where thinking suddenly stops in a configuration pregnant with tensions, it gives that configuration a shock, by which it crystalizes into a monad. A historical materialist approaches a historical subject only where he recognizes the sign of a Messianic cessation of happening, or, put differently, a revolutionary chance in the fight for the oppressed past. He takes cognizance of it in order to blast a specific era out of the homogenous course of history—blasting a specific life out of the era or a specific work out of the lifework. As a result of this method the lifework is preserved in this work and at the same time canceled, in the lifework, the era; and in the era, the entire course of history. The nourishing fruit of the historically understood contains time as a precious but tasteless seed.

"In relation to the history of organic life on earth," writes a modern biologist, "the paltry fifty millennia of *homo sapiens* constitute something like two seconds at the close of a twenty-four-hour day. On this scale, the history of civilized mankind would fill one-fifth of the last second of the last hour." The present, which, as a model of Messianic time, comprises the entire history of mankind in an enormous abridgment, coincides exactly with the stature which the history of mankind has in the universe.

Historicism contents itself with establishing a causal connection between various moments in history. But no fact that is a cause is for that very reason historical. It became historical posthumously, as it were, through events that may be separated from it by thousands of years. A historian who takes this as his point of departure stops telling the sequence of events like the beads of a rosary. Instead, he grasps the constellation which his own era has formed with a definite earlier one. Thus, he establishes a conception of the present as the "time of the now" which is shot through with chips of Messianic time.

The soothsayers who found out from time what it had in store certainly did not experience time as either homogeneous or empty. Anyone who keeps this in mind will perhaps get an idea of how past times were experienced in remembrance—namely, in just the same way. We know that the Jews were prohibited from investigating the future. The Torah and the prayers instruct them in rememberance, however. This stripped the future of its magic, to which all those succumb who turn to the soothsayers for enlightenment. This does not imply, however, that for the Jews the future turned into homogeneous, empty time. For every second of time was the strait gate through which the Messiah might enter.

HERBERT MARCUSE

Liberation from the Affluent Society

I am very happy to see so many flowers here and that is why I want to remind you that flowers, by themselves, have no power whatsoever, other than the power of men and women who protect them and take care of them against aggression and destruction.

As a hopeless philosopher for whom philosophy has become inseparable from politics, I am afraid I have to give here today a rather philosophical speech, and I must ask your indulgence. We are dealing with the dialectics of liberation (actually a redundant phrase, because I believe that all dialectic is liberation) and not only liberation in an intellectual sense, but liberation involving the mind and the body, liberation involving entire human existence. Think of Plato: the liberation from the existence in the cave. Think of Hegel: liberation in the sense of progress and freedom on the historical scale. Think of Marx. Now, in what sense is all dialectic liberation? It is liberation from the repressive, from a bad, a false system—be it an organic system, be it a social system, be it a mental or intellectual system: liberation by forces developing within such a system. That is a decisive point. And liberation by virtue of the contradiction generated by the system, precisely because it is a bad, a false system.

I am intentionally using here moral, philosophical terms, values: "bad," "false." For without an objectively justifiable goal of a better, a free human existence, all liberation must remain meaningless—at best, progress in servitude. I believe that in Marx too socialism *ought* to be. This "ought" belongs to the very essence of scientific socialism. It *ought* to be; it is, we may almost say, a biological, sociological, and political necessity. It is a biological necessity inasmuch as a socialist society, according to Marx, would conform with the very *logos* of life, with the essential possibilities of a human existence, not only mentally, not only intellectually, but also organically.

Now, as to today and our own situation. I think we are faced with a novel situation in history, because today we have to be liberated from a relatively well-functioning, rich, powerful society. I am speaking here about liberation from the affluent society, that is to say, the advanced industrial societies. The problem we are facing is the need for liberation not from a poor society, not from a disintegrating society, not even in most cases from a terroristic society, but from a society which develops to a great extent the material and even cultural needs of man—a society which, to use a slogan, delivers the goods to an ever larger part of the population. And that implies, we are facing liberation from a society where liberation is apparently without a mass basis. We know very well the social mechanisms of manipulation, indoctrination, repression which are responsible for this lack of a mass basis, for the integration of the majority of the oppositional forces into the established social system. But I must emphasize again that this is not merely an ideological integration; that it is not merely a social integration; that it takes place precisely on the strong and rich basis which enables the society to develop and satisfy material and cultural needs better than before.

But knowledge of the mechanisms of manipulation or repression, which go down into the very unconscious of man, is not the whole story. I believe that we (and I will use "we" throughout my talk) have been too hesitant, that we have been too ashamed, understandably ashamed, to insist on the integral, radical features of a socialist society, its qualitative difference from all the established societies: the qualitative difference by virtue of which socialism is indeed the negation of the established systems, no matter how productive, no matter how powerful they are or they may appear. In other words—and this is one of the many points where I disagree with Paul Goodman—our fault was not that we have been too immodest, but that we have been too modest. We have, as it were, repressed a great deal of what we should have said and what we should have emphasized.

If today these integral features, these truly radical features which make a socialist society a definite negation of the existing societies, if this qualitative difference today appears as utopian, as idealistic, as metaphysical, this is precisely the form in which these radical features must appear if they are really to be a definite negation of the established society: if socialism is indeed the rupture of history, the radical break, the leap into the realm of freedom—a total rupture.

Let us give one illustration of how this awareness, or half-awareness, of the need for such a total rupture was present in some of the great social struggles of our period. Walter Benjamin quotes reports that during the Paris Commune, in all corners of the city of Paris there were people shooting at the clocks on the towers of the churches, palaces, and so on, thereby consciously or half-consciously expressing the need that somehow time has to be arrested: that at least the prevailing, the established time continuum has to be arrested, and that a new time has to begin—a very strong emphasis on the qualitative difference and on the totality of the rupture between the new society and the old.

In this sense, I should like to discuss here with you the repressed prerequisites of qualitative change. I say intentionally "of qualitative change," not "of revolution," because we know of too many revolutions through which the continuum of repression has been sustained, revolutions which have replaced one system of domination by another. We must become aware of the essentially new features which distinguish a free society as a definite negation of the established societies, and we must begin formulating these features, no matter how metaphysical, no matter how utopian. I would even say no matter how ridiculous we may appear to the normal people in all camps, on the right as well as on the left.

What is the dialectic of liberation with which we here are concerned? It is the con-

struction of a free society, a construction which depends in the first place on the prevalence of the vital need for abolishing the established systems of servitude: and secondly,
and this is decisive, it depends on the vital commitment, the striving, conscious as well as
sub- and unconscious, for the qualitatively different values of a free human existence.
Without the emergence of such new needs and satisfactions, the needs and satisfactions of
free men, all change in the social institutions, no matter how great, would only replace one
system of servitude by another system of servitude. Nor can the emergence—and I should
like to emphasize this—nor can the emergence of such new needs and satisfactions be
envisaged as a mere by-product, the mere result, of changed social institutions. We have
seen this: it is a fact of experience. The development of the new institutions must already
be carried out and carried through by men with the new needs. That, by the way, is the
basic idea underlying Marx's own concept of the proletariat as the historical agent of revolution. He saw the industrial proletariat as the historical agent of revolution, not only
because it was the basic class in the material process of production, not only because it was
at that time the majority of the population, but also because this class was "free" from the
repressive and aggressive competitive needs of capitalist society and therefore, at least
potentially, the carrier of essentially new needs, goals, and satisfactions.

We can formulate this dialectic of liberation also in a more brutal way, as a vicious circle. The transition from voluntary servitude (as it exists to a great extent in the affluent
society) to freedom presupposes the abolition of the institutions and mechanisms of repression. And the abolition of the institutions and mechanisms of repression already presupposes liberation from servitude, prevalence of the need for liberation. As to needs, I think
we have to distinguish between the need for changing intolerable conditions of existence,
and the need for changing the society as a whole. The two are by no means identical, they
are by no means in harmony. *If* the need is for changing intolerable conditions of existence, with at least a reasonable chance that this can be achieved within the established
society, with the growth and progress of the established society, then this is merely quantitative change. Qualitative change is a change of the very system as a whole.

I would like to point out that the distinction between quantitative and qualitative
change is not identical with the distinction between reform and revolution. Quantitative
change can mean and can lead to revolution. Only the conjunction, I suggest, of these
two is revolution in the essential sense of the leap from prehistory into the history of man.
In other words, the problem with which we are faced is the point where quantity can turn
into quality, where the quantitative change in the conditions and institutions can become
a qualitative change affecting all human existence.

Today the two potential factors of revolution which I have just mentioned are dis-
jointed. The first is most prevalent in the underdeveloped countries, where quantitative
change—that is to say, the creation of human living conditions—is in itself qualitative
change, but is not yet freedom. The second potential factor of revolution, the prerequisites
of liberation, are potentially there in the advanced industrial countries, but are contained
and perverted by the capitalist organization of society.

I think we are faced with a situation in which this advanced capitalist society has
reached a point where quantitative change can technically be turned into qualitative

change, into authentic liberation. And it is precisely against this truly fatal possibility that the affluent society, advanced capitalism, is mobilized and organized on all fronts, at home as well as abroad.

Before I go on, let me give a brief definition of what I mean by an affluent society. A model, of course, is American society today, although even in the U.S. it is more a tendency, not yet entirely translated into reality. In the first place, it is a capitalist society. It seems to be necessary to remind ourselves of this because there are some people, even on the left, who believe that American society is no longer a class society. I can assure you that it is a class society. It is a capitalist society with a high concentration of economic and political power; with an enlarged and enlarging sector of automation and coordination of production, distribution, and communication; with private ownership in the means of production, which however depends increasingly on ever more active and wide intervention by the government. It is a society in which, as I mentioned, the material as well as cultural needs of the underlying population are satisfied on a scale larger than ever before—but they are satisfied in line with the requirements and interests of the apparatus and of the powers which control the apparatus. And it is a society growing on the condition of accelerating waste, planned obsolescence, and destruction, while the substratum of the population continues to live in poverty and misery.

I believe that these factors are internally interrelated, that they constitute the syndrome of late capitalism: namely, the apparently inseparable unity—inseparable for the system—of productivity and destruction, of satisfaction of needs and repression, of liberty within a system of servitude—that is to say, the subjugation of man to the apparatus, and the inseparable unity of rational and irrational. We can say that the rationality of the society lies in its very insanity, and that the insanity of the society is rational to the degree to which it is efficient, to the degree to which it delivers the goods.

Now the question we must raise is: Why do we need liberation from such a society if it is capable—perhaps in the distant future, but apparently capable—of conquering poverty to a greater degree than ever before, of reducing the toil of labor and the time of labor, and of raising the standard of living? If the price for all goods delivered, the price for this comfortable servitude, for all these achievements, is exacted from people far away from the metropolis and far away from its affluence? If the affluent society itself hardly notices what it is doing, how it is spreading terror and enslavement, how it is fighting liberation in all corners of the globe?

We know the traditional weakness of emotional, moral, and humanitarian arguments in the face of such technological achievement, in the face of the irrational rationality of such a power. These arguments do not seem to carry any weight against the brute facts— we might say brutal facts—of the society and its productivity. And yet, it is only the insistence on the real possibilities of a free society, which is blocked by the affluent society—it is only this insistence in practice as well as in theory, in demonstration as well as in discussion, which still stands in the way of the complete degradation of man to an object, or rather subject/object, of total administration. It is only this insistence which still stands in the way of the progressive brutalization and moronization of man. For—and I should like to emphasize this—the capitalist Welfare State is a Warfare State. It must have an Enemy, with a capital E, a total Enemy: because the perpetuation of servitude, the perpetuation of the miserable struggle for existence in the very face of the new possibilities of freedom, activates and intensifies in this society a primary aggressiveness to a degree, I think, hitherto unknown in history. And this primary aggressiveness must be mobilized in socially useful ways, lest it explode the system itself. Therefore the need for an Enemy, who must be there, and who must be created if he does not exist. Fortunately, I dare say, the Enemy does exist. But his image and his power must, in this society, be inflated beyond all proportions in order to be able to mobilize this aggressiveness of the affluent society in socially useful ways.

The result is a mutilated, crippled, and frustrated human existence: a human existence that is violently defending its own servitude.

We can sum up the fatal situation with which we are confronted. Radical social change is objectively necessary, in the dual sense that it is the only chance to save the possibilities of human freedom and, furthermore, in the sense that the technical and material resources for the realization of freedom are available. But while this objective need is demonstrably there, the subjective need for such a change does not prevail. It does not prevail precisely among those parts of the population that are traditionally considered the agents of historical change. The subjective need is repressed, again on a dual ground: firstly, by virtue of the actual satisfaction of needs, and secondly, by a massive scientific manipulation and administration of needs—that is, by a systematic social control not only of the consciousness, but also of the unconscious of man. This control has been made possible by the very achievements of the greatest liberating sciences of our time, in psychology, mainly psychoanalysis and psychiatry. That they could become and have become at the same time powerful instruments of suppression, one of the most effective engines of suppression, is again one of the terrible aspects of the dialectic of liberation.

This divergence between the objective and the subjective need changes completely, I suggest, the basis, the prospects, and the strategy of liberation. This situation presupposes the emergence of new needs, qualitatively different and even opposed to the prevailing aggressive and repressive needs: the emergence of a new type of man, with a vital, biological drive for liberation, and with a consciousness capable of breaking through the material as well as ideological veil of the affluent society. In other words, liberation seems to be predicated upon the opening and the activation of a depth dimension of human existence, this side of and underneath the traditional material base: not an idealistic dimension, over and above the material base, but a dimension even more material than the material base, a dimension underneath the material base. I will illustrate presently what I mean.

The emphasis on this new dimension does not mean replacing politics by psychology, but rather the other way around. It means finally taking account of the fact that society has invaded even the deepest roots of individual existence, even the unconscious of man. We must get at the roots of society in the individuals themselves, the individuals who, because of social engineering, constantly reproduce the continuum of repression even through the great revolution.

This change is, I suggest, not an ideological change. It is dictated by the actual development of an industrial society, which has introduced factors which our theory could formerly correctly neglect. It is dictated by the actual development of industrial society, by the tremendous growth of its material and technical productivity, which has surpassed and rendered obsolete the traditional goals and preconditions of liberation.

Here we are faced with the question: Is liberation from the affluent society identical with the transition from capitalism to socialism? The answer I suggest is: It is not identical, if socialism is defined merely as the planned development of the productive forces and the rationalization of resources (although this remains a precondition for all liberation). It is identical with the transition from capitalism to socialism, if socialism is defined in its most utopian terms: namely, among others, the abolition of labor, the termination of the struggle for existence—that is to say, life as an end in itself and no longer as a means to an end—and the liberation of human sensibility and sensitivity, not as a private factor, but as a force for transformation of human existence and of its environment. To give sensitivity and sensibility their own right is, I think, one of the basic goals of integral socialism. These are the qualitatively different features of a free society. They presuppose, as you may already have seen, a total transvaluation of values, a new anthropology. They presuppose a type of man who rejects the performance principles governing the established societies; a type of man who has rid himself of the aggressiveness and brutality that are inherent in the organization of established society, and in their hypocritical, puritan morality: a type of man who is biologically incapable of fighting wars and creating suffering; a type of man who has a good conscience of joy and pleasure, and who works, collectively and individually, for a social and natural environment in which such an existence becomes possible.

The dialectic of liberation, as turned from quantity into quality, thus involves, I repeat, a break in the continuum of repression which reaches into the depth dimension of the organism itself. Or, we may say that today qualitative change, liberation, involves organic, instinctual, biological changes at the same time as political and social changes.

The new needs and satisfactions have a very material basis, as I have indicated. They are not thought out but are the logical derivation from the technical, material, and intellectual possibilities of advanced, industrial society. They are inherent in, and the expression of, the productivity of advanced industrial society, which has long since made obsolete all kinds of innerwordly asceticism, the entire work discipline on which Judaeo-Christian morality has been based.

Why is this society surpassing and negating this type of man, the traditional type of man, and the forms of his existence, as well as the morality to which it owes much of its origins and foundations? This new, unheard-of, and not anticipated productivity allows the concept of a technology of liberation. Here I can only briefly indicate what I have in mind: such amazing and indeed apparently utopian tendencies as the convergence of technique and art, the convergence of work and play, the convergence of the realm of necessity and the realm of freedom. How? No longer subjected to the dictates of capitalist profitability and of efficiency, no longer to the dictates of scarcity, which today are perpetuated by the capitalist organization of society; socially necessary labor, material production, would and could become (we see the tendency already) increasingly scientific. Technical experimentation, science, and technology would and could become a play with the hitherto hidden—methodically hidden and blocked—potentialities of men and things, of society and nature.

This means one of the oldest dreams of all radical theory and practice. It means that the creative imagination, and not only the rationality of the performance principle, would become a productive force applied to the transformation of the social and natural universe. It would mean the emergence of a form of reality which is the work and the medium of the developing sensibility and sensitivity of man.

And now I throw in the terrible concept: it would mean an "aesthetic" reality—society as a work of art. This is the most utopian, the most radical possibility of liberation today.

What does this mean, in concrete terms? I said, we are not concerned here with private sensitivity and sensibility, but with sensitivity and sensibility, creative imagination and play, becoming forces of transformation. As such they would guide, for example, the total reconstruction of our cities and of the countryside; the restoration of nature after the elimination of the violence and destruction of capitalist industrialization; the creation of internal and external space for privacy, individual autonomy, tranquility; the elimination of noise, of captive audiences, of enforced togetherness, of pollution, of ugliness. These are not—and I cannot emphasize this strongly enough—snobbish and romantic demands. Biologists today have emphasized that these are organic needs for the human organism, and that their arrest, their perversion and destruction by capitalist society, actually mutilates the human organism, not only in a figurative way but in a very real and literal sense.

I believe that it is only in such a universe that man can be truly free, and truly human relationships between free beings can be established. I believe that the idea of such a universe guided also Marx's concept of socialism, and that these aesthetic needs and goals must from the beginning be present in the reconstruction of society, and not only at the end or in the far future. Otherwise, the needs and satisfactions which reproduce a repressive society would be carried over into the new society. Repressive men would carry over their repression into the new society.

Now, at this farthest point, the question is: How can we possibly envisage the emergence of such qualitatively different needs and goals as organic, biological needs and goals and not as superimposed values? How can we envisage the emergence of these needs and satisfactions within and against the established society—that is to say, prior to liberation? That was the dialectic with which I started, that in a very definite sense we have to be free from in order to create a free society.

Needless to say, the dissolution of the existing system is the precondition for such qualitative change. And the more efficiently the repressive apparatus of the affluent societies operates, the less likely is a gradual transition from servitude to freedom. The fact that today we cannot identify any specific class or any specific group as a revolutionary force—this fact is no excuse for not using any and every possibility and method to arrest the engines of repression in the individual. The diffusion of potential opposition among the entire underlying population corresponds precisely to the total character of our advanced capitalist society. The internal contradictions of the system are as grave as ever before and likely to be aggravated by the violent expansion of capitalist imperialism. Not only the most general contradictions between the tremendous social wealth on the one hand, and the destructive, aggressive, and wasteful use of this wealth on the other: but far more concrete contradictions such as the necessity for the system to automate, the continued reduction of the human base in physical labor-power in the material reproduction of society, and thereby the tendency towards the draining of the sources of surplus profit. Finally, there is the threat of technological unemployment which even the most affluent society may no longer be capable of compensating by the creation of ever more parasitic and unproductive labor: all these contradictions exist. In reaction to them suppression, manipulation and integration are likely to increase.

But fulfillment is there, the ground can and must be prepared. The mutilated consciousness and the mutilated instincts must be broken. The sensitivity and the awareness of the new transcending, antagonistic values—they are there. And they are there, they are here, precisely among the still nonintegrated social groups and among those who, by virtue of their privileged position, can pierce the ideological and material veil of mass communication and indoctrination—namely, the intelligentsia.

We all know the fatal prejudice, practically from the beginning, in the labor movement against the intelligentsia as catalyst of historical change. It is time to ask whether this prejudice against the intellectuals, and the inferiority complex of the intellectuals resulting from it, was not an essential factor in the development of the capitalist as well as the socialist societies: in the development and weakening of the opposition. The intellectuals usually went out to organize the others, to organize in the communities. They certainly did not use the potentiality they had to organize themselves, to organize among themselves not only on a regional, not only on a national, but on an international level. That is, in my view, today one of the most urgent tasks. Can we say that the intelligentsia is the agent of historical change? Can we say that the intelligentsia today is a revolutionary class? The answer I would give is: No, we cannot say that. But we can say, and I think we must say, that the intelligentsia has a decisive preparatory function, not more; and I suggest that this is plenty. By itself it is not and cannot be a revolutionary class, but it can become the catalyst, and it has a preparatory function—certainly not for the first time; that is in fact the way all revolution starts—but more, perhaps, today than ever before. Because—and for this too we have a very material and very concrete basis—it is from this group that the holders of decisive positions in the productive process will be recruited, in the future even more than hitherto. I refer to what we may call the increasingly scientific character of the material process of production, by virtue of which the role of the intelligentsia changes. It is the group from which the decisive holders of decisive positions will be recruited: scientists, researchers, technicians, engineers, even psychologists—because psychology will continue to be a socially necessary instrument, either of servitude or of liberation.

This class, this intelligentsia has been called the new working class. I believe this term is at best premature. They are—and this we should not forget—today the pet beneficiaries of the established system. But they are also at the very source of the glaring contradictions between the liberating capacity of science and its repressive and enslaving use. To activate the repressed and manipulated contradiction, to make it operate as a catalyst of change, that is one of the main tasks of the opposition today. It remains and must remain a political task.

Education is our job, but education in a new sense. Being theory as well as practice, political practice, education today is more than discussion, more than teaching and learning and writing. Unless and until it goes beyond the classroom, until and unless it goes beyond the college, the school, the university, it will remain powerless. Education today must involve the mind and the body, reason and imagination, the intellectual and the instinctual needs, because our entire existence has become the subject/object of politics, of social engineering. I emphasize, it is not a question of making the schools and universities, of making the educational system political. The educational system is political already. I need only remind you of the incredible degree to which (I am speaking of the U.S.) universities are involved in huge research grants (the nature of which you know in many cases) by the government and the various quasi-governmental agencies.

The educational system *is* political, so it is not we who want to politicize the educational system. What we want is a counterpolicy against the established policy. And in this sense we must meet this society on its own ground of total mobilization. We must confront indoctrination in servitude with indoctrination in freedom. We must each of us generate in ourselves, and try to generate in others, the instinctual need for a life without fear, without brutality, and without stupidity. And we must see that we can generate the instinctual and intellectual revulsion against the values of an affluence which spreads aggressiveness and suppression throughout the world.

Before I conclude I would like to say my bit about the Hippies. It seems to me a serious phenomenon. If we are talking of the emergence of an instinctual revulsion against the values of the affluent society, I think here is a place where we should look for it. It seems to me that the Hippies, like any nonconformist movement on the left, are split. That there are two parts, or parties, or tendencies. Much of it is mere masquerade and clownery on the private level, and therefore indeed, as Gerassi suggested, completely harmless, very nice and charming in many cases, but that is all there is to it. But that is not the whole story. There is in the Hippies, and especially in such tendencies in the Hippies as the Diggers and the Provos, an inherent political element—perhaps even more so in the U.S. than here. It is the appearance indeed of new instinctual needs and values. This experience is there. There is a new sensibility against efficient and insane reasonableness. There is the refusal to play by the rules of a rigged game, a game which one knows is rigged from the beginning, and the revolt against the compulsive cleanliness of puritan morality and the aggression bred by this puritan morality as we see it today in Vietnam among other things.

At least this part of the Hippies, in which sexual, moral, and political rebellion are somehow united, is indeed a nonaggressive form of life: a demonstration of an aggressive nonaggressiveness which achieves, at least potentially, the demonstration of qualitatively different values, a transvaluation of values.

All education today is therapy: therapy in the sense of liberating man by all available means from a society in which, sooner or later, he is going to be transformed into a brute, even if he doesn't notice it any more. Education in this sense is therapy, and all therapy today is political theory and practice. What kind of political practice? That depends entirely on the situation. It is hardly imaginable that we should discuss this here in detail. I will only remind you of the various possibilities of demonstrations, of finding out flexible modes of demonstration which can cope with the use of institutionalized violence, of boycott, many other things—anything goes which is such that it indeed has a reasonable chance of strengthening the forces of the opposition.

We can prepare for it as educators, as students. Again, I say, our role is limited. We are no mass movement. I do not believe that in the near future we will see such a mass movement.

I want to add one word about the so-called Third World. I have not spoken of the Third World because my topic was strictly liberation from the affluent society. I agree entirely with Paul Sweezy, that without putting the affluent society in the framework of the Third World it is not understandable. I also believe that here and now our emphasis must be on the advanced industrial societies—not forgetting to do whatever we can and in whatever way we can to support, theoretically and practically, the struggle for liberation in the neocolonial countries which, if again they are not the final force of liberation, at least contribute their share—and it is a considerable share—to the potential weakening and disintegration of the imperialist world system.

Our role as intellectuals is a limited role. On no account should we succumb to any illusions. But even worse than this is to succumb to the widespread defeatism which we witness. The preparatory role today is an indispensable role. I believe I am not being too optimistic—I have not in general the reputation of being too optimistic—when I say that we can already see the signs, not only that *They* are getting frightened and worried but that there are far more concrete, far more tangible manifestations of the essential weakness of the system. Therefore, let us continue with whatever we can—no illusions, but even more, no defeatism.

POSTMODERNISM AND POSTSTRUCTURALISM

Postmodernism and poststructuralism are often used interchangeably. The former usually refers to various trends expressive of a new historical phase in which the structures and assumptions of modernity are no longer valid. The latter usually deals with the methodological ways in which these structures and assumptions are exposed as arbitrary and as serving a particular form of domination. Neither postmodernism nor poststructuralism should be understood as a unified or coherent doctrine. Nevertheless, the following selections should provide some insight into the more generally accepted tenets, influences, and beliefs of this new understanding of society.

Jean-François Lyotard views the postmodern as an "incredulity toward metanarrative" in the introduction to his enormously influential *The Postmodern Condition*. He means by this a skepticism toward all general claims, universal theories of history, and attempts to view society as a coherent totality with a fixed or stable "subject." The postmodern condition, in this way, fosters a new sensitivity to the differences among individuals and groups even as it reinforces toleration of the "incommensurable."

Michel Foucault makes these insights concrete with respect to the role of the intellectual. The author of *Discipline and Punish*, *The History of Sexuality*, and numerous other works suggests that the Enlightenment notion of the "universal intellectual" is no longer relevant. Intellectuals must now become "specific" and deal with problems emanating from "where their own condition of life and work situates them." Women must primarily speak for women or gays for gays, even as intellectuals must make make use of their disciplinary knowledge to solve particular problems.

Truth is always a social construct, however, and it thus has no anchoring or "foundation." No epistemological "starting points" or discursive presuppositions exist for dealing with others. "Contingency" is seen as undermining every philosophical "foundation." Judith Butler argues, however, in her well-known essay "Contingent Foundations" that the two terms are not antithetical. She retains a concern for the foundational or universal even though such terms always legitimate dominant social interests. The foundation is therefore always contingent and the point is to recognize it as such. Genuine political criticism, instead of treating categories as absolute of immutable, must subsequently insist on keeping them "open." Even the notion of "woman," for example, hides the differences between various women. Nevertheless, establishing the foundation or the universal is necessary precisely in order to contest it in the name of the contingent and the particular.

JEAN-FRANÇOIS LYOTARD

Introduction to
The Postmodern Condition:
A Report on Knowledge

The object of this study is the condition of knowledge in the most highly developed societies. I have decided to use the word *postmodern* to describe that condition. The word is in current use on the American continent among sociologists and critics; it designates the state of our culture following the transformations which, since the end of the nineteenth century, have altered the game rules for science, literature, and the arts. The present study will place these transformations in the context of the crisis of narratives.

Science has always been in conflict with narratives. Judged by the yardstick of science, the majority of them prove to be fables. But to the extent that science does not restrict itself to stating useful regularities and seeks the truth, it is obliged to legitimate the rules of its own game. It then produces a discourse of legitimation with respect to its own status, a discourse called philosophy. I will use the term *modern* to designate any science that legitimates itself with reference to a metadiscourse of this kind making an explicit appeal to some grand narrative, such as the dialectics of Spirit, the hermeneutics of meaning, the emancipation of the rational or working subject, or the creation of wealth. For example, the rule of consensus between the sender and addressee of a statement with truth-value is deemed acceptable if it is cast in terms of a possible unanimity between rational minds: this is the Enlightenment narrative, in which the hero of knowledge works toward a good ethico-political end—universal peace. As can be seen from this example, if a metanarrative implying a philosophy of history is used to legitimate knowledge, questions are raised concerning the validity of the institutions governing the social bond: these must be legitimated as well. Thus justice is consigned to the grand narrative in the same way as truth.

Simplifying to the extreme, I define *postmodern* as incredulity toward metanarratives. This incredulity is undoubtedly a product of progress in the sciences: but that progress in turn presupposes it. To the obsolescence of the metanarrative apparatus of legitimation corresponds, most notably, the crisis of metaphysical philosophy and of the university institution which in the past relied on it. The narrative function is losing its functors, its great hero, its great dangers, its great voyages, its great goal. It is being dispersed in clouds of narrative language elements—narrative, but also denotative, prescriptive, descriptive, and so on. Conveyed within each cloud are pragmatic valencies specific to its kind. Each of us lives at the intersection of many of these. However, we do not necessarily establish stable language combinations, and the properties of the ones we do establish are not necessarily communicable.

Thus the society of the future falls less within the province of a Newtonian anthropology (such as stucturalism or systems theory) than a pragmatics of language particles. There are many different language games—a heterogeneity of elements. They only give rise to institutions in patches—local determinism.

The decision makers, however, attempt to manage these clouds of sociality according to input/output matrices, following a logic which implies that their elements are commensurable and that the whole is determinable. They allocate our lives for the growth of power. In matters of social justice and of scientific truth alike, the legitimation of that power is based on its optimizing the system's performance—efficiency. The application of this criterion to all of our games necessarily entails a certain level of terror, whether soft or hard: be operational (that is, commensurable) or disappear.

The logic of maximum performance is no doubt inconsistent in many ways, particularly with respect to contradiction in the socioeconomic field: it demands both less work (to lower production costs) and more (to lessen the social burden of the idle population). But our incredulity is now such that we no longer expect salvation to rise from these inconsistencies, as did Marx.

Still, the postmodern condition is as much a stranger to disenchantment as it is to the blind positivity of delegitimation. Where, after the metanarratives, can legitimacy reside? The operativity criterion is technological; it has no relevance for judging what is true or just. Is legitimacy to be found in consensus obtained through discussion, as Jürgen Habermas thinks? Such consensus does violence to the heterogeneity of language games. And invention is always born of dissension. Postmodern knowledge is not simply a tool of the authorities; it refines our sensitivity to differences and reinforces our ability to tolerate the incommensurable. Its principle is not the expert's homology, but the inventor's paralogy.

Here is the question: is a legitimation of the social bond, a just society, feasible in terms of a paradox analogous to that of scientific activity? What would such a paradox be?

The text that follows is an occasional one. It is a report on knowledge in the most highly developed societies and was presented to the Conseil des Universitiés of the government of Quebec at the request of its president. I would like to thank him for his kindness in allowing its publication.

It remains to be said that the author of the report is a philosopher, not an expert. The latter knows what he knows and what he does not know: the former does not. One concludes, the other questions—two very different language games. I combine them here with the result that neither quite succeeds.

The philosopher at least can console himself with the thought that the formal and pragmatic analysis of certain philosophical and ethico-political discourses of legitimation, which underlies the report, will subsequently see the light of day. The report will have

INTRODUCTION TO *THE POSTMODERN CONDITION* [241]

served to introduce that analysis from a somewhat sociologizing slant, one that truncates but at the same time situates it.

Such as it is, I dedicate this report to the Institut Polytechnique de Philosophie of the Université de Paris VIII (Vincennes)—at this very postmodern moment that finds the University nearing what may be its end, while the Institute may just be beginning.

MICHEL FOUCAULT

Truth and Power

For a long period, the 'left' intellectual spoke and was acknowledged the right of speaking in the capacity of master of truth and justice. He was heard, or purported to make himself heard, as the spokesman of the universal. To be an intellectual meant something like being the consciousness/conscience of us all. I think we have here an idea transposed from Marxism, from a faded Marxism indeed. Just as the proletariat, by the necessity of its historical situation, is the bearer of the universal (but its immediate, unreflected bearer, barely conscious of itself as such), so the intellectual, through his moral, theoretical and political choice, aspires to be the bearer of this universality in its conscious, elaborated form. The intellectual is thus taken as the clear, individual figure of a universality whose obscure, collective form is embodied in the proletariat.

Some years have now passed since the intellectual was called upon to play this role. A new mode of the 'connection between theory and practice' has been established. Intellectuals have got used to working, not in the modality of the 'universal', the 'exemplary', the 'just-and-true-for-all', but within specific sectors, at the precise points where their own conditions of life or work situate them (housing, the hospital, the asylum, the laboratory, the university, family and sexual relations). This has undoubtedly given them a much more immediate and concrete awareness of struggles. And they have met here with problems which are specific, 'non-universal', and often different from those of the proletariat or the masses. And yet I believe intellectuals have actually been drawn closer to the proletariat and the masses, for two reasons. Firstly, because it has been a question of real, material, everyday struggles, and secondly because they have often been confronted, albeit in a different form, by the same adversary as the proletariat, namely the multinational corporations, the judicial and police apparatuses, the property speculators, etc. This is what I would call the 'specific' intellectual as opposed to the 'universal' intellectual.

This new configuration has a further political significance. It makes it possible, if not to integrate, at least to rearticulate categories which were previously kept separate. The intellectual *par excellence* used to be the writer: as a universal consciousness, a free subject, he was counterposed to those intellectuals who were merely *competent instances* in the service of the State or Capital—technicians, magistrates, teachers. Since the time when each individual's specific activity began to serve as the basis for politicisation, the threshold of *writing*, as the sacralising mark of the intellectual, has disappeared. And it has become possible to develop lateral connections across different forms of knowledge and from one focus of politicisation to another. Magistrates and psychiatrists, doctors and social workers, laboratory technicians and sociologists have become able to participate, both within their own fields and through mutual exchange and support, in a global process of politicisation of intellectuals. This process explains how, even as the writer tends to disappear as a figurehead, the university and the academic emerge, if not as principal elements, at least as 'exchangers', privileged points of intersection. If the universities and education have become politically ultrasensitive areas, this is no doubt the reason why. And what is called the crisis of the universities should not be interpreted as a loss of power, but on the contrary as a multiplication and re-inforcement of their power-effects as centres in a polymorphous ensemble of intellectuals who virtually all pass through and relate themselves to the academic system. The whole relentless theorisation of writing which we saw in the 1960s was doubtless only a swansong. Through it, the writer was fighting for the preservation of his political privilege; but the fact that it was precisely a matter of theory, that he needed scientific credentials, founded in linguistics, semiology, psychoanalysis, that this theory took its references from the direction of Saussure, or Chomsky, etc., and that it gave rise to such mediocre literary products, all this proves that the activity of the writer was no longer at the focus of things.

It seems to me that this figure of the 'specific' intellectual has emerged since the Second World War. Perhaps it was the atomic scientist (in a word, or rather a name: Oppenheimer) who acted as the point of transition between the universal and the specific intellectual. It's because he had a direct and localised relation to scientific knowledge and institutions that the atomic scientist could make his intervention; but, since the nuclear threat affected the whole human race and the fate of the world, his discourse could at the same time be the discourse of the universal. Under the rubric of this protest, which concerned the entire world, the atomic expert brought into play his specific position in the order of knowledge. And for the first time, I think, the intellectual was hounded by political powers, no longer on account of a general discourse which he conducted, but because of the knowledge at his disposal: it was at this level that he constituted a political threat. I am only speaking here of Western intellectuals. What happened in the Soviet Union is analogous with this on a number of points, but different on many others. There is certainly a whole study that needs to be made of scientific dissidence in the West and the socialist countries since 1945.

It is possible to suppose that the 'universal' intellectual, as he functioned in the nineteenth and early twentieth centuries was in fact derived from a quite specific historical figure: the man of justice, the man of law, who counterposes to power, despotism and the abuses and arrogance of wealth the universality of justice and the equity of an ideal law. The great political struggles of the eighteenth century were fought over law, right, the constitution, the just in reason and law, that which can and must apply universally. What we call today 'the intellectual' (I mean the intellectual in the political, not the sociological sense of the word, in other words the person who utilises his knowledge, his competence and his relation to truth in the field of political struggles) was, I think, an offspring of the jurist, or at any rate of the man who invoked the universality of a just law, if necessary against the legal professions themselves (Voltaire, in France, is the prototype of such intellectuals). The 'universal' intellectual derives from the jurist or notable, and finds his fullest manifestation in the writer, the bearer of values and significations in which all can recognise themselves. The 'specific' intellectual derives from quite another figure, not the jurist or notable, but the savant or expert. I said just now that it's with the atomic scientists that this latter figure comes to the forefront. In fact, it was preparing in the wings for some time before, and was even present on at least a corner of the stage from about the end of the nineteenth century. No doubt it's with Darwin or rather with the post-Darwinian evolutionists that this figure begins to appear clearly. The stormy relationship between evolutionism and the socialists, as well as the highly ambiguous effects of evolutionism (on sociology, criminology, psychiatry and eugenics, for example) mark the important moment when the savant begins to intervene in contemporary political struggles in the name of a 'local' scientific truth—however important the latter may be. Historically, Darwin represents this point of inflection in the history of the Western intellectual. (Zola is very significant from this point of view: he is the type of the 'universal' intellectual, bearer of law and militant of equity, but he ballasts his discourse with a whole invocation of nosology and evolutionism, which he believes to be scientific, grasps very poorly in any case, and whose political effects on his own discourse are very equivocal.) If one were to study this closely, one would have to follow how the physicists, at the turn of the century, re-entered the field of political debate. The debates between the theorists of socialism and the theorists of relativity are of capital importance in this history.

At all events, biology and physics were to a privileged degree the zones of formation of this new personage, the specific intellectual. The extension of technico-scientific structures in the economic and strategic domain was what gave him his real importance. The figure in which the functions and prestige of this new intellectual are concentrated is no longer that of the 'writer of genius', but that of the 'absolute savant', no longer he who bears the values of all, opposes the unjust sovereign or his ministers and makes his cry resound even beyond the grave. It is rather he who, along with a handful of others, has at his disposal, whether in the service of the State or against it, powers which can either benefit or irrevocably destroy life. He is no longer the rhapsodist of the eternal, but the strategist of life and death. Meanwhile we are at present experiencing the disappearance of the figure of the 'great writer.'

Now let's come back to more precise details. We accept, alongside the development of technico-scientific structures in contemporary society, the importance gained by the specific intellectual in recent decades, as well as the acceleration of this process since around 1960. Now the specific intellectual encounters certain obstacles and faces certain dangers. The danger of remaining at the level of conjunctural struggles, pressing demands restricted to particular sectors. The risk of letting himself be manipulated by the political parties or trade union apparatuses which control these local struggles. Above all, the risks of being unable to develop these struggles for lack of a global strategy or outside support; the risk too of not being followed, or only by very limited groups. In France we can see at the moment an example of this. The struggle around the prisons, the penal system and the police-judicial system, because it has developed 'in solitary', among social workers and ex-prisoners, has tended increasingly to separate itself from the forces which would have enabled it to grow. It has allowed itself to be penetrated by a whole naive, archaic ideology which makes the criminal at once into the innocent victim and the pure rebel—society's scapegoat—and the young wolf of future revolutions. This return to anarchist themes of the late nineteenth century was possible only because of a failure of integration of current strategies. And the result has been a deep split between this campaign with its monotonous, lyrical little chant, heard only among a few small groups, and the masses who have good reason not to accept it as valid political currency, but who also—thanks to the studiously cultivated fear of criminals—tolerate the maintenance, or rather the reinforcement, of the judicial and police apparatuses.

It seems to me that we are now at a point where the function of the specific intellectual needs to be reconsidered. Reconsidered but not abandoned, despite the nostalgia of some for the great 'universal' intellectuals and the desire for a new philosophy, a new world-view. Suffice it to consider the important results which have been achieved in psychiatry: they prove that these local, specific struggles haven't been a mistake and haven't led to a dead end. One may even say that the role of the specific intellectual must become more and more important in proportion to the political responsibilities which he is obliged willy-nilly to accept, as a nuclear scientist, computer expert, pharmacologist, etc. It would be a dangerous error to discount him politically in his specific relation to a local form of power, either on the grounds that this is a specialist matter which doesn't concern the masses (which is doubly wrong: they are already aware of it, and in any case implicated in it), or that the specific intellectual serves the interests of State or Capital (which is true, but at the same time shows the strategic position he occupies), or, again, on the grounds that he propagates a scientific ideology (which isn't always true, and is anyway certainly a secondary matter compared with the fundamental point: the effects proper to true discourses).

The important thing here, I believe, is that truth isn't outside power, or lacking in power: contrary to a myth whose history and functions would repay further study, truth isn't the reward of free spirits, the child of protracted solitude, nor the privilege of those who have succeeded in liberating themselves. Truth is a thing of this world: it is produced only by virtue of multiple forms of constraint. And it induces regular effects of power. Each society has its régime of truth, its 'general politics' of truth: that is, the types of discourse which it accepts and makes function as true; the mechanisms and instances which enable one to distinguish true and false statements, the means by which each is sanctioned; the techniques and procedures accorded value in the acquisition of truth; the status of those who are charged with saying what counts as true.

In societies like ours, the 'political economy' of truth is characterised by five important traits. 'Truth' is centred on the form of scientific discourse and the institutions which produce it; it is subject to constant economic and political incitement (the demand for truth, as much for economic production as for political power); it is the object, under diverse forms, of immense diffusion and consumption (circulating through apparatuses of education and information whose extent is relatively broad in the social body, not withstanding certain strict limitations); it is produced and transmitted under the control, dominant if not exclusive, of a few great political and economic apparatuses (university, army, writing, media); lastly, it is the issue of a whole political debate and social confrontation ('ideological' struggles).

It seems to me that what must now be taken into account in the intellectual is not the 'bearer of universal values'. Rather, it's the person occupying a specific position—but whose specificity is linked, in a society like ours, to the general functioning of an apparatus of truth. In other words, the intellectual has a three-fold specificity: that of his class position (whether as petty-bourgeois in the service of capitalism or 'organic' intellectual of the proletariat); that of his conditions of life and work, linked to his condition as an intellectual (his field of research, his place in a laboratory, the political and economic demands to which he submits or against which he rebels, in the university, the hospital, etc.); lastly, the specificity of the politics of truth in our societies. And it's with this last factor that his position can take on a general significance and that his local, specific struggle can have effects and implications which are not simply professional or sectoral. The intellectual can operate and struggle at the general level of that régime of truth which is so essential to the structure and functioning of our society. There is a battle 'for truth', or at least 'around truth'—it being understood once again that by truth I do not mean 'the ensemble of truths which are to be discovered and accepted', but rather 'the ensemble of rules according to which the true and the false are separated and specific effects of power attached to the true', it being understood also that it's not a matter of a battle 'on behalf' of the truth, but of a battle about the status of truth and the economic and political role it plays. It is necessary to think of the political problems of intellectuals not in terms of 'science' and 'ideology', but in terms of 'truth' and 'power'. And thus the question of the professionalisation of intellectuals and the division between intellectual and manual labour can be envisaged in a new way.

All this must seem very confused and uncertain. Uncertain indeed, and what I am saying here is above all to be taken as a hypothesis. In order for it to be a little less confused, however, I would like to put forward a few 'propositions'—not firm assertions, but simply suggestions to be further tested and evaluated.

'Truth' is to be understood as a system of ordered procedures for the production, regulation, distribution, circulation and operation of statements.

'Truth' is linked in a circular relation with systems of power which produce and sustain it, and to effects of power which it induces and which extend it. A 'régime' of truth.

This régime is not merely ideological or superstructural; it was a condition of the formation and development of capitalism. And it's this same régime which, subject to certain modifications, operates in the socialist countries (I leave open here the question of China, about which I know little).

The essential political problem for the intellectual is not to criticise the ideological contents supposedly linked to science, or to ensure that his own scientific practice is accompanied by a correct ideology, but that of ascertaining the possibility of constituting a new politics of truth. The problem is not changing people's consciousnesses—or what's in their heads—but the political, economic, institutional régime of the production of truth.

It's not a matter of emancipating truth from every system of power (which would be a chimera, for truth is already power) but of detaching the power of truth from the forms of hegemony, social, economic and cultural, within which it operates at the present time.

The political question, to sum up, is not error, illusion, alienated consciousness or ideology, it is truth itself. Hence the importance of Nietzsche.

JUDITH BUTLER

Contingent Foundations

The question of postmodernism is surely a question, for is there, after all, something called postmodernism? Is it an historical characterization, a certain kind of theoretical position, and what does it mean for a term that has described a certain aesthetic practice now to apply to social theory and to feminist social and political theory in particular? Who are these postmodernists? Is this a name that one takes on for oneself, or is it more often a name that one is called if and when one offers a critique of the subject, a discursive analysis, or questions the integrity or coherence of totalizing social descriptions?

I know the term from the way it is used, and it usually appears on my horizon embedded in the following critical formulations: "if discourse is all there is . . . ," or "if everything is a text . . . ," or "if the subject is dead . . . ," of "if real bodies do not exist . . . ." The sentence begins as a warning against an impending nihilism, for if the conjured content of these series of conditional clauses proves to be true, then, and there is always a then, some set of dangerous consequences will surely follow. So 'postmodernism' appears to be articulated in the form of a fearful conditional or sometimes in the form of paternalistic disdain toward that which is youthful and irrational. Against this postmodernism, there is an effort to shore up the primary premises, to establish in advance that any theory of politics requires a subject, needs from the start to presume its subject, the referentiality of language, the integrity of the institutional descriptions it provides. For politics is unthinkable without a foundation, without these premises. But do these claims seek to secure a contingent formation of politics that requires that these notions remain unproblematized features of its own definition? Is it the case that all politics, and feminist politics in particular, is unthinkable without these premises? Or is it rather that a specific version of politics is shown in its contingency once those premises are problematically thematized?

To claim that politics requires a stable subject is to claim that there can be no *political* opposition to that claim. Indeed, that claim implies that a critique of the subject cannot be a politically informed critique but, rather, an act which puts into jeopardy politics as his work, then can that quotation serve as an "example" of postmodernism, symptomatic of the whole?

But if I understand part of the project of postmodernism, it is to call into question the ways in which such "examples" and "paradigms" serve to subordinate and erase that which they seek to explain. For the "whole," the field of postmodernism in its supposed breadth, is effectively "produced" by the example which is made to stand as a symptom and exemplar of the whole; in effect, if in the example of Lyotard we think we have a representation of postmodernism, we have then forced a substitution of the example for the entire field, effecting a violent reduction of the field to the one piece of text the critic is willing to read, a piece which, conveniently, uses the term "postmodern."

In a sense, this gesture of conceptual mastery that groups together a set of positions under the postmodern, that makes the postmodern into an epoch or a synthetic whole, and that claims that the part can stand for this artificially constructed whole, enacts a certain self-congratulatory ruse of power. It is paradoxical, at best, that the act of conceptual mastery that effects this dismissive grouping of positions under the postmodern wants to ward off the peril of political authoritarianism. For the assumption is that some piece of the text is representational, that it stands for the phenomenon, and that the structure of "these" positions can be properly and economically discerned in the structure of the one. What authorizes such an assumption from the start? From the start we must believe that theories offer themselves in bundles or in organized totalities, and that historically a set of theories which are structurally similar emerge as the articulation of an historically specific condition of human reflection. This Hegelian trope, which continues through Adorno, assumes from the start that these theories can be substituted for one another because they variously symptomatize a common structural preoccupation. And yet, that presumption can no longer be made, for the Hegelian presumption that a synthesis is available from the start is precisely what has come under contest in various ways by some of the positions happily unified under the sign of postmodernism. One might argue that if, and to the extent that, the postmodern functions as such a unifying sign, then it is a decidedly "modern" sign, which is why there is some question whether one can debate for or against this postmodernism. To install the term as that which can be only affirmed or negated is to force it to occupy one position within a binary, and so to affirm a logic of noncontradication over and against some more generative scheme.

Perhaps the reason for this unification of positions is occasioned by the very unruliness of the field, by the way in which the differences among these positions cannot be rendered symptomatic, exemplary, or representative of each other and of some common structure called postmodernism. If postmodernism as a term has some force or meaning within social theory, or feminist social theory in particular, perhaps it can be found in the critical exercise that seeks to show how theory, how philosophy, is always implicated in power, and perhaps that is precisely what is symptomatically at work in the effort to domesticate and refuse a set of powerful criticisms under the rubric of postmodernism. That the philosophical apparatus in its various conceptual refinements is always engaged in exercising power is not a new insight, but then again the postmodern ought not to be confused with the new; after all, the pursuit of the "new" is the preoccupation of high modernism; if anything, the postmodern casts doubt upon the possibility of a "new" that is not in some way already implicated in the "old".

But the point articulated forcefully by some recent critics of normative political philosophy is that the recourse to a position—hypothetical, counterfactual, or imaginary—that places itself beyond the play of power, and which seeks to establish the metapolitical basis for a negotiation of power relations, is perhaps the most insidious ruse of power. That this position beyond power lays claim to its legitimacy through recourse to a prior and implicitly universal agreement does not in any way circumvent the charge, for what rationalist project will designate in advance what courts as agreement? What form of insidious cultural imperialism here legislates itself under the sign of the universal?[4]

I don't know about the term "postmodern," but if there is a point, and a fine point, to what I perhaps better understand as poststructuralism, it is that power pervades the very conceptual apparatus that seeks to negotiate its terms, including the subject position of the critic; and further, that this implication of the terms of criticism in the field of power is not the advent of a nihilistic relativism incapable of furnishing norms, but, rather, the very precondition of a politically engaged critique. To establish a set of norms that are beyond power or force is itself a powerful and forceful conceptual practice that sublimates, disguises and extends its own power play through recourse to tropes of normative universality. And the point is not to do away with foundations, or even to champion a position that goes under the name of antifoundationalism. Both of those positions belong together as different versions of foundationalism and the skeptical problematic it engenders. Rather, the task is to interrogate what the theoretical move that establishes foundations *authorizes,* and what precisely it excludes or forecloses.

It seems that theory posits foundations incessantly, and forms implicit metaphysical commitments as a matter of course, even when it seeks to guard against it; foundations function as the unquestioned and the unquestionable within any theory. And yet, are these "foundations," that is, those premises that function as authorizing grounds, are they themselves not constituted through exclusions which, taken into account, expose the foundational premises as a contingent and contestable presumption. Even when we claim that there is some implied universal basis for a given foundation, that implication and that universality simply constitute a new dimension of unquestionability.

How is it that we might ground a theory or politics in a speech situation or subject position which is "universal," when the very category of the universal has only begun to be exposed for its own highly ethnocentric biases? How many "universalities" are there[5] and to what extent is cultural conflict understandable as the clashing of a set of presumed and intransigent "universalities," a conflict which cannot be negotiated through recourse to a culturally imperialist notion of the "universal" or, rather, which will only be solved through such recourse at the cost of violence? We have, I think, witnessed the conceptual and material violence of this practice in the United States's war against Iraq, in which the Arab "other" is understood to be radically "outside" the universal structures of reason and democracy and, hence, calls to be brought forcibly within. Significantly, the U.S. had to abrogate the democratic principles of political sovereignty and free speech, among others, to effect this forcible return of Iraq to the "democratic" fold, and this violent move reveals, among other things, that such notions of universality are installed through the abrogation of the very universal principles to be implemented. Within the political context of contemporary postcoloniality more generally, it is perhaps especially urgent to underscore the very category of the "universal" as a site of insistent contest and resignification.[6] Given the contested character of the term, to assume from the start a procedural or substantive notion of the universal is of necessity to impose a culturally hegemonic notion on the social field. To herald that notion then as the philosophical instrument that will negotiate between conflicts of power is precisely to safeguard and reproduce a position of hegemonic power by installing it in the metapolitical site of ultimate normativity.

It may at first seem that I am simply calling for a more concrete and internally diverse "universality," a more synthetic and inclusive notion of the universal, and in that way committed to the very foundational notion that I seek to undermine. But my task is, I think, significantly different from that which would articulate a comprehensive universality. In the first place, such a totalizing notion could only be achieved at the cost of producing new and further exclusions. The term "universality" would have to be left permanently open, permanently contested, permanently contingent, in order not to foreclose in advance future claims for inclusion. Indeed, from my position and from any historically constrained perspective, any totalizing concept of the universal will shut down rather than authorize the unanticipated and unanticipatable claims that will be made under the sign of "the universal." In this sense, I am not doing away with the category, but trying to relieve the category of its foundationalist weight in order to render it as a site of permanent political contest.

A social theory committed to democratic contestation within a postcolonial horizon needs to find a way to bring into question the foundations it is compelled to lay down. It is this movement of interrogating that ruse of authority that seeks to close itself off from contest that is, in my view, at the heart of any radical political project. Inasmuch as poststructuralism offers a mode of critique that effects this contestation of the foundationalist move, it can be used as a part of such a radical agenda. Note that I have said, "it can be used": I think there are no necessary political consequences for such a theory, but only a possible political deployment.

If one of the points associated with postmodernism is that the epistemological point of departure in philosophy is inadequate, then it ought not to be a question of subjects who claim to know and theorize under the sign of the postmodern pitted against other subjects who claim to know and theorize under the sign of the modern. Indeed, it is that very way of framing debate that is being contested by the suggestion that the position articulated by the subject is always in some way constituted by what must be displaced for that position to take hold, and that the subject who theorizes is constituted as a "theorizing subject" by a set of exclusionary and selective procedures. For, indeed, who is it that gets constituted as the feminist theorist whose framing of the debate will get publicity? Is it not always the case that power operates in advance, in the very procedures that establish who will be the subject who speaks in the name of feminism, and to whom? And is it not also clear that a process of subjection is presupposed in the subjectivating process that produces before you one speaking subject of feminist debate? What speaks when "I" speak to you? What are the institutional histories of subjection and subjectivation that "position" me here now? If there is something called "Butler's position," is this one that I devise, publish, and defend, that belongs to me as a kind of academic property? Or is there a grammar of the subject that merely encourages us to position me as the proprietor of those theories?

Indeed, how is it that a position becomes a position, for clearly not every utterance qualifies as such. It is clearly a matter of a certain authorizing power, and that clearly does not emanate from the position itself. My position is mine to the extent that "I"—and I do not shirk from the pronoun—replay and resignify the theoretical positions that have constituted me, working the possibilities of their convergence, and trying to take account of the possibilities that they systematically exclude. But it is clearly not the case that "I" preside over the positions that have constituted me, shuffling through them instrumentally, casting some aside, incorporating others, although some of my activity may take that form. The "I" who would select between them is always already constituted by them. The "I" is the transfer point of that replay, but it is simply not a strong enough claim to say that the "I" is situated; the "I," this "I," is *constituted* by these positions, and these "positions" are not merely theoretical products, but fully embedded organizing principles of material practices and institutional arrangements, those matrices of power and discourse that produce me as a viable "subject." Indeed, this "I" would not be a thinking, speaking "I" if it were not for the very positions that I oppose, for those positions, the ones that claim that the subject must be given in advance, that discourse is an instrument or reflection of that subject, are already part of what constitutes me.

No subject is its own point of departure; and the fantasy that it is one can only disavow its constitutive relations by recasting them as the domain of a countervailing externality. Indeed, one might consider Luce Irigaray's claim that the subject, understood as a fantasy of autogenesis, is always already masculine. Psychoanalytically, that version of the subject is constituted through a kind of disavowal or through the primary repression of its dependency on the maternal. And to become a subject on this model is surely not a feminist goal.

The critique of the subject is not a negation or repudiation of the subject, but, rather, a way of interrogating its construction as a pregiven or foundationalist premise. At the outset of the war against Iraq, we almost all saw strategists who placed before us maps of the Middle East, objects of analysis and targets of instrumental military action. Retired and active generals were called up by the networks to stand in for the generals on the field whose intentions would be invariably realized in the destruction of various Iraqi military bases. The various affirmations of the early success of these operations were delivered with great enthusiasm, and it seemed that this hitting of the goal, this apparently seamless realization of intention through an instrumental action without much resistance or hindrance was the occasion, not merely to destroy Iraqi military installations, but also to champion a masculinized Western subject whose will immediately translates into a deed, whose utterance or order materializes in an action which would destroy the very possibility of a reverse strike, and whose obliterating power at once confirms the impenetrable contours of its own subjecthood. . . .

In a sense, the subject is constituted through an exclusion and differentiation, perhaps a repression, that is subsequently concealed, covered over, by the effect of autonomy. In this sense, autonomy is the logical consequence of a disavowed dependency, which is to say that the autonomous subject can maintain the illusion of its autonomy insofar as it covers over the break out of which it is constituted. This dependency and this break are already social relations, ones which precede and condition the formation of the subject. As a result, this is not a relation in which the subject finds itself, as one of the relations that forms its situation. The subject is constructed through acts of differentiation that distinguish the subject from its constitutive outside, a domain of abjected alterity conventionally associated with the feminine, but clearly not exclusively. Precisely in this recent war we saw "the Arab" figured as the abjected other as well as a site of homophobic fantasy made clear in the abundance of bad jokes grounded in the linguistic sliding from Saddam to Sodom.

There is no ontologically intact reflexivity to the subject which is then placed within a cultural context; that cultural context, as it were, is already there as the disarticulated process of that subject's production, one that is concealed by the frame that would situate a ready-made subject in an external web of cultural relations.

We may be tempted to think that to assume the subject in advance is necessary in order to safeguard the *agency* of the subject. But to claim that the subject is constituted is not to claim that it is determined; on the contrary, the constituted character of the subject is the very precondition of its agency. For what is it that enables a purposive and significant reconfiguration of cultural and political relations, if not a relation that can be turned against itself, reworked, resisted? Do we need to assume theoretically from the start a subject with agency *before* we can articulate the terms of a significant social and political task of transformation, resistance, radical democratization? If we do not offer in advance the theoretical guarantee of that agent, are we doomed to give up transformation and meaningful political practice? My suggestion is that agency belongs to a way of thinking about persons as instrumental actors who confront an external political field. But if we agree that politics and power exist already at the level at which the subject and its agency are articulated and made possible, then agency can be *presumed* only at the cost of refusing to inquire into its construction. Consider that "agency" has no formal existence or, if it does, it has no bearing on the question at hand. In a sense, the epistemological model that offers us a pre-given subject or agent is one that refuses to acknowledge that *agency is always and only a political prerogative*. As such, it seems crucial to question the conditions of its possibility, not to take it for granted as an a priori guarantee. We need instead to ask, what possibilities of mobilization are produced on the basis of existing configurations of discourse and power? Where are the possibilities of reworking that very matrix of power by which we are constituted, of reconstituting the legacy of that constitution, and of working against each other those processes of regulation that can destabilize existing power regimes? For if the subject is constituted by power, that power does not cease at the moment the subject is constituted, for that subject is never fully constituted, but is subjected and produced time and again. That subject is neither a ground nor a product, but the permanent possibility of a certain resignifying process, one which gets detoured and stalled through other mechanisms of power, but which is power's own possibility of being reworked. It is not enough to say that the subject is invariably engaged in a political field; that phenomenological phrasing misses the point that the subject is an accomplishment regulated and produced in advance. And is as such fully political; indeed, perhaps *most* political at the point in which it is claimed to be prior to politics itself. To perform this kind of Foucaultian critique of the subject is not to do away with the subject or pronounce its death, but merely to claim that certain versions of the subject are politically insidious.

For the subject to be a pregiven point of departure for politics is to defer the question of the political construction and regulation of the subject itself; for it is important to remember that subjects are constituted through exclusion, that is, through the creation of a domain of deauthorized subjects, presubjects, figures of abjection, populations erased from view. This becomes clear, for instance, within the law when certain qualifications must first be met in order to be, quite literally, a claimant in sex discrimination or rape cases. Here it becomes quite urgent to ask, who qualifies as a "who," what systematic structures of disempowerment make it impossible for certain injured parties to invoke the "I" effectively within a court of law? Or less overtly, in a social theory like Albert Memmi's *The Colonizer and the Colonized*, an otherwise compelling call for radical enfranchisement, the category of women falls into neither category, the oppressor or the oppressed.[7] How do we theorize the exclusion of women from the category of the oppressed? Here the construction of subject-positions works to exclude women from the description of oppression, and this constitutes a different kind of oppression, one that is effected by the very *erasure* that grounds the articulation of the emancipatory subject. As Joan Scott makes clear in *Gender and the Politics of History*, once it is understood that subjects are formed through exclusionary operations, it becomes politically necessary to trace the operations of that construction and erasure.[8]

The above sketches in part a Foucaultian reinscription of the subject, an effort to resignify the subject as a site of resignification. As a result, it is not a "bidding farewell" to the subject per se, but, rather, a call to rework that notion outside the terms of an epistemological given. But perhaps Foucault is not really postmodern; after all, his is an analytics of *modern* power. There is, of course, talk about the death of the subject, but *which* subject is that? And what is the status of the utterance that announces its passing? What speaks now that the subject is dead? That there is a speaking seems clear, for how else could the utterance be heard? So clearly, the death of that subject is not the end of agency, of speech, or of political debate. There is the refrain that, just now, when women are beginning to assume the place of subjects, postmodern positions come along to announce that the subject is dead (there is a difference between positions of poststructuralism which claim that the subject *never* existed, and postmodern positions which claim that the subject *once* had integrity, but no longer does). Some see this as a conspiracy against women and other disenfranchised groups who are now only beginning to speak on their own behalf. But what precisely is meant by this, and how do we account for the very strong criticisms of the subject as an instrument of Western imperialist hegemony theorized by Gloria Anzaldua,[9] Gayatri Spivak[10] and various theorists of postcoloniality? Surely there is a caution offered here, that in the very struggle toward enfranchisement and democratization, we might adopt the very models of domination by which we were oppressed, not realizing that one way that domination works is through the regulation and production of subjects. Through what exclusions has the feminist subject been constructed, and how do those excluded domains return to haunt the "integrity" and "unity" of the feminist "we"? And how is it that the very category, the subject, the "we," that is supposed to be presumed for the purpose of solidarity, produces the very factionalization it is supposed to quell? Do women want to become subjects on the model which requires and produces an anterior region of abjection, or must feminism become a process which is self-critical about the processes that produce and destabilize identity categories? To take the construction of the subject as a political problematic is not the same as doing away with the subject; to deconstruct the subject is not to negate or throw away the concept; on the contrary, deconstruction implies only that we suspend all commitments to that to which the term, "the subject," refers, and that we consider the linguistic functions it serves in the consolidation and concealment of authority. To deconstruct is not to negate or to dismiss, but to call into question and, perhaps most importantly, to open up a term, like the subject, to a reusage or redeployment that previously has not been authorized.

Within feminism, it seems as if there is some political necessity to speak as and for *women,* and I would not contest that necessity. Surely, that is the way in which representational politics operates, and in this country, lobbying efforts are virtually impossible without recourse to identity politics. So we agree that demonstrations and legislative efforts and radical movements need to make claims in the name of women.

But this necessity needs to be reconciled with another. The minute that the category of women is invoked as *describing* the constituency for which feminism speaks, an internal debate invariably begins over what the descriptive content of that term will be. There are those who claim that there is an ontological specificity to women as childbearers that forms the basis of a specific legal and political interest in representation, and then there are others who understand maternity to be a social relation that is, under current social circumstances, the specific and cross-cultural situation of women. And there are those who seek recourse to Gilligan and others to establish a feminine specificity that makes itself clear in women's communities or ways of knowing. But every time that specificity is articulated, there is resistance and factionalization within the very constituency that is supposed to be *unified* by the articulation of its common element. In the early 1980s, the feminist "we" rightly came under attack by women of color who claimed that the "we" was invariably white, and that that "we" that was meant to solidify the movement was the very source of a painful factionalization. The effort to characterize a feminine specificity through recourse to maternity, whether biological or social, produced a similar factionalization and even a disavowal of feminism althogether. For surely all women are not mothers; some cannot be, some are too young or too old to be, some choose not to be, and for some who are mothers, that is not necessarily the rallying point of their politicization in feminism.

I would argue that any effort to give universal or specific content to the category of women, presuming that that guarantee of solidarity is required *in advance,* will necessarily produce factionalization, and that "identity" as a point of departure can never hold as the solidifying ground of a feminist political movement. Identity categories are never merely descriptive, but always normative, and as such, exclusionary. This is not to say that the term "women" ought not to be used, or that we ought to announce the death of the category. On the contrary, if feminism presupposes that "women" designates an undesignatable field of differences, one that cannot be totalized or summarized by a descriptive identity category, then the very term becomes a site of permanent openness and resignifiability. I would argue that the rifts among women over the content of the term ought to be safeguarded and prized, indeed, that this constant rifting ought to be affirmed as the ungrounded ground of feminist theory. To deconstruct the subject of feminism is not, then, to censure its usage, but, on the contrary, to release the term into a future of multiple significations, to emancipate it from the maternal or racialist ontologies to which it has been restricted, and to give it play as a site where unanticipated meanings might come to bear.

Paradoxically, it may be that only through releasing the category of women from a fixed referent that something like 'agency' becomes possible. For if the term permits of a resignification, if its referent is not fixed, then possibilities for new configurations of the term become possible. In a sense, what women signify has been taken for granted for too long, and what has been fixed as the 'referent' of the term has been "fixed," normalized, immobilized, paralyzed in positions of subordination. In effect, the signified has been conflated with the referent, whereby a set of meanings have been taken to inhere in the real nature of women themselves. To recast the referent as the signified, and to authorize or safeguard the category of women as a site of possible resignifications is to expand the possibilities of what it means to be a woman and in this sense to condition and enable an enhanced sense of agency.

One might well ask: but doesn't there have to be a set of norms that discriminate between those descriptions that ought to adhere to the category of women and those that do not? The only answer to that question is a counter-question: who would set those norms, and what contestations would they produce? To establish a normative foundation for settling the question of what ought properly to be included in the description of women would be only and always to produce a new site of political contest. That foundation would settle nothing, but would of its own necessity founder on its own authoritarian ruse. This is not to say that there is no foundation, but rather, that wherever there is one, there will also be a foundering, a contestation. That such foundations exist only to be put into question is, as it were, the permanent risk of the process of democratization. To refuse that contest is to sacrifice the radical democratic impetus of feminist politics. That the category is unconstrained, even that it comes to serve antifeminist purposes, will be part of the risk of this procedure. But this is a risk that is produced by the very foundationlism that seeks to safeguard feminism against it. In a sense, this risk is the foundation, and hence is not, of any feminist practice.

NOTES

1. Here it is worth noting that in some recent political theory, notably in the writings of Ernesto Laclau and Chantal Mouffe (*Hegemony and Socialist Strategy*, London: Verso, 1986) and William Connolly (*Political Theory and Modernity,* Madison: University of Wisconsin Press, 1988) as well as Jean-Luc Nancy and Philippe Lacoue-Labarthe ("Le retrait du politique" in *Le Retrait due politique*, Paris: Editions galilée, 1983), there is an insistence that the political field is of necessity constructed through the production of a

determining exterior. In other words, the very domain of politics constitutes itself through the production and naturalization of the "pre-" or "non" political. In Derridean terms, this is the production of a "constitutive outside." Here I would like to suggest a distinction between the constitution of a political field that produces *and naturalizes* that constitutive outside and a political field that produces and *renders contingent* the specific parameters of that constitutive outside. Although I do not think that the differential relations through which the political field itself is constituted can ever be fully elaborated (precisely because the status of that elaboration would have to be elaborated as well *ad infinitum*), I do find useful William Connolly's notion of constitutive antagonisms, a notion that finds a parallel expression in Laclau and Mouffe, which suggests a form of political struggle which puts the parameters of the political itself into question. This is especially important for feminist concerns insofar as the grounds of politics ('universality,' 'equality,' the subject of rights) have been constructed through unmarked racial and gender exclusions and by a conflation of politics with public life that renders the private (reproduction, domains of "feminity") prepolitical.

2. Julia Kristeva, *Black Sun: Depression and Melancholy* (New York: Columbia University Press, 1989), pp. 258–59.

3. The conflation of Lyotard with the array of thinkers summarily positioned under the rubric of "postmodernism" is performed by the title and essay by Seyla Benhabib: "Epistemologies of Postmodernism: A Rejoinder to Jean-Françcois Lyotard," in *Feminism/Postmodernism*, edited by Linda Nicholson (New York: Routledge, 1989).

4. This is abundantly clear in feminist criticisms of Jürgen Habermas as well as Catharine MacKinnon. See Iris Young. "Impartiality and the Civil Public: Some Implications of Feminist Criticisms of Modern Political Theory," in Seyla Benhabib and Drucilla Cornell, eds., *Feminism as Critique: Essays on the Politics of Gender in Late-Capitalism* (Oxford-Basil Blackwell, 1987); Nancy Fraser, *Unruly Practices: Power and Gender in Contemporary Social Theory* (Minneapolis: University of Minnesota Press, 1989), especially "What's Critical about Critical Theory: The Case of Habermas and Gender." Wendy Brown, "Razing Consciousness," *The Nation*, 250:2, January 8/15m. 1990.

5. See Ashis Nandy on the notion of alternative universalities in the preface to *The Intimate Enemy: Loss and Recovery of Self under Colonialism* (New Delhi: Oxford University Press, 1983).

6. Homi Bhabha's notion of "hybridity" is important to consider in this context.

7. "At the height of the revolt," Memmi writes, "the colonized still bears the traces and lessons of prolonged cohabitation (just as the smile or movements of a wife, even during divorce proceedings, remind one strangely of those of her husband)." Here Memmi sets up an analogy which presumes that colonizer and colonized exist in a parallel and separate relation to the divorcing husband and wife. The analogy simultaneously and paradoxically suggests the feminization of the colonized, where the colonized is presumed to be the subject of men, and the exclusion of the women from the category of the colonized subject. Albert Memmi, *The Colonizer and the Colonized* (Boston: Beacon Press, 1965), p. 129.

8. Joan W. Scott, *Gender and the Politics of History*. (New York: Columbia University Press, 1988), introduction.

9. Gloria Anzaldua, *Borderlands/La Frontera* (San Francisco: Spinsters Ink, 1988).

10. Gayatri Spivak, "Can the Subaltern Speak?" in *Marxism and the Interpretation of Culture,* eds. Nelson and Grossberg (Chicago: University of Illinois Press, 1988).

PostColonial
Political Theory

Eurocentrism creates the world in its image. It presents itself as universalist, but it is in fact particular. Edward W. Said makes this clear in the introduction to his *Orientalism* when he writes that neither the Orient nor the Occident is simply "there." The Orient was, according to Said, "orientalized" in the western popular media and its academic presses. It has become an idea through which Western cultural and political hegemony legitimate themselves.

Eurocentrism calls upon other continents to imitate the European model of development. But this model is precisely what Mahatma Gandhi calls into question with his religious ethic of nonviolence and sacrifice. Violence is seen as a Western import insofar as Gandhi considers nonviolence "the root of Hinduism." Upon its acceptance, the dignity of the colonized and a new form of spiritual freedom present themselves.

But this is not the view of Frantz Fanon in his famous chapter "Concerning Violence," from *The Wretched of the Earth*. Fanon sees decolonization as pitting two incompatible forces and two mutually exclusive worldviews against one another. It calls for replacing one "species" of man with another. Violence alone is capable of obliterating the settler. It assumes a cathartic quality for the native, and in this way violence serves to bring about the "new man" even as it is brought about by him.

The "new man" is intertwined with the idea of revolution. A genuinely radical social transformation not only transforms "objective conditions," but liberates the masses from the reactionary habits and sentiments of the past. A better world lies on the horizon devoid of the consumerism and individualism associated with advanced industrial society. The new revolutionary societies must overcome the commodity form and the old divisions generated by imperialism with new forms of utopian solidarity and commitment to the future. Indeed, such was the vision of the Cuban Revolution painted by the romantic figure of Che Guevara in his essay "Building the New Man."

EDWARD W. SAID

Introduction to *Orientalism*

I have begun with the assumption that the Orient is not an inert fact of nature. It is not merely *there*, just as the Occident itself is not just *there* either. We must take seriously Vico's great observation that men make their own history, that what they can know is what they have made, and extend it to geography: as both geographical and cultural entities—to say nothing of historical entities—such locales, regions, geographical sectors as "Orient" and "Occident" are man-made. Therefore as much as the West itself, the Orient is an idea that has a history and a tradition of thought, imagery, and vocabulary that have given it reality and presence in and for the West. The two geographical entities thus support and to an extent reflect each other.

Having said that, one must go on to state a number of reasonable qualifications. In the first place, it would be wrong to conclude that the Orient was *essentially* an idea, or a creation with no corresponding reality. When Disraeli said in his novel *Tancred* that the East was a career, he meant that to be interested in the East was something bright young Westerners would find to be an all-consuming passion; he should not be interpreted as saying that the East was *only* a career for Westerners. There were—and are—cultures and nations whose location is in the East, and their lives, histories, and customs have a brute reality obviously greater than anything that could be said about them in the West. About that fact this study of Orientalism has very little to contribute, except to acknowledge it tacitly. But the phenomenon of Orientalism as I study it here deals principally, not with a correspondence between Orientalism and Orient, but with the internal consistency of Orientalism and its ideas about the Orient (the East as career) despite or beyond correspondence, or lack thereof, with a "real" Orient. My point is that Disraeli's statement about the East refers mainly to that created consistency, that regular constellation of ideas as the pre-eminent thing about the Orient, and not to its mere being, as Wallace Stevens's phrase has it.

A second qualification is that ideas, cultures, and histories cannot seriously be understood or studied without their force, or more precisely their configurations of power, also being studied. To believe that the Orient was created—or, as I call it, "Orientalized"—and to believe that such things happen simply as a necessity of the imagination, is to be disingenuous. The relationship between Occident and Orient is a relationship of power, of domination, of varying degrees of a complex hegemony, and is quite accurately indicated in the title of K. M. Panikkar's classic *Asia and Western Dominance*. The Orient was Orientalized not only because it was discovered to be "Oriental" in all those ways considered common-place by an average nineteenth-century European, but also because it *could be*—that is, submitted to being—*made* Oriental. There is very little consent to be found, for example, in the fact that Flaubert's encounter with an Egyptian courtesan produced a widely influential model of the Oriental woman; she never spoke of herself, she never represented her emotions, presence, or history. *He* spoke for and represented her. He was foreign, comparatively wealthy, male, and these were historical facts of domination that allowed him not only to possess Kuchuk Hanem physically but to speak for her and tell his readers in what way she was "typically Oriental." My argument is that Flaubert's situation of strength in relation to Kuchuk Hanem was not an isolated instance. It fairly stands for the pattern of relative strength between East and West, and the discourse about the Orient that it enabled.

This brings us to a third qualification. One ought never to assume that the structure of Orientalism is nothing more than a structure of lies or of myths which, were the truth about them to be told, would simply blow away. I myself believe that Orientalism is more particularly valuable as a sign of European-Atlantic power over the Orient than it is as a veridic discourse about the Orient (which is what, in its academic or scholarly form, it claims to be). Nevertheless, what we must respect and try to grasp is the sheer knitted-together strength of Orientalist discourse, its very close ties to the enabling socio-economic and political institutions, and its redoubtable durability. After all, any system of ideas that can remain unchanged as teachable wisdom (in academies, books, congresses, universities, foreign-service institutes) from the period of Ernest Renan in the late 1840s until the present in the United States must be something more formidable than a mere collection of lies. Orientalism, therefore, is not an airy European fantasy about the Orient, but a created body of theory and practice in which, for many generations, there has been a considerable material investment. Continued investment made Orientalism, as a system of knowledge about the Orient, an accepted grid for filtering through the Orient into Western consciousness, just as that same investment multiplied—indeed, made truly productive—the statements proliferating out from Orientalism into the general culture.

Gramsci has made the useful analytic distinction between civil and political society in which the former is made up of voluntary (or at least rational and noncoercive) affiliations like schools, families, and unions, the latter of state institutions (the army, the police, the central bureaucracy) whose role in the polity is direct domination. Culture, of course, is to be found operating within civil society, where the influence of ideas, of institutions, and of other persons works not through domination but by what Gramsci calls consent. In any society not totalitarian, then, certain cultural forms predominate over others, just as certain ideas are more influential than others; the form of this cultural leadership is what Gramsci has identified as *hegemony*, an indispensable concept for any understanding of cultural life in the industrial West. It is hegemony, or rather the result of cultural hegemony at work, that gives Orientalism the durability and the strength I have been speaking about so far. Orientalism is never far from what Denys Hay has called the idea of Europe, a collective notion identifying "us" Europeans as against all "those" non-Europeans, and indeed it can be argued that the major component in European culture is precisely what made that culture hegemonic both in and outside Europe: the idea of European identity as a superior one in comparison with all the non-European peoples and cultures. There is in addition the hegemony of European ideas about the Orient, themselves reiterating European superiority over Oriental backwardness, usually overriding the possibility that a more independent, or more skeptical, thinker might have had different views on the matter.

In a quite constant way, Orientalism depends for its strategy on this flexible *positional* superiority, which puts the Westerner in a whole series of possible relationships with the Orient without ever losing him the relative upper hand. And why should it have been otherwise, especially during the period of extraordinary European ascendancy from the late Renaissance to the present? The scientist, the scholar, the missionary, the trader, or the soldier was in, or thought about, the Orient because he *could be there*, or could think about it, with very little resistance on the Orient's part. Under the general heading of knowledge of the Orient, and within the umbrella of Western hegemony over the Orient during the period from the end of the eighteenth century, there emerged a complex Orient suitable for study in the academy, for display in the museum, for reconstruction in the colonial office, for theoretical illustration in anthorpological, biological, linguistic, racial, and historical theses about mankind and the universe, for instances of economic and sociological theories of development, revolution, cultural personality, national or religious character. Additionally, the imaginative examination of things Oriental was based more or less exclusively upon a sovereign Western consciousness out of whose unchallenged centrality an Oriental world emerged, first according to general ideas about who or what was an Oriental, then according to a detailed logic governed not simply by empirical reality but by a battery of desires, repressions, investments, and projections. If we can point to great Orientalist works of genuine scholarship like Silvestre de Sacy's *Chrestomathie arabe* or Edward William Lane's *Account of the Manners and Customs of the Modern Egyptians*, we need also to note that Renan's and Gobineau's racial ideas came out of the same impulse, as did a great many Victorian pornographic novels (see the analysis by Steven Marcus of "The Lustful Turk").

And yet, one must repeatedly ask oneself whether what matters in Orientalism is the general group of ideas overriding the mass of material—about which who could deny that they were shot through with doctrines of European superiority, various kinds of racism, imperialism, and the like, dogmatic views of "the Oriental" as a kind of ideal and unchanging abstraction?—or the much more varied work produced by almost uncountable individual writers, whom one would take up as individual instances of authors dealing with the Orient. In a sense the two alternatives, general and particular, are really two perspectives on the same material: in both instances one would have to deal with pioneers in the field like William Jones, with great artists like Nerval or Flaubert. And why would it not be possible to employ both perspectives together, or one after the other? Isn't there an obvious danger of distortion (of precisely the kind that academic Orientalism has always been prone to) if either too general or too specific a level of description is maintained systematically?

My two fears are distortion and inaccuracy, or rather the kind of inaccuracy produced by too dogmatic a generality and too positivistic a localized focus. In trying to deal with these problems I have tried to deal with three main aspects of my own contemporary reality that seem to me to point the way out of the methodological or perspectival difficulties I have been discussing, difficulties that might force one, in the first instance, into writing a coarse polemic on so unacceptably general a level of description as not to be worth the effort, or in the second instance, into writing so detailed and atomistic a series of analyses as to lose all track of the general lines of force informing the field, giving it its special cogency. How then to recognize individually and to reconcile it with its intelligent, and by no means passive or merely dictatorial, general and hegemonic context?

MOHANDAS K. GANDHI

The Doctrine of the Sword

In this age of the rule of brute force, it is almost impossible for any one to believe that any one else could possibly reject the law of the final supremacy of brute force. And so I receive anonymous letters advising me that I must not interfere with the progress of non-co-operation even though popular violence may break out. Others come to me and, assuming that secretly I must be plotting violence, inquire when the happy moment for declaring open violence will arrive. They assure me that the English will never yield to anything but violence secret or open. Yet others, I am informed, believe that I am the most rascally person living in India because I never give out my real intention, and that they have not a shadow of doubt that I believe in violence just as much as most people do.

Such being the hold that the doctrine of the sword has on the majority of mankind, and as success of non-co-operation depends principally on absence of violence during its pendency, and as my views in this matter affect the conduct of a large number of people, I am anxious to state them as clearly as possible.

I do believe that where there is only a choice between cowardice and violence I would advise violence. Thus when my eldest son asked me what he should have done, had he been present when I was almost fatally assaulted in 1908, whether he should have run away and seen me killed or whether he should have used his physical force which he could and wanted to use, and defended me, I told him that it was his duty to defend me even by using violence. Hence it was that I took part in the Boer War, the so-called Zulu rebellion and the late War. Hence also do I advocate training in arms for those who believe in the method of violence. I would rather have India resort to arms in order to defend her honour than that she should in a cowardly manner become or remain a helpless witness to her own dishonour.

But I believe that non-violence is infinitely superior to violence, forgiveness is more manly than punishment. (Forgiveness adorns a soldier.) But abstinence is forgiveness only when there is the power to punish; it is meaningless when it pretends to proceed from a helpless creature. A mouse hardly forgives a cat when it allows itself to be torn to pieces by her. I therefore appreciate the sentiment of those who cry out for the condign punishment of General Dyer and his ilk. They would tear him to pieces if they could. But I do not believe India to be helpless. I do not believe myself to be a helpless creature. Only I want to use India's and my strength for a better purpose.

Let me not be misunderstood. Strength does not come from physical capacity. It comes from an indomitable will. An average Zulu is any way more than a match for an average Englishman in bodily capacity. But he flees from an English boy, because he fears the boy's revolver or those who will use it for him. He fears death and is nerveless in spite of his burly figure. We in India may in a moment realize that one hundred thousand English-men need not frighten three hundred million human beings. A definite forgiveness would therefore mean a definite recognition of our strength. With enlightened forgiveness must come a mighty wave of strength in us, which would make it impossible for a Dyer and a Frank Johnson to heap affront upon India's devoted head. It matters little to me that for the moment I do not drive my point home. We feel too downtrodden not to be angry and revengeful. But I must not refrain from saying that India can gain more by waiving the right of punishment. We have better work to do, a better mission to deliver to the world.

I am not a visionary. I claim to be a practical idealist. The religion of non-violence is not meant merely for *rishis* and saints. It is meant for the common people as well. Non-violence is the law of our species as violence is the law of the brute. The spirit lies dormant in the brute and he knows no law but that of physical might. The dignity of man requires obedience to a higher law—to the strength of the spirit.

I have therefore ventured to place before India the ancient law of self-sacrifice. For Satyagraha and its offshoots, non-co-operation and civil resistance are nothing but new names for the law of suffering. The *rishis,* who discovered the law of non-violence in the midst of violence, were greater geniuses than Newton. They were themselves greater war-riors than Wellington. Having themselves known the use of arms, they realized their use-lessness and taught a weary world that its salvation lay not through violence but through non-violence.

Non-violence in its dynamic condition means conscious suffering. It does not mean meek submission to the will of the evil-doer, but it means the pitting of one's whole soul against the will of the tyrant. Working under this law of our being, it is possible for a sin-gle individual to defy the whole might of an unjust empire, to save his honour, his reli-gion, his soul and lay the foundation for that empire's fall or its regeneration.

And so I am not pleading for India to practise non-violence because she is weak. I want her to practise non-violence being conscious of her strength and power. No training in arms is required for realization of her strength. We seem to need it because we seem to think that we are but a lump of flesh. I want India to recognize that she has a soul that cannot perish and that can rise triumphant above every physical weakness and defy the physical combination of a whole world. What is the meaning of Rama, a mere human being, with his host of monkeys, pitting himself against the insolent strength of ten-headed Ravana surrounded in supposed safety by the raging waters on all sides of Lanka? Does it not mean the conquest of physical might by spiritual strength? However, being a practical man, I do not wait till India recognizes the practicability of the spiritual life in the political world. India considers herself to be powerless and paralyzed before the machine guns, the tanks and the aeroplanes of the English. And she takes up non-cooperation out of her weakness. It must still serve the same purpose, namely, bring her delivery from the crushing weight of British injustice if a sufficient number of people practise it.

I isolate this non-cooperation from Sinn Feinism, for, it is so conceived as to be incapable of being offered side by side with violence. But I invite even the school of violence to give this peaceful non-cooperation a trial. It will not fail through its inherent weakness. It may fail because of poverty of response. Then will be the time for real danger. The high-souled men, who are unable to suffer national humiliation any longer, will want to vent their wrath. They will take to violence. So far as I know, they must perish without delivering themselves or their country from the wrong. If India takes up the doctrine of the sword, she may gain momentary victory. Then India will cease to be the pride of my heart. I am wedded to India because I owe my all to her. I believe absolutely that she has a mission for the world. She is not to copy Europe blindly. India's acceptance of the doctrine of the sword will be the hour of my trial. I hope I shall not be found wanting. My religion has no geographical limits. If I have a living faith in it, it will transcend my love for India herself. My life is dedicated to service of India through the religion of non-violence which I believe to be the root of Hinduism.

Meanwhile I urge those who distrust me not to disturb the even working of the struggle that has just commenced, by inciting to violence in the belief that I want violence. I detest secrecy as a sin. Let them give non-violent non-cooperation a trial and they will find that I had no mental reservation whatsoever.

FRANTZ FANON

Concerning Violence

National liberation, national renaissance, the restoration of nationhood to the people, commonwealth: whatever may be the headings used or the new formulas introduced, decolonization is always a violent phenomenon. At whatever level we study it—relationships between individuals, new names for sports clubs, the human admixture at cocktail parties, in the police, on the directing boards of national or private banks—decolonization is quite simply the replacing of a certain "species" of men by another "species" of men. Without any period of transition, there is a total, complete, and absolute substitution. It is true that we could equally well stress the rise of a new nation, the setting up of a new state, its diplomatic relations, and its economic and political trends. But we have precisely chosen to speak of that kind of tabula rasa which characterizes at the outset all decolonization. Its unusual importance is that it constitutes, from the very first day, the minimum demands of the colonized. To tell the truth, the proof of success lies in a whole social structure being changed from the bottom up. The extraordinary importance of this change is that it is willed, called for, demanded. The need for this change exists in its crude state, impetuous and compelling, in the consciousness and in the lives of the men and women who are colonized. But the possibility of this change is equally experienced in the form of a terrifying future in the consciousness of another "species" of men and women: the colonizers.

Decolonization, which sets out to change the order of the world, is, obviously, a program of complete disorder. But it cannot come as a result of magical practices, nor of a natural shock, nor of a friendly understanding. Decolonization, as we know, is a historical process: that is to say that it cannot be understood, it cannot become intelligible nor clear to itself except in the exact measure that we can discern the movements which give it historical form and content. Decolonization is the meeting of two forces, opposed to each other by their very nature, which in fact owe their originality to that sort of substantification which results from and is nourished by the situation in the colonies. Their first encounter was marked by violence and their existence together—that is to say the exploitation of the native by the settler—was carried on by dint of a great array of bayonets and cannons. The settler and the native are old acquaintances. In fact, the settler is right when he speaks of knowing "them" well. For it is the settler who has brought the native into existence and who perpetuates his existence. The settler owes the fact of his very existence, that is to say, his property, to the colonial system.

Decolonization never takes place unnoticed, for it influences individuals and modifies them fundamentally. It transforms spectators crushed with their inessentiality into privileged actors, with the grandiose glare of history's floodlights upon them. It brings a natural rhythm into existence, introduced by new men, and with it a new language and a new humanity. Decolonization is the veritable creation of new men. But this creation owes nothing of its legitimacy to any supernatural power; the "thing" which has been colonized becomes man during the same process by which it frees itself.

In decolonization, there is therefore the need of a complete calling in question of the colonial situation. If we wish to describe it precisely, we might find it in the well-known words: "The last shall be first and the first last." Decolonization is the putting into practice of this sentence. That is why, if we try to describe it, all decolonization is successful.

The naked truth of decolonization evokes for us the searing bullets and bloodstained knives which emanate from it. For if the last shall be first, this will only come to pass after a murderous and decisive struggle between the two protagonists. That affirmed intention to place the last at the head of things, and to make them climb at a pace (too quickly, some say) the well-known steps which characterize an organized society, can only triumph if we use all means to turn the scale, including, of course, that of violence.

You do not turn any society, however primitive it may be, upside down with such a program if you have not decided from the very beginning, that is to say from the actual formulation of that program, to overcome all the obstacles that you will come across in so doing. The native who decides to put the program into practice, and to become its moving force, is ready for violence at all times. From birth it is clear to him that this narrow world, strewn with prohibitions, can only be called in question by absolute violence.

The colonial world is a world divided into compartments. It is probably unnecessary to recall the existence of native quarters and European quarters, of schools for natives and schools for Europeans; in the same way we need not recall apartheid in South Africa. Yet, if we examine closely this system of compartments, we will at least be able to reveal the lines of force it implies. This approach to the colonial world, its ordering and its geographical layout will allow us to mark out the lines on which a decolonized society will be reorganized.

The colonial world is a world cut in two. The dividing line, the frontiers are shown by barracks and police stations. In the colonies it is the policeman and the soldier who are the official, instituted go-betweens, the spokesmen of the settler and his rule of oppression. In capitalist societies the educational system, whether lay or clerical, the structure of moral reflexes handed down from father to son, the exemplary honesty of workers who are given a medal after fifty years of good and loyal service, and the affection which springs from harmonious relations and good behavior—all these aesthetic expressions of respect for the established order serve to create around the exploited person an atmosphere of submission and of inhibition which lightens the task of policing considerably. In the capitalist countries a multitude of moral teachers, counselors and "bewilderers" separate the exploited from those in power. In the colonial countries, on the contrary, the policeman and the soldier, by their immediate presence and their frequent and direct action maintain contact with the native and advise him by means of rifle butts and napalm not to budge. It is obvious here that the agents of government speak the language of pure force. The intermediary does not lighten the oppression, nor seek to hide the domination; he shows them up and puts them into practice with the clear conscience of an upholder of the peace; yet he is the bringer of violence into the home and into the mind of the native.

The zone where the natives live is not complementary to the zone inhabited by the settlers. The two zones are opposed, but not in the service of a higher unity. Obedient to the rules of pure Aristotelian logic, they both follow the principle of reciprocal exclusivity. No conciliation is possible, for of the two terms, one is superfluous. The settlers' town is a strongly built town, all made of stone and steel. It is a brightly lit town; the streets are covered with asphalt, and the garbage cans swallow all the leavings, unseen, unknown and hardly thought about. The settler's feet are never visible, except perhaps in the sea; but there you're never close enough to see them. His feet are protected by strong shoes although the streets of his town are clean and even, with no holes or stones. The settler's town is a well-fed town, an easygoing town; its belly is always full of good things. The settlers' town is a town of white people, of foreigners.

The town belonging to the colonized people, or at least the native town, the Negro village, the medina, the reservation, is a place of ill fame, peopled by men of evil repute. They are born there, it matters little where or how; they die there, it matters not where, nor how. It is a world without spaciousness; men live there on top of each other, and their huts are built one on top of the other. The native town is a hungry town, starved of bread, of meat, of shoes, of coal, of light. The native town is a crouching village, a town of its knees, a town wallowing in the mire. It is a town of niggers and dirty Arabs. The look that the native turns on the settler's town is a look of lust, a look of envy; it expresses his dreams of possession—all manner of possession: to sit at the settler's table, to sleep in the settler's bed, with his wife if possible. The colonized man is an envious man. And this the settler knows very well; when their glances meet he ascertains bitterly, always on the defensive, "They want to take our place." It is true, for there is no native who does not dream at least once a day of setting himself up in the settler's place.

This world divided into compartments, this world cut in two is inhabited by two different species. The originality of the colonial context is that economic reality, inequality, and the immense difference of ways of life never come to mask the human realities. When you examine at close quarters the colonial context, it is evident that what parcels out the world is to begin with the fact of belonging to or not belonging to a given race, a given species. In the colonies the economic substructure is also a superstructure. The cause is the consequence; you are rich because you are white, you are white because you are rich. This is why Marxist analysis should always be slightly stretched every time we have to do with the colonial problem.

Everything up to and including the very nature of precapitalist society, so well explained by Marx, must here be thought out again. The serf is in essence different from the knight, but a reference to divine right is necessary to legitimize this statutory difference. In the colonies, the foreigner coming from another country imposed his rule by means of guns and machines. In defiance of his successful transplantation, in spite of his appropriation, the settler still remains a foreigner. It is neither the act of owning factories, nor estates, nor a bank balance which distinguishes the governing classes. The governing race is first and foremost those who come from elsewhere, those who are unlike the original inhabitants, "the others."

The violence which has ruled over the ordering of the colonial world, which has ceaselessly drummed the rhythm for the destruction of native social forms and broken up without reserve the systems of reference of the economy, the customs of dress and external life, that same violence will be claimed and taken over the native at the moment when, deciding to embody history in his own person, he surges into the forbidden quarters. To wreck the colonial world is henceforward a mental picture of action which is very clear, very easy to understand and which may be assumed by each one of the individuals which constitute the colonized people. To break up the colonial world does not mean that after the frontiers have been abolished lines of communication will be set up between the two zones. The destruction of the colonial world is no more and no less that the abolition of one zone, its burial in the depths of the earth or its expulsion from the country.

The natives' challenge to the colonial world is not a rational confrontation of points of view. It is not a treatise on the universal, but the untidy affirmation of an original idea propounded as an absolute. The colonial world is a Manichean world. It is not enough for the settler to delimit physically, that is to say with the help of the army and the police force, the place of the native. As if to show the totalitarian character of colonial exploitation the settler paints the native as a sort of quintessence of evil. Native society is not simply described as a society lacking in values. It is not enough for the colonist to affirm that those values have disappeared from, or still better never existed in, the colonial world. The native is declared insensible to ethics; he represents not only the absence of values, but also the negation of values. He is, let us dare to admit, the enemy of values, and in this sense he is the absolute evil. He is the corrosive element, destroying all that comes near him; he is the deforming element, disfiguring all that has to do with beauty or mortality; he is the depository of maleficent powers, the unconscious and irretrievable instrument of blind forces. Monsieur Meyer could thus state seriously in the French National Assembly that the Republic must not be prostituted by allowing the Algerian people to become part of it. All values, in fact, are irrevocably poisoned and diseased as soon as they are allowed in contact with the colonized race. The customs of the colonized people, their traditions, their myths—above all, their myths—are the very sign of that poverty of spirit and of their constitutional depravity. That is why we must put the DDT which destroys parasites, the bearers of disease, on the same level as the Christian religion which wages war on embryonic heresies and instincts, and on evil as yet unborn. The recession of yellow fever and the advance of evangelization form part of the same balance sheet. But the triumphant communiqués from the missions are in fact a source of information concerning the implantation of foreign influences in the core of the colonized people. I speak of the Christian religion, and no one need be astonished. The Church in the colonies is the white people's Church, the foreigner's Church. She does not call the native to God's ways but to the ways of the white man, of the master, of the oppressor. And as we know, in this matter many are called but few chosen.

At times this Manicheism goes to its logical conclusion and dehumanizes the native, or to speak plainly, it turns him into an animal. In fact, the terms the settler uses when he mentions the native are zoological terms. He speaks of the yellow man's reptilian motions, of the stink of the native quarter, of breeding swarms, of foulness, of spawn, of gesticulations. When the settler seeks to describe the native fully in exact terms he constantly refers to the bestiary. The European rarely hits on a picturesque style; but the native, who knows what is in the mind of the settler, guesses at once what he is thinking of. Those hordes of vital statistics, those hysterical masses, those faces bereft of all humanity, those distended bodies which are like nothing on earth, that mob without beginning or end, those children who seem to belong to nobody, that laziness stretched out in the sun, that vegetative rhythm of life—all this forms part of the colonial vocabulary. General de Gaulle speaks of "the yellow multitudes" and François Mauriac of the black, brown, and yellow masses which soon will be unleashed. The native knows all this, and laughs to himself every time he spots an allusion to the animal world in the other's words. For he knows that he is not an animal; and it is precisely at the moment he realizes his humanity that he begins to sharpen the weapons with which he will secure its victory.

As soon as the native begins to pull on his moorings, and to cause anxiety to the settler, he is handed over to well-meaning souls who in cultural congresses point out to him the specificity and wealth of Western values. But every time Western values are mentioned they produce in the native a sort of stiffening or muscular lockjaw. During the period of decolonization, the native's reason is appealed to. He is offered definite values, he is told frequently that decolonization need not mean regression, and that he must put his trust in qualities which are well-tried, solid, and highly esteemed. But it so happens that when the native hears a speech about Western culture he pulls out his knife—or at least he makes sure it is within reach. The violence with which the supremacy of white values is affirmed and the aggressiveness which has permeated the victory of these values over the ways of life and of thought of the native mean that, in revenge, the native laughs in mockery when Western values are mentioned in front of him. In the colonial context the settler only ends his work of breaking in the native when the latter admits loudly and intelligibly the supremacy of the white man's values. In the period of decolonization, the colonized masses mock at these very values, insult them, and vomit them up.

This phenomenon is ordinarily masked because, during the period of decolonization, certain colonized intellectuals have begun a dialogue with the bourgeoisie of the colonialist country. During this phase, the indigenous population is discerned only as an indistinct mass. The few native personalities whom the colonialist bourgeois have come to know here and there have not sufficient influence on that immediate discernment to give rise to nuances. On the other hand, during the period of liberation, the colonialist bourgeoisie looks feverishly for contacts with the elite and it is with these elite that the familiar dialogue concerning values is carried on. The colonialist bourgeoisie, when it realizes that it is impossible for it to maintain its domination over the colonial countries, decides to carry out a rearguard action with regard to culture, values, techniques, and so on. Now what we must never forget is that the immense majority of colonized peoples is oblivious to these problems. For a colonized people the most essential value, because the most concrete, is first and foremost the land: the land which will bring them bread and, above all, dignity. But this dignity has nothing to do with the dignity of the human individual: for that human individual has never heard tell of it. All that the native has seen in his country is that they can freely arrest him, beat him, starve him; and no professor of ethics, no priest has ever come to be beaten in his place, nor to share their bread with him. As far as the native is concerned, morality is very concrete; it is to silence the settler's defiance, to break his flaunting violence—in a word, to put him out of the picture. The well-known principle that all men are equal will be illustrated in the colonies from the moment that the native claims that he is the equal of the settler. One step more, and he is ready to fight to be more than the settler. In fact, he has already decided to eject him and to take his place; as we see it, it is a whole material and moral universe which is breaking up. The intellectual who for his part has followed the colonialist with regard to the universal abstract will fight in order that the settler and the native may live together in peace in a new world. But the thing he does not see, precisely because he is permeated by colonialism and all its ways of thinking, is that the settler, from the moment that the colonial context disappears, has no longer any interest in remaining or in co-existing. It is not by chance that, even before any negotiation between the Algerian and French governments has taken place, the European minority which calls itself "liberal" has already made its position clear: it demands nothing more nor less than twofold citizenship. By setting themselves apart in an abstract manner, the liberals try to force the settler into taking a very concrete jump into the unknown. Let us admit it, the settler knows perfectly well that no phraseology can be a substitute for reality.

Thus the native discovers that his life, his breath, his beating heart are the same as those of the settler. He finds out that the settler's skin is not of any more value than a native's skin; and it must be said that this discovery shakes the world in a very necessary manner. All the new, revolutionary assurance of the native stems from it. For if, in fact, my life is worth as much as the settler's, his glance no longer shrivels me up nor freezes me, and his voice no longer turns me into stone. I am no longer on tenterhooks in his presence; in fact, I don't give a damn for him. Not only does his presence no longer trouble me, but I am already preparing such efficient ambushes for him that soon there will be no way out but that of flight.

We have said that the colonial context is characterized by the dichotomy which it imposes upon the whole people. Decolonization unifies that people by the radical decision to remove from it its heterogeneity, and by unifying it on a national, sometimes a racial, basis. We know the fierce words of the Senegalese patriots, referring to the maneuvers of their president, Senghor: "We have demanded that the higher posts should be given to Africans; and now Senghor is Africanizing the Europeans." That is to say that the native can see clearly and immediately if decolonization has come to pass or not, for his minimum demands are simply that the last shall be first.

CHE GUEVARA

Building New Men

The new society being formed has to compete fiercely with the past. The latter makes itself felt in the consciousness in which the residue of an education systematically oriented towards isolating the individual still weighs heavily, and also through the very character of the transitional period in which the market relationships of the past still persist. The commodity is the economic cell of capitalist society; so long as it exists its effects will make themselves felt in the organization of production and, consequently, in consciousness.

Marx outlined the period of transition as a period which results from the explosive transformation of the capitalist system of a country destroyed by its own contradictions. However in historical reality we have seen that some countries, which were weak limbs of the tree of imperialism, were torn off first—a phenomenon foreseen by Lenin.

In these countries capitalism had developed to a degree sufficient to make its effects felt by the people in one way or another; but, having exhausted all its possibilities, it was not its internal contradictions which caused these systems to explode. The struggle for liberation from a foreign oppressor, the misery caused by external events like war whose consequences make the privileged classes bear down more heavily on the oppressed, liberation movements aimed at the overthrow of neo-colonial regimes—these are the usual factors in this kind of explosion. Conscious action does the rest.

In these countries a complete education for social labor has not yet taken place, and wealth is far from being within the reach of the masses simply through the process of appropriation. Underdevelopment on the one hand, and the inevitable flight of capital on the other, make a rapid transition impossible without sacrifices. There remains a long way to go in constructing the economic base, and the temptation to follow the beaten track of material interest as the moving lever of accelerated development is very great....

... To build communism, you must build new men as well as the new economic base.

Hence it is very important to choose correctly the instrument for mobilizing the masses. Basically, this instrument must be moral in character, without neglecting, however, a correct utilization of the material stimulus—especially of a social character....

In our case direct education acquires a much greater importance. The explanation is convincing because it is true; no subterfuge is needed. It is carried on by the state's educational apparatus as a function of general, technical and ideological culture through such agencies as the Ministry of Education and the party's informational apparatus.

Education takes hold of the masses and the new attitude tends to become a habit; the masses continue to absorb it and to influence those who have not yet educated themselves. This is the indirect form of educating the masses, as powerful as the other.

But the process is a conscious one; the individual continually feels the impact of the new social power and perceives that he does not entirely measure up to its standards. Under the pressure of indirect education, he tries to adjust himself to a norm which he feels is just and which his own lack of development had prevented him from reaching theretofore. He educates himself.

In this period of the building of socialism we can see the new man being born. His image is not yet completely finished—it never could be—since the process goes forward hand in hand with the development of new economic forms.

Leaving out of consideration those whose lack of education makes them take the solitary road toward satisfying their own personal ambitions, there are those, even within this new panorama of a unified march forward, who have a tendency to remain isolated from the masses accompanying them. But what is important is that everyday men are continuing to acquire more consciousness of the need for their incorporation into society and, at the same time, of their importance as the movers of society.

They no longer travel completely alone over trackless routes toward distant desires. They follow their vanguard, consisting of the party, the advanced workers, the advanced men who walk in unity with the masses and in close communion with them. The vanguard has its eyes fixed on the future and its rewards, but this is not seen as something personal. The reward is the new society in which men will have attained new features: the society of communist man.

The road is long and full of difficulties. At times we wander from the path and must turn back; at other times we go too fast and separate ourselves from the masses; on occasions we go too slow and feel the hot breath of those treading on our heels. In our zeal as revolutionists we try to move ahead as fast as possible, clearing the way, but knowing we must draw our sustenance from the mass and that it can advance more rapidly only if we inspire it by our example.

The fact that there remains a division into two main groups (excluding, of course, that minority not participating for one reason or another in the building of socialism), despite the importance given to moral stimuli, indicates the relative lack of development of social consciousness.

The vanguard group is ideologically more advanced than the mass; the latter understands the new values, but not sufficiently. While among the former there has been a qualitative change which enables them to make sacrifices to carry out their function as an advance guard, the latter go only half way and must be subjected to stimuli and pressures of a certain intensity. That is the dictatorship of the proletariat operating not only on the defeated class but also on individuals of the victorious class.

All of this means that for total success a series of mechanisms, of revolutionary institutions, is needed. Fitted into the pattern of the multitudes marching towards the future is the concept of a harmonious aggregate of channels, steps, restraints, and smoothly working mechanisms which would facilitate that advance by ensuring the efficient selection of those destined to march in the vanguard which, itself, bestows rewards on those who fulfill their duties, and punishments on those who attempt to obstruct the development of the new society.

This institutionalization of the revolution has not yet been achieved. We are looking for something which will permit a perfect identification between the government and the community in its entirety, something appropriate to the special conditions of the building of socialism, while avoiding to the maximum degree a mere transplanting of the commonplace places of bourgeois democracy—like legislative chambers—into the society in formation.

Some experiments aimed at the gradual development of institutionalized forms of the revolution have been made, but without undue haste. The greatest obstacle has been our fear lest any appearance of formality might separate us from the masses and from the individual, might make us lose sight of the ultimate and most important revolutionary aspiration, which is to see man liberated from his alienation.

Despite the lack of institutions, which must be corrected gradually, the masses are now making history as a conscious aggregate of individuals fighting for the same cause. Man under socialism, despite his apparent standardization, is more complete; despite the lack of perfect machinery for it, his opportunities for expressing himself and making himself felt in the social organism are infinitely greater.

It is still necessary to strengthen his conscious participation, individual and collective, in all the mechanisms of management and production, and to link it to the idea of the need for technical and ideological education, so that he sees how closely interdependent these processes are and how their advancement is parallel. In this way he will reach total consciousness of his social function, which is equivalent to his full realization as a human being, once the chains of alienation are broken.

This will be translated concretely into the regaining of his true nature through liberated labor, and the expression of his proper human condition through culture and art.

In order for him to develop in the first of the above categories, labor must acquire a new status. Man dominated by commodity relationships will cease to exist, and a system will be created which establishes a quota for the fulfillment of his social duty. The means of production belong to society, and the machine will merely be the trench where duty is fulfilled.

Man will begin to see himself mirrored in his work and to realize his full stature as a human being through the object created, through the work accomplished. Work will no longer entail surrendering a part of his being in the form of labor-power sold, which no longer belongs to him, but will represent an emanation of himself reflecting his contribution to the common life, the fulfillment of his social duty.

We are doing everything possible to give labor this new status of social duty and to link it on the one side with the development of a technology which will create the conditions for greater freedom, and on the other side with voluntary work based on a Marxist appreciation of the fact that man truly reaches a full human condition when he produces without being driven by the physical need to sell his labor as a commodity.

Of course there are other factors involved even when labor is voluntary: Man has not transformed all the coercive factors around him into conditioned reflexes of a social character, and he still produces under the pressures of his society. (Fidel calls this moral compulsion.)

Man still needs to undergo a complete spiritual rebirth in his attitude towards his work, freed from the direct pressure of his social environment, through linked to it by his new habits. That will be communism.

[T]he need for the creation of a new man has not been understood, a new man who would represent neither the ideas of the nineteenth century nor those of our own decadent and morbid century.

What we must create is the man of the twenty-first century, although this is still a subjective and not a realized aspiration. It is precisely this man of the next century who is one of the fundamental objectives of our work; and to the extent that we achieve concrete successes on a theoretical plane—or, vice versa, to the extent we draw theoretical conclusions of a broad character on the basis of our concrete research—we shall have made an important contribution to Marxism-Leninism, to the cause of humanity.

Reaction against the man of the nineteeth century has brought us a relapse into the decadence of the twentieth century; it is not a fatal error, but we must overcome it lest we open a breach for revisionism.

The great multitudes continue to develop; the new ideas continue to attain their proper force within society; the material possibilities for the full development of all members of society make the task much more fruitful. The present is a time for struggle; the future is ours.

To sum up, the fault of our artists and intellectuals lies in their original sin: They are not truly revolutionary. We can try to graft the elm tree so that it will bear pears, but at the same time we must plant pear trees. New generations will come who will be free of the original sin. The probabilities that great artists will appear will be greater to the degree that the field of culture and the possibilities for expression are broadened.

Our task is to prevent the present generation, torn asunder by its conflicts, from becoming perverted and from perverting new generations. We must not bring into being either docile servants of official thought, or scholarship students who live at the expense of the state—practicing "freedom." Already there are revolutionaries coming who will sing the song of the new man in the true voice of the people. This is a process which takes time.

such. To require the subject means to foreclose the domain of the political, and that fore-closure, installed analytically as an essential feature of the political, enforces the bound-aries of the domain of the political in such a way that that enforcement is protected from political scrutiny. The act which unilaterally establishes the domain of the political func-tions, then, as an authoritarian ruse by which political contest over the status of the sub-ject is summarily silenced.[1]

To refuse to assume, that is, to require a notion of the subject from the start is not the same as negating or dispensing with such a notion altogether; on the contrary, it is to ask after the process of its construction and the political meaning and consequentiality of tak-ing the subject as a requirement or presupposition of theory. But have we arrived yet at a notion of postmodernism?

A number of positions are ascribed to postmodernism, as if it were the kind of thing that could be the bearer of a set of positions: discourse is all there is, as if discourse were some kind of monistic stuff out of which all things are composed; the subject is dead, I can never say "I" again; there is no reality, only representations. These characterizations are variously imputed to postmodernism or postsructuralism, which are conflated with each other and sometimes conflated with deconstruction, and sometimes understood as an indiscriminate assemblage of French feminism, deconstruction, Lacanian psychoanalysis, Foucaultian analysis, Rorty's conversationalism and cultural studies. On this side of the Atlantic and in recent discourse, the terms "postmodernism" or "poststructuralism" settle the differences among those positions in a single stroke, providing a substantive, a noun, that includes those positions as so many of its modalities or permutations. It may come as a suprise to some purveyors of the Continental scene to learn that Lacanian psychoanalysis in France positions itself officially against poststructuralism, that Kristeva denounces postmodernism,[2] that Foucaultians rarely relate to Derrideans, that Cixous and Irigaray are fundamentally opposed, and that the only tenuous connection between French Femi-nism and deconstruction exists between Cixous and Derrida, although a certain affinity in textual practices is to be found between Derrida and Irigaray. Biddy Martin is also right to point out that almost all of French feminism adheres to a notion of high modernism and the avant-garde, which throws some question on whether these theories or writings can be grouped simply under the category of postmodernism.

I propose that the question of postmodernism be read not merely as the question that postmodernism poses for feminism, but as the question, what is postmodernism? What kind of existence does it have? Jean-François Lyotard champions the term, but he cannot be made into the example of what all the rest of the purported postmodernists are doing.[3] Lyotard's work is, for instance, seriously at odds with that of Derrida, who does not affirm the notion of "the postmodern," and with others for whom Lyotard is made to stand. Is he paradigmatic? Do all these theories have the same structure (a comforting notion to the critic who would dispense with them all at once)? Is the effort to colonize and domesticate these theories under the sign of the same, to group them synthetically and masterfully under a single rubric, a simple refusal to grant the specificity of these positions, an execuse not to read, and not to read closely? For if Lyotard uses the term, and if he can be conve-niently grouped with a set of writers, and if some problematic quotation can be found in

Part IV

NEW SOCIAL MOVEMENTS

THE AFRICAN-AMERICAN HERITAGE

"Socialism and the American Negro," by W.E.B. DuBois, a speech given in 1960 by the great scholar and activist, provides a wonderful impressionistic account of the African-American movement in the United States. It also shows a realistic awareness of the growing economic differences between blacks and whites as well as the emergence of class contradictions within the African-American community itself. Indeed, DuBois anticipates the growing disillusionment with a liberal movement incapable of extending its successful legal battles for civil rights into an assault on material inequality.

The classic "Letter from Birmingham Jail," by Rev. Dr. Martin Luther King, Jr., is a committed liberal response to those who thought the civil rights movement was "going too fast" and who opposed the idea of outsiders seeking to change the South. He emphasizes the need to distinguish between just and unjust laws, and he justifies civil disobedience. According to Dr. King, however, dissidents must accept punishment for breaking the law and refrain from violence. The religious and ethical assumptions of his outlook become obvious along with his belief that justice is more important than public order.

"The Ballot or the Bullet," by Malcolm X, takes a different tone and has a different purpose. This speech, given shortly after Malcolm's break with the Nation of Islam, seeks to give the battle for civil rights a new interpretation. It makes no ethical commitment to nonviolence, no bow to the democratic institutions in the United States, and no concession to either of the two reigning political parties. It begins by assuming, in fact, that the prevailing democratic government and white liberals have failed black people. The response is a "black nationalism" predicated on uniting all currents in the black community, giving them greater control over its politics and economy, and creating an international alliance among people of color.

There are points of convergence between these three positions, but they are fundamentally different. Some combination of them, however, will surely inform the new theoretical developments in the African-American community.

W.E.B. DuBois

Socialism and the American Negro

Democracy has so disappeared in the United States that there are some subjects that cannot even be disccussed. The essence of the democratic process is free discussion. There was a time when men were not allowed to talk of universal suffrage, education for women, or freedom for Negro slaves. Today communism is the dirty word and socialism is suspect. I often refer to my education in democracy. In the little New England town where I was born, we had a high school of about 25 pupils. I entered it in 1880, at the age of 12. As I attended town-meeting, annually in the spring, there used regularly to appear one of the dirtiest old men I ever saw. He was fat and greasy, and every year he made a fierce attack on wasting his taxes on a high school. I was always furious. I wondered why the citizens sat silent and let him rant, but they did, and then quietly they voted money for the high school. There I learned my lesson in democracy. Listen to the other side.

In this state, and in our time, occurred one of the worst blows to the democratic process which our nation has suffered. Senator McCarthy succeeded in making America afraid to discuss socialism, or to recognize communism as aught but a conspiracy. And this, in the state of Robert LaFollette. I knew LaFollette and his valiant wife. I voted for him for president in 1924, and saw him give his life fighting monopolized wealth and asking world peace. For a quarter of a century, I edited a little monthly magazine, *The Crisis,* and despite opposition, I spoke plainly. I was criticized as being "bitter," as seeking not simply political, but social equality for Negroes. For favoring the teachings of Karl Marx, and for joining the socialist party. These accusations were true, but largely as a result of my work, and the work of others, the Negro made progress toward equal citizenship. Progress, but not complete success.

The collapse of the capitalist system after the first World War brought poverty, unemployment and distress, worse than America had ever seen, and then came a surge toward socialism, called the "New Deal." The Nation relieved distress, built public works, helped agriculture and trade, encouraged literature and art. It joined the Soviet Union in overthrowing Hitler, Mussolini and Japan. And in forming the United Nations to avoid future war.

With the death of Roosevelt, came reaction. The United States not only stopped progress toward socialism, but ceased to discuss or study it and came to regard the object of socialism and communism as a crime. Especially American Negroes, still as a mass, poor, ignorant and sick, were given no opportunity to know the sort of progress the world was making to ameliorate the plight of the unfortunate working people, the world over, who were in [a] condition similar to ours. American Negroes were not socialists, nor did they know what communism was or was doing. But they knew that Negro education must be better; that Negroes must have better opportunity to work and to receive a wage which would let them enjoy a decent standard of life.

They were victims of disease, and drifting into crime. To remedy this, they sought to pattern their life after successful Americans. They must work hard, save money, become employers, and property owners and investors. This they thought would bring them recognition, as American citizens equal to others. But America has changed. There was still a chance for some to rise and get rich, but the working classes were no longer generally able to buy land. Their wages did not amount to what they in reality earned, and those handicapped by race prejudice had small chance to overcome poverty, ignorance and disease. A class structure began to arise within the Negro group which produced haves and have nots, and tended to encourage more successful Negroes to join the forces of monopoly and exploitation, and help victimize their own lower classes.

To remedy this situation, thinking Negroes still regarded their first step toward emancipation as being political power. They felt that their present plight was due to the fact that they had never become voting citizens of the country, and their first efforts were toward gaining the real right to vote.

The young colored men in 1905 emphasized this. The group meeting, at Niagara Falls, Canada, in June 1905, demanded freedom of speech and criticism, manhood suffrage, the abolition of all distinctions based on race. Recognition of basic principles of human brotherhood and respect for the working man. They called themselves the Niagara Movement and, despite violent attack on all sides, met again at Harpers Ferry the next year. There they said: "In the past year the work of the Negro hater has flourished in the land. Step by step, the defenders of the rights of American citizens have retreated. The work of stealing the Black man's ballot has progressed and fifty and more representatives, of stolen votes, still sit in the nation's capital. Never before in the modern age has a great and civilized folk threatened to adopt so cowardly a creed in the treatment of its fellow-citizens, born and bred on its soil. Stripped of verbose subterfuge, and in its naked nastiness, the new American creed says: fear to let black men even try to rise, lest they become, the equals of the white. And this is the land, that professes to follow Jesus Christ. The blasphemy of such a course is only matched by its cowardice."

The NAACP, organized in 1909, added to the program of the Niagara Movement the realization that the fight for Negro freedom could not be carried on by Negroes alone but by a national movement which united Negroes and whites. They emphasized the role which prejudice played, a prejudice often unconscious but nevertheless effective.

The NAACP made a nationwide fight against the horror of lynching and mob violence, and then more and more, it began to concentrate on the legal aspects of race discrimination, and the fact that the Negro was oppressed because the constitution of the United States was not being enforced. This fight had unprecedented success and culminated in 1954, in the unanimous decision of the Supreme Court against segregation.

But during all this struggle, we knew that something still was lacking. If we harked back, to the cry of the French Revolution, Liberty, equality and brotherhood, it was clear that there was not and could not be, *Liberty* of individual action, under the great industrial organization which was growing up in the world led by the United States. Production in industry and trade involved planning and planning curtailed liberty. Moreover our inequality was a matter of fact. Negroes with their ignorance, poverty and sickness, were distinctly below the average of those of their white neighbors who were educated, well-to-do and healthy.

Finally, despite all propaganda, we saw democracy failing in America. Fewer and fewer people went to the polls. It was increasingly difficult to know for whom, or for what, one was voting, and the cost of elections arose to suspicious heights. The election in which Abraham Lincoln became president of the United States cost about $100,000. The election which made Dwight Eisenhower president probably cost more than $100 million. Indeed it is possible that it cost twice that amount. Election expenses today include not only direct bribery, but indirect influences, monopoly, propaganda, and deception. Under these circumstances the appeal of socialism to all Americans increased. But the answer to the doctrines of Karl Marx, and the Utopias of Fourier and others, was that, with human nature as it is, socialism simply would not work.

To me, the obvious approach to socialism seemed consumers' cooperation. I tried to plan an organization among Negroes as consumers, which would furnish employment, help savings, and bring unity of action. But it was soon evident, as many of my fellow workers warned me from the beginning, that individual action alone could not bring consumers' cooperation. That without the power of the government, it would fail, and with government cooperation it was socialism. My own training in this thought came from travel: my two years sojourn in Germany, at the end of the 19th century, where I saw the rise of the social democratic party. My repeated visits to England and France, in the first decade of this century. My visits to the Soviet Union, in 1926, 1936 and 1949. Then, as a peculiar aftermath of the two world wars, and my advocacy of peace, my travel abroad was stopped, from 1950 and 1958. In 1958, I was able to make a trip, covering eleven months, in which I visited western Europe, eastern Europe including the Soviet Union, and the Republic of China. This trip completely transformed my thinking. I started on it believing that socialism was a possible form of government, and economic organization, and was being carried on successfully in eastern Europe. That capitalism was also a successful form of organization, and while it might degenerate into fascism, and the rule of wealth, nevertheless it could, as had been proven, by Franklin Roosevelt, become a progressive organization. I returned with completely changed ideas. I saw socialism as the most successful form of government today possible in the Soviet Union, and in the Chinese republic. I saw it evolving into communism, to an astonishingly successful degree.

On the other hand, I was frightened and am still alarmed at the degeneracy of capitalism, and the possibility of it becoming a force so destructive, that it cannot be endured.

One of my first experiences was in England. I had in London a severe attack of intestinal disorder. A young physician, summoned at midnight, came and treated me. He made six or more visits, within the next few days, until he had me completely on my feet. When I asked for my bill, I was told that there was no charge. That his services were paid for by the British government. I reminded him that I was an American, and that in America we were repeatedly informed that socialized medicine in Great Britain was a failure. He smiled: the only cost of my illness was the medicine which he prescribed, and that was less than $5.

On the other hand, I found Great Britain, France, Holland and Belgium, countries which for past centuries had built their comfort, prosperity and civilization mainly on the free land and materials, and cheap labor, partly of their own working class, but mainly of colored people overseas, whom they dominated, by their colonial empires. In 1958 it was clear that the end of this colonialism was in sight. Already most of the colonies of Holland had become independent. Britain had lost the empire of India, and France was fighting in vain to hold North Africa. Yet despite the fact that the colonial organization must end, these three great countries of western Europe, and others like Italy, West Germany, and Portugal, were depending for their future life on materials which they underpriced in the world market. On stolen land, and on labor wretchedly underpaid. The political power to carry on this process depended upon the laboring class in western Europe and America, and that laboring class was being bribed by political power and high wages which came, not so much out of the profits of the employers, as out of the low wages of colored labor. I did not sense in western Europe, and certainly I had not seen in America, any disposition so to improve the organization of work and the distribution of income as to make any essential change in the present capitalist system. On the other hand, I was astonished and encouraged by what I saw socialism doing. Not only did I see results of socialized medicine in England, progress in housing, health and workers, pensions in Sweden, Holland, Belgium and France, but in the Soviet Union, Czechoslovakia and East Germany, I saw a change of attitude which regarded the masses of people not as the wards and beneficiaries of the rulers of the nation, but as the main body, which itself owned the nation, and for which the nation existed; and as the reservoir, out of which were being recruited, those who were making civilization.

In China, it seemed to me that the process was going even further and that human nature was being so changed that instead of the self-seeking and class-hatred, which so characterized the West, there was coming a sense of partnership in a vast and growing nation, of willing cooperation and of a widespread content and happiness, which I had seen nowhere else in the world. All this was my deep and firm impression. I cannot prove it, particularly not to you, who have been poisoned by lies and distortion for ten years. After all, I saw these countries only partially and for brief visits. Yet I am a traveller of experience, and I know personally the trials of the poor and despised. I was given unusual opportunity for observation and thus my conclusions are of value.

I saw the spread of socialism and communism. Today more than half the people of the world live under socialism, which is growing toward complete communism. In my mind, there is no doubt that the world of the twenty-first century will be overwhelmingly communistic.

Returning now to the United States, I look again upon the scene. The legal fight led by the NAACP has been astonishing success. But its very success shows the limitations of law, and law enforcement, unless it has an economic program; unless the mass of Negro people have not simply legal rights, but have such rights to work and wage that enable them to live decently. Here in the United States, we have had a stirring, in the Negro population, which emphasized these facts. In the slave south, Negroes impoverished and mistreated, have sought remedy by pouring into the cities of the south and especially the great cities of the north. There they have caused problems of housing and of crime, poverty and disease. It spells the damnation of youth, and death of children, and the degradation of women. Through this, the American Negro is passing. It emphasizes our national problem of gambling, prostitution, drug using, murder and suicide. On the other hand, the Negroes who have grown in intelligence and awareness of their handicaps have begun to fight back by the use of the boycott and passive resistance. The experience in Montgomery, the extraordinary uprising of the students, all over the south and beginning in the north, shows an awareness of our situation which is most encouraging. But it still does not reach the center of the problem. And that center is not simply the right of Americans to spend their money as they wish and according to law, but the chance for American Negroes to have money to spend, because of employment, in which they can make a decent wage. What then is the next step? It is for American Negroes in increasing numbers, and more and more widely, to insist upon the legal rights which are already theirs, and to add to that, increasingly a socialistic form of government, an insistence upon the welfare state, which denies the further carrying on of industry for the profit of those corporations which monopolize wealth and power. The stopping of a government of wealth for wealth, and by wealth, and a returning of governmental power to the individual voter, with all the freedom of action which can be preserved, along with an industry carefully organized for the good of the masses of people and not for the manufacture of millionaires. Does capitalism offer such a program? It does not. It offers war.

We have gone insane with the idea that we are going to rule the world by physical force. More than any other nation on earth, or in time, we are spending fantastic sums of money to prepare for war, and basing this necessity of war preparation on dislike, distrust and contempt for most of the human beings who inhabit the world. We have no peace movement in the United States that deserves the name. We have almost no men of intelligence and prestige who dare speak up for peace. Cowed and silent, we face immeasurable catastrophe and the first duty of Americans is to realize this fact.

To illustrate what I am trying to say, let me remind you of certain recent occurrences. On October 27, 1951, eight and half years ago, *Collier's Magazine*, a flamboyant pictorial with a circulation claimed to be a million and a half, published a number to which the leaders of American science and literature contributed. This at a time when few socialists in the United States dared open their mouths, and many were in jail, when economics and social science were being taught in our colleges with the utmost caution, and when I was being handcuffed, for advocating peace with the Soviet Union. This extraordinary magazine was on every newsstand, and on radio and television. It predicted and described in 130 pages, the aggressive war of the United States against the Soviet Union. The editors and contributors said that this year, 1960, would see the utter destruction of communism the world over and the victorious American troops walking the streets of Moscow.

Who wrote these words and made these prophecies? The editors say, "This historical report, was written by many of the West's top historians, political, economic and military experts, commentators and artists." Among them were Allan Nevins, "one of the foremost American historians," Stuart Chase, Edward R. Murrow, Robert Sherwood, J. B. Priestley, and Margaret Chase Smith. Senator Smith wrote on "Russia's rebirth" which she pictured as being accomplished by American soldiers presumably like those then raping Korean women and burning Korean children alive and dropping disease germs on China.

For myself I knew that these writers were wrong. I had been in the Soviet Union in 1926 and 1936. In 1949, twenty-five Americans had been invited to attend, expenses paid, a Soviet Peace Congress. I was the only one who accepted. I addressed a cross-section of that great nation. I did not, as I would have been justified in doing, devote this opportunity to describing the plight of my people. On the contrary, I contended that I was speaking for those Americans who did not want war. And that they were a majority of the nation. No one visiting the Soviet Union, at that time could for a moment doubt its peaceful intentions. The reply to my thesis was this extraordinary article, which broke all rules of international decency, told lies and spread misinformation, and yet was received with applause in most quarters and unforgivable silence in others.

The year 1960 has come and is over a third gone. What has happened? *Collier's* Magazine has gone. Its vaunted million and a half readers have ceased to subscribe because the "reduced prices" which they charged for *Collier's* and a dozen other flashy periodicals which are thrust down our throats are not needed by the publishers, save as bait to advertisers who pay millions to make you buy their goods. The day will come, when *Life* and *Look* will pay their subscribers to allow the use of their names.

American troops are not in Moscow, and are not planning to be there. But the President of the United States is going, and we hope on an errand of peace to which he has been graciously invited, by the head of the Soviet State, in one of the greatest speeches of our day.

On the other hand, there are signs in this nation which should give us pause: there is stealing, cheating, poisoning, gambling and killing, to a frightening degree; our exports do not pay for our imports and we are settling the deficit by exporting $4 billion. Adulteration of food, and over-pricing of medicines, have reached alarming heights and the cost of living is continuously rising.

Perhaps our most unforgivable deed today, is our attitude toward China. Historically in America, "Chinks" have always rated below "Wops" and "Niggers." Negroes were lazy and jolly, and thus infuriated slave-drivers; but Chinese coolies worked like dumb, driven cattle. They were valuable, because they worked hard for almost nothing. During the nineteenth century, they were not only worked at home, but were transported in droves overseas like slaves to work for white folk. When they showed signs of rebellion in China, we began to steal their land, make them buy opium, and we planned to distribute the Chinese empire among the superior white nations. America willingly agreed so long as we got equal entry through this "open door." The Christian world sent droves of missionaries to make Chinese submission quick and easy. Then just as we were stretching our claws to pluck the rich fruit of the "white man's burden," Sun Yat Sen led the last revolt. The Soviet Union helped, and Chiang Kai Shek assumed leadership. Our way was clear, despite the advice of our own General Stillwell. We bribed Chiang to betray and murder communists. We gave him money and arms, and yet with desperate determination, China won its independence, and drove the murderous traitor into the sea, where he still squats on an island, protected by our money and guns. We hate China. We propose never to forgive the Chinese. We count them outside humanity. We charge them with every crime we can invent. I was on the borders of Tibet, last year, when China saved Tibetan slaves, and we shed crocodile tears. We have sympathy and money for the slave-drivers who hold the Dalai Lama as prisoner; but for the prisoners in our own overcrowded jails, who rebel each day, and cry in vain for justice and mercy, our only remedy is more jails. This shows the increase in our religion. This shows why we tax Americans into crime, poverty and suicide, and spend ten times more for war than for education, health and social security. Our national debt for war is greater than possibly we ever will or can pay.

This nation tries to prove its prosperity by balancing the monopolized wealth of the owners of its great corporations against the poverty of our lower third. What does this call for? Not for a compulsory rush toward socialism. Many of us believe and hope that socialism will and must come to this land. We see no other way. But scores of others do not believe this, and that is their right. But they have no right to prevent the truth about socialism from being told. They have no right to prevent students from studying the remarkable philosophy of Karl Marx. They have no right to prevent Americans from travel in China. Especially Americans of eminence must stop the spreading of lies about the socialist world. A few years ago, I was invited to the Harvard Club of New York to hear a former president of Harvard lecture on Soviet education. I was loath to accept because no Harvard Club has ever admitted a Negro to membership. But it was my duty to go. Knowledge always costs something and this is the kind of currency I have often had to pay in order to know.

President Conant, former commissioner of Germany, and largely responsible for present conditions there, told his audience that after two visits to the Soviet Union he had been unable to learn on what basis of examination Russian students were graduated into the University. Now on his return to America, he had learned the truth: the communist party had refused to allow students to be examined in order to promote only followers of the party. He had hardly got his mouth closed before sputnik had crossed the heavens, and the back of the moon had been photographed, proving beyond doubt the leadership of a communist state in modern science. The superiority of the Soviet Union in the education of children became indisputable and her lead in industry seems soon inevitable.

America must let youth know. American students must dare study the Soviet Union and China as carefully as they study Great Britain and France. But especially American

Negroes must know what is going on in the world today, and learn for themselves, what this has to teach them, in order that they may preserve their culture, get rid of poverty, ignorance and disease, and help America live up at least to a shadow of its vain boast as the land of the free and the home of the brave. Remember how once Browning sang

"O to be in England, now that April's there!"
Today in Wisconsin one hears the winds of spring
But listen low and long: The wails we hear are not all spring
There moans beneath the swish of whips the lithe thongs of South Africa
 Lashing civilization into Niggers: With drip of blood and roar of guns
And sob of mother and babies!
This is part of the system you defend
Americans have three hundred and fifty million invested in South Africa
It must make profit even as England's April does
For our profit the Blacks must work for what we offer. Chant Jew and Christian:
"Come unto me, all ye that labor and are heavy laden," and I will give you hell.
Take my yoke upon you or I will bash your Black faces in.
Listen to the winds
Hear the wail of death
And weep

MARTIN LUTHER KING, JR.

Letter from Birmingham Jail

While confined here in the Birmingham city jail, I came across your recent statement calling my present activities "unwise and untimely." Seldom do I pause to answer criticism of my work and ideas. If I sought to answer all the criticisms that cross my desk, my secretaries would have little time for anything other than such correspondence in the course of the day, and I would have no time for constructive work. But since I feel that you are men of genuine good will and that your criticisms are sincerely set forth, I want to try to answer your statement in what I hope will be patient and reasonable terms.

I think I should indicate why I am here in Birmingham, since you have been influenced by the view which argues against "outsiders coming in." I have the honor of serving as president of the Southern Christian Leadership Conference, an organization operating in every southern state, with headquarters in Atlanta, Georgia. We have some eighty-five affiliated organizations across the South, and one of them is the Alabama Christian Movement for Human Rights. Frequently we share staff, educational and financial resources with our affiliates. Several months ago the affiliate here in Birmingham asked us to be on call to engage in a nonviolent direct-action program if such were deemed necessary. We readily consented, and when the hour came we lived up to our promise. So I, along with several members of my staff, am here because I was invited here. I am here because I have organizational ties here.

But more basically, I am in Birmingham because injustice is here. Just as the prophets of the eighth century B.C. left their villages and carried their "thus saith the Lord" far beyond the boundaries of their home towns, and just as the Apostle Paul left his village of Tarsus and carried the gospel of Jesus Christ to the far corners of the Greco-Roman world, so am I compelled to carry the gospel of freedom beyond my own home town. Like Paul, I must constantly respond to the Macedonian call for aid.

Moreover, I am cognizant of the interrelatedness of all communities and states. I cannot sit idly by in Atlanta and not be concerned about what happens in Birmingham.

Injustice anywhere is a threat to justice everywhere. We are caught in an inescapable network of mutuality, tied in a single garment of destiny. Whatever affects one directly, affects all indirectly. Never again can we afford to live with the narrow, provincial "outside agitator" idea. Anyone who lives inside the United States can never be considered an outsider anywhere within its bounds.

You deplore the demonstrations taking place in Birmingham. But your statement, I am sorry to say, fails to express a similar concern for the conditions that brought about the demonstrations. I am sure that none of you would want to rest content with the superficial kind of social analysis that deals merely with effects and does not grapple with underlying causes. It is unfortunate that demonstrations are taking place in Birmingham, but it is even more unfortunate that the city's white power structure left the Negro community with no alternative.

In any nonviolent campaign there are four basic steps: collection of the facts to determine whether injustices exist; negotiation; self-purification; and direct action. We have gone through all these steps in Birmingham. There can be no gainsaying the fact that racial injustice engulfs this community. Birmingham is probably the most thoroughly segregated city in the United States. Its ugly record of brutality is widely known. Negroes have experienced grossly unjust treatment in the courts. There have been more unsolved bombings of Negro homes and churches in Birmingham than in any other city in the nation. These are the hard, brutal facts of the case. On the basis of these conditions, Negro leaders sought to negotiate with the city fathers. But the latter consistently refused to engage in good-faith negotiation.

Then, last September, came the opportunity to talk with leaders of Birmingham's economic community. In the course of the negotiations, certain promises were made by the merchants—for example, to remove the stores' humiliating racial signs. On the basis of these promises, the Reverend Fred Shuttlesworth and the leaders of the Alabama Christian Movement for Human Rights agreed to a moratorium on all demonstrations. As the weeks and months went by, we realized that we were the victims of a broken promise. A few signs, briefly removed, returned; the others remained.

As in so many past experiences, our hopes had been blasted, and the shadow of deep disappointment settled upon us. We had no alternative except to prepare for direct action, whereby we would present our very bodies as a means of laying our case before the conscience of the local and the national community. Mindful of the difficulties involved, we decided to undertake a process of self-purification. We began a series of workshops on nonviolence, and we repeatedly asked ourselves: "Are you able to accept blows without retaliating?" "Are you able to endure the ordeal of jail?" We decided to schedule our direct-action program for the Easter season, realizing that except for Christmas, this is the main shopping period of the year. Knowing that a strong economic-withdrawal program would be the by-product of direct action, we felt that this would be the best time to bring pressure to bear on the merchants for the needed change.

Then it occurred to us that Birmingham's mayoralty election was coming up in March, and we speedily decided to postpone action until after election day. When we discovered that the Commissioner of Public Safety, Eugene "Bull" Connor, had piled up enough votes to be in the run-off, we decided again to postpone action until the day after the run-off so that the demonstrations could not be used to cloud the issues. Like many others, we waited to see Mr. Connor defeated, and to this end we endured postponement after postponement. Having aided in this community need, we felt that our direct-action program could be delayed no longer.

You may well ask: "Why direct action? Why sit-ins, marches and so forth? Isn't negotiation a better path?" You are quite right in calling for negotiation. Indeed, this is the very purpose of direct action. Nonviolent direct action seeks to create such a crisis and foster such a tension that a community which has constantly refused to negotiate is forced to confront the issue. It seeks so to dramatize the issue that it can no longer be ignored. My citing the creation of tension as part of the work of the nonviolent-resister may sound rather shocking. But I must confess that I am not afraid of the word "tension." I have earnestly opposed violent tension, but there is a type of constructive, nonviolent tension which is necessary for growth. Just as Socrates felt that it was necessary to create a tension in the mind so that individuals could rise from the bondage of myths and half-truths to the unfettered realm of creative analysis and objective appraisal, so must we see the need for nonviolent gadflies to create the kind of tension in society that will help men rise from the dark depths of prejudice and racism to the majestic heights of understanding and brotherhood.

The purpose of our direct-action program is to create a situation so crisis-packed that it will inevitably open the door to negotiation. I therefore concur with you in your call for negotiation. Too long has our beloved Southland been bogged down in a tragic effort to live in monologue rather than dialogue.

One of the basic points in your statement is that the action that I and my associates have taken in Birmingham is untimely. Some have asked: "Why didn't you give the new city administration time to act?" The only answer that I can give to this query is that the new Birmingham administration must be prodded about as much as the outgoing one, before it will act. We are sadly mistaken if we feel that the election of Albert Boutwell as mayor will bring the millennium to Birmingham. While Mr. Boutwell is a much more gentle person than Mr. Connor, they are both segregationists, dedicated to maintenance of the status quo. I have hope that Mr. Boutwell will be reasonable enough to see the futility of massive resistance to desegregation. But he will not see this without pressure from devotees of civil rights. My friends, I must say to you that we have not made a single gain in civil rights without determined legal and nonviolent pressure. Lamentably, it is an historical fact that privileged groups seldom give up their privileges voluntarily. Individuals may see the moral light and voluntarily give up their unjust posture; but, as Reinhold Niebuhr has reminded us, groups tend to be more immoral than individuals.

We know through painful experience that freedom is never voluntarily given by the oppressor; it must be demanded by the oppressed. Frankly, I have yet to engage in a direct-action campaign that was "well timed" in the view of those who have not suffered unduly from the disease of segregation. For years now I have heard the word "Wait!" It rings in the ear of every Negro with piercing familiarity. This "Wait" has almost always meant "Never." We must come to see, with one of our distinguished jurists, that "justice too long delayed is justice denied."

We have waited for more than 340 years for our constitutional and God-given rights. The nations of Asia and Africa are moving with jetlike speed toward gaining political independence, but we still creep at horse-and-buggy pace toward gaining a cup of coffee at a lunch counter. Perhaps it is easy for those who have never felt the stinging darts of segregation to say, "Wait." But when you have seen vicious mobs lynch your mothers and fathers at will and down your sisters and brothers at whim; when you have seen hate-filled policemen curse, kick and even kill your black brothers and sisters; when you see the vast majority of your twenty million Negro brothers smothering in an airtight cage of poverty in the midst of an affluent society; when you suddenly find your tongue twisted and your speech stammering as you seek to explain to your six-year-old daughter why she can't go to the public amusement park that has just been advertised on television, and see tears welling up in her eyes when she is told that Funtown is closed to colored children, and see ominous clouds of inferiority beginning to form in her little mental sky, and see her beginning to distort her personality by developing an unconscious bitterness toward white people; when you have to concoct an answer for a five-year-old son who is asking: "Daddy, why do white people treat colored people so mean?"; when you take a cross-country drive and find it necessary to sleep night after night in the uncomfortable corners of your automobile because no motel will accept you; when you are humiliated day in and day out by nagging signs reading "white" and "colored"; when your first name becomes "nigger," your middle name becomes "boy" (however old you are) and your last name becomes "John," and your wife and mother are never given the respected title "Mrs."; when you are harried by day and haunted by night by the fact that you are a Negro, living constantly at tiptoe stance, never quite knowing what to expect next, and are plagued with inner fears and outer resentments; when you are forever fighting a degenerating sense of "nobodiness"—then you will understand why we find it difficult to wait. There comes a time when the cup of endurance runs over, and men are no longer willing to be plunged into the abyss of despair. I hope, sirs, you can understand our legitimate and unavoidable impatience.

You express a great deal of anxiety over our willingness to break laws. This is certainly a legitimate concern. Since we so diligently urge people to obey the Supreme Court's decision of 1954 outlawing segregation in the public schools, at first glance it may seem rather paradoxical for us consciously to break laws. One may well ask: "How can you advocate breaking some laws and obeying others?" The answer lies in the fact that there are two types of laws: just and unjust. I would be the first to advocate obeying just laws. One has not only a legal but a moral responsibility to obey just laws. Conversely, one has a moral responsibility to disobey unjust laws. I would agree with St. Augustine that "an unjust law is no law at all."

Now, what is the difference between the two? How does one determine whether a law is just or unjust? A just law is a man-made code that squares with the moral law or the law of God. An unjust law is a code that is out of harmony with the moral law. To put it in the terms of St. Thomas Aquinas: An unjust law is a human law that is not rooted in eternal law and natural law. Any law that uplifts human personality is just. Any law that degrades human personality is unjust. All segregation statutes are unjust because segregation distorts the soul and damages the personality. It gives the segregator a false sense of superiority and the segregated a false sense of inferiority. Segregation, to use the terminology of the Jewish philosopher Martin Buber, substitutes an "I—it" relationship for an "I—thou" relationship and ends up relegating persons to the status of things. Hence segregation is not only politically, economically and sociologically unsound, it is morally wrong and sinful. Paul Tillich has said that sin is separation. Is not segregation an existential expression of man's tragic separation, his awful estrangement, his terrible sinfulness? Thus it is that I can urge men to obey the 1954 decision of the Supreme Court, for it is morally right; and I can urge them to disobey segregation ordinances, for they are morally wrong.

Let us consider a more concrete example of just and unjust laws. An unjust law is a code that a numerical or power majority group compels a minority group to obey but does not make binding on itself. This is *difference* made legal. By the same token, a just law is a code that a majority compels a minority to follow and that it is willing to follow itself. This is *sameness* made legal.

Let me give another explanation. A law is unjust if it is inflicted on a minority that, as a result of being denied the right to vote, had no part in enacting or devising the law. Who can say that the legislature of Alabama which set up that state's segregation laws was democratically elected? Throughout Alabama all sorts of devious methods are used to prevent Negroes from becoming registered voters, and there are some counties in which, even though Negroes constitute a majority of the population, not a single Negro is registered. Can any law enacted under such circumstances be considered democratically structured?

Sometimes a law is just on its face and unjust in its application. For instance, I have been arrested on a charge of parading without a permit. Now, there is nothing wrong in having an ordinance which requires a permit for a parade. But such an ordinance becomes unjust when it is used to maintain segregation and to deny citizens the First-Amendment privilege of peaceful assembly and protest.

I hope you are able to see the distinction I am trying to point out. In no sense do I advocate evading or defying the law, as would the rabid segregationist. That would lead to anarchy. One who breaks an unjust law must do so openly, lovingly, and with a willingness to accept the penalty. I submit that an individual who breaks a law that conscience tells him is unjust, and who willingly accepts the penalty of imprisonment in order to arouse the conscience of the community over its injustice, is in reality expressing the highest respect for law.

Of course, there is nothing new about this kind of civil disobedience. It was evidenced sublimely in the refusal of Shadrach, Meshach and Abednego to obey the laws of Nebuchadnezzar, on the ground that a higher moral law was at stake. It was practiced superbly by the early Christians, who were willing to face hungry lions and the excruciating pain of chopping blocks rather than submit to certain unjust laws of the Roman Empire. To a degree, academic freedom is a reality today because Socrates practiced civil disobedience. In our own nation, the Boston Tea Party represented a massive act of civil disobedience.

We should never forget that everything Adolf Hitler did in Germany was "legal" and everything the Hungarian freedom fighters did in Hungary was "illegal." It was "illegal" to aid and comfort a Jew in Hitler's Germany. Even so, I am sure that, had I lived in Germany at the time, I would have aided and comforted my Jewish brothers. If today I lived in a Communist country where certain principles dear to the Christian faith are suppressed, I would openly advocate disobeying that country's antireligious laws.

I must make two honest confessions to you, my Christian and Jewish brothers. First, I must confess that over the past few years I have been gravely disappointed with the white moderate. I have almost reached the regrettable conclusion that the Negro's great stumbling block in his stride toward freedom is not the White Citizen's Counciler or the Ku Klux Klanner, but the white moderate, who is more devoted to "order" than to justice; who prefers a negative peace which is the absence of tension to a positive peace which is the presence of justice; who constantly says: "I agree with you in the goal you seek, but I cannot agree with your methods of direct action"; who paternalistically believes he can set the timetable for another man's freedom; who lives by a mythical concept of time and who constantly advises the Negro to wait for a "more convenient season." Shallow understanding from people of good will is more frustrating than absolute misunderstanding from people of ill will. Lukewarm acceptance is much more bewildering than outright rejection.

I had hoped that the white moderate would understand that law and order exist for the purpose of establishing justice and that when they fail in this purpose they become the dangerously structured dams that block the flow of social progress. I had hoped that the white moderate would understand that the present tension in the South is a necessary phase of the transition from an obnoxious negative peace, in which the Negro passively accepted his unjust plight, to a substantive and positive peace, in which all men will respect the dignity and worth of human personality. Actually, we who engage in nonviolent direct action are not the creators of tension. We merely bring to the surface the hidden tension that is already alive. We bring it out in the open, where it can be seen and dealt with. Like a boil that can never be cured so long as it is covered up but must be opened with all its ugliness to the natural medicines of air and light, injustice must be exposed, with all the tension its exposure creates, to the light of human conscience and the air of national opinion before it can be cured.

In your statement you assert that our actions, even though peaceful, must be condemned because they precipitate violence. But is this a logical assertion? Isn't this like condemning a robbed man because his possession of money precipitated the evil act of robbery? Isn't this like condemning Socrates because his unswerving commitment to truth and his philosophical inquiries precipitated the act by the misguided populace in which they made him drink hemlock? Isn't this like condemning Jesus because his unique God-consciousness and never-ceasing devotion to God's will precipitated the evil act of crucifixion? We must come to see that, as the federal courts have consistently affirmed, it is wrong to urge an individual to cease his efforts to gain his basic constitutional rights because the quest may precipitate violence. Society must protect the robbed and punish the robber.

I had also hoped that the white moderate would reject the myth concerning time in relation to the struggle for freedom. I have just received a letter from a white brother in Texas. He writes: "All Christians know that the colored people will receive equal rights eventually, but it is possible that you are in too great a religious hurry. It has taken Christianity almost two thousand years to accomplish what it has. The teachings of Christ take time to come to earth." Such an attitude stems from a tragic misconception of time, from the strangely irrational notion that there is something in the very flow of time that will inevitably cure all ills. Actually, time itself is neutral; it can be used either destructively or constructively. More and more I feel that the people of ill will have used time much more effectively than have the people of good will. We will have to repent in this generation not merely for the hateful words and actions of the bad people but for the appalling silence of the good people. Human progress never rolls in on wheels of inevitability; it comes through the tireless efforts of men willing to be co-workers with God, and without this hard work, time itself becomes an ally of the forces of social stagnation. We must use time creatively, in the knowledge that the time is always ripe to do right. Now is the time to make real the promise of democracy and transform our pending national elegy into a creative psalm of brotherhood. Now is the time to lift our national policy from the quicksand of racial injustice to the solid rock of human dignity.

You speak of our activity in Birmingham as extreme. At first I was rather disappointed that fellow clergymen would see my nonviolent efforts as those of an extremist. I began thinking about the fact that I stand in the middle of two opposing forces in the Negro community. One is a force of complacency, made up in part of Negroes who, as a result of long years of oppression, are so drained of self-respect and a sense of "somebodiness" that they have adjusted to segregation; and in part of a few middle-class Negroes who, because of a degree of academic and economic security and because in some ways they profit by segregation, have become insensitive to the problems of the masses. The other force is one of bitterness and hatred, and it comes perilously close to advocating violence. It is expressed in the various black nationalist groups that are springing up across the nation, the largest and best-known being Elijah Muhammad's Muslim movement. Nourished by the Negro's frustration over the continued existence of racial discrimination, this movement is made up of people who have lost faith in America, who have absolutely repudiated Christianity, and who have concluded that the white man is an incorrigible "devil."

I have tried to stand between these two forces, saying that we need emulate neither the "do-nothingism" of the complacent nor the hatred and despair of the black nationalist. For there is the more excellent way of love and nonviolent protest. I am grateful to God that, through the influence of the Negro church, the way of nonviolence became an integral part of our struggle.

If this philosophy had not emerged, by now many streets of the South would, I am convinced, be flowing with blood. And I am further convinced that if our white brothers dismiss as "rabble-rousers" and "outside agitators" those of us who employ nonviolent direct action, and if they refuse to support our nonviolent efforts, millions of Negroes will, out of frustration and despair, seek solace and security in black-nationalist ideologies—a development that would inevitably lead to a frightening racial nightmare.

Oppressed people cannot remain oppressed forever. The yearning for freedom eventually manifests itself, and that is what has happened to the American Negro. Something within has reminded him of his birthright of freedom, and something without has reminded him that it can be gained. Consciously or unconsciously, he has been caught up by the *Zeitgeist*, and with his black brothers of Africa and his brown and yellow brothers of Asia, South America and the Caribbean, the United States Negro is moving with a sense of great urgency toward the promised land of racial justice. If one recognizes this vital urge that has engulfed the Negro community, one should readily understand why public demonstrations are taking place. The Negro has many pent-up resentments and latent frustrations, and he must release them. So let him march; let him make prayer pilgrimages to the city hall; let him go on freedom rides—and try to understand why he must do so. If his repressed emotions are not released in nonviolent ways, they will seek expression through violence; this is not a threat but a fact of history. So I have not said to my people: "Get rid of your discontent." Rather, I have tried to say that this normal and healthy discontent can be channeled into the creative outlet of nonviolent direct action. And now this approach is being termed extremist.

But though I was initially disappointed at being categorized as an extremist, as I continued to think about the matter I gradually gained a measure of satisfaction from the label. Was not Jesus an extremist for love: "Love your enemies, bless them that curse you, do good to them that hate you, and pray for them which despitefully use you, and persecute you." Was not Amos an extremist for justice: "Let justice roll down like waters and righteousness like an ever-flowing stream." Was not Paul an extremist for the Christian gospel: "I bear in my body the marks of the Lord Jesus." Was not Martin Luther an extremist: "Here I stand; I cannot do otherwise, so help me God." And John Bunyan: "I will stay in jail to the end of my days before I make a butchery of my conscience." And Abraham Lincoln: This nation cannot survive half slave and half free." And Thomas Jefferson: "We hold these truths to be self-evident, that all men are created equal . . ." So the question is not whether we will be extremists, but what kind of extremists we will be. Will we be extremists for hate or for love? Will we be extremists for the preservation of injustive or for the extension of justice? In that dramatic scene on Calvary's hill three men were crucified. We must never forget that all three were crucified for the same crime—the crime of extremism. Two were extremists for immorality, and thus fell below their environment. The other, Jesus Christ, was an extremist for love, truth and goodness, and thereby rose above his environment. Perhaps the South, the nation and the world are in dire need of creative extremists.

I had hoped that the white moderate would see this need. Perhaps I was too optimistic; perhaps I expected too much. I suppose I should have realized that few members of the oppressor race can understand the deep groans and passionate yearnings of the oppressed race, and still fewer have the vision to see that injustice must be rooted out by strong, persistent and determined action. I am thankful, however, that some of our white brothers in the South have grasped the meaning of this social revolution and committed themselves to it. They are still all too few in quantity, but they are big in quality. Some—such as Ralph McGill, Lillian Smith, Harry Golden, James McBride Dabbs, Ann Braden and Sarah Patton Boyle—have written about our struggle in eloquent and prophetic terms. Others have marched with us down nameless streets of the South. They have languished in filthy, roach-infested jails, suffering the abuse and brutality of policemen who view them as "dirty nigger-lovers." Unlike so many of their moderate brothers and sisters, they have recognized the urgency of the moment and sensed the need for powerful "action" antidotes to combat the disease of segregation.

Let me take note of my other major disappointment. I have been so greatly disappointment with the white church and its leadership. Of course, there are some notable exceptions. I am not unmindful of the fact that each of you has taken some significant stands on this issue. I commend you, Reverend Stallings, for your Christian stand on this past Sunday, in welcoming Negroes to your worship service on a nonsegregated basis. I commend the Catholic leaders of this state for integrating Spring Hill College several years ago.

But despite these notable exceptions, I must honestly reiterate that I have been disappointed with the church. I do not say this as one of those negative critics who can always find something wrong with the church. I say this as a minister of the gospel, who loves the church; who was nurtured in its bosom; who has been sustained by its spiritual blessings and who will remain true to it as long as the cord of life shall lengthen.

When I was suddenly catapulted into the leadership of the bus protest in Montgomery, Alabama, a few years ago, I felt we would be supported by the white church. I felt that the white ministers, priests and rabbis of the South would be among our strongest allies. Instead, some have been outright opponents, refusing to understand the freedom movement and misrepresenting its leaders; all too many others have been more cautious than courageous and have remained silent behind the anesthetizing security of stained-glass windows.

In spite of my shattered dreams, I came to Birmingham with the hope that the white religious leadership of this community would see the justice of our cause and, with deep moral concern, would serve as the channel through which our just grievances could reach the power structure. I had hoped that each of you would understand. But again I have been disappointed.

I have heard numerous southern religious leaders admonish their worshipers to comply with a desegregation decision because it is the law, but I have longed to hear white ministers declare: "Follow this decree because integration is morally right and because the Negro is your brother." In the midst of blatant injustices inflicted upon the Negro, I have watched white churchmen stand on the sideline and mouth pious irrelevancies and sanctimonious trivialities. In the midst of a mighty struggle to rid our nation of racial and economic injustice, I have heard many ministers say: "Those are social issues, with which the gospel has no real concern." And I have watched many churches commit themselves to a completely other-worldly religion which makes a strange, un-Biblical distinction between body and soul, between the sacred and the secular.

I have traveled the length and breadth of Alabama, Mississippi and all the other southern states. On sweltering summer days and crisp autumn mornings I have looked at the South's beautiful churches with their lofty spires pointing heavenward. I have beheld the impressive outlines of her massive religious-education buildings. Over and over I have found myself asking: "What kind of people worship here? Who is their God? Where were their voices when the lips of Governor Barnett dripped with words of interposition and nullification? Where were they when Governor Wallace gave a clarion call for defiance and hatred? Where were their voices of support when brusied and weary Negro men and women decided to rise from the dark dungeons of complacency to the bright hills of creative protest?"

Yes, these questions are still in my mind. In deep disappointment I have wept over the laxity of the church. But be assured that my tears have been tears of love. There can be no deep disappointment where there is not deep love. Yes, I love the church. How could I do otherwise? I am in the rather unique position of being the son, the grandson and the great-grandson of preachers. Yes, I see the church as the body of Chirst. But, oh! How we have blemished and scarred that body through social neglect and through fear of being nonconformists.

There was a time when the church was very powerful—in the time when the early Christians rejoiced at being deemed worthy to suffer for what they believed. In those days the church was not merely a thermometer that recorded the ideas and principles of popular opinion; it was a thermostat that transformed the mores of society. Whenever the early Christians entered a town, the people in power became disturbed and immediately sought to convict the Christians for being "distrubers of the peace" and "outside agitators." But the Christians pressed on, in the conviction that they were "a colony of heaven," called to obey God rather than man. Small in number, they were big in commitment. They were too God-intoxicated to be "astronomically intimidated." By their effort and example they brought an end to such ancient evils as infanticide and gladiatorial contests.

Things are different now. So often the contemporary church is a weak, ineffectual voice with an uncertain sound. So often it is an archdefender of the status quo. Far from being disturbed by the presence of the church, the power structure of the average community is consoled by the church's silent—and often even vocal—sanction of things as they are.

But the judgment of God is upon the church as never before. If today's church does not recapture the sacrificial spirit of the early church, it will lose its authenticity, forfeit the loyalty of millions, and be dismissed as an irrelevant social club with no meaning for the twentieth century. Every day I meet young people whose disappointment with the church has turned into outright disgust.

Perhaps I have once again been too optimistic. Is organized religion too inextricably bound to the status quo to save our nation and the world? Perhaps I must turn my faith to the inner spiritual church, the church within the church, as the true *ekklesia* and the hope of the world. But again I am thankful to God that some noble souls from the ranks of organized religion have broken loose from the paralyzing chains of conformity and joined us as active partners in the struggle for freedom. They have left their secure congregations and walked the streets of Albany, Georgia, with us. They have gone down the highways of the South on tortuous rides for freedom. Yes, they have gone to jail with us. Some have been dismissed from their churches, have lost the support of their bishops and fellow ministers. But they have acted in the faith that right defeated is stronger than evil triumphant. Their witness has been the spiritual salt that has preserved the true meaning of the gospel in these troubled times. They have carved a tunnel of hope through the dark mountain of disappointment.

I hope the church as a whole will meet the challenge of this decisive hour. But even if the church does not come to the aid of justice, I have no despair about the future. I have no fear about the outcome of our struggle in Birmingham, even if our motives are at present misunderstood. We will reach the goal of freedom in Birmingham and all over the nation, because the goal of America is freedom. Abused and scorned though we may be, our destiny is tied up with America's destiny. Before the pilgrims landed at Plymouth, we were here. Before the pen of Jefferson etched the majestic words of the Declaration of Independence across the pages of history, we were here. For more than two centuries our forebears labored in this country without wages; they made cotton king; they built the homes of their masters while suffering gross injustice and shameful humiliation—and yet out of a bottomless vitality they continued to thrive and develop. If the inexpressible cruelties of slavery could not stop us, the opposition we now face will surely fail. We will win our freedom because the sacred heritage of our nation and the eternal will of God are embodied in our echoing demands.

Before closing I feel impelled to mention one other point in your statement that has troubled me profoundly. You warmly commended the Birmingham police force for keeping "order" and "preventing violence." I doubt that you would have so warmly commended the police force if you had seen its dogs sinking their teeth into unarmed, nonviolent Negroes. I doubt that you would so quickly commend the policemen if you were to observe their ugly and inhumane treatment of Negroes here in the city jail; if you were to watch them push and curse old Negro women and young Negro girls; if you were to see them slap and kick old Negro men and young boys; if you were to observe them, as they did on two occasions, refuse to give us food because we wanted to sing our grace together. I cannot join you in your praise of the Birmingham police department.

It is true that the police have exercised a degree of discipline in handling the demonstrators. In this sense they have conducted themselves rather "nonviolently" in public. But for what purpose? To preserve the evil system of segregation. Over the past few years I have consistently preached that nonviolence demands that the means we use must be as pure as the ends we seek. I have tried to make clear that it is wrong to use immoral means to attain moral ends. But now I must affirm that it is just as wrong, or perhaps even more so, to use moral means to preserve immoral ends. Perhaps Mr. Connor and his policemen have been rather nonviolent in public, as was Chief Pritchett in Albany, Georgia, but they have used the moral means of nonviolence to maintain the immoral end of racial injustice. As T. S. Eliot has said: "The last temptation is the greatest treason: To do the right deed for the wrong reason."

I wish you had commended the Negro sit-inners and demonstrators of Birmingham for their sublime courage, their willingness to suffer and their amazing discipline in the midst of great provocation. One day the South will recognize its real heroes. They will be the James Merediths, with the noble sense of purpose that enables them to face jeering and hostile mobs, and with the agonizing loneliness that characterizes the life of the pioneer. They will be old, oppressed, battered Negro women, symbolized in a seventy-two-year-old woman in Montgomery, Alabama, who rose up with a sense of dignity and with her people decided not to ride segregated buses, and who responded with ungrammatical profundity to one who inquired about her weariness: "My feets is tired, but my soul is at rest." They will be the young high school and college students, the young ministers of the gospel and a host of their elders, courageously and nonviolently sitting in at lunch counters and willingly going to jail for conscience' sake. One day the South will know that when these disinherited children of God sat down at lunch counters, they were in reality standing up for what is best in the American dream and for the most sacred values in our Judaeo-Christian heritage, thereby bringing our nation back to those great wells of democracy which were dug deep by the founding fathers in their formulation of the Constitution and the Declaration of Independence.

Never before have I written so long a letter. I'm afraid it is much too long to take your precious time. I can assure you that it would have been much shorter if I had been writing from a comfortable desk, but what else can one do when he is alone in a narrow jail cell, other than write long letters, think long thoughts and pray long prayers?

If I have said anything in this letter that overstates the truth and indicates an unreasonable inpatience, I beg you to forgive me. If I have said anything that understates the truth and indicates my having a patience that allows me to settle for anything less than brotherhood, I beg God to forgive me.

I hope this letter finds you strong in the faith. I also hope that circumstances will soon make it possible for me to meet each of you, not as an integrationist or a civil-rights leader but as a fellow clergyman and a Christian brother. Let us all hope that the dark clouds of racial prejudice will soon pass away and the deep fog of misunderstanding will be lifted from our fear-drenched communities, and in some not too distant tomorrow the radiant stars of love and brotherhood will shine over our great nation with all their scintillating beauty.

Yours for the cause of Peace and Brotherhood,
Martin Luther King, Jr.

AUTHOR'S NOTE

This response to a published statement by eight fellow clergy men from Alabama (Bishop C. C. J. Carpenter, Bishop Joseph A. Durick, Rabbi Hilton L. Grafman, Bishop Paul Hardin, Bishop Holan B. Harmon, the Reverend George M. Murray, the Reverend Edward V. Ramage and the Reverend Earl Stallings) was composed under somewhat constricting circumstances. Begun on the margins of the newspaper in which the statement appeared while I was in jail, the letter was continued on scraps of writing paper supplied by a friendly Negro trusty, and concluded on a pad my attorneys were eventually permitted to leave me. Although the text remains in substance unaltered, I have indulged in the author's prerogative of polishing it for publication.

MALCOLM X

The Ballot or the Bullet

Mr. Moderator, Brother Lomax, brothers and sisters, friends and enemies: I just can't believe everyone in here is a friend and I don't want to leave anybody out. The question tonight, as I understand it, is "The Negro Revolt, and Where Do We Go From Here?" or "What Next?" In my little humble way of understanding it, it points toward either the ballot or the bullet.

Before we try and explain what is meant by the ballot or the bullet, I would like to clarify something concerning myself. I'm still a Muslim, my religion is still Islam. That's my personal belief. Just as Adam Clayton Powell is a Christian minister who heads the Abyssinian Bapist Church in New York, but at the same time takes part in the political struggles to try and bring about rights to the black people in this country; and Dr. Martin Luther King is a Christian minister down in Atlanta, Georgia, who heads another organization fighting for the civil rights of black people in this country; and Rev. Galamison, I guess you've heard of him, is another Christian minister in New York who has been deeply involved in the school boycotts to eliminate segregated education; well, I myself am a minister, not a Christian minister, but a Muslim minister; and I believe in action on all fronts by whatever means necessary.

Although I'm still a Muslim, I'm not here tonight to discuss my religion. I'm not here to try and change your religion. I'm not here to argue or discuss anything that we differ about, because it's time for us to submerge our differences and realize that it is best for us to first see that we have the same problem, a common problem—a problem that will make you catch hell whether you're a Baptist, or a Methodist, or a Muslim, or a nationalist. Whether you're educated or illiterate, whether you live on the boulevard or in the alley, you're going to catch hell just like I am. We're all in the same boat and we all are going to catch the same hell from the same man. He just happens to be a white man. All of us have suffered here, in this country, political oppression at the hands of the white man, economic exploitation at the hands of the white man, and social degradation at the hands of the white man.

Now in speaking like this, it doesn't mean that we're anti-white, but it does mean we're anti-exploitation, we're anti-degradation, we're anti-oppression. And if the white man doesn't want us to be anti-him, let him stop oppressing and exploiting and degrading us. Whether we are Christians or Muslims or nationalists or agnostics or atheists, we must first learn to forget our differences. If we have differences, let us differ in the closet; when we come out in front, let us not have anything to argue about until we get finished arguing with the man. If the late President Kennedy could get together with Khrushchev and exchange some wheat, we certainly have more in common with each other than Kennedy and Khrushchev had with each other.

If we don't do something real soon, I think you'll have to agree that we're going to be forced either to use the ballot or the bullet. It's one or the other in 1964. It isn't that time is running out—time has run out! 1964 threatens to be the most explosive year America has ever witnessed. The most explosive year. Why? It's also a political year. It's the year when all of the white politicians will be back in the so-called Negro community jiving you and me for some votes. The year when all of the white political crooks will be right back in your and my community with their false promises, building up our hopes for a let-down, with their trickery and their treachery, with their false promises which they don't intend to keep. As they nourish these dissatisfactions, it can only lead to one thing, an explosion; and now we have the type of black man on the scene in America today—I'm sorry, Brother Lomax—who just doesn't intend to turn the other cheek any longer.

Don't let anybody tell you anything about the odds are against you. If they draft you, they send you to Korea and make you face 800 million Chinese. If you can be brave over there, you can be brave right here. These odds aren't as great as those odds. And if you fight here, you will at least know what you're fighting for.

I'm not a politician, not even a student of politics; in fact, I'm not a student of much of anything. I'm not a Democrat, I'm not a Republican, and I don't even consider myself an American. If you and I were Americans, there'd be no problem. Those Hunkies that just got off the boat, they're already Americans; Polacks are already Americans; the Italian refugees are already Americans. Everything that came out of Europe, every blue-eyed thing, is already an American. And as long as you and I have been over here, we aren't Americans yet.

Well, I am one who doesn't believe in deluding myself. I'm not going to sit at your table and watch you eat, with nothing on my plate, and call myself a diner. Sitting at the table doesn't make you a diner, unless you eat some of what's on that plate. Being here in America doesn't make you an American. Being born here in America doesn't make you an American. Why, if birth made you American, you wouldn't need any legislation, you wouldn't need any amendments to the Constitution, you wouldn't be faced with civil-rights filibustering in Washington, D.C., right now. They don't have to pass civil-rights legislation to make a Polack an American.

No, I'm not an American. I'm one of the 22 million black people who are the victims of Americanism. One of the 22 million black people who are the victims of democracy, nothing but disguised hypocrisy. So, I'm not standing here speaking to you as an American, or a patriot, or a flag-saluter, or a flag-waver—no, not I. I'm speaking as a victim of this American system. And I see America through the eyes of the victim. I don't see any American dream; I see an American nightmare.

These 22 million victims are waking up. Their eyes are coming open. They're beginning to see what they used to only look at. They're becoming politically mature. They are realizing that there are new political trends from coast to coast. As they see these new political trends, it's possible for them to see that every time there's an election the races are so close that they have to have a recount. They had to recount in Massachusetts to see who was going to be governor, it was so close. It was the same way in Rhode Island, in Minnesota, and in many other parts of the country. And the same with Kennedy and Nixon when they ran for president. It was so close they had to count all over again. Well, what does this mean? It means that when white people are evenly divided, and black people have a bloc of votes of their own, it is left up to them to determine who's going to sit in the White House and who's going to be in the dog house.

It was the black man's vote that put the present administration in Washington, D.C. Your vote, your dumb vote, your ignorant vote, your wasted vote put in an administration in Washington, D.C., that has seen fit to pass every kind of legislation imaginable, saving you until last, then filibustering on top of that. And your and my leaders have the audacity to run around clapping their hands and talk about how much progress we're making. And what a good president we have. If he wasn't good in Texas, he sure can't be good in Washington, D.C. Because Texas is a lynch state. It is in the same breath as Mississippi, no different; only they lynch you in Texas with a Texas accent and lynch you in Mississippi with a Mississippi accent. And these Negro leaders have the audacity to go and have some coffee in the White House with a Texan, a Southern cracker—that's all he is—and then come out and tell you and me that he's going to be better for us because, since he's from the South, he knows how to deal with the Southerners. What kind of logic is that? Let Eastland be president, he's from the South too. He should be better able to deal with them than Johnson.

In this present administration they have in the House of Representatives 257 Democrats to only 177 Republicans. They control two-thirds of the House vote. Why can't they pass something that will help you and me? In the Senate, there are 67 senators who are of the Democratic Party. Only 33 of them are Republicans. Why, the Democrats have got the government sewed up, and you're the one who sewed it up for them. And what have they given you for it? Four years in office, and just now getting around to some civil-rights legislation. Just now, after everything else is gone, out of the way, they're going to sit down now and play with you all summer long—the same old giant con game that they call filibuster. All those are in cahoots together. Don't you ever think they're not in cahoots together, for the man that is heading the civil-rights filibuster is a man from Georgia named Richard Russell. When Johnson became president, the first man he asked for when he got back to Washington, D.C., was "Dicky"—that's how tight they are. That's his boy, that's his pal, that's his buddy. But they're playing that old con game. One of them makes believe he's for you, and he's got it fixed where the other one is so tight against you, he never has to keep his promise.

So it's time in 1964 to wake up. And when you see them coming up with that kind of conspiracy, let them know your eyes are open. And let them know you got something else that's wide open too. It's got to be the ballot or the bullet. The ballot or the bullet. If you're afraid to use an expression like that, you should get on out of the country, you should get back in the cotton patch, you should get back in the alley. They get all the Negro vote, and after they get it, the Negro gets nothing in return. All they did when they got to Washington was give a few big Negroes big jobs. Those big Negroes didn't need big jobs, they already had jobs. That's camouflage, that's trickery, that's treachery, window-dressing. I'm not trying to knock out the Democrats for the Republicans, we'll get to them in a minute. But it is true—you put the Democrats first and the Democrats put you last.

Look at it the way it is. What alibis do they use, since they control Congress and the Senate? What alibi do they use when you and I ask, "Well, when are you going to keep your promise?" They blame the Dixiecrats. What is a Dixiecrat? A Democrat. A Dixiecrat is nothing but a Democrat in disguise. The titular head of the Democrats is also the head of the Dixiecrats, because the Dixiecrats are a part of the Democratic Party. The Democrats have never kicked the Dixiecrats out of the party. The Dixiecrats bolted themselves once, but the Democrats didn't put them out. Imagine, these lowdown Southern segregations put the Northern Democrats down. But the Northern Democrats have never put the Dixiecrats down. No, look at that thing the way it is. They have got a con game going on, a political con game, and you and I are in the middle. It's time for you and me to wake up and start looking at it like it is, and trying to understand it like it is; and then we can deal with it like it is.

The Dixiecrats in Washington, D.C., control the key committees that run the government. The only reason the Dixiecrats control these committees is because they have seniority. The only reason they have seniority is because they come from states where Negroes can't vote. This is not even a government that's based on democracy. It is not a government that is made up of representatives of the people. Half of the people in the South can't even vote. Eastland is not even supposed to be in Washington. Half of the senators and congressmen who occupy these key positions in Washington, D.C., are there illegally, are there unconstitutionally.

I was in Washington, D.C., a week ago Thursday, when they were debating whether or not they should let the bill come onto the floor. And in the back of the room where the Senate meets, there's a huge map of the United States, and on that map it shows the location of Negroes throughout the country. And it shows that the Southern section of the country, the states that are most heavily concentrated with Negroes, are the ones that have senators and congressmen standing up filibustering and doing all other kinds of trickery to keep the Negro from being able to vote. This is pitiful. But it's not pitiful for us any longer; it's actually pitiful for the white man, because soon now, as the Negro awakens a little more and sees the vise that he's in, sees the bag that he's in, sees the real game that he's in, then the Negro's going to develop a new tactic.

These senators and congressmen actually violate the constitutional amendments that guarantee the people of that particular state or county the right to vote. And the Constitution itself has within it the machinery to expel any representative from a state where the voting rights of the people are violated. You don't even need new legislation. Any person in Congress right now, who is there from a state or a district where the voting rights of the people are violated, that particular person should be expelled from Congress. And when you expel him, you've removed one of the obstacles in the path of any real meaningful legislation in this country. In fact, when you expel them, you don't need new legislation, because they will be replaced by black representatives from countries and districts where the black man is in the majority, not in the minority.

If the black man in these Southern states had his full voting rights, the key Dixiecrats in Washington, D.C., which means the key Democrats in Washington, D.C., would lose their seats. The Democratic Party itself would lose its power. It would cease to be powerful as a party. When you see the amount of power that would be lost by the Democratic Party if it were to lose the Dixiecrat wing, or branch, or element, you can see where it's against the interests of the Democrats to give voting rights to Negroes in states where the Democrats have been in complete power and authority ever since the Civil War. You just can't belong to that party without analyzing it.

I say again, I'm not anti-Democrat, I'm not anti-Republican, I'm not anti-anything. I'm just questioning their sincerity, and some of the strategy that they've been using on our people by promising them promises that they don't intend to keep. When you keep the Democrats in power, you're keeping the Dixiecrats in power. I doubt that my good Brother Lomax will deny that. A vote for a Democrat is a vote for a Dixiecrat. That's why, in 1964, it's time now for you and me to become more politically mature and realize what the ballot is for; what we're supposed to get when we cast a ballot; and that if we don't cast a ballot, it's going to end up in a situation where we're going to have to cast a bullet. It's either a ballot or a bullet.

In the North, they do it a different way. They have a system that's known as gerrymandering, whatever that means. It means when Negroes become too heavily concentrated in a certain area, and begin to gain too much political power, the white man comes along and changes the district lines. You may say, "Why do you keep saying white man?" Because it's the white man who does it. I haven't ever seen any Negro changing any lines. They don't let him get near the line. It's the white man who does this. And usually, it's the white man who grins at you the most, and pats you on the back, and is supposed to be your friend. He may be friendly, but he's not your friend.

So, what I'm trying to impress upon you, in essence, is this: You and I in America are faced not with a segregationist conspiracy, we're faced with a government conspiracy. Everyone who's filibustering is a senator—that's the government. Everyone who's finagling in Washington, D.C., is a congressman—that's the government. You don't have anybody putting blocks in your path but people who are a part of the government. The same government that you go abroad to fight for and die for is the government that is in a conspiracy to deprive you of your voting rights, deprive you of your economic opportunities, deprive you of decent housing, deprive you of decent education. You don't need to go to the employer alone, it is the government itself, the government of America, that is responsible for the oppression and exploitation and degradation of black people in this country. And you should drop it in their lap. This government has failed the Negro. This so-called democracy has failed the Negro. And all these white liberals have definitely failed the Negro.

So, where do we go from here? First, we need some friends. We need some new allies. The entire civil-rights struggle needs a new interpretation, a broader interpretation. We need to look at this civil-rights thing from another angle—from the inside as well as from the outside. To those of us whose philosophy is black nationalism, the only way you can get involved in the civil-rights struggle is give it a new interpretation. That old interpretation excluded us. It kept us out. So, we're giving a new interpretation to the civil-rights struggle, an interpretation that will enable us to come into it, take part in it. And these handkerchief-heads who have been dillydallying and pussy-footing and compromising— we don't intend to let them pussyfoot and dillydally and compromise any longer.

How can you thank a man for giving you what's already yours? How then can you thank him for giving you only part of what's already yours? You haven't even made progress, if what's being given to you, you should have had already. That's not progress. And I love my Brother Lomax, the way he pointed out we're right back where we were in 1954. We're not even as far up as we were in 1954. We're behind where we were in 1954. There's more segregation now than there was in 1954. There's more racial animosity, more racial hatred, more racial violence today in 1964, than there was in 1954. Where is the progress?

And now you're facing a situation where the young Negro's coming up. They don't want to hear that "turn-the-other-cheek" stuff, no. In Jacksonville, those were teenagers, they were throwing Molotov cocktails. Negroes have never done that before. But it shows you there's a new deal coming in. There's new thinking coming in. There's new strategy coming in. It'll be Molotov cocktails this month, hand grenades next month, and something else next month. It'll be ballots, or it'll be bullets. It'll be liberty, or it will be death. The only difference about this kind of death—it'll be reciprocal. You know what is meant by "reciprocal"? That's one of Brother Lomax's words, I stole it from him. I don't usually deal with those big words because I don't usually deal with big people. I deal with small people. I find you can get a whole lot of small people and whip hell out of a whole lot of big people. They haven't got anything to lose, and they've got everything to gain. And they'll let you know in a minute: "It takes two to tango; when I go, you go."

The black nationalists, those whose philosophy is black nationalism, in bringing about this new interpretation of the entire meaning of civil rights, look upon it as meaning, as Brother Lomax has pointed out, equality of opportunity. Well, we're justified in seeking civil rights, if it means equality of opportunity, because all we're doing there is trying to collect for our investment. Our mothers and fathers invested sweat and blood. Three hundred and ten years we worked in this country without a dime in return—I mean without a *dime* in return. You let the white man walk around here talking about how rich this country is, but you never stop to think how it got rich so quick. It got rich because you made it rich.

You take the people who are in this audience right now. They're poor, we're all poor as individuals. Our weekly salary individually amounts to hardly anything. But if you take the salary of everyone in here collectively it'll fill up a whole lot of baskets. It's a lot of wealth. If you can collect the wages of just these people right here for a year, you'll be rich—richer than rich. When you look at it like that, think how rich Uncle Sam had to become, not with this handful, but millions of black people. Your and my mother and father, who didn't work an eight-hour shift, but worked from "can't see" in the morning until "can't see" at night, and worked for nothing making the white man rich, making Uncle Sam rich.

This is our investment. This is our contribution—our blood. Not only did we give of our free labor, we gave of our blood. Every time he had a call to arms, we were the first ones in uniform. We died on every battlefield the white man had. We have made a greater sacrifice than anybody who's standing up in America today. We have made a greater contribution and have collected less. Civil rights, for those of us whose philosophy is black nationalism, means: "Give it to us now. Don't wait for next year. Give it to us yesterday, and that's not fast enough."

I might stop right here to point out one thing. Whenever you're going after something that belongs to you, anyone who's depriving you of the right to have it is a criminal. Understand that. Whenever you are going after something that is yours, you are within your legal rights to lay claim to it. And anyone who puts forth any effort to deprive you of that which is yours, is breaking the law, is a criminal. And this was pointed out by the Supreme Court decision. It outlawed segregation. Which means segregation is against the law. Which means a segregationist is breaking the law. A segregationist is a criminal. You can't label him as anything other than that. And when you demonstrate against segregation, the law is on your side. The Supreme Court is on your side.

Now, who is it that opposes you in carrying out the law? The police department itself. With police dogs and clubs. Whenever you demonstrate against segregation, whether it is segregated education, segregated housing, or anything else, the law is on your side, and anyone who stands in the way is not the law any longer. They are breaking the law, they are not representatives of the law. Any time you demonstrate against segregation and a man has the audacity to put a police dog on you, kill that dog, kill him, I'm telling you, kill that dog. I say it, if they put me in jail tomorrow, kill—that—dog. Then you'll put a stop to it. Now, if these white people in here don't want to see that kind of action, get down and tell the mayor to tell the police department to pull the dogs in. That's all you have to do. If you don't do it, someone else will.

If you don't take this kind of stand, your little children will grow up and look at you and think "shame." If you don't take an uncompromising stand—I don't mean go out and get violent; but at the same time you should never be nonviolent unless you run into some nonviolence. I'm nonviolent with those who are nonviolent with me. But when you drop that violence on me, then you've made me go insane, and I'm not responsible for what I do. And that's the way every Negro should get. Any time you know you're within the law, within your legal rights, within your moral rights, in accord with justice, then die for what you believe in. But don't die alone. Let your dying be reciprocal. This is what is meant by equality. What's good for the goose is good for the gander.

When we begin to get in this area, we need new friends, we need new allies. We need to expand the civil-rights struggle to a higher level—to the level of human rights.

Whenever you are in a civil-rights struggle, whether you know it or not, you are confining yourself to the jurisdiction of Uncle Sam. No one from the outside world can speak out in your behalf as long as your struggle is a civil-rights struggle. Civil rights comes within the domestic affairs of this country. All of our African brothers and our Asian brothers and our Latin-American brothers cannot open their mouths and interfere in the domestic affairs of the United States. And as long as it's civil rights, this comes under the jurisdiction of Uncle Sam.

But the United Nations has what's known as the charter of human rights, it has a committee that deals in human rights. You may wonder why all of the atrocities that have been committed in Africa and in Hungary and in Asia and in Latin America are brought before the UN, and the Negro problem is never brought before the UN. This is part of the conspiracy. This old, tricky, blue-eyed liberal who is supposed to be your and my friend, supposed to be in our corner, supposed to be subsidizing our struggle, and supposed to be acting in the capacity of an adviser, never tells you anything about human rights. They keep you wrapped up in civil rights. And you spend so much time barking up the civil-rights tree, you don't even know there's a human-rights tree on the same floor.

When you expand the civil-rights struggle to the level of human rights, you can then take the case of the black man in this country before the nations in the UN. You can take it before the General Assembly. You can take Uncle Sam before a world court. But the only level you can do it on is the level of human rights. Civil rights keeps you under his restrictions, under his jurisdiction. Civil rights keeps you in his pocket. Civil rights means you're asking Uncle Sam to treat you right. Human rights are something you were born with. Human rights are your God-given rights. Human rights are the rights that are recognized by all nations of this earth. And any time any one violates your human rights, you can take them to the world court. Uncle Sam's hands are dripping with blood, dripping with the blood of the black man in this country. He's the earth's number-one hypocrite. He has the audacity—yes, he has—imagine him posing as the leader of the free world. The free world!—and you over here singing "We Shall Overcome." Expand the civil-rights struggle to the level of human rights, take it into the United Nations, where our African brothers can throw their weight on our side, where our Asian brothers can throw their weight on our side, where our Latin-American brothers can throw their weight on our side, and where 800 million Chinamen are sitting there waiting to throw their weight on our side.

Let the world know how bloody his hands are. Let the world know the hypocrisy that's practiced over here. Let it be the ballot or the bullet. Let him know that it must be the ballot or the bullet.

When you take your case to Washington, D.C., you're taking it to the criminal who's responsible; it's like running from the wolf to the fox. They're all in cahoots together. They all work political chicanery and make you look like a chump before the eyes of the world. Here you are walking around in America, getting ready to be drafted and sent abroad, like a tin soldier, and when you get over there, people ask you what are you fighting for, and you have to stick your tongue in your cheek. No, take Uncle Sam to court, take him before the world.

By ballot I only mean freedom. Don't you know—I disagree with Lomax on this issue—that the ballot is more important than the dollar? Can I prove it? Yes. Look in the UN. There are poor nations in the UN; yet those poor nations can get together with their voting power and keep the rich nations from making a move. They have one nation—one vote, everyone has an equal vote. And when those brothers from Asia, and Africa and the darker parts of this earth get together, their voting power is sufficient to hold Sam in check. Or Russia in check. Or some other section of the earth in check. So, the ballot is most important.

Right now, in this country, if you and I, 22 million African-Americans—that's what we are—Africans who are in America. You're nothing but Africans. Nothing but Africans. In fact, you'd get farther calling yourself African instead of Negro. Africans don't catch hell. You're the only one catching hell. They don't have to pass civil-rights bills for Africans. An African can go anywhere he wants right now. All you've got to do is tie your head up. That's right, go anywhere you want. Just stop being a Negro. Change your name to Hoogagagooba. That'll show you how silly the white man is. You're dealing with a silly man. A friend of mine who's very dark put a turban on his head and went into a restaurant in Atlanta before they called themselves desegregated. He went into a white restaurant, he sat down, they served him, and he said, "What would happen if a Negro came in here?" And there he's sitting, black as night, but because he had his head wrapped up the waitress looked back at him and says, "Why, there wouldn't no nigger dare come in here."

So, you're dealing with a man whose bias and prejudice are making him lose his mind, his intelligence, every day. He's frightened. He looks around and sees what's taking place on this earth, and he sees that the pendulum of time is swinging in your direction. The dark people are waking up. They're losing their fear of the white man. No place where he's fighting right now is he winning. Everywhere he's fighting, he's fighting someone your and my complexion. And they're beating him. He can't win any more. He's won his last battle. He failed to win the Korean War. He couldn't win it. He had to sign a truce. That's a loss. Any time Uncle Sam, with all his machinery for warfare, is held to a draw by some rice-eaters, he's lost the battle. He had to sign a truce. America's not supposed to sign a truce. She's supposed to be bad. But she's not bad any more. She's bad as long as she can use her hydrogen bomb, but she can't use hers for fear Russia might use hers. Russia can't use hers, for fear that Sam might use his. So, both of them are weaponless. They can't use the weapon because each's weapon nullifies the other's. So the only place where action can take place is on the ground. And the white man can't win another war fighting on the ground. Those days are over. The black man knows it, the brown man knows it, the red man knows it, and the yellow man knows it. So they engage him in guerrilla warfare. That's not his style. You've got to have heart to be a guerrilla warrior, and he hasn't got any heart. I'm telling you now.

I just want to give you a little briefing on guerrilla warfare because, before you know it, before you know it—It takes heart to be a guerrilla warrior because you're on your own. In conventional warfare you have tanks and a whole lot of other people with you to back you up, planes over your head and all that kind of stuff. But a guerrilla is on his own. All you have is a rifle, some sneakers and a bowl of rice, and that's all you need—and a lot of heart. The Japanese on some of those islands in the Pacific, when the American soldiers landed, one Japanese sometimes could hold the whole army off. He'd just wait until the sun went down, and when the sun went down they were all equal. He would take his little blade and slip from bush to bush, and from American to American. The white soldiers couldn't cope with that. Whenever you see a white soldier that fought in the Pacific, he has the shakes, he has a nervous condition, because they scared him to death.

The same thing happened to the French up in French Indochina. People who just a few years previously were rice farmers got together and ran the heavily-mechanized French army out of Indochina. You don't need it—modern warfare today won't work. This is the day of the guerrilla. They did the same thing in Algeria. Algerians, who were nothing but Bedouins, took a rifle and sneaked off to the hills, and de Gaulle and all of his highfalutin' war machinery couldn't defeat those guerrillas. Nowhere on this earth does the white man win in a guerrilla warfare. It's not his speed. Just as guerrilla warfare is prevailing in Asia and in parts of Africa and in parts of Latin America, you've got to be mighty naive, or you've got to play the black man cheap, if you don't think some day he's going to wake up and find that it's got to be the ballot or the bullet.

I would like to say, in closing, a few things concerning the Muslim Mosque, Inc., which we established recently in New York City. It's true we're Muslims and our religion is Islam, but we don't mix our religion with our politics and our economics and our social and civil activities—not any more. We keep our religion in our mosque. After our religious services are over, then as Muslims we become involved in political action, economic action and social and civic action. We become involved with anybody, anywhere, any time and in any manner that's designed to eliminate the evils, the political, economic and social evils that are afflicting the people of our community.

The political philosophy of black nationalism means that the black man should control the politics and the politicians in his own community; no more. The black man in the black community has to be re-educated into the science of politics so he will know what politics is supposed to bring him in return. Don't be throwing out any ballots. A ballot is like a bullet. You don't throw your ballots until you see a target, and if that target is not within your reach, keep your ballot in your pocket. The political philosophy of black nationalism is being taught in the Christian church. It's being taught in the NAACP. It's being taught in CORE meetings. It's being taught in SNCC [Student Non-violent Coordinating Committee] meetings. It's being taught in Muslim meetings. It's being taught where nothing but atheists and agnostics come together. It's being taught everywhere. Black people are fed up with the dillydallying, pussyfooting, compromising approach that we've been using toward getting our freedom. We want freedom *now*, but we're not going to get it saying "We Shall Overcome." We've got to fight until we overcome.

The economic philosophy of black nationalism is pure and simple. It only means that we should control the economy of our community. Why should white people be running all the stores in our community? Why should white people be running the banks of our community? Why should the economy of our community be in the hands of the white man? Why? If a black man can't move his store into a white community, you tell me why a white man should move his store into a black community. The philosophy of black nationalism involves a re-education program in the black community in regards to economics. Our people have to be made to see that any time you take your dollar out of your community and spend it in a community where you don't live, the community where you live will get poorer and poorer, and the community where you spend your money will get richer and richer. Then you wonder why where you live is always a ghetto or a slum area. And where you and I are concerned, not only do we lose it when we spend it out of the community, but the white man has got all our stores in the community tied up; so that though we spend it in the community, at sundown the man who runs the store takes it over across town somewhere. He's got us in a vise.

So the economic philosophy of black nationalism means in every church, in every civic organization, in every fraternal order, it's time now for our people to become conscious of the importance of controlling the economy of our community. If we own the stores, if we operate the businesses, if we try and establish some industry in our community, then we're developing to the position where we are creating employment for our own kind. Once you gain control of the economy of your own community, then you don't have to picket and boycott and beg some cracker downtown for a job in his business.

The social philosophy of black nationalism only means that we have to get together and remove the evils, the vices, alcoholism, drug addiction, and other evils that are destroying the moral fiber of our community. We ourselves have to lift the level of our community, the standard of our community to a higher level, make our own society beautiful so that we will be satisfied in our own social circles and won't be running around here trying to knock our way into a social circle where we're not wanted.

So I say, in spreading a gospel such as black nationalism, it is not designed to make the black man re-evaluate the white man—you know him already—but to make the black man re-evaluate himself. Don't change the white man's mind—you can't change his mind, and that whole thing about appealing to the moral conscience of America—America's conscience is bankrupt. She lost all conscience a long time ago. Uncle Sam has no conscience. They don't know what morals are. They don't try and eliminate an evil because it's evil, or because it's illegal, or because it's immoral; they eliminate it only when it threatens their existence. So you're wasting your time appealing to the moral conscience of a bankrupt man like Uncle Sam. If he had a conscience, he'd straighten this thing out with no more pressure being put upon him. So it is not necessary to change the white man's mind. We have to change our own mind. You can't change his mind about us. We've got to change our own minds about each other. We have to see each other with new eyes. We have to see each other as brothers and sisters. We have to come together with warmth so we can develop unity and harmony that's necessary to get this problem solved ourselves. How can we do this? How can we avoid jealousy? How can we avoid the suspicion and the divisions that exist in the community? I'll tell you how.

I have watched how Billy Graham comes into a city, spreading what he calls the gospel of Christ, which is only white nationalism. That's what he is. Billy Graham is a white nationalist; I'm a black nationalist. But since it's the natural tendency for leaders to be jealous and look upon a powerful figure like Graham with suspicion and envy, how is it possible for him to come into a city and get all the cooperation of the church leaders? Don't think because they're church leaders that they don't have weaknesses that make them envious and jealous—no, everybody's got it. It's not an accident that when they want to choose a cardinal [as Pope] over there in Rome, they get in a closet so you can't hear them cussing and fighting and carrying on.

Billy Graham comes in preaching the gospel of Christ, he evangelizes the gospel, he stirs everybody up, but he never tries to start a church. If he came in trying to start a church, all the churches would be against him. So, he just comes in talking about Christ and tells everybody who gets Christ to go to any church where Christ is; and in this way the church cooperates with him. So we're going to take a page from his book.

Our gospel is black nationalism. We're not trying to threaten the existence of any organization, but we're spreading the gospel of black nationalism. Anywhere there's a church that is also preaching and practicing the gospel of black nationalism, join that church. If the NAACP is preaching and practicing the gospel of black nationalism, join the NAACP. If CORE is spreading and practicing the gospel of black nationalism, join CORE. Join any organization that has a gospel that's for the uplift of the black man. And when you get into it and see them pussyfooting or compromising, pull out of it because that's not black nationalism. We'll find another one.

And in this manner, the organizations will increase in number and in quantity and in quality, and by August, it is then our intention to have a black nationalist convention which will consist of delegates from all over the country who are interested in the political, economic and social philosophy of black nationalism. After these delegates convene, we will hold a seminar, we will hold discussions, we will listen to everyone. We want to hear new ideas and new solutions and new answers. And at that time, if we see fit then to form a black nationalist party, we'll form a black nationalist party. If it's necessary to form a black nationalist army, we'll form a black nationalist army. It'll be the ballot or the bullet. It'll be liberty or it'll be death.

It's time for you and me to stop sitting in this country, letting some cracker senators, Northern crackers and Southern crackers, sit there in Washington, D.C., and come to a conclusion in their mind that you and I are supposed to have civil rights. There's no white man going to tell me anything about *my* rights. Brothers and sisters, always remember, if it doesn't take senators and congressmen and presidential proclamations to give freedom to the white man, it is not necessary for legislation or proclamation or Supreme Court decisions to give freedom to the black man. You let that white man know, if this is a country of freedom, let it be a country of freedom; and if it's not a country of freedom, change it.

We will work with anybody, anywhere, at any time, who is genuinely interested in tackling the problem head-on, nonviolently as long as the enemy is nonviolent, but violent when the enemy gets violent. We'll work with you on the voter-registration drive, we'll work with you on rent strikes, we'll work with you on school boycotts—I don't believe in any kind of integration; I'm not even worried about it because I know you're not going to get it anyway; you're not going to get it because you're afraid to die; you've got to be ready to die if you try and force yourself on the white man, because he'll get just as violent as those crackers in Mississippi, right here in Cleveland. But we will still work with you on the school boycotts because we're against a segregated school system. A segregated school system produces children who, when they graduate, graduate with crippled minds. But this does not mean that a school is segregated because it's all black. A segregated school means a school that is controlled by people who have no real interest in it whatsoever.

Let me explain what I mean. A segregated district or community is a community in which people live, but outsiders control the politics and the economy of that community. They never refer to the white section as a segregated community. It's the all-Negro section that's a segregated community. Why? The white man controls his own school, his own bank, his own economy, his own politics, his own everything, his own community—but he also controls yours. When you're under someone else's control, you're segregated. They'll always give you the lowest or the worst that there is to offer, but it doesn't mean you're segregated just because you have your own. You've got to *control* your own. Just like the white man has control of his, you need to control yours.

You know the best way to get rid of segregation? The white man is more afraid of separation than he is of integration. Segregation means that he puts you away from him, but not far enough for you to be out of his jurisdiction; separation means you're gone. And the white man will integrate faster than he'll let you separate. So we will work with you against the segregated school system because it's criminal, because it is absolutely destructive, in every way imaginable, to the minds of the children who have to be exposed to that type of crippling education.

Last but not least, I must say this concerning the great controversy over rifles and shotguns. The only thing that I've ever said is that in areas where the government has proven itself either unwilling or unable to defend the lives and the property of Negroes, it's time for Negroes to defend themselves. Article number two of the constitutional amendments provides you and me the right to own a rifle or a shotgun. It is constitutionally legal to own a shotgun or a rifle. This doesn't mean you're going to get a rifle and form battalions and go out looking for white folks, although you'd be within your rights—I mean, you'd be justified; but that would be illegal and we don't do anything illegal. If the white man doesn't want the black man buying rifles and shotguns, then let the government do its job. That's all. And don't let the white man come to you and ask you what you think about what Malcolm says—why, you old Uncle Tom. He would never ask you if he thought you were going to say, "Amen!" No, he is making a Tom out of you.

So, this doesn't mean forming rifle clubs and going out looking for people, but it is time, in 1964, if you are a man, to let that man know. If he's not going to do his job in running the government and providing you and me with the protection that our taxes are supposed to be for, since he spends all those billions for his defense budget, he certainly can't begrudge you and me spending $12 or $15 for a single-shot, or double-action. I hope you understand. Don't go out shooting people, but any time, brothers and sisters, and especially the men in this audience—some of you wearing Congressional Medals of Honor, with shoulders this wide, chests this big, muscles that big—any time you and I sit around and read where they bomb a church and murder in cold blood, not some grownups, but four little girls while they were praying to the same god the white man taught them to pray to, and you and I see the government go down and can't find who did it.

Why, this man—he can find Eichmann hiding down in Argentina somewhere. Let two or three American soldiers, who are minding somebody else's business way over in South Vietnam, get killed, and he'll send battleships, sticking his nose in their business. He wanted to send troops down to Cuba and make them have what he calls free elections—this old cracker who doesn't have free elections in his own country. No, if you never see me another time in your life, if I die in the morning, I'll die saying one thing: the ballot or the bullet, the ballot or the bullet.

If a Negro in 1964 has to sit around and wait for some cracker senator to filibuster when it comes to the rights of black people, why, you and I should hang our heads in shame. You talk about a march on Washington in 1963, you haven't seen anything. There's some more going down in '64. And this time they're not going like they went last year. They're not going singing "We Shall Overcome." They're not going with white friends. They're not going with placards already painted for them. They're not going with round-trip tickets. They're going with one-way tickets.

And if they don't want that non-nonviolent army going down there, tell them to bring the filibuster to a halt. The black nationalists aren't going to wait. Lyndon B. Johnson is the head of the Democratic Party. If he's for civil rights, let him go into the Senate next week and declare himself. Let him go in there right now and declare himself. Let him go in there and denounce the Southern branch of his party. Let him go in there right now and take a moral stand—right now, not later. Tell him, don't wait until election time. If he waits too long, brothers and sisters, he will be responsible for letting a condition develop in this country which will create a climate that will bring seeds up out of the ground with vegetation on the end of them looking like something these people never dreamed of. In 1964, it's the ballot or the bullet. Thank you.

GENDERED EXPERIENCES

Among the most influential works of feminism is surely *The Second Sex*, originally published in 1949, by Simone de Beauvoir. Its elegant and wide-ranging introduction states the overriding problem clearly: women have been defined purely in relation to men, not as autonomous beings. Man has thus become the subject and woman "the Other." The choice, for de Beauvoir, is between accepting or rejecting that point of view. The anthropological oppression of women is mutuable, but changing it will demand a new form of solidarity among women themselves. Indeed, just as with blacks or proletarians, female solidarity begins with the ability to say "we."

De Beauvoir establishes an existential as well as a social rationale for a feminist "movement"; almost from the first, feminism should deal with both the personal and the social. But the interplay between the two is complex. The selection here from the introduction to *The Politics of Women's Liberation*, by Jo Freeman, illuminates some of the problems. It also shows how political institutions reshape the movement as they change long-range ideals into short-term reforms or leave radicals who are concerned with more profound transformation "isolated in a splendid ideological purity, which gains nothing for anyone." The proper tactic for what is actually an interest group, according to this liberal analysis, involves balancing personal with social issues as well as the "politics" with the "vision" of the movement.

But this becomes exceptionally difficult once structural issues like patriarchy are brought into play. Sheila Rowbotham makes the difficulty clear in her conclusion to *Women's Consciousness, Man's World*, one of the classic volumes of socialist feminism. Rowbotham also tries to connect issues of gender with those of class and race. Her book emphasizes the unique character of the women's movement and the exploited position of women, particularly working-class women, in the capitalist economy. It is also among the first to grapple with the problem of difference versus equality and to consider the difficulty of "translating the experience of one group to another without merely annexing the weaker to the stronger."

This translation is the preeminent concern of the following speech by Audre Lorde, which she delivered in September 1979 at a panel entitled "The Personal and the Political" for the Second Sex Conference in New York. "The Master's Tools Will Never Dismantle the Master's House" blasts the academic and conformist currents of feminism. It calls not merely for the toleration of difference but for a new emphasis on the mutuality between women and a new vision of interdependence. Lorde also insists on highlighting the differences in race, sexuality, class, and age among women. Community is based on difference, in her view, and ultimately "divide and conquer must become define and empower."

Introduction to *The Second Sex*

For a long time I have hesitated to write a book on woman. The subject is irritating, especially to women; and it is not new. Enough ink has been spilled in the quarreling over feminism, now practically over, and perhaps we should say no more about it. It is still talked about, however, for the voluminous nonsense uttered during the last century seems to have done little to illuminate the problem. After all, is there a problem? And if so, what is it? Are there women, really? Most assuredly the theory of the eternal feminine still has its adherents who will whisper in your ear: "Even in Russia women still are *women*"; and other erudite persons—sometimes the very same—say with a sigh: "Woman is losing her way, woman is lost." One wonders if women still exist, if they will always exist, whether or not it is desirable that they should, what place they occupy in this world, what their place should be. "What has become of women?" was asked recently in an ephemeral magazine.

But first we must ask: what is a woman? "*Tota mulier in utero*," says one, "woman is a womb." But in speaking of certain women, connoisseurs declare that they are not women, although they are equipped with a uterus like the rest. All agree in recognizing the fact that females exist in the human species; today as always they make up about one half of humanity. And yet we are told that femininity is in danger; we are exhorted to be women, remain women, become women. It would appear, then, that every female human being is not necessarily a woman; to be so considered she must share in that mysterious and threatened reality known as femininity. Is this attribute something secreted by the ovaries? Or is it a Platonic essence, a product of the philosophic imagination? Is a rustling petticoat enough to bring it down to earth? Although some women try zealously to incarnate this essence, it is hardly patentable. It is frequently described in vague and dazzling terms that seem to have been borrowed from the vocabulary of the seers, and indeed in the times of St. Thomas it was considered an essence as certainly defined as the somniferous virtue of the poppy.

But conceptualism has lost ground. The biological and social sciences no longer admit the existence of unchangeably fixed entities that determine given characteristics, such as those ascribed to woman, the Jew, or the Negro. Science regards any characteristic as a reaction dependent in part upon a *situation*. If today feminity no longer exists, then it never existed. But does the word *woman*, then, have no specific content? This is stoutly affirmed by those who hold to the philosophy of the enlightenment, of rationalism, of nominalism; women, to them, are merely the human beings arbitrarily designated by the word *woman*. Many American women particularly are prepared to think that there is no longer any place for woman as such; if a backward individual still takes herself for a woman, her friends advise her to be psychoanalyzed and thus get rid of this obsession. In regard to a work, *Modern Woman: The Lost Sex*, which in other respects has its irritating features, Dorothy Parker has written: "I cannot be just to books which treat of woman as woman. . . . My idea is that all of us, men as well as women, should be regarded as human beings." But nominalism is a rather inadequate doctrine, and the antifemininists have had no trouble in showing that women simply *are not* men. Surely woman is, like man, a human being; but such a declaration is abstract. The fact is that every concrete human being is always a singular, separate individual. To decline to accept such notions as the eternal feminine, the black soul, the Jewish character, is not to deny that Jews, Negroes, women exist today—this denial does not represent a liberation for those concerned, but rather a flight from reality. Some years ago a well-known woman writer refused to permit her portrait to appear in a series of photographs especially devoted to women writers; she wished to be counted among the men. But in order to gain this privilege she made use of her husband's influence! Women who assert that they are men lay claim none the less to masculine consideration and respect. I recall also a young Trotskyite standing on a platform at a boisterous meeting and getting ready to use her fists, in spite of her eviident fragility. She was denying her feminine weakness; but it was for love of a militant male whose equal she wished to be. The attitude of defiance of many American women proves that they are haunted by a sense of their femininity. In truth, to go for a walk with one's eyes open is enough to demonstrate that humanity is divided into two classes of individuals whose clothes, faces, bodies, smiles, gaits, interests, and occupations are manifestly different. Perhaps these differences are superficial, perhaps they are destined to disappear. What is certain is that right now they do most obviously exist.

If her functioning as a female is not enough to define woman, if we decline also to explain her through "the eternal feminine," and if nevertheless we admit, provisionally, that women do exist, then we must face the question: what is a woman?

To state the question is, to me, to suggest, at once, a preliminary answer. The fact that I ask it is in itself significant. A man would never get the notion of writing a book on the peculiar situation of the human male. But if I wish to define myself, I must first of all say: "I am a woman"; on this truth must be based all further discussion. A man never begins by presenting himself as an individual of a certain sex; it goes without saying that he is a man. The terms *masculine* and *feminine* are used symmetrically only as a matter of form, as on legal papers. In actuality the relation of the two sexes is not quite like that of two electrical poles, for man represents both the positive and the neutral, as is indicated by the common use of *man* to designate human beings in general; whereas woman represents only the negative, defined by limiting criteria, without reciprocity. In the midst of an abstract discussion it is vexing to hear a man say: "You think thus and so because you are a woman"; but I know that my only defense is to reply: "I think thus and so because it is true," thereby removing my subjective self from the argument. It would be out of the question to reply: "And you think the contrary because you are a man," for it is understood that the fact of being a man is no peculiarity. A man is in the right in being a man; it is the woman who is in the wrong. It amounts to this: just as for the ancients there was an absolute vertical with reference to which the oblique was defined, so there is an absolute human type, the masculine. Woman has ovaries, a uterus; these peculiarities imprison her in her subjectivity, circumscribe her within the limits of her own nature. It is often said that she thinks with her glands. Man superbly ignores the fact that his anatomy also includes glands, such as the testicles, and that they secrete hormones. He thinks of his body as a direct and normal connection with the world, which he believes he apprehends objectively, whereas he regards the body of woman as a hindrance, a prison, weighed down by everything peculiar to it. "The female is a female by virtue of a certain *lack* of qualities," said Aristotle; "we should regard the female nature as afflicted with a natural defectiveness." And St. Thomas for his part pronounced woman to be an "imperfect man," an "incidental" being. This is symbolized in Genesis where Eve is depicted as made from what Bossuet called "a supernumerary bone" of Adam.

Thus humanity is male and man defines woman not in herself but as relative to him; she is not regarded as an autonomous being. Michelet writes: "Woman, the relative being...." And Benda is most positive in his *Rapport d'Uriel*: "The body of man makes sense in itself quite apart from that of woman, whereas the latter seems wanting in significance by itself.... Man can think of himself without woman. She cannot think of herself without man." And she is simply what man decrees; thus she is called "the sex," by which is meant that she appears essentially to the male as a sexual being. For him she is sex—absolute sex, no less. She is defined and differentiated with reference to man and not he with reference to her; she is the incidental, the inessential as opposed to the essential. He is the Subject, he is the Absolute—she is the Other.

The category of the *Other* is as primordial as consciousness itself. In the most primitive societies, in the most ancient mythologies, one finds the expression of a duality—that of the Self and the Other. This duality was not originally attached to the division of the sexes; it was not dependent upon any empirical facts. It is revealed in such works as that of Granet on Chinese thought and those of Dumézil on the East Indies and Rome. The feminine element was at first no more involved in such pairs as Varuna-Mitra, Uranus-Zeus, Sun-Moon, and Day-Night than it was in the contrasts between Good and Evil, lucky and unlucky auspices, right and left, God and Lucifer. Otherness is a fundamental category of human thought.

Thus it is that no group ever sets itself up as the One without at once setting up the Other over against itself. If three travelers change to occupy the same compartment, that is enough to make vaguely hostile "others" out of all the rest of the passengers on the train. In small-town eyes all persons not belonging to the village are "strangers" and suspect; to the native of a country all who inhabit other countries are "foreigners"; Jews are "different" for the anti-Semite, Negroes are "inferior" for American racists, aborigines are "native" for colonists, proletarians are the "lower class" for the privileged.

Lévi-Strauss, at the end of a profound work on the various forms of primitive societies, reaches the following conclusion: "Passage from the state of Nature to the state of Culture is marked by man's ability to view biological relations as a series of contrasts; duality, alternation, opposition, and symmetry, whether under definite or vague forms, constitute not so much phenomena to be explained as fundamental and immediately given data of social reality." These phenomena would be incomprehensible if in fact human society were simply a *Mitsein* or fellowship based on solidarity and friendliness. Things become clear, on the contrary, if, following Hegel, we find in consciousness itself a fundamental hostility toward every other consciousness; the subject can be posed only in being opposed—he sets himself up as the essential, as opposed to the other, the inessential, the object.

But the other consciousness, the other ego, sets up a reciprocal claim. The native traveling abroad is shocked to find himself in turn regarded as a "stranger" by the natives of neighboring countries. As a matter of fact, wars, festivals, trading, treaties, and contests among tribes, nations, and classes tend to deprive the concept *Other* of its absolute sense and to make manifest its relativity; willy-nilly, individuals and groups are forced to realize the reciprocity of their relations. How is it, then, that this reciprocity has not been recognized between the sexes, that one of the contrasting terms is set up as the sole essential, denying any relativity in regard to its correlative and defining the latter as pure otherness? Why is it that women do not dispute male sovereignty? No subject will readily volunteer to become the object, the inessential; it is not the Other who, in defining himself as the Other, establishes the One. The Other is posed as such by the One in defining himself as the One. But if the Other is not to regain the status of being the One, he must be submissive enough to accept this alien point of view. Whence comes this submission in the case of woman?

There are, to be sure, other cases in which a certain category has been able to dominate another completely for a time. Very often this privilege depends upon inequality of numbers—the majority imposes its rule upon the minority or persecutes it. But women are not a minority, like the American Negroes or the Jews; there are as many women as men on earth. Again, the two groups concerned have often been originally independent; they may have been formerly unaware of each other's existence, or perhaps they recognized each other's autonomy. But a historical event has resulted in the subjugation of the weaker by the stronger. The scattering of the Jews, the introduction of slavery into America, the conquests of imperialism are examples in point. In these cases the oppressed retained at least the memory of former days; they possessed in common a past, a tradition, sometimes a religion or a culture.

The parallel drawn by Bebel between women and the proletariat is valid in that neither ever formed a minority or a separate collective unit of mankind. And instead of a single historical event it is in both cases a historical development that explains their status as a class and accounts for the membership of *particular individuals* in that class. But proletarians have not always existed, whereas there have always been women. They are women in virtue of their anatomy and physiology. Throughout history they have always been subordinated to men, and hence their dependency is not the result of a historical event or a social change—it was not something that *occurred*. The reason why otherness in this case seems to be an absolute is in part that it lacks the contingent or incidental nature of historical facts. A condition brought about at a certain time can be abolished at some other times, as the Negroes of Haiti and others have proved; but it might seem that a natural condition is beyond the possibility of change. In truth, however, the nature of things is no more immutably given, once and for all, than is historical reality. If woman seems to be the inessential which never becomes the essential, it is because she herself fails to bring about this change. Proletarians say "We"; Negroes also. Regarding themselves as subjects, they transform the bourgeois, the whites, into "others." But women do not say "We," except at some congress of feminists or similar formal demonstration; men say "women," and women use the same word in referring to themselves. They do not authentically assume a subjective attitude. The proletarians have accomplished the revolution in Russia, the Negroes in Haiti, the Indo-Chinese are battling for it in Indo-China; but the women's effort has never been anything more than a symbolic agitation. They have gained only what men have been willing to grant; they have taken nothing, they have only received.

The reason for this is that women lack concrete means for organizing themselves into a unit which can stand face to face with the correlative unit. They have no past, no history, no religion of their own; and they have no such solidarity of work and interest as that of the proletariat. They are not even promiscuously herded together in the way that creates community feeling among the American Negroes, the ghetto Jews, the workers of Saint-Denis, or the factory hands of Renault. They live dispersed among the males, attached through residence, housework, economic condition, and social standing to certain men—fathers or husbands—more firmly than they are to other women. If they belong to the bourgeoisie, they feel solidarity with men of that class, not with proletarian women; if they are white, their allegiance is to white men, not to Negro women. The proletariat can propose to massacre the ruling class, and a sufficiently fanatical Jew or Negro might dream of getting sole possession of the atomic bomb and making humanity wholly Jewish or black; but woman cannot even dream of exterminating the males. The bond that unites her to her oppressors is not comparable to any other. The division of the sexes is a biological fact, not an event in human history. Male and female stand opposed within a primordial *Mitsein*, and woman has not broken it. The couple is a fundamental unity with its two halves riveted together, and the cleavage of society along the line of sex is impossible. Here is to be found the basic trait of woman: she is the Other in a totality of which the two components are necessary to one another.

One could suppose that this reciprocity might have facilitated the liberation of woman. When Hercules sat at the feet of Omphale and helped with her spinning, his desire for her held him captive; but why did she fail to gain a lasting power? To revenge herself on Jason, Medea killed their children; and this grim legend would seem to suggest that she might have obtained a formidable influence over him through his love for his offspring. In *Lysistrata* Aristophanes gaily depicts a band of women who joined forces to gain social ends through the sexual needs of their men; but this is only a play. In the legend of the Sabine women, the latter soon abandoned their plan of remaining sterile to punish their ravishers. In truth woman has not been socially emancipated through man's need—sexual desire and the desire for offspring—which makes the male dependent for satisfaction upon the female.

Master and slave, also, are united by a reciprocal need, in this case economic, which does not liberate the slave. In the relation of master to slave the master does not make a point of the need that he has for the other; he has in his grasp the power of satisfying this need through his own action; whereas the slave, in his dependent condition, his hope and fear, is quite conscious of the need he has for his master. Even if the need is at bottom equally urgent for both, it always works in favor of the oppressor and against the oppressed. That is why the liberation of the working class, for example, has been slow.

Now, woman has always been man's dependent, if not his slave; the two sexes have never shared the world in equality. And even today woman is heavily handicapped, though her situation is beginning to change. Almost nowhere is her legal status the same as man's, and frequently it is much to her disadvantage. Even when her rights are legally recognized in the abstract, long-standing custom prevents their full expression in the mores. In the economic sphere men and women can almost be said to make up two castes; other things being equal, the former hold the better jobs, get higher wages, and have more opportunity for success than their new competitors. In industry and politics men have a great many more positions and they monopolize the most important posts. In addition to all this, they enjoy a traditional prestige that the education of children tends in every way to support, for the present enshrines the past—and in the past all history has been made by men. At the present time, when women are beginning to take part in the affairs of the world, it is still a world that belongs to men—they have no doubt of it at and women have scarcely any. To decline to be the Other, to refuse to be a party to the deal—this would be for women to renounce all the advantages conferred upon them by their alliance with the superior caste. Man-the-sovereign will provide woman-the-liege with material protection and will undertake the moral justification of her existence; thus she can evade at once both economic risk and the metaphysical risk of a liberty in which ends and aims must be contrived without assistance. Indeed, along with the ethical urge of each individual to affirm his subjective existence, there is also the temptation to forgo liberty and become a thing. This is an inauspicious road, for he who takes it—passive, lost, ruined—becomes henceforth the creature of another's will, frustrated in his transcendence and deprived of every value. But it is an easy road; on it one avoids the strain involved in undertaking an authentic existence. When man makes of woman the *Other*, he may, then, expect her to manifest deep-seated tendencies toward complicity. Thus, woman may fail to lay claim to the status of subject because she lacks definite resources, because she feels the necessary bond that ties her to man regardless of reciprocity, and because she is often very well pleased with her role as the *Other*.

But it will be asked at once: how did all this begin? It is easy to see that the duality of the sexes, like any duality, gives rise to conflict. And doubtless the winner will assume the status of absolute. But why should man have won from the start? It seems possible that women could have won the victory; or that the outcome of the conflict might never have been decided. How is it that this world has always belonged to the men and that things have begun to change only recently? Is this change a good thing? Will it bring about an equal sharing of the world between men and women?

These questions are not new, and they have often been answered. But the very fact that woman *is the Other* tends to cast suspicion upon all the justifications that men have ever been able to provide for it. These have all too evidently been dictated by men's interest. A little-known feminist of the seventeenth century, Poulain de la Barre, put it this way: "All that has been written about women by men should be suspect, for the men are at once judge and party to the lawsuit." Everywhere, at all times, the males have displayed their satisfaction in feeling that they are the lords of creation. "Blessed be God . . . that He did not make me a woman," say the Jews in their morning prayers, while their wives pray on a note of resignation: "Blessed be the Lord, who created me according to His will." The first among the blessings for which Plato thanked the gods was that he had been created free, not enslaved; the second, a man, not a woman. But the males could not enjoy this privilege fully unless they believed it to be founded on the absolute and the eternal; they sought to make the fact of their supremacy into a right. "Being men, those who have made and compiled the laws have favored their own sex, and jurists have elevated these laws into principles," to quote Poulain de la Barre once more.

Legislators, priests, philosophers, writers, and scientists have striven to show that the subordinate position of woman is willed in heaven and advantageous on earth. The religions invented by men reflect this wish for domination. In the legends of Eve and Pandora men have taken up arms against women. They have made use of philosophy and theology, as the quotations from Aristotle and St. Thomas have shown. Since ancient times satirists and moralists have delighted in showing up the weaknesses of women. We are familiar with the savage indictments hurled against women throughout French literature. Montherlant, for example, follows the tradition of Jean de Meung, though with less gusto. This hostility may at times be well founded, often it is gratuitous; but in truth it more or less successfully conceals a desire for self-justification. As Montaigne says, "It is easier to accuse one sex than to excuse the other." Sometimes what is going on is clear enough. For instance, the Roman law limiting the rights of woman cited "the imbecility, the instability of the sex" just when the weakening of family ties seemed to threaten the interests of male heirs. And in the effort to keep the married woman under guardianship, appeal was made in the sixteenth century to the authority of St. Augustine, who declared that "woman is a creature neither decisive nor constant," at a time when the single woman was thought capable of managing her property. Montaigne understood clearly how arbitrary and unjust was woman's appointed lot: "Women are not in the wrong when they decline to accept the rules laid down for them, since the men make these rules without consulting them. No wonder intrigue and strife abound." But he did not go so far as to champion their cause.

It was only later, in the eighteenth century, that genuinely democratic men began to view the matter objectively. Diderot, among others, strove to show that woman is, like man, a human being. Later John Stuart Mill came fervently to her defense. But these philosophers displayed unusual impartiality. In the nineteenth century the feminist quarrel became again a quarrel of partisans. One of the consequences of the industrial revolution was the entrance of women into productive labor, and it was just here that the claims of the feminists emerged from the realm of theory and acquired an economic basis, while their opponents became the more aggressive. Although landed property lost power to some extent, the bourgeoisie clung to the old morality that found the guarantee of private property in the solidity of the family. Woman was ordered back into the home the more harshly as her emancipation became a real menace. Even within the working class the men endeavored to restrain woman's liberation, because they began to see the women as dangerous competitors—the more so because they were accustomed to work for lower wages.

In proving woman's inferiority, the antifeminists then began to draw not only upon religion, philosophy, and theology, as before, but also upon science—biology, experimental psychology, etc. At most they were willing to grant "equality in difference" to the *other* sex. That profitable formula is most significant; it is precisely like the "equal but separate" formula of the Jim Crow laws aimed at the North American Negroes. As is well known, this so-called equalitarian segregation has resulted only in the most extreme discrimination. The similarity just noted is in no way due to chance, for whether it is a race, a caste, a class, or a sex that is reduced to a position of inferiority, the methods of justification are the same. "The eternal feminine" corresponds to "the black soul" and to "the Jewish character." True, the Jewish problem is on the whole very different from the other two—to the anti-Semite the Jew is not so much an inferior as he is an enemy for whom there is to be granted no place on earth, for whom annihilation is the fate desired. But there are deep similarities between the situation of woman and that of the Negro. Both are being emancipated today from a like paternalism, and the former master class wishes to "keep them in their place"—that is, the place chosen for them. In both cases the former masters lavish more or less sincere eulogies, either on the virtues of "the good Negro" with his dormant, childish, merry soul—the submissive Negro—or on the merits of the woman who is "truly feminine"—that is, frivolous, infantile, irresponsible—the submissive woman. In both cases the dominant class bases its argument on a state of affairs that it has itself created. As George Bernard Shaw puts it, in substance, "The American white relegates the black to the rank of shoeshine boy; and he concludes from this that the black is good for nothing but shining shoes." This vicious circle is met with in all analogous circumstances; when an individual (or a group of individuals) is kept in a situation of inferiority, the fact is that he *is* inferior. But the significance of the verb *to be* must be rightly understood here; it is in bad faith to give it a static value when it really has the dynamic Hegelian sense of "to have become." Yes, women on the whole *are* today inferior to men; that is, their situation affords them fewer possibilities. The question is: should that state of affairs continue?

Many men hope that it will continue; not all have given up the battle. The conservative bourgeoisie still see in the emancipation of women a menace to their morality and their interests. Some men dread feminine competition. Recently a male student wrote in the *Hebdo-Latin*: Every woman student who goes into medicine or law robs us of a job." He never questioned his rights in this world. And economic interests are not the only ones concerned. One of the benefits that oppression confers upon the oppressors is that the most humble among them is made to *feel* superior; thus, a "poor white" in the South can console himself with the thought that he is not a "dirty nigger"—and the more prosperous whites cleverly exploit this pride. . . . Here is miraculous balm for those afflicted with an inferiority complex, and indeed no one is more arrogant toward women, more aggressive or scornful, than the man who is anxious about his virility. Those who are not fear-ridden in the presence of their fellow men are much more disposed to recognize a fellow creature in woman; but even to these the myth of Woman, the Other, is precious for many reasons. They cannot be blamed for not cheerfully relinquishing all the benefits they derive from the myth, for they realize what they would lose in relinquishing woman as they fancy her to be, while they fail to realize what they have to gain from the woman of tomorrow. Refusal to pose oneself as the Subject, unique and absolute, requires great self-denial. Furthermore, the vast majority of men make no such claim explicitly. They do not *postulate* woman as inferior, for today they are too thoroughly imbued with the ideal of democracy not to recognize all human beings as equals.

In the bosom of the family, woman seems in the eyes of childhood and youth to be clothed in the same social dignity as the adult males. Later on, the young man, desiring and loving, experiences the resistance, the independence of the woman desired and loved; in marriage, he respects woman as wife and mother, and in the concrete events of conjugal life she stands there before him as a free being. He can therefore feel that social subordination as between the sexes no longer exists and that on the whole, in spite of differences, woman is an equal. As, however, he observes some points of inferiority—the most important being unfitness for the professions—he attributes these to natural causes. When he is in a co-operative and benevolent relation with woman, his theme is the principle of abstract equality, and he does not base his attitude upon such inequality as may exist. But when he is in conflict with her, the situation is reversed: his theme will be the existing inequality, and he will even take it as justification for denying abstract equality.

So it is that many men will affirm as if in good faith that women *are* the equals of man and that they have nothing to clamor for, while *at the same time* they will say that women can never be the equals of man and that their demands are in vain. It is, in point of fact, a difficult matter for man to realize the extreme importance of social discriminations which seem outwardly insignificant but which produce in woman moral and intellectual effects so profound that they appear to spring from her original nature. The most sympathetic of men never fully comprehend woman's concrete situation. And there is no reason to put much trust in the men when they rush to the defense of privileges whose full extent they can hardly measure. We shall not, then, permit ourselves to be intimidated by the number and violence of the attacks launched against women, nor to be entrapped by the self-seeking eulogies bestowed on the "true woman," nor to profit by the enthusiasm for woman's destiny manifested by men who would not for the world have any part of it. . . .

But it is doubtless impossible to approach any human problem with a mind free from bias. The way in which questions are put, the points of view assumed, presuppose a relativity of interest; all characteristics imply values, and every objective description, so called, implies an ethical background. Rather than attempt to conceal principles more or less definitely implied, it is better to state them openly at the beginning. This will make

it unneccessary to specify on every page in just what sense one uses such words as *superior,
inferior, better, worse, progress, reaction*, and the like. If we survey some of the works on
woman, we note that one of the points of view most frequently adopted is that of the public good, the general interest; and one always means by this the benefit of society as one
wishes it to be maintained or established. For our part, we hold that the only public good
is that which assures the private good of the citizens; we shall pass judgment on institutions according to their effectiveness in giving concrete opportunities to individuals. But
we do not confuse the idea of private interest with that of happiness, although that is
another common point of view. Are not women of the harem more happy than women
voters? Is not the housekeeper happier than the working-woman? It is not too clear just
what the word *happy* really means and still less what true values it may mask. There is no
possibility of measuring the happiness of others, and it is always easy to describe as happy
the situation in which one wishes to place them.

In particular those who are condemned to stagnation are often pronounced happy on
the pretext that happiness consists in being at rest. This notion we reject, for our perspective is that of existentialist ethics. Every subject plays his part as such specifically through
exploits or projects that serve as a mode of transcendence; he achieves liberty only through
a continual reaching out toward other liberties. There is no justification for present existence other than its expansion into an indefinitely open future. Every time transcendence
falls back into immanence, stagnation, there is a degradation of existence into the *"en-
soi"*—the brutish life of subjection to given conditions—and of liberty into constraint and
contingence. This downfall represents a moral fault if the subject consents to it; if it
inflicted upon him, it spells frustration and oppression. In both cases it is an absolute evil.
Every individual concerned to justify his existence feels that his existence involves an
undefined need to transcend himself, to engage in freely chosen projects.

Now, what peculiarly signalizes the situation of woman is that she—a free and
autonomous being like all human creatures—nevertheless finds herself living in a world
where men compel her to assume the status of the Other. They propose to stabilize her as
object and to doom her to immanence since her transcendence is to be overshadowed and
forever transcended by another ego (*conscience*) which is essential and sovereign. The drama
of woman lies in this conflict between the fundamental aspirations of every subject (ego)—
who always regards the self is the essential—and the compulsions of a situation in which
she is the inessential. How can a human being in woman's situation attain fulfillment?
What roads are open to her? Which are blocked? How can independence be recovered in a
state of dependency? What circumstances limit woman's liberty and how can they be overcome? These are the fundamental questions on which I would fain throw some light. This
means that I am interested in the fortunes of the individual as defined not in terms of happiness but in terms of liberty.

Quite evidently this problem would be without significance if we were to believe that
woman's destiny is inevitably determined by physiological, psychological, or economic
forces. Hence I shall discuss first of all the light in which woman is viewed by biology, psychoanalysis, and historical materialism. Next I shall try to show exactly how the concept of
the "truly feminine" has been fashioned—why woman has been defined as the Other—and

what have been the consequences from man's point of view. Then from woman's point of view I shall describe the world in which women must live; and thus we shall be able to envisage the difficulties in their way as, endeavoring to make their escape from the sphere hitherto assigned them, they aspire to full membership in the human race.

JO FREEMAN

Introduction to
The Politics of Women's Liberation

The study of social movements and that of public policy are two fields that have heretofore been treated primarily as distinct and unrelated areas in the scholarly literature. While some writers have envisioned social movements as incipient interest groups and/or political parties[1] and thus as having a potential effect on policy, no one has tried to trace out the exact relationships between the two and the way in which each affects the other.[2] The examination of such a mutual relationship is both the hypothesis and purpose of this thesis. Nonetheless, it will be impossible to convey the degree of complexity of the relationship as many of the intervening and contributory variables will be dealt with cursorily. In particular, the effects of the general atmospheric changes caused by the movement will be more assumed than delineated. Instead the focus will be on the specific relationship. It is understood that while the same social conditions which create a social movement may have a direct effect on policy, it is when the people most strongly affected by changes in social conditions are not already part of the policy making process that they must organize themselves for political action. Thus a social movement becomes the vehicle by which policy makers are influenced directly, as well as indirectly through general social change.

Concomitantly, while policy has an indirect effect on social movements by altering the conditions which gave rise to them, it has a more immediate and direct effect as well. As Schattschneider has pointed out, the outcome of a conflict is determined by its scope, and "the socialization of conflict is the essential democratic process."[3] Social movements are one of the primary means of socializing conflict; of taking private disputes and making them political ones.[4] This is why a successful movement provides an *intersection* between personal and social change. Personal changes can be a *vehicle* to more concrete social changes, and are also often a result; but if a movement restricts itself to change purely on the personal level, its impact on society remains minimal. It is only when private disputes that result from personal changes are translated into public demands that a movement enters the political arena and can make use of political institutions to reach its goals of social change.

Once a social movement enters the political realm, however, it is usually constrained by the limitations of that realm. There already exist many concrete, accepted "rules of the game" which newcomers are expected to abide by.[5] These rules are manifested not only in norms of behavior but in the very institutions which govern the system and manage the conflicts within it.

> The function of institutions is to channel conflict; institutions do not treat all forms of conflict impartially, just as football rules do not treat all forms of violence with indiscriminate equality.[6]

These institutions in turn, by their ability to "reward" or "punish" efforts for change with "success" or "defeat," often reshape the structure, the activities, and even the goals of social movements.[7]

It is here that we encounter a paradox. Movements that conform themselves to the norms of behavior in order to participate successfully in political institutions often find themselves forsaking their major goals for social change. Long-range ideals are warped for the sake of short-range gains. But movements that hold steadfast to their radical goals and disdain political participation of any kind in an "evil" system often find themselves isolated in a splendid ideological purity which gains nothing for any one. They are paralyzed by their own fear of cooptation; and such paralysis is in turn the ultimate cooptation as inactive revolutionaries are a good deal more innocuous than active "reformists." Thus a successful movement must not only maintain a balance between personal and political change, but also a creative tension between its "politics" and its "vision."[8] It must keep well in mind where it wants to go while accepting the necessity of often following a twisted and tortured road in order to get there.

Ironically, a successful political system must do the same—though its vision if not its politics do not always coincide with those of the groups conflicting within it. It must manage its conflicts in such a way that it maintains its basic values while not necessarily maintaining the given positions of power of the partisans within it. To do this it must provide for the emergence and growth to power of new elements which are compatible with its basic values while guarding itself against being totally overwhelmed by them. Concomitantly it must maintain its old supporters without allowing itself to be totally controlled by them. It must provide for both continuity and change.[9]

No political system to date has been completely successful in this effort. With the exception of one major schism, the American system has managed more or less so far; though not always with much ease or grace. But it is young yet and will still have many opportunities to stagnate in its own complacency—provided new political elements cease in their constant efforts to keep it from doing so.

NOTES

1. E.g., Rudolph Heberle, *Social Movements* (New York: Appleton-Century-Crofts, 1951); Lowi, *The Politics of Disorder*; Harmon Zeigler, *Interest Groups in American Society* (Englewood Cliffs, N.J.: Prentice-Hall, 1964).

2. Juliet Z. Saltman, *Open Housing as a Social Movement* (Lexington, Mass.: D. C. Heath, 1971), presents data which could be used to develop such an analysis, but it is not a major theme of her book. Paul Schumaker, in "Protest Groups, Environmental Characteristics and Policy-Responsiveness" (paper given at the 1974 convention of the Midwest Political Science Association), argues that "the policy-responsiveness of urban communities to protest group demands is enhanced, either directly or indirectly, by . . . : (1) private-regarding political cultures, (2) economic development, (3) unreformed governmental institutions and (4) dispersed structures of influence." However, his measures of these variables are crude, their relationships weak, and the specific means by which they effect policy are ignored.

3. E. E. Schattschneider, *The Semi-Sovereign People* (New York: Holt, Rinehart & Winston, 1960), p. 142.

4. McWilliams argues that "previously nonpolitical issues will almost inevitably become political whenever two conditions apply: (a) when reality comes to be perceptibly discordant with social myths . . . and (b) when there is the opportunity to compare notes on personal unhappiness." Nancy McWilliams, "Contemporary Feminism, Consciousness-Raising, and Changing Views of the Political," in *Women in Politics*, ed. Jane Jaquette (New York: Wiley, 1974), p. 160.

5. Needless to say, not all social movements play by the rules because those rules do not fit their needs and their resources. The civil rights movement would have died an early death if it had done so, as would the labor movement and many others. Those movements which opt out of playing the game inevitably subject themselves to the criticism that "I agree with your goals but not with your methods." Fortunately, such movements usually have the sense to ignore this criticism, occasionally to the benefit of everyone. Many new tactics created by dissident movements that violated the rules of their day have since become enshrined into the accepted pantheon of political activities. The illegal device of political pamphleteering developed in seventeenth- and eighteenth-century England is now the stalwart democratic concept of freedom of press. The labor movement gave us the strike and boycott, formerly seditious activities now protected by law. The civil rights movement has developed the sit-in, which has not yet become as respectable as many of its predecessors, but might very well through time and use.

6. Schattschneider, *The Semi-Sovereign People*, p. 72.

7. This is merely using the language of operant conditioning to express an institutional perspective on the Weber-Michels hypothesis of goal transformation of social movements. The latter will be explained and utilized more fully in a later chapter.

8. My thanks to Sheldon Wolin for this unintended use of his terminology.

9. For an extensive analysis of the relationship between what he labels the "influence" and "social control" perspectives, see William A. Gamson, *Power and Discontent* (Homewood, Ill.: Dorsey Press, 1968). A different approach to this problem is taken by Lipset who asserts that: "A principal problem for a theory of democratic systems is: Under what conditions can a society have 'sufficient' participation to maintain the democratic system without introducing sources of cleavage which will undermine the cohesion?" Seymour Martin Lipset, *Political Man: The Social Bases of Politics* (New York: Doubleday, 1960), p. 14.

SHEILA ROWBOTHAM

Conclusion to
Woman's Consciousness, Man's World

Capitalism moves. The capitalist mode of production has penetrated farther and deeper than any other form of production. Geographically it has extended its technology in search of markets; politically it has devised the most ingenious methods of control in its own interests; economically it has created means of production which are wonderful in their productive capacity and terrifying in their devastation. Its industry has devoured human labour power and human intelligence. In its search for raw materials it has laid waste the land and is beginning to exhaust even the sea. Worse, its version of itself has entered the souls and spirits of millions of men and women, so we no longer know what is our own and what is alienated to capital.

This indiscriminate hunger of capital destroys but it also provokes resistance. The antagonisms it generates produce the shifts and fissures which make the growth of new movements possible. In quiet times the hope of liberation grows lichen-like on the inhospitable rock. In times of upheaval the new growths can take root.

In order to change capitalism we have to understand how it is made, how it moves and how it came into being. We have to see how it is different from, or related to, other forms of production, how it is hinged together. It is a foxy old thing, wily at dealing with the opposition it brings into being, whether its opponent is the working class or movements for black or women's liberation.

We have to start off where we came in. The predicament of being born a woman in capitalism is specific. The social situation of women and the way in which we learn to be feminine is peculiar to us. Men do not share it, consequently we cannot be simply included under the general heading of 'mankind'. The only claim that this word has to be general comes from the dominance of men in society. As the rulers they presume to define others by their own criteria.

Women are not the same as other oppressed groups. Unlike the working class, who have no need for the capitalist under socialism, the liberation of women does not mean that men will be eliminated. Sex and class are not the same. Similarly people from oppressed races have a memory of a cultural alternative somewhere in the past. Women have only myths made by men.

We have to recognize our biological distinctness but this does not mean that we should become involved in an illusory hunt for our lost 'nature'. There are so many social accretions round our biology. All conceptions of female 'nature' are formed in cultures dominated by men, and like all abstract ideas of human nature are invariably used to deter the oppressed from organizing effectively against that most unnatural of systems, capitalism.

The oppression of women differs too from class and race because it has not come out of capitalism and imperialism. The sexual division of labour and the possession of women by men predates capitalism. Patriarchal authority is based on male control over the woman's productive capacity, and over her person. This control existed before the development of capitalist commodity production. It belonged to a society in which the persons of human beings were owned by others. Patriarchy, however, is contradicted by the dominant mode of production in capitalism because in capitalism the owner of capital owns and controls the labour power but not the persons of his labourers.

What form female oppression took in the distant past is impossible to verify and the search for it rapidly becomes a chimerical pursuit of origins. We can only guess that the physical weakness of women and the need of protection during pregnancy enabled men to gain domination.

More relevant to us are the consequences of opposing a form of oppression which has taken a specific shape in capitalism, but which nevertheless existed in precapitalist society. In order to act effectively we have to try to work out the precise relationship between the patriarchal dominance of men over women, and the property relations which come from this, to class exploitation and racism.

In order to understand the traces of patriarchy which have persisted into the present, it is essential to see what part patriarchy played in precapitalist society. The dominance of men over women in the past was more clearly a property relation than it is now. We usually think of property as things. However, animals and people can also be possessions. The word 'stock' still covers the breeding of animals and people as well as assets on the stock exchange. But women are no longer so clearly means of production owned by men. When a man married in a society in which production was only marginally beyond subsistence, he married a 'yoke-fellow' whose labour was crucial if he were to prosper. Her procreative capacity was important not only because of the high infant mortality rate but also because children meant more hands to labour. The wife's role in production was much greater because although tasks were already sexually divided many more goods were produced in the household. Women who were too high up in the social scale to work with their own hands supervised household production.

The family was a collective working group. The father was its head, but for survival the labour of wife and children was necessary. Notions of leisure were necessarily restricted in a situation of scarcity when the surplus produced was very small. Consequently, the economic and social cohesion of the family was more important than what individuals in the family might want or regard as their right. Indeed the notion that women and children had individual interests which could not be included in those of the father is a modern concept that belongs to capitalism. It would have seemed bizarre, atomistic and socially destructive in earlier times. The productive forces of capital thus made the concept of individual development possible even though it was still confined in practice to the lives of those who belonged to the dominant class.

The introduction of individual wages and the end of the ownership of people in serfdom did not dissolve the economic and social control of men over women. The man remained the head of the family unit of production and he retained control over the ownership of property through primogeniture. Both his wife's capacity to labour and her capacity to bear his children were still part of his stock in the world. Moreover, the notion that this was part of the order of things was firmly embedded in all political, religious and educational institutions.

Although capitalism temporarily strengthened the control over women by the middle- and upper-class men in the nineteenth century by removing them from production, it has tended to whittle away at the economic and ideological basis of patriarchy. As wage labour became general and the idea spread in society that it was unjust to own other people, although the exploitation of their labour power was perfectly fair, the position of the daughter and the wife appeared increasingly anomalous. Ironically, middle-class women came to the conviction that their dependence on men and the protection of patriarchal authority were intolerable precisely at a time when the separation of work from home was shattering the economic basis of patriarchy among the working class. The factories meant that the economic hold of men over women in the working-class family was weakened. Machinery meant that tasks formerly done by men could be done by women. The woman's wage packet gave her some independence. Ideologically, however, men's hold persisted among the workers and was nurtured by the male ruling class.

Subsequently by continually reducing the scope of production, by developing the separation between home and work, and by reducing the time spent in procreation, a great army of women workers has been 'freed' for exploitation in the commodity system. This integration of married women into the labour market has been especially noticeable in the advanced capitalist countries since the Second World War and testifies to the tendency for capital to seek new reserves of labour. The result in terms of women's consciousness at work is only now beginning to be felt. While the dissolution of the extended kinship networks has produced in the nuclear family a streamlined unit suitable for modern capitalism, it has forced an examination of the relationships of man to woman and parent to child.

The struggle of the early feminist movement for legal and political equality and the assumptions it has bequeathed to women now, despite the degeneration of its radical impulse, have strained the hold of patriarchy in the capitalist state, though without dislodging it. The power of the working class within capitalism and the growth of new kinds of political movements recently, particularly for black liberation, have touched the consciousness of women and brought many of us to question the domination of men over women. This has taken a political shape, in the new feminism of women's liberation.

The development of contraceptive technology in capitalism means that ideas of sexual liberation can begin to be realized. The fact that sexual pleasure now need not necessarily result in procreation means a new dimension of liberation in the relation of men and women to nature is possible. It also removes some of patriarchy's most important sanctions against rebellion. The right to determine our own sexuality, to control when or if we want to give birth, and to choose who and how we want to love are central in both women's liberation and in gay liberation. All these are most subversive to patriarchy.

However, although capitalism has itself eroded patriarchy and has brought into being movements and ideas which are both anti-capitalist and anti-patriarchal, it still maintains the subordination of women as a group. Patriarchy has continued in capitalism as an ever present prop in time of need. Although women are not literally the property of men, the continuation of female production in the family means that women have not yet even won the right to be exploited equally. The wage system in capitalism has continued to be structured according to the assumption that women's labour is worth half that of men on the market. Behind this is the idea that women are somehow owned by men who should support them. Women are thus seen as economic attachments to men, not quite as free labourers. Their wage is still seen as supplementary. If a woman has no man she is seen as a sexual failure and the inference is often that she is a slut as well. She also has to struggle to bring up a family alone, on half a man's income. This very simple economic fact about the position of women in capitalism acts as a bribe to keep women with men: it has no regard for feeling or suffering and makes a mockery of any notion of choice or control over how we live. It also means that women make up a convenient reserve army which will work at half pay and can be reabsorbed back into the family if there is unemployment.

Our sexual conditioning means that we submit more readily than men to this intolerable state of affairs. We are brought up to think not only that it is just that the private owner of capital can extract profit from the surplus we produce but also that it is legitimate for the capitalist to return to us in the form of wages about half the sum he has to pay a man. Equal pay is obviously only the beginning of an answer to this—though even the chances of the limited measures in the Equal Pay Act in Britain look doubtful if the Tories have their way. The inequality of women at work is built into the structure of capitalist production and the division of labour in industry and in the family. The equality of women to men, even the equal *exploitation* of women in capitalism, would require such fundamental changes in work and at home that it is very hard to imagine how they could be effected while capitalism survives.

Our labour in the family goes unrecognized except as an excuse to keep us out of the better jobs in industry and accuse us of absenteeism and unreliability. This separation between home and work, together with the responsibility of women for housework and child care, serves to perpetuate inequality. Women, as a group in the labour force, are badly paid and underprivileged. This is not only economically profitable to capitalism, it has proved a useful political safety valve. There are many aspects of women's consciousness which have never fully come to terms with the capitalist mode of production. There is no reason why these should not take a radical and critical form in the context of a movement for liberation but in the past they have been used against women and against the working class. It is quite handy for capitalism if wives can be persuaded to oppose their husbands on strike, or if men console themselves for their lack of control at work with the right to be master in their own home. When this happens patriarchy is earning its keep. Similarly, when men and women do not support each other at work both patriarchy and capitalism are strengthened.

Because production in the family differs from commodity production we learn to feel that it is not quite work. This undermines our resentment and makes it harder to stress that it should be eliminated as much as possible not only by technology but by new styles of living, new buildings, and new forms of social care for the young, the sick and the old.

In capitalism housework and child care are lumped together. In fact they are completely different. Housework is drudgery which is best reduced by mechanizing and socializing it, except for cookery, which can be shared. Caring for small children is important and absorbing work, which does not mean that one person should have to do it all the time. But we are taught to think there is something wrong with us if we seek any alternative. The lack of nurseries and of other facilities for children and the rigid structuring of work and the division of labour between the sexes again makes choice impossible.

Propaganda about our feminine role helps to make us accept this state of affairs. Values linger on after the social structures which conceived them. Our ideas of what is 'feminine' are a strange bundle of assumptions, some of which belong to the Victorian middle class and others which simply rationalize the form patriarchy assumes in capitalism now. Either way the notion of 'femininity' is a convenient means of making us believe submission is somehow natural. When we get angry we are called hysterical.

Thus, although capitalism has eroded the forms of production and property ownership which were the basis of patriarchy, it has still retained the domination of men over women in society. This domination continues to pervade economic, legal, social and sexual life.

It is not enough to struggle for particular reforms, important as these are. Unless we understand the relationship of the various elements within the structure of male-dominated capitalism, we will find the improvements we achieve are twisted against us, or serve one group at the expense of the rest. For example, the wider dissemination of contraceptive information and the weakening of guilt about our sexuality have meant a major improvement in the lives of many women. However, the removal of fear alone is not enough because relations between the sexes are based on the ownership of property, property consisting not only of the woman's labour in procreation, but also of her body. Therefore, while class, race and sex domination remain a constituent element of relations between men and women, women and women, and men and men, these relations will continue to be distorted. Sexual liberation in capitalism can thus continue to be defined by men and also continue to be competitive. The only difference between this and the old set-up is that when patriarchy was secure men measured their virility by the number of children they produced, now they can apply more suitable means of assessing masculinity in a use-and-throw-away society and simply notch up sexual conquests.

There are other examples of feminist reforms being distorted by the structure of capitalist society. We are far from the situation of baby farms and state-controlled breeding but these are the lines along which a pure capitalism, shorn of the remnants of earlier forms of production, would develop. Similarly, one group of women can be bought off at the expense of another, young women against old, middle class against working class. If we are ready to settle for a slightly bigger bite of the existing cake for a privileged section we will merely create gradations among the underprivileged. We will not change the context in which women are inferior. For instance, in Britain there has been some recent discussion about giving women better jobs in management and promoting secretaries because they will work harder for less pay.

Capitalism is not based on the organization of production for people but simply on the need to secure maximum profit. It is naïve to expect that it will make exceptions of women. It is impossible now to predict whether capitalism could accommodate itself to the complete elimination of all earlier forms of property and production and specifically to the abolition of patriarchy. But it is certain that the kind of accommodation it could make would provide no real solution for women when we are unable to labour in commodity production because we are pregnant: socially helpless people protected in capitalism are not only treated as parasites who are expected to show gratitude but are under the direct power of the bourgeois state. Also class and race cut across sexual oppression. A feminist movement which is confined to the specific oppression of women cannot, in isolation, end exploitation and imperialism.

We have to keep struggling to go beyond our own situation. This means recognizing that the emphases which have come out of women's liberation are important not only to ourselves. The capacity to bring into conscious combination the unorganizable, those who distrust one another, who have been taught to despise themselves, and the connection which comes out of our practice between work and home, personal and political, are of vital significance to other movements in advanced capitalism. Similarly, the comprehension in women's liberation of the delicate mechanism of communication between the structures of capitalist society and the most hidden part of our secret selves is too important not to become part of the general theory and practice of the Left. Women's liberation has mounted an attack on precisely those areas where socialists have been slow to resist capitalism: authoritarian social relationships, sexuality and the family. 'Personal' relations within capitalism, where the labour force is reproduced, are becoming increasingly crucial in the modern organization of industry. We have to struggle for control not merely over the means of production but over the conditions of reproduction.

The predicament of working-class women is the most potentially subversive to capitalism because it spans production and reproduction, class exploitation and sex oppression. The movement of working-class women is thus essential for the emergence of socialist feminism because the necessary connections are forced upon women who are working-class when they take action. When they occupy or strike they have their own conditioning as women, the attitude of husbands, the care of the family, the sexual patronage of union officials, the ridicule of the popular press about petticoat pickets and Mrs Mopps, the overwhelming contempt from the middle class for their sex and their class. They are thus compelled to develop both sisterhood and solidarity or be crushed. They need each other, they need the support of male workers, and their fight at work connects immediately to their situation at home. Their organization and militancy is vital not only for women's liberation but for the whole socialist and working-class movement.

The problem about how a revolutionary theory can come out of a day-to-day practice defined by the existence of capitalism has long bedevilled revolutionary socialism. The concept of the Leninist party as the conscious embodiment of an alternative has become dubious, because the party in reality will still express the viewpoint of sections which are the stronger within capitalism, most obviously men, for example. Moreover, the party itself can become absorbed in the immediate problem of surviving within capitalism rather than in the task of exposing contradictions and seeking revolutionary transformation. The mobilization of new groups within capitalism against a specific form of oppression is thus very important, but more important still is the means of translating the experience of one group to another without merely annexing the weaker to the stronger.

Thus it is not just groups which have a position of power at the point of production in the advanced sectors of the capitalist economy, but the organization of groups whose consciousness spans several dimensions of oppression which becomes crucial in a revolutionary movement.

This is not an idealization of weakness. Women as a group are extremely vulnerable within capitalism, but because of our social situation we are forced to find the means of going beyond our own specific oppression. The blocks against us are very real; male domination permeates every organization within capitalism including trade unions and revolutionary groups, and the problem of how to safeguard our autonomy while making a strategy of organizing with men is a persistent dilemma in the women's movement.

Nor is this an evasion of the urgent problem of making an offensive organization which is capable of overcoming the tremendous resources of the advanced capitalist state. The substitution of the women's movement for such an organization would be most evidently absurd. Although we have the capacity to go beyond our own predicament, and although alternatives must be continually drawn out of our day-to-day struggle to defend women against capitalism, neither our structure, nor our politics, are the same as those of a revolutionary organization. We come into women's liberation out of our specific predicament as women, not as people who necessarily are committed to the creation of socialism. We are, moreover, essentially a partial organization representing a specific group. Such a substitution is both dishonest and foolhardy. It implies imposing a consciousness on other women and exposing ourselves to the full repression of the state.

There are no short-cuts. The making of a revolutionary socialist organization which is capable of taking the offensive without being either absorbed or smashed, which can at once safeguard the interests of the groups within it and not simply reproduce the structures of authority and domination which belong to capitalism, is a gigantic task. Autonomy and cohesive organization in the face of repression go uncomfortably together. The models of the past can help us but do not fit the special problems of the modern capitalist state. However, the political process of making an effective movement for the liberation of women—which means a movement in which working-class women are in the majority—is an essential part of this task.

AUDRE LORDE

The Master's Tools

I agreed to take part in a New York University Institute for the Humanities conference a year ago, with the understanding that I would be commenting upon papers dealing with the role of difference within the lives of american women: difference of race, sexuality, class, and age. The absence of these considerations weakens any feminist discussion of the personal and the political.

It is a particular academic arrogance to assume any discussion of feminist theory without examining our many differences, and without a significant input from poor women, Black and Third World women, and lesbians. And yet, I stand here as a Black lesbian feminist, having been invited to comment within the only panel at this conference where the input of Black feminists and lesbians is represented. What this says about the vision of this conference is sad, in a country where racism, sexism, and homophobia are inseparable. To read this program is to assume that lesbian and Black women have nothing to say about existentialism, the erotic, women's culture and silence, developing feminist theory, or heterosexuality and power. And what does it mean in personal and political terms when even the two Black women who did present here were literally found at the last hour? What does it mean when the tools of a racist patriarchy are used to examine the fruits of that same partiarchy? It means that only the most narrow perimeters of change are possible and allowable.

The absence of any consideration of lesbian consciousness or the consciousness of Third World women leaves a serious gap within this conference and within the papers presented here. For example, in a paper on material relationships between women, I was conscious of an either/or model of nurturing which totally dismissed my knowledge as a Black lesbian. In this paper there was no examination of mutuality between women, no systems of shared support, no interdependence as exists between lesbians and women-identified women. Yet it is only in the patriarchal model of nurturance that women "who attempt to emancipate themselves pay perhaps too high a price for the results," as this paper states.

For women, the need and desire to nurture each other is not pathological but redemptive, and it is within that knowledge that our real power is rediscovered. It is this real connection which is so feared by a patriarchal world. Only within a patriarchal structure is maternity the only social power open to women.

Interdependency between women is the way to a freedom which allows the *I* to *be*, not in order to be used, but in order to be creative. This is a difference between the passive *be* and the active *being*.

Advocating the mere tolerance of difference between women is the grossest reformism. It is a total denial of the creative function of difference in our lives. Difference must be not merely tolerated, but seen as a fund of necessary polarities between which our creativity can spark like a dialectic. Only then does the necessity for interdependency become unthreatening. Only within that interdependency of different strengths, acknowledged and equal, can the power to seek new ways of being in the world generate, as well as the courage and sustenance to act where there are no charters.

Within the interdependence of mutual (nondominant) differences lies that security which enables us to descend into the chaos of knowledge and return with true visions of our future, along with the concomitant power to effect those changes which can bring that future into being. Difference is that raw and powerful connection from which our personal power is forged.

As women, we have been taught either to ignore our differences, or to view them as causes for separation and suspicion rather than as forces for change. Without community there is no liberation, only the most vulnerable and temporary armistice between an individual and her oppression. But community must not mean a shedding of our differences, nor the pathetic pretense that these differences do not exist.

Those of us who stand outside the circle of this society's definition of acceptable women; those of us who have been forged in the crucibles of difference—those of us who are poor, who are lesbians, who are Black, who are older—know that *survival is not an academic skill*. It is learning how to stand alone, unpopular and sometimes reviled, and how to make common cause with those others identified as outside the structures in order to define and seek a world in which we can all flourish. It is learning how to take our differences and make them strengths. *For the master's tools will never dismantle the master's house.* They may allow us temporarily to beat him at his own game, but they will never enable us to bring about genuine change. And this fact is only threatening to those women who still define the master's house as their only source of support.

Poor women and women of Color know there is a difference between the daily manifestations of marital slavery and prostitution because it is our daughters who line 42nd Street. If while american feminist theory need not deal with the differences between us, and the resulting difference in our oppressions, then how do you deal with the fact that the women who clean your houses and tend your children while you attend conferences on feminist theory are, for the most part, poor women and women of Color? What is the theory behind racist feminism?

In world of possibility for us all, our personal visions help lay the groundwork for political action. The failure of academic feminists to recognize difference as a crucial strength is a failure to reach beyond the first patriarchal lesson. In our world, divide and conquer must become define and empower.

Why weren't other women of Color found to participate in this conference? Why were two phone calls to me considered a consultation? Am I the only possible source of names of Black feminists? And although the Black panelist's paper ends on an important and powerful connection of love between women, what about interracial cooperation between feminists who don't love each other?

In academic feminist circles, the answer to these questions is often, "We did not know who to ask." But that is the same evasion of responsibility, the same cop-out, that keeps Black women's art out of women's exhibitions, Black women's work out of most feminist publications except for the occasional "Special Third World Women's Issue," and Black women's texts off your reading lists. But as Adrienne Rich pointed out in a recent talk, white feminists have educated themselves about such an enormous amount over the past ten years, how come you haven't also educated yourselves about Black women and the differences between us—white and Black—when it is key to our survival as a movement?

Women of today are still being called upon to stretch across the gap of male ignorance and to educate men as to our existence and our needs. This is an old and primary tool of all oppressors to keep the oppressed occupied with the master's concerns. Now we hear that it is the task of women of Color to educate white women—in the face of tremendous resistance—as to our existence, our differences, our relative roles in our joint survival. This is a diversion of energies and a tragic repetition of racist patriarchal thought.

Simone de Beauvoir once said: "It is in the knowledge of the genuine conditions of our lives that we must draw our strength to live and our reasons for acting."

Racism and homophobia are real conditions of all our lives in this place and time. *I urge each one of us here to reach down into that deep place of knowledge inside herself and touch that terror and loathing of any difference that lives there. See whose face it wears.* Then the personal as the political can begin to illuminate all our choices.

ECOLOGICAL VISIONS

Nature stands in danger, and with it the prospects for civilization itself. The most economically advanced societies, according to Andre Gorz in the following selections from his *Ecology as Politics,* are undermining the infrastructure of our planet. Oceans are becoming sterile, soil infertile, and air unbreathable. Capitalist growth is now encountering not merely economic limits, but physical ones. It is no longer enough to refrain from consuming more; it is time to begin consuming less. A new form of "ecological realism," which examines the material prerequisites for economic activity, is required in order to both contest capitalist rationality and conceive of socialism as a genuinely antiauthoritarian and democratic alternative to the status quo.

Carolyn Merchant deals with precisely these issues in the conclusion to her influential *The Death of Nature.* She criticizes the traditional positivistic model and advances a new "holistic" perspective. There is nothing neutral about mathematical formalism, according to Merchant, and its limits become evident in its mechanical equation of the whole with the sum of its parts. Nature must instead be seen as alive, and its parts must be considered in their interconnectedness. All living things have rights, a recognition that necessitates new priorities for science and production. In this sense, ecology is understood as involving an extension of the principles inherited from the democratic revolutions of the last centuries.

Ulrich Beck, similarly, connects ecology and the Enlightenment. Author of the already classic *Risk Society* and among the most important contemporary sociologists, Beck notes how ignorance grows in concert with knowledge. Rejecting those who take their stand either "for" or "against" progress, and noting that doubt is the "inside ally" for any future reformation of science, Beck maintains that the advances of science itself have demolished the assumptions and certainties usually associated with scientific rationality. It is no longer possible, for example, to differentiate between theoretical and applied science. The one presupposes the other, and for this very reason political interests necessarily inform scientific development. These are what Beck hopes to question in terms of a new "risk calculus" and an ongoing public discussion of the fundamental question raised by ecology: How do we want to live?

ANDRE GORZ

Ecology and Freedom

1. ECOLOGICAL REALISM

Growth-oriented capitalism is dead. Growth-oriented socialism, which closely resembles it, reflects the distorted image of our past, not of our future. Marxism, although irreplaceable as an instrument of analysis, has lost its prophetic value.

The development of the forces of production, which was supposed to enable the working class to cast off its chains and establish universal freedom, has instead dispossessed the workers of the last shreds of their sovereignty, deepened the division between manual and intellectual labor, and destroyed the material and existential bases of the producers' power.

Economic growth, which was supposed to ensure the affluence and well-being of everyone, has created needs more quickly than it could satisfy them, and has led to a series of dead ends which are not solely economic in character: capitalist growth is in crisis not only because it is capitalist but also because it is encountering physical limits.

It is possible to imagine palliatives for one or another of the problems which have given rise to the present crisis. But its distinctive character is that it will inevitably be aggravated by each of the successive and partial solutions by which it seeks to overcome them.

While it has all the characteristics of a classical crisis of overproduction, the current crisis also possesses a number of new dimensions which Marxists, with rare exceptions, have not foreseen, and for which what has until now been understood as "socialism" does not contain adequate answers. It is a crisis in the relation between the individual and the economic sphere as such; a crisis in the character of work; a crisis in our relations with nature, with our bodies, with our sexuality, with society, with future generations, with history; a crisis of urban life, of habitat, of medical practice, of education, of science.

We know that our present mode of life is without future; that the children we will bring into the world will use neither oil nor a number of now-familiar metals during their adult lives; that if current nuclear programs are implemented, uranium reserves will be exhausted by them.

We know that *our* world is ending; that if we go on as before, the oceans and the rivers will be sterile, the soil infertile, the air unbreathable in the cities, and life a privilege reserved for the selected specimens of a new race of humans, adapted by chemical conditioning and genetic programming to survive in a new ecological niche, carved out and sustained by biological engineering.

We know that for a hundred and fifty years industrial society has developed through the accelerated looting of reserves whose creation required tens of millions of years; and that until very recently all economists, whether classical or Marxist, have rejected as irrelevant or "reactionary" all questions concerning the longer-term future—that of the planet, that of the biosphere, that of civilizations. "In the long run we shall all be dead," said Keynes, wryly asserting that the temporal horizon of the economist should not exceed the next ten or twenty years. "Science," we were assured, would find new paths; engineering would discover new processes undreamt of today.

But science and technology have ended up making this central discovery: all productive activity depends on borrowing from the finite resources of the planet and on organizing a set of exchanges within a fragile system of multiple equilibriums.

The point is not to deify nature or to "go back" to it, but to take account of a simple fact: human activity finds in the natural world its external limits. Disregarding these limits sets off a backlash whose effects we are already experiencing in specific, though still widely misunderstood, ways: new diseases and new forms of dis-ease, maladjusted children (but maladjusted to what?), decreasing life expectancy, decreasing physical yields and economic pay-offs, and a decreasing quality of life despite increasing levels of material consumption.

The response of economists up to now has essentially consisted of dismissing as "utopian" or "irresponsible" those who have focused attention on these symptoms of a crisis in our fundamental relation to the natural world, a relation in which all economic activity is grounded. The boldest concept which modern political economy dared envisage was that of "zero growth" in physical consumption. Only one economist, Nicholas Georgesco-Roegen, has had the common sense to point out that, even at zero growth, the continued consumption of scarce resources will inevitably result in exhausting them completely. The point is not to refrain from consuming more and more, but to consume less and less—there is no other way of conserving the available reserves for future generations.

This is what ecological realism is about.

The standard objection is that any effort to arrest or reverse the process of growth will perpetuate or even worsen existing inequalities, and result in a deterioration in the material conditions of those who are already poor. But the idea that growth reduces inequality is a faulty one—statistics show that, on the contrary, the reverse is true. It may be objected that these statistics apply only to capitalist countries and that socialism would produce greater social justice; but why then should it be necessary to produce more things? Would it not be more rational to improve the conditions and the quality of life by making more efficient use of available resources, by producing different things differently, by eliminating waste, and by refusing to produce socially those goods which are so expensive that they can never be available to all, or which are so cumbersome or polluting that their costs outweigh their benefits as soon as they become accessible to the majority?

Radicals who refuse to examine the question of equality without growth merely demonstrate that "socialism," for them, is nothing but the continuation of capitalism by other means—an extension of middle class values, lifestyles, and social patterns (which the more enlightened members of that class, under pressure from their daughters and sons, are already beginning to reject).

Today a lack of realism no longer consists in advocating greater well-being through the inversion of growth and the subversion of the prevailing way of life. Lack of realism consists in imagining that economic growth can still bring about increased human welfare, and indeed that it is still physically possible.

2. POLITICAL ECONOMY AND ECOLOGY

Political economy, as a specific discipline, applies neither to the family nor to those communities small enough to settle by common agreement the cooperation of their members and their exchange (or pooling) of goods and mutual services. Political economy begins only where free cooperation and reciprocity cease. It begins only with *social production*, i.e., production founded upon a social division of labor and regulated by mechanisms external to the will and consciousness of individuals—by market processes or by central planning (or by both).

"Economic man," i.e., the abstract individual who underpins economic reasoning, has the unique characteristic of not consuming what he or she produces and not producing what he or she consumes. Consequently he or she is never troubled by questions of quality, usefulness, charm, beauty, happiness, freedom, or morality, but is affected only by exchange values, flows, and quantitative aggregates and balances.

Economists do not concern themselves with what individuals think, feel, and desire, but only with the material processes which, independently of their own will, human activities give rise to in a (social) context of limited resources.

It is impossible to derive an ethic from economic reasoning. Marx was one of the first to understand this. The choice he discerned was, very schematically, as follows:

• either individuals manage to unite and, in order to subordinate the economic process to their collective will, replace the social division of labor with the voluntary cooperation of associated producers;

• or else they remain dispersed and divided, in which case the economic process will prevail over people's aims and goals, and sooner or later a strong central state will, in the pursuit of its own rationality, impose by force the cooperation which the people were unable to achieve for themselves. The choice is simple: "socialism or barbarism."

The ecologist stands in the same relation to economic activity as the economist to the convivial cooperation which rules family or community activities. Ecology, as a specific discipline, does not apply to those communities or peoples whose ways of producing have no lasting or irremediable effects on the environment—natural resources appear inexhaustible, the impact of human activity negligible. In the ideal case, the stewardship of nature is, like the art of healthy living, based on the unwritten rules of generally accepted wisdom.

Ecology does not appear as a separate discipline until economic activity destroys or permanently disturbs the environment and, in so doing, compromises the pursuit of economic activity itself, or significantly changes its conditions. Ecology is concerned with the external limits which economic activity must respect so as to avoid producing effects contrary to its aims or incompatible with its continuation.

In the same way that economics is concerned with the external constraints that *individual* activities give rise to when they generate unwanted *collective* results, ecology is concerned with the external constraints which economic activity gives rise to when it produces environmental alterations which upset the calculation of costs and benefits.

In the same way that economics belongs to a realm beyond reciprocity and voluntary cooperation, ecology belongs to a realm beyond that of economic activity and calculation, *but without including it*—it is not the case that ecology is a superior rationality which subsumes that of economics. Ecology has a different rationality: it makes us aware that the efficiency of economic activity is a limited one and that it rests upon extraeconomic conditions. It enables us to discover, in particular, that the economic effort to overcome *relative* scarcities engenders, beyond a certain threshold, *absolute and insurmountable* scarcities. The returns become negative: production destroys more than it produces. This inversion occurs when economic activity infringes upon the equilibrium of primary ecological cycles and/or destroys resources which it is incapable of regenerating or reconstituting.

To this type of situation, the economic system has in the past invariably responded by additional productive efforts; it tries to compensate with increased production for the scarcities engendered by increased production. It does not recognize that this response necessarily exacerbates these scarcities: that, beyond a certain threshold, measures favoring the circulation of automobiles increase congestion; that the increased consumption of medicine increases morbidity while displacing its causes; that the increased consumption of energy creates forms of pollution which, as long as they remain uncontrolled at their source, can only be fought in ways which involve a new increase in energy consumption, itself polluting, and so on.

To understand and overcome these "counterproductivities," one has to break with economic rationality. This is what ecology does: it reveals to us that an appropriate response to the scarcities and disease, to the bottlenecks and dead-ends of industrial civilization, must be sought not in growth but in the limitation or reduction of material production. It demonstrates that it can be more effective and "productive" to conserve natural resources than to exploit them, to sustain natural cycles rather than interfere with them.

It is nevertheless impossible to derive an ethic from ecology. Ivan Illich is one of the first to have understood this. The alternatives which he sees before us can be stated schematically as follows:

• either we agree to impose limits on technology and industrial production so as to conserve natural resources, preserve the ecological balances necessary to life, and favor the development and autonomy of communities and individuals (this is the convivial option);

• or else the limits necessary to the preservation of life will be centrally determined and planned by ecological engineers, and the programmed production of an "optimal" environment will be entrusted to centralized institutions and hard technologies (this is the technofascist option, the path along which we are already halfway engaged). The choice is simple: "conviviality or technofascism."

Ecology, as a purely scientific discipline, does not necessarily imply the rejection of authoritarian, technofascist solutions. The rejection of technofascism does not arise from a scientific understanding of the balances of nature, but from a political and cultural choice. Environmentalists *use* ecology as the lever to push forward a radical critique of our civilization and our society. But ecological arguments can also be used to justify the application of biological engineering to human systems.

3. ECOLOGY AND THE INVERSION OF TOOLS

The preference for natural, self-regulating systems over systems relying on experts and institutions need not imply a quasireligious exaltation of nature. It is not impossible for artificial systems to be, in certain respects, more efficient than natural ones. The preference for the latter should be defended as a *rational choice*, in both political and ethical terms—a preference for decentralized self-regulation over centralized other-regulation. The field of "health policy" provides us with a particularly striking example, which can serve as a paradigm.

Natural selection is the perfect case of decentralized self-regulation. It can be circumvented by the increasingly sophisticated interventions of the medical-care apparatus, which can save the lives of babies who would otherwise die in their first days or months. These individuals, however, will in turn tend to have offspring of whom a growing proportion will display hereditary defects or diseases. The resulting deterioration of the genetic stock is already leading some geneticists to advocate a state-enforced policy of eugenics—that is, a regulation of the freedom to mate and procreate.

The abolition of natural self-regulation thus leads to the necessity for administrative regulation. Natural selection is in the end to be replaced by social selection.

The latter can, in certain respects, be regarded as more efficient than the former: eugenics would prevent the conception of deformed or non-viable individuals, whereas natural selection eliminates them only after conception or, often, only after birth. But there is another difference: natural selection occurs spontaneously, without any planned intervention. Eugenics, on the other hand, assumes a technobureaucracy capable of enforcing the administrative norms which it lays down. Natural self-regulation can only be replaced by regulating *authority*.

This example, in no way fanciful, is intended to illustrate the ecological principle that *it is better to leave nature to work itself out than to seek to correct it at the cost of a growing submission of individuals to institutions, to the domination of others.* For the ecologist's objection to system engineering is not that it violates nature (which is not sacred), but that it substitutes new forms of domination for existing natural processes.

Politically, the implication is obvious: the ecological perspective is incompatible with the rationality of capitalism. It is also wholly incompatible with the authoritarian socialism which (whether it relies on central economic planning or not) is the only kind which exists in the world today on a governmental level. The ecologist's position is not, by contrast, incompatible with a libertarian or democratic socialism: but it should not be confused with it. The ecologist's concern is working at another and more fundamental level:

that of the material prerequisites of the economic system. In particular, it is concerned with the character of prevailing technologies, for the techniques on which the economic system is based are not neutral. In fact, they reflect and determine the relations of the producers of their products, of the workers to their work, of the individual to the group and the society, of people to the environment. Technology is the matrix in which the distribution of power, the social relations of production, and the hierarchical division of labor are embedded.

Societal choices are continually being imposed upon us under the guise of technical choices. These technical choices are rarely the only ones possible, nor are they necessarily the most efficient ones. For capitalism develops only those technologies which correspond to its logic and which are compatible with its continued domination. It eliminates those technologies which do not strengthen prevailing social relations, even where they are more rational with respect to stated objectives. Capitalist relations of production and exchange are already inscribed in the technologies which capitalism bequeaths to us.

The struggle for different technologies is essential to the struggle for a different society. The institutions and structures of the state are to a large extent determined by the nature and weight of its technologies. Nuclear energy, for example—whether "capitalist" or "socialist"—presupposes and imposes a centralized, hierarchical, police-dominated society.

The inversion of tools is a fundamental condition of the transformation of society. The development of voluntary cooperation, the self-determination and freedom of communities and individuals, requires the development of technologies and methods of production which:

- can be used and controlled at the level of the neighborhood or community;
- are capable of generating increased economic autonomy for local and regional collectivities;
- are not harmful to the environment; and
- are compatible with the exercise of joint control by producers and consumers over products and production processes.

Of course, it can be objected that it is impossible to change the tools without transforming society as a whole, and that this cannot be accomplished without gaining control over the state. This objection is valid providing it is not taken to mean that societal change and the acquisition of state power must *precede* technological change. For without changing the technology, the transformation of society will remain formal and illusory. The theoretical and practical definition of alternative technologies, and the struggle of communities and individuals to win, collectively and individually, control over their own destinies, must be the permanent focus of political action. If they are not, the seizure of state power by people calling themselves socialists will not change fundamentally either the system of domination or the relations of men and women to each other and to nature. Socialism is not immune to technofascism. It will, on the contrary, fall prey to it whenever and wherever it sets out to enhance and multiply the powers of the state without developing simultaneously the autonomy of civil society.

This is why the ecological struggle is in its present form, an indispensable dimension of the struggle against capitalism. It cannot be subordinated to the political objectives of socialism. Only where the left is committed to a fully decentralized and democratic socialism can it give political expression to ecological demands. The organized left, in France as in other countries, has not yet reached this stage; it has not incorporated ecological principles in either its practice or its program. It is for this reason that the ecological movement must continue to assert its specificity and its autonomy.

Ecological concerns are fundamental; they cannot be compromised or postponed. Socialism is no better than capitalism if it makes use of the same tools. The total domination of nature inevitably entails a domination of people by the techniques of domination. If there were no other options, it would be preferable to have a non-nuclear capitalism than to have a nuclear socialism, for the former would weigh less heavily upon future generations.

CAROLYN MERCHANT

Epilogue to *The Death of Nature*

The mechanistic view of nature, developed by the seventeeth-century natural philosophers and based on a Western mathematical tradition going back to Plato, is still dominant in science today. This view assumes that nature can be divided into parts and that the parts can be rearranged to create other species of being. "Facts" or information bits can be extracted from the environmental context and rearranged according to a set of rules based on logical and mathematical operations. The results can then be tested and verified by resubmitting them to nature, the ultimate judge of their validity. Mathematical formalism provides the criterion for rationality and certainty, nature the criterion for empirical validity and acceptance or rejection of the theory.

The work of historians and philosophers of science notwithstanding, it is widely assumed by the scientific community that modern science is objective, value-free, and context-free knowledge of the external world. To the extent to which the sciences can be reduced to this mechanistic mathematical model, the more legitimate they become as sciences. Thus the reductionist hierarchy of the validity of the sciences first proposed in the nineteenth century by French positivist philosopher August Comte is still widely assumed by intellectuals, the most mathematical and highly theoretical sciences occupying the most revered position.

The mechanistic approach to nature is as fundamental to the twentieth-century revolution in physics as it was to classical Newtonian science, culminating in the nineteenth-century unification of mechanics, thermodynamics, and electromagnetic theory. Twentieth-century physics still views the world in terms of fundamental particles—electrons, protons, neutrons, mesons, muons, pions, taus, thetas, sigmas, pis, and so on. The search for the ultimate unifying particle, the quark, continues to engage the efforts of the best theoretical physicists.

Mathematical formalism isolates the elements of a given quantum mechanical problem, places them in a latticelike matrix, and rearranges them through a mathematical function called an *operator*. Systems theory extracts possibly relevant information bits from the environmental context and stores them in a computer memory for later use. But since it cannot store an infinite number of "facts," it must select a finite number of potentially relevant pieces of data according to a theory or set of rules governing the selection process. For any given solution, this mechanistic approach very likely excludes some potentially relevant factors.

Systems theorists claim for themselves a holistic outlook, because they believe that they are taking into account the ways in which all the parts in a given system affect the whole. Yet the formalism of the calculus of probabilities excludes the possibility of mathematizing the gestalt—that is, the ways in which each part at any given instant take their meaning from the whole. The more open, adaptive, organic, and complex the system, the less successful is the formalism. It is most successful when applied to closed, artificial, precisely defined, relatively simple systems. Mechanistic assumptions about nature push us increasingly in the direction of artificial environments, mechanized control over more and more aspects of human life, and a loss of the quality of life itself.

In the social sphere, the mechanistic model helps to guide technological and industrial development. In *The Technological Society,* Jacques Ellul discussed the techniques of economics and the mechanistic organization of specialities inherent in and entailed by the machines and mathematical methods themselves. The calculating machine, punch card machine, microfilm, and computer transform statistical methods and administrative organization into specialized agencies centered around one or more statistical categories.

Econometric models and stochastics are used to operate on statistical data in order to analyze, compare, and predict. In social applications, attempts to predict public reaction through the calculus of probabilities may make a public informed of its conformation to a trend act in the inverse manner.

> But the public, by so reacting falls under the influence of a new prediction which is completely determinable. . . . It must be assumed, however, that one remains within the framework of rational behavior. The system works all the better when it deals with people who are better integrated into the mass . . . whose consciousness is partially paralyzed, who lend themselves willingly to statistical observations and systematization.

Such attempts to reduce human behavior to statistical probabilities and to condition it by such psychological techniques as those developed by B. F. Skinner are manifestations of the pervasiveness of the mechanistic mode of thought developed by the seventeenth-century scientists.

Holism was proposed as a philosophical alternative to mechanism by J. C. Smuts in his book *Holism and Evolution* (1926), in which he attempted to define the essential characteristics of holism and to differentiate it from nineteenth-century mechanism. He attempts to show that

> Taking a plant or animal as a type of whole, we notice the fundamental holistic characters as a unity of parts which is so close and intense as to be more than a sum of its

parts; which not only gives a particular conformation or structure to the parts but so relates and determines them in their synthesis that their functions are altered; the synthesis affects and determines the parts so that they function toward the "whole"; and the whole and the parts therefore reciprocally influence and determine each other and appear more or less to merge their individual characters.

Smuts saw a continuum of relationships among parts from simple physical mixtures and chemical compounds to organisms and minds in which the unity among parts was affected and changed by the synthesis. "Holism is a process of creative synthesis; the resulting wholes are not static, but dynamic, evolutionary, creative. . . . The explanation of nature can therefore not be purely mechanical; and the mechanistic concept of nature has its place and justification only in the wider setting of holism."

The most important example of holism today is provided by the science of ecology. Although ecology is a relatively new science, its philosophy of nature, holism, is not. Historically, holistic presuppositions about nature have been assumed by communities of people who have succeeded in living in equilibrium with their environments. The idea of cyclical processes, of the interconnectedness of all things, and the assumption that nature is active and alive are fundamental to the history of human thought. No element of an interlocking cycle can be removed without the collapse of the cycle. The parts themselves thus take their meaning from the whole. Each particular part is defined by and dependent on the total context. The cycle itself is a dynamic interactive relationship of all its parts, and process is a dialectical relation between part and whole. Ecology necessarily must consider the complexities and the totality. It cannot isolate the parts into simplified systems that can be studied in a laboratory, because such isolation distorts the whole.

External forces and stresses on a balanced ecosystem, whether natural or man made, can make some parts of the cycle act faster than the systems' own natural oscillations. Depending on the strength of the external disturbance, the metabolic and reproductive reaction rates of the slowest parts of the cycle, and the complexity of the system, it may or may not be able to absorb the stresses without collapsing. At various times in history, civilizations which have put too much external stress on their environments have caused long-term or irrevocable alterations.

By pointing up the essential role of every part of an ecosystem, that if one part is removed the system is weakened and loses stability, ecology has moved in the direction of the leveling of value hierarchies. Each part contributes equal value to the healthy functioning of the whole. All living things, as integral parts of a viable ecosystem, thus have rights. The necessity of protecting the ecosystem from collapse due to the extinction of vital members was one argument for the passage of the Endangered Species Act of 1973. The movement toward egalitarianism manifested in the democratic revolutions of the eighteenth century, the extension of citizens' rights to blacks, and finally, voting rights to women was thus carried a step further. Endangered species became equal to the Army Corps of Engineers: the sails darter had to have a legal hearing before the Tellico Dam could be approved, the Furbish lousewort could block construction of the Dickey-Lincoln Dam in Maine, the red-cockaded woodpecker must be considered in Texas timber management, and the El Segundo Blue Butterfly in California airport expansion.

The conjunction of conservation and ecology movements with women's rights and liberation has moved in the direction of reversing both the subjugation of nature and women. In the late nineteenth and early twentieth centuries, the strong feminist movement in the United States begun in 1842 pressed for women's suffrage first in the individual states and then in the nation. Women activists also formed conservation committees in the many women's organizations that were part of the Federation of Women's Clubs established in 1890. They supported the preservationist movement for national, state, and city parks and wilderness areas led by John Muir and Frederick Law Olmsted, eventually splitting away from the managerial, utilitarian wing headed by Gifford Pinchot and Theodore Roosevelt.

Today the conjunction of the women's movement with the ecology movement again brings the issue of liberation into focus. Mainstream women's groups such as the League of Women Voters took an early lead in studying and pressing for clean air and water legislation. Socialist-feminist and "science for the people" groups worked toward revolutionizing economic structures in a direction that would equalize female and male work options and reform a capitalist system that creates profits at the expense of nature and working people.

The March 1979 accident at the Three-Mile Island nuclear reactor near Harrisburg, Pennsylvania, epitomized the problems of the "death of nature" that have become apparent since the Scientific Revolution. The manipulation of nuclear processes in an effort to control and harness nature through technology backfired into disaster. The long-range economic interests and public image of the power company and the reactor's designer were set above the immediate safety of the people and the health of the earth. The hidden effects of radioactive emissions, which by concentrating in the food chain could lead to an increase in cancers over the next several years, were initially downplayed by those charged with responsibility for regulating atomic power.

Three-Mile Island is a recent symbol of the earth's sickness caused by radioactive wastes, pesticides, plastics, photochemical smog, and fluorocarbons. The pollution "of her purest streams" has been supported since the Scientific Revolution by an ideology of "power over nature," an ontology of interchangeable atomic and human parts, and a methodology of "penetration" into her innermost secrets. The sick earth, "yea dead, yea putrified," can probably in the long run be restored to health only by a reversal of mainstream values and a revolution in economic priorities. In this sense, the world must once again be turned upside down.

As natural resources and energy supplies diminish in the future, it will become essential to examine alternatives of all kinds so that, by adopting new social styles, the quality of the environment can be sustained. Decentralization, nonhierarchical forms of organization, recycling of wastes, simpler living styles involving less-polluting "soft" technologies, and labor-intensive rather than capital-intensive economic methods are possibilities only beginning to be explored. The future distribution of energy and resources among communities should be based on the integration of human and natural ecosystems. Such a restructuring of priorities may be crucial if people and nature are to survive.

ULRICH BECK

The World As Laboratory

Any contemplation of the interlocking of progress and destruction or the growth of hazards and the economy must struggle with a word that sticks to these efforts like a bad smell: "repetition." Everything has been said, exchanged, balanced, repeated. For some time we have been stuck in the repetition of repetition, and any contribution that gets readers' attention can claim to be original only if there are big gaps in what people have read—but such a claim can count on success particularly because of scientific specialization and detail work. What would have been left out anyway? What thought is not already turning brown somewhere in the dusty corners of libraries?

Science and the technology spree, with which the industrial age feeds and irresistibly drives its transformation of the world into world markets, take place as a kind of undemocratic, permanent change in all areas of life, and may even openly contradict the schoolbook rules of democracy. We know this and have thoroughly discussed it, but that has not really kept us from accepting the contradiction. Consider as an example the tinkering advances in knowledge in genetic technology and human genetics and their impending large-scale utilization: there is no site and no subject for decision making in this area of progress, an area that will touch, change, and quite possibly endanger the human substance of our social life.

New technology weasels its way in, advancing here and there, as support for points of view that are motivated by completely different priorities (curiosity, career, competition, opening markets, protecting investments). Making such an amorphous process the business of parliament is as absurd as Eskimo's wish to take a summer vacation to Greenland. One can criticize science and technology again and again, in philosophical journals, in articles for the art-and-living sections of newspapapers, and again in trade-union monthlies. There are honors and academies for doing so; perhaps there will someday be almost professionally protected Cassandra careers, with opportunities for streets to be named posthumously in one's honor. But who really cares about that?

Overpowering objections await anyone who questions the status quo: Should seeking the truth perhaps be replaced by voting? And all this talk of an *alternative* science! Is logic flexible? Can it be laid out broadly or narrowly, violently or gently?

Such prickly arguments lie in wait everywhere to burst the soap-bubble dreams of an alternative development of technology and industry. Does the call for control and shared decision making not throttle freedom of research? Isn't it therefore in the same unsavory group as the Inquisition, facism, and Stalinism, which also subjugated the freedom of scientific judgment, albeit in different ways? To complete the triumph over the critic of science, already down for the count: what will be the source of the social force and power, the rationality, that are needed to break the spell over the Sorcerer's Apprentice? Doesn't all the puzzling over possibilities for political direction and co-decision seem ridiculous in view of a global, autonomous mechanism of progress? Doesn't shaking up the somnambulistic certainty of techno-scientific civilization just rouse the spirits of irrationalism? How in the world is the ecological catastrosphe to be mastered, if not by an upward turn in technological development? But that means *more*, rather than less, technological rule is required, so that any critique of progress, if it is fortunate enough to succeed, only raises the technological programming and planning of society to a higher level. Isn't the call for alternatives just a cheap way to create new world markets? Isn't the dramatization of ecological threats already introducing a new technological imperialism of the First World over the Third and Fourth Worlds? This is how the questions march over the critics of progress.

Here I introduce and test a question so obviously banal that it might again be worth wasting one's attention on it.

PROGRESS ALSO MEANS: FROM THE SCIENCE OF TRUTH TO SCIENCE AS IF AND BUT

The power that can counter the autonomous development of science and technology does not, in the first instance, consist of politics, parliament, law, the public sphere, or meetings of citizens' initiative groups. All these countervailing institutions can only gain influence to the extent that they recognize and politically use science itself to undermine the autonomous course of science and technology. Science and technology, with their inherent thoroughness, reveal possible starting points for their own reformation. The still unseen side effect of the techno-scientific revolution is the revolutionizing of the sciences themselves, the overthrow of their foundations and the claims with which they started and established their autonomous course.

To restate it bluntly, all attempts to attribute a logic to the progress of the sciences, to base their judgment-making ability on the infallibility of experiments, to represent the sciences as, in a way, nature's finding a voice, all these have failed. It was always—and this is important—the advances in science itself that demolished the designs of scientific rationality. Modern physics destroyed the old mechanistic causal understanding of nature and human beings. Epistemology and the theory of science have cut off any path leading to reality in and of itself, without the surmising and erring recourse to knowledge. Progress in science, after all, means the continual refutation of older conceptions, and thus it is a constant testimony within our memory, reaching beyond the present moment, to human and scientific inadequacy.

The self-abdication of science is not, therefore, bad science, some sort of flaw or mistake that could be removed. It is the product of the law of "further, more, better" that is an intrinsic part of science, and only through a temporary forgetting occasioned by the elation of current knowledge can it be distorted into infinite progress. We are largely concerned with a development of science and technology that charges forward without benefit of truth or methodological certainty in its statements and projects. This is a science, then, that has metamorphosed by virtue of its own judgment, its own mechanism of progress, from a science of truth into a science of if and but.

In a certain way, the ancient Greek Skeptics' surmise that our ignorance grows with our knowledge is being confirmed today. The result of scientific progress is not security but uncertainty, although a considered, questioned, and more conscious uncertainty. We know less because we know more. Ignorance and the awareness of ignorance grow along with knowledge, and this publicly reflected doubt, which is the quintessence of science on the leading edge of research, is the core of the uneasiness that shakes techno-scientific civilization today. Cultural critique and the critique of science would have remained unsuccessful, as in the past, if science had not entered a stage of published and objectified self-doubt as a consequence of its specialized autonomy. The doubt that resides in the deepest recess of scientific rationality constitutes it, and is (involuntarily) unleashed in its most advanced stage is the inside ally, the door-opener, for a future reformation of science in a society that is becoming mature with and against science.

SOCIETY AS LABORATORY: DEMOCRACY SNEAKS IN

These considerations sound very philosophical, which nowadays means remote. The opposite is true: these are stumbling blocks in laboratory and research practice.

Schoolbooks distinguish between pure science and applied science. The former is research and the latter is technology. The former is free (value-free) and the latter is determined by and interlocked with economics and politics. Rationality protects pure research under the honorary title of "basic research"; the term claims first, a sequential, and second, a derivational, relationship between research and application, between experiment and technical utilization. This entire ideal world of scientific rationality has collapsed, like a house of cards, under the weight of the largest, deepest, and most economically ambitious advances of recent years. Theories on the operation and safety of nuclear power plants, for instance, can only be tested *after* construction. Experimental mega-technology must be stage-managed and monitored after implementation *as* the manufacture of a new, unknown, and unexplored reality.

Practice as research and running risks for their own sake are two sides of the same thing in the adventure of technological civilization.

We now know that many, at least two hundred, experiments of "destructive embryonic research" were needed to achieve the first test-tube baby. Nuclear reactors must be *built*, artificial biotechnical creatures must be *released into* the environment, and chemical products must be *put into circulation* for their properties, safety, and long-term effects to be studied. Moral, political, and logical problems lurk in this reversal of experiment and application, in this fusion of research and technology into a new type of *manufacturing tinker-science*, in a society that is itself becoming experimental. So far, only the ethical problems have been (cautiously) revealed in public. They are as evident in embryonic research as in open-air experiments, and they lead to difficult trade-offs and conflicts whose insolubility creates a virtually predictable obscurity that is considered worthy of encouragement, for it then allows one to write off ethical problems as lost causes. In this sense, the establishment of ethics chairs at universities is the second way of preserving a green light for research.

The dilemma lies in the fact that the experiment is exported and *society is made into a laboratory*, which has two consequences.

First, research becomes a kind of groping in the fog. Laboratory experiments assume that variables are controllable. To the extent the boundaries of the laboratory are opened this controllability is cancelled. Experiments in the open air and on people (as represented not only by genetic engineering, research into human genetics, and reproductive medicine, but also by ecological catastrophes) raise not only ethical problems but also theoretical questions about the logic of research. When the controllability of the laboratory situation is lost, so is the very framework that makes a precise conceptualization and determination of variables possible at all. Checking hypotheses becomes blurred, fictive, because the opening of the laboratory boundaries requires one to assume theoretically and practically uncontrollable influences.

Second, manufacturing as technology research becomes politically dependent on consent and responses to public questions and doubts, which scientific authority and scientific logic cannot answer or defuse. Active science needs deeds, manufactured realities, to correct its mistakes. It becomes a layperson in its own case, however, when what is at stake is deciding whether it is acceptable to risk the adventure of a science that is first an initially practical and only second empirical and theoretical science and that at the same time cancels the cultural constants of life. The precondition for manufacturing as research is a consensus that cannot be based on science, but only on politics.

The risk of a technology research that studies created facts can never be logically and morally legitimized in a scientific sense. Genetic engineers, human geneticists, reactor researchers, practitioners of reproductive medicine and the like become beggars or solicitors for their own cause. Their activity becomes dependent on public and political consent, without a hint of scientific justification. Politics comes before research, and research really and literally becomes politics itself, because it must produce and change something in order to develop its scientific rationality at all.

Where science robs itself of its own scientific character, however, it opens the door to public disputes, fears, and viewpoints and to shared decisions. Democracy sneaks in, not only in the implementation but also in the uncertainty and conflict over the direction of research itself, before that research can develop and stage-manage its own objective course of events. In starting research, the scientist is a layperson, ignorant like other observers and affected people. No, more than that: he is a layperson *with interests*. His research interests *compel* him to prove that the experiment is harmless. Bias is a professional necessity, because questions and doubts, now ruthless and fundamental, can literally starve technological research. To put it metaphorically, the suspected thief passes judgment on a robbery.

We have arrived at the central problem. We can learn from our mistakes; according to Popper, this is the core of scientific rationality. Who will decide, however—how, when and upon what basis—whether a social experiment of production as technological research has failed? Research that must become practice in order to be research has leveraged away its conditions of falsification. The boundaries between production, research, and use are blurring. Furthermore, all accidents and disruptions—for instance, in nuclear power plants all over the world—are experimental findings in a continuing, perhaps undecidable concrete experiment.

But many voices are involved in this experiment. Differing, antagonistic worldviews appear. The technical people are interested in technical success, which may well be independent of health effects, social and political turbulence and responsibilities, and lest we forget, the verdict of profitability. A chorus of voices and viewpoints argues about the course and outcome of such experiments.

Two things stand out here. The experiment, nuclear energy for instance, becomes *inconcludable, temporally, spatially and socially.* At the same time, however, there is no experimenter in charge, *no decision maker* to decide on the validity of the initial hypothesis with scientific authority. In the limiting case, we are concerned with all-inclusive experiments on humanity itself (therefore not experiments at all), whose unwritten, controversial history, across time, disciplines, and nations, corresponds to the results of earlier experiments.

If we apply Popper's rather antiquarian-sounding dictum to this situation, which has existed for some time and is by now well established, then scientific rationality hangs on the silk thread of the revisability and the fallibility of research that creates its own reality. Nuclear power plants could still be shut down and removed from the power grid, although with great difficulty and at high costs. What will happen, however, to the flesh-and-blood "mistakes" of the genetic engineers and human geneticists? How can research be kept capable of learning when to admit mistakes not only destroys billion-dollar investments but is tantamount to the self-annihilation of an entire specialized discipline? The new research installations know the laboratory only as a way station; they need practice, open-air experiments, and social change to test their assumptions. Hence they are struggling in a totally new way with dogma, not in terms of their objective intentions but in view of the displaced, inverted, interest constellations of their production as research. There is justified suspicion that the ability to make mistakes and learn is fundamentally truncated. Science has said goodbye to its logic and now comes under the power of dogmas that it itself created and cultivated. Furthermore, this is occurring in those scientific fields and research issues that touch and change the very form of existence of life and humankind.

THE RISK CALCULUS; OR, HOW DO WE WANT TO LIVE?

We know how these issues are treated *de facto*. People form special installations for risk calculations, which are attempts to produce, by technical means, answers to the very questions that elude purely technical answers. The currently ubiquitous talk of risks is a mathematically concealed form of moralizing. Accepted risks are compared with risks that one proposes to accept, whereby the legitimation that the former enjoy is supposed to be transferred to the latter.

It is undeniable that the calculus of risks trips some of the excitement from the adventure of industrialism. Unpredictable future events become calculable in the present. Their effects are elevated above the suffering of the individuals involved and become events predicted probabilistically, and therefore parts of the system that require general regulation, through insurance policies, for instance, or technical precautions, burden sharing, preventive medical care, and so on. This does not change the fact that technology cannot, by inherent, mathematical means, on its own responsibility, as it were, solve the political and ethical questions that assail it.

On the contrary, risk calculations are a kind of bankruptcy declaration of technical rationality. They never lead to what they were supposed to produce, namely, acceptance. Specialists depend on cultural and ethical standards to investigate the limits of what is tolerable and acceptable. "Maximum allowable levels" are traffic rules, basic laws for dealing with predictably unpredictable effects of techno-industrial developments. Special knowledge of reactions, processes, and medical effects contribute to them, but answers to the question "How should we live?" also contribute. Not only can that question be answered differently from one country to another, from one culture to another, but further, in a democratically governed society, it does not belong just in the hands of engineers. Nevertheless, technology and engineers have a monopoly on questions of risk in Germany as in other industrialized countries. Even reservations about the risks of a technology are almost always formulated on the basis of techno-scientific thinking. The therapies and alternatives offered also originate in the arsenal of technology.

There are demands for scrubbing technologies to eliminate emissions containing sulfur dioxide, and catalytic converters are supposed to prevent harmful automobile exhaust gases. From recycling plans to containment devices for nuclear power plants, the call for legislation usually demands nothing more than changing the signals in environmental policy in favor of an allegedly better *technical* solution. Many petitions presented in court demand nothing more, as the complaints understand it, than making the insights of natural science legally binding. Acceptable levels for pollution are cast into doubt because the scientific knowledge on which they rest seems to be outdated or the measuring procedures are technologically obsolete. The emissions of older facilities are subject to criticism whenever the people affected suspect that they exceed what is "inevitable" according to the state of the art.

The engineers have hung their society-creating role on a simple-minded social nail. They are conceded the right, obligatory for law and politics, to decide, on their own standards, what the state of the art requires. But since this general restriction is the standard for legally required safety, private organizations and committees (for example in Germany, the Society of German Engineers or the German Standards Institute) decide *de facto* what amount of threat all of us should accept.

In air pollution policy, noise protection, water policy, and so on, one finds the same pattern over and over again. Laws specify the general political plan, but only the fine print reveals what ration of standardized pollution the citizens are subject to. Even the classical instruments of political control—statutes and administrative regulations—are hollow, juggling with the state of the art and thereby undermining their own jurisdiction. At the same time they install "techno-scientific expert knowledge" on the throne of risk civilization.

WHAT IS TO BE DONE? PERSPECTIVES ON AN ECOLOGICAL ENLIGHTENMENT

All the arguments that I have highlighted here can be turned around and read the other way. In its most advanced stage, science has become an undertaking of involuntary self-subversion not in narrow-minded specialization but in the interrelationship between disciplines, times, theories, schools, and methods. It is scientific meticulousness that honeycombs the armor protecting the scientific monopoly on knowledge. In the same measure, external agencies gain opportunities to influence not just the evaluation but also the design of scientific knowledge. This must be used for a democratic opening and shared decision making.

Society itself has become a laboratory; that is, finding the truth has become both polyvocal and public. There are specialists for the technical matters and the effects; social and functional realities split apart and compete. The "simple" (i.e., traditional and monopolistic) concept of science and a "reflexive" (i.e., self-critical) one begin to orient and organize themselves *inside* the disciplines. In matters of risk, and this is important, no one is an expert. If the engineers have the say here *de facto*, then it is important to open the committees and the circles of experts and evaluators to the pluralism of disciplines, extradisciplinary modes of judgment, and shared decision making that have already been speaking out for some time and have begun to organize themselves.

The principle of the separation of powers needs to be enforced against the technocratic unity of culprits and judges (expert witnesses). Precisely because the investigation of effects and risks presumes their production, others—laypeople, the public sphere, the parliament, and politics—must also have a say; they must regain the power to make decisions in a society that has gone over to shaping its future through technology. The investigation of threats and risks is a necessary first step from the isolation of scientific social change into the public sphere.

Scientific activity requires justification on the basis of standards, which are concealed in the Trojan Horse of shared decision making. And yet it must be seen just as clearly that risk is a concept of only limited use for restraining or steering an autonomous, dynamic technologizing of society.

Risks can be minimized technically. Anyone who depends on them as the only lever to gain and expand some public say in the techno-scientific adventure puts pressure on himself to consent when the safety concerns are alleviated. Democracy beyond expertocracy— and expertocracy is a particular danger when hazards are dramatized—begins where debate and decision making are opened about whether we *want* a life under the conditions that are being presented to us even by those technologies that are growing steadily safer.

How do we want to live? The concentration on risks and safety can wrest this question away from public responsibility, which alone is qualified to answer it in a democracy that does not wish to capitulate to the shaping power of technology. A key question for present and future social development is, Can—or, more optimistically, how can—the industrial system learn from its mistakes? That the industrial system can *profit* from its mistakes is proved by the expanding market for anything labeled "environmentally safe" (from shoelaces to motor oil). Recruiting industrial production's interest in technology and using economic recovery to solve questions of survival is an obvious step toward a successful pragmatic policy, in the best sense of the word, of preventing and overcoming hazards. The industrial system and its productivity, set on an ecological path, point the way out of the dilemma of an industrial production trapped between growth and destruction. The magic formula is this: we need not just a social but also an *ecological* market economy.

In his most recent book, *Der Ökologische Umbau der Industriegesellschaft* (*The Ecological Reconstruction of Industrial Society*, 1989), Joschka Fischer (who represents many in the Social Democratic Party and the Christian Democratic Union as well as his fellow Greens), clearly and with laudable specificity sketched this one logically possible way. One can feel a lot of sympathy for his pragmatism, precisely because it is so nicely un-German and dismisses purism as ridiculous in favor of an orientation toward practical effect, which means the detailed treatment of hazards. This realism is also what may finally make the Greens electable.

None of this, however, must prevent us from seeing pragmatism as the fundamental mistake, which stands out when one considers the question, "To what hazard targets should the ecological reconstruction of industrial society be oriented?" To those that may or may not be brought into the open, into public view in ten years, or today, or tomorrow? The recent history of mega-hazards is enough to make one suspicious here. How long was nuclear energy generally welcomed? When were the ozone hole and forest destruction estimated, or statistically discounted, and what were the counter-arguments, the loaded counter-questions?

It becomes clear that a pragmatic approach to techno-economic hazards is taken in by ad-hoc definitions, forgets its own historical origin and uses the highly changeable media image of recognized hazards, or those struggling for recognition, as the plumb-line of a substantive social reconstruction. The category error lies in the technological verification of hazards and the concomitant exclusion of their social genesis of hazards and their conditions.

Only by breaking the law of unseen side effects, by elevating decision making on technologies to public and political processes before and during the genesis of hazards, can we return the fate of the hazard civilization to the realm of action and decision-making. We must reverse the prevailing practice of developing and financing new technologies first, and then investigating the effects and the hazards, and finally publicly discussing them under the guillotine of manufactured objective constraints. Only in that way could we minimize the hazards *and* open the possibilities for people to have a say in the matter. This time (for once) the political and democratic opening of hazard technocracy is also a way to prevent the hazards.

Part V
———

Conclusion:

The End of History?

CONCLUSION:
THE END OF HISTORY?

A new millennium begins with the year 2000. But has history come to an end? In a provocative article, Francis Fukuyama answered this question affirmatively and unleashed a torrent of controversy. This senior social scientist at the Rand Corporation, formerly an official in the U.S. State Department, basically sees at this moment the elimination of all alternatives to the liberal capitalist state. In short, the age of the grand design and the great deed is over. Mediocrity, individualism, and consumerism will mark a future that is itself nothing more than an elaboration of the past.

But the global transition to capitalism has not been smooth, and disturbing nationalistic and religious trends have appeared in the West no less than in the East. Economic differences between states and regions are growing, environmental degeneration threatens the planet, and there is still a need for transnational institutions to negotiate grievances between states and even minorities within states. The liberal capitalist state is incapable of solving such problems by itself; bitter conflicts will also ever more surely emerge over its policies and the degree of freedom accorded the market.

None of these transformations are merely incidental or transitory. Tensions will become increasingly manifest between transnational and national or regional and local organizations. Differences will also increasingly appear between the forms of liberal capitalism. A critical perspective that can distinguish between seemingly similar phenomena and provide criteria for making judgments about crucial issues has become more necessary than ever before. There is, in short, a deep need for new ways of thinking—even about old ideas—and new forms of commitment as the next century dawns.

FRANCIS FUKUYAMA

The End of History?

In watching the flow of events over the past decade or so, it is hard to avoid the feeling that something very fundamental has happened in world history. The past year has seen a flood of articles commemorating the end of the Cold War, and the fact that "peace" seems to be breaking out in many regions of the world. Most of these analyses lack any larger conceptual framework for distinguishing between what is essential and what is contingent or accidental in world history, and are predictably superficial. If Mr. Gorbachev were ousted from the Kremlin or a new Ayatollah proclaimed the millennium from a desolate Middle Eastern capital, these same commentators would scramble to announce the rebirth of a new era of conflict.

And yet, all of these people sense dimly that there is some larger process at work, a process that gives coherence and order to the daily headlines. The twentieth century saw the developed world descend into a paroxysm of ideological violence, as liberalism contended first with the remnants of absolutism, then bolshevism and fascism, and finally an updated Marxism that threatened to lead to the ultimate apocalypse of nuclear war. But the century that began full of self-confidence in the ultimate triumph of Western liberal democracy seems at its close to be returning full circle to where it started: not to an "end of ideology" or a convergence between capitalism and socialism, as earlier predicted, but to an unabashed victory of economic and political liberalism.

The triumph of the West, of the Western *idea,* is evident first of all in the total exhaustion of viable systematic alternatives to Western liberalism. In the past decade, there have been unmistakable changes in the intellectual climate of the world's two largest communist countries, and the beginnings of significant reform movements in both. But this phenomenon extends beyond high politics and it can be seen also in the ineluctable spread of consumerist Western culture in such diverse contexts as the peasants' markets and color televisions sets now omnipresent throughout China, the cooperative restaurants and clothing stores opened in the past year in Moscow, the Beethoven piped into Japanese department stores, and the rock music enjoyed alike in Prague, Rangoon, and Tehran.

What we may be witnessing is not just the end of the Cold War, or the passing of a particular period of postwar history, but the end of history as such: that is, the end point of mankind's ideological evolution and the universalization of Western liberal democracy as the final form of human government. This is not to say that there will no longer be events to fill the pages of *Foreign Affair's* yearly summaries of international relations, for the victory of liberalism has occurred primarily in the realm of ideas or consciousness and is as yet incomplete in the real or material world. But there are powerful reasons for believing that it is the ideal that will govern the material world *in the long run.* To understand how this is so, we must first consider some theoretical issues concerning the nature of historical change.

I

The notion of the end of history is not an original one. Its best-known propagator was Karl Marx, who believed that the direction of historical development was a purposeful one determined by the interplay of material forces, and would come to an end only with the achievement of a communist utopia that would finally resolve all prior contradictions. But the concept of history as a dialectical process with a beginning, a middle, and an end was borrowed by Marx from his great German predecessor, George Wilhelm Friedrich Hegel.

For better or worse, much of Hegel's historicism has become part of our contemporary intellectual baggage. The notion that mankind has progressed through a series of primitive stages of consciousness on his path to the present, and that these stages corresponded to concrete forms of social organization, such as tribal, slave-owning, theocratic, and finally democratic-egalitarian societies, has become inseparable from the modern understanding of man. Hegel was the first philosopher to speak the language of modern social science, insofar as man for him was the product of his concrete historical and social environment and not, as earlier natural right theorists would have it, a collection of more or less fixed "natural" attributes. The mastery and transformation of man's natural environment through the application of science and technology was originally not a Marxist concept, but a Hegelian one. Unlike later historicists whose historical relativism degenerated into relativism *tour court,* however, Hegel believed that history culminated in an absolute moment—a moment in which a final, rational form of society and state became victorious.

It is Hegel's misfortune to be known now primarily as Marx's precursor, and it is our misfortune that few of us are familiar with Hegel's work from direct study, but only as it has been filtered through the distorting lens of Marxism. In France, however, there has been an effort to save Hegel from his Marxist interpreters and to resurrect him as the philosopher who most correctly speaks to our time. Among those modern French interpreters of Hegel, the greatest was certainly Alexandre Kojève, a brilliant Russian emigre who taught a highly influential series of seminars in Paris in the 1930s at the *Ecole Practique des Hautes Etudes.*[1] While largely unknown in the United States, Kojève had a major impact on the intellectual life of the continent. Among his students ranged such future luminaries as Jean-Paul Sartre on the Left and Raymond Aron on the Right; postwar existentialism borrowed many of its basic categories from Hegel via Kojève.

Kojève sought to resurrect the Hegel of the *Phenomenology of Mind*, the Hegel who proclaimed history to be at an end in 1806. For as early as this Hegel saw in Napoleon's defeat of the Prussian monarchy at the Battle of Jena the victory of the ideals of the French Revolution, and the imminent universalization of the state incorporating the principles of liberty and equality. Kojève, far from rejecting Hegel in light of the turbulent events of the next century and a half, insisted that the latter had been essentially correct.[2] The Battle of Jena marked the end of history because it was at that point that the *vanguard* of humanity (a term quite familiar to Marxists) actualized the principles of the French Revolution. While there was considerable work to be done after 1806—abolishing slavery and the slave trade, extending the franchise to workers, women, blacks, and other racial minorities, etc.—the basic *principles* of the liberal democratic state could not be improved upon. The two world wars in this century and their attendant revolutions and upheavals simply had the effect of extending those principles spatially, such that the various provinces of human civilization were brought up to the level of its most advanced outposts, and of forcing those societies in Europe and North America at the vanguard of civilization to implement their liberalism more fully.

The state that emerges at the end of history is liberal insofar as it recognizes and protects through a system of law man's universal right to freedom, and democratic insofar as it exists only with the consent of the governed. For Kojève, this so-called "universal homogenous state" found real-life embodiment in the countries of postwar Western Europe—precisely those flabby, prosperous, self-satisfied, inward-looking, weak-willed states whose grandest project was nothing more heroic than the creation of the Common Market.[3] But this was only to be expected. For human history and the conflict that characterized it was based on the existence of "contradictions": primitive man's quest for mutual recognition, the dialectic of the master and slave, the transformation and mastery of nature, the struggle for the universal recognition of rights, and the dichotomy between proletarian and capitalist. But in the universal homogenous state, all prior contradictions are resolved and all human needs are satisfied. There is no struggle or conflict over "large" issues, and consequently no need for generals or statesmen; what remains is primarily economic activity. And indeed, Kojève's life was consistent with his teaching. Believing that there was no more work for philosophers as well, since Hegel (correctly understood) had already achieved absolute knowledge, Kojève left teaching after the war and spent the remainder of his life working as a bureaucrat in the European Economic Community, until his death in 1968.

To his contemporaries at mid-century, Kojève's proclamation of the end of history must have seemed like the typical eccentric solipsism of a French intellectual, coming as it did on the heels of World War II and at the very height of the Cold War. To comprehend how Kojève could have been so audacious as to assert that history has ended, we must first of all understand the meaning of Hegelian idealism.

II

For Hegel, the contradictions that drive history exist first of all in the realm of human consciousness, i.e., on the level of ideas[4]—not the trivial election year proposals of American politicians, but ideas in the sense of large unifying world views that might best be understood under the rubric of ideology. Ideology in this sense is not restricted to the sec-ular and explicit political doctrines we usually associate with the term, but can include religion, culture, and the complex of moral values underlying any society as well.

Hegel's view of the relationship between the ideal and the real or material world was an extremely complicated one, beginning with the fact that for him the distinction between the two was only apparent.[5] He did not believe that the real world conformed or could be made to conform to ideological preconceptions of philosophy professors in any simpleminded way, or that the "material" world could not impinge on the ideal. Indeed, Hegel the professor was temporarily thrown out of work as a result of a very material event, the Battle of Jena. But while Hegel's writing and thinking could be stopped by a bullet from the material world, the hand on the trigger of the gun was motivated in turn by the ideas of liberty and equality that had driven the French Revolution.

For Hegel, all human behavior in the material world, and hence all human history, is rooted in a prior state of consciousness—an idea similar to the one expressed by John Maynard Keynes when he said that the views of men of affairs were usually derived from defunct economists and academic scribblers of earlier generations. This consciousness may not be explicit and self-aware, as are modern political doctrines, but may rather take the form of religion or simple cultural or moral habits. And yet this realm of consciousness *in the long run* necessarily becomes manifest in the material world, indeed creates the mater-ial world in its own image. Consciousness is cause and not effect, and can develop autonomously from the material world; hence the real subtext underlying the apparent jumble of current events is the history of ideology.

Hegel's idealism has fared poorly at the hands of later thinkers. Marx reversed the pri-ority of the real and the ideal completely, relegating the entire realm of consciousness—religion, art, culture, philosophy itself—to a "superstructure" that was determined entirely by the prevailing material mode of production. Yet another unfortunate legacy of Marxism is our tendency to retreat into materialist or utilitarian explanations of political or historical phenomena, and our disinclination to believe in the autonomous power of ideas. A recent example of this is Paul Kennedy's hugely successful *The Rise and Fall of the Great Powers*, which ascribes the decline of great powers to simple economic overexten-sion. Obviously, this is true on some level: an empire whose economy is barely above the level of subsistence cannot bankrupt its treasury indefinitely. But whether a highly pro-ductive modern industrial society chooses to spend 3 or 7 percent of its GNP on defense rather than consumption is entirely a matter of that society's political priorities, which are in turn determined in the realm of consciousness.

The materialist bias of modern thought is characteristic not only of people on the Left who may be sympathetic to Marxism, but of many passionate anti-Marxists as well. Indeed, there is on the Right what one might label the *Wall Street Journal* school of deter-ministic materialism that discounts the importance of ideology and culture and sees man as essentially a rational, profit-maximizing individual. It is precisely this kind of individ-ual and his pursuit of material incentives that is posited as the basis for economic life as such in economic textbooks.[6] One small example will illustrate the problematic character of such materialist views.

Max Weber begins his famous book, *The Protestant Ethic and the Spirit of Capitalism*, by noting the different economic performance of Protestant and Catholic communities throughout Europe and America, summed up in the proverb that Protestants eat well while Catholics sleep well. Weber notes that according to any economic theory that posited man as a rational profit-maximizer, raising the piece-work rate should increase labor productivity. But in fact, in many traditional peasant communities, raising the piece-work rate actually had the opposite effect of *lowering* labor productivity: at the higher rate, a peasant accustomed to earning two and one-half marks per day found he could earn the same amount by working less, and did so because he valued leisure more than income. The choices of leisure over income, or of the militaristic life of the Spartan hoplite over the wealth of the Athenian trader, or even the ascetic life of the early capitalist entrepreneur over that of a traditional leisured aristocrat, cannot possibly be explained by the impersonal working of material forces, but come preeminently out of the sphere of consciousness—what we have labeled here broadly as ideology. And indeed, a central theme of Weber's work was to prove that contrary to Marx, the material mode of production, far from being the "base," was itself a "superstructure" with roots in religion and culture, and that to understand the emergence of modern capitalism and the profit motive one had to study their antecedents in the realm of the spirit.

As we look around the contemporary world, the poverty of materialist theories of economic development is all too apparent. The *Wall Street Journal* school of deterministic materialism habitually points to the stunning economic success of Asia in the past few decades as evidence of the viability of free market economics, with the implication that all societies would see similar development were they simply to allow their populations to pursue their material self-interest freely. Surely free markets and stable political systems are a necessary precondition to capitalist economic growth. But just as surely the cultural heritage of those Far Eastern societies, the ethic of work and saving and family, a religious heritage that does not, like Islam, place restrictions on certain forms of economic behavior, and other deeply ingrained moral qualities, are equally important in explaining their economic performance.[7] And yet the intellectual weight of materialism is such that not a single respectable contemporary theory of economic development addresses consciousness and culture seriously as the matrix within which economic behavior is formed.

Failure to understand that the roots of economic behavior lie in the realm of consciousness and culture leads to the common mistake of attributing material causes to phenomena that are essentially ideal in nature. For example, it is commonplace in the West to interpret the reform movements first in China and most recently in the Soviet Union as the victory of the material over the ideal—that is, a recognition that ideological incentives could not replace material ones in stimulating a highly productive modern economy, and that if one wanted to prosper one had to appeal to baser forms of self-interest. But the deep defects of socialist economies were evident thirty or forty years ago to anyone who chose to look. Why was it that these countries moved away from central planning only in the 1980s? The answer must be found in the consciousness of the elites and leaders ruling them, who decided to opt for the "Protestant" life of wealth and risk over the "Catholic" path of poverty and security.[8] That change was in no way made inevitable by the material conditions in which either country found itself on the eve of the reform, but instead came about as the result of the victory of one idea over another.[9]

For Kojève, as for all good Hegelians, understanding the underlying processes of history requires understanding developments in the realm of consciousness or ideas, since consciousness will ultimately remake the material world in its own image. To say that history ended in 1806 meant that mankind's ideological evolution ended in the ideals of the French or American Revolutions: while particular regimes in the real world might not implement these ideals fully, their theoretical truth is absolute and could not be improved upon. Hence it did not matter to Kojève that the consciousness of the postwar generation of Europeans had not been universalized throughout the world; if ideological development had in fact ended, the homogenous state would eventually become victorious throughout the material world.

I have neither the space nor, frankly, the ability to defend in depth Hegel's radical idealist perspective. The issue is not whether Hegel's system was right, but whether his perspective might uncover the problematic nature of many materialist explanations we often take for granted. This is not to deny the role of material factors as such. To a literal-minded idealist, human society can be built around any arbitrary set of principles regardless of their relationship to the material world. And in fact men have proven themselves able to endure the most extreme material hardships in the name of ideas that exist in the realm of the spirit alone, be it the divinity of cows or the nature of the Holy Trinity.[10]

But while man's very perception of the material world is shaped by his historical consciousness of it, the material world can clearly affect in return the viability of a particular state of consciousness. In particular, the spectacular abundance of advanced liberal economies and the infinitely diverse consumer culture made possible by them seem to both foster and preserve liberalism in the political sphere. I want to avoid the materialist determinism that says that liberal economics inevitably produces liberal politics, because I believe that both economics and politics presuppose an autonomous prior state of consciousness that makes them possible. But that state of consciousness that permits the growth of liberalism seems to stabilize in the way one would expect at the end of history if it is underwritten by the abundance of a modern free market economy. We might summarize the content of the universal homogenous state as liberal democracy in the political sphere combined with easy access to *VCRs* and stereos in the economic.

III

Have we in fact reached the end of history? Are there, in other words, any fundamental "contradictions" in human life that cannot be resolved in the context of modern liberalism, that would be resolvable by an alternative political-economic structure? If we accept the idealist premises laid out above, we must seek an answer to this question in the realm of ideology and consciousness. Our task is not to answer exhaustively the challenges to liberalism promoted by every crackpot messiah around the world, but only those that are embodied in important social or political forces and movements, and which are therefore part of world history. For our purposes, it matters very little what strange thoughts occur to people in Albania or Burkina Faso, for we are interested in what one could in some sense call the common ideological heritage of mankind.

In the past century, there have been two major challenges to liberalism, those of fascism and of communism. The former[11] saw the political weakness, materialism, anomie, and lack of community of the West as fundamental contradictions in liberal societies that could only be resolved by a strong state that forged a new "people" on the basis of national exclusiveness. Fascism was destroyed as a living ideology by World War II. This was a defeat, of course, on a very material level, but it amounted to a defeat of the idea as well. What destroyed fascism as an idea was not universal moral revulsion against it, since plenty of people were willing to endorse the idea as long as it seemed the wave of the future, but its lack of success. After the war, it seemed to most people that German fascism as well as its other European and Asian variants were bound to self-destruct. There was no material reason why new fascist movements could not have sprung up again after the war in other locales, but for the fact that expansionist ultranationalism, with its promise of unending conflict leading to disastrous military defeat, had completely lost its appeal. The ruins of the Reich chancellory as well as the atomic bombs dropped on Hiroshima and Nagasaki killed this ideology on the level of consciousness as well as materially, and all of the proto-fascist movements spawned by the German and Japanese examples like the Peronist movement in Argentina or Subhas Chandra Bose's Indian National Army withered after the war.

The ideological challenge mounted by the other great alternative to liberalism, communism, was far more serious. Marx, speaking Hegel's language, asserted that liberal society contained a fundamental contradiction that could not be resolved within its context, that between capital and labor, and this contradiction has constituted the chief accusation against liberalism ever since. But surely, the class issue has actually been successfully resolved in the West. As Kojève (among others) noted, the egalitarianism of modern America represents the essential achievement of the classless society envisioned by Marx. This is not to say that there are not rich people and poor people in the United States, or that the gap between them has not grown in recent years. But the root causes of economic inequality do not have to do with the underlying legal and social structure of our society, which remains fundamentally egalitarian and moderately redistributionist, so much as with the cultural and social characteristics of the groups that make it up, which are in turn the historical legacy of premodern conditions. Thus black poverty in the United States is not the inherent product of liberalism, but is rather the "legacy of slavery and racism" which persisted long after the formal abolition of slavery.

As a result of the receding of the class issue, the appeal of communism in the developed Western world, it is safe to say, is lower today than any time since the end of the First World War. This can be measured in any number of ways: in the declining membership parties, and their overtly revisionist programs; in the corresponding electoral success of conservative parties from Britain and Germany to the United States and Japan, which are unabashedly pro-market and antistatist; and in an intellectual climate whose most "advanced" members no longer believe that bourgeois society is something that ultimately needs to be overcome. This is not to say that the opinions of progressive intellectuals in Western countries are not deeply pathological in any number of ways. But those who believe that the future must inevitably be socialist tend to be very old, or very marginal to the real political discourse of their societies.

One may argue that the socialist alternative was never terribly plausible for the North Atlantic world, and was sustained for the last several decades primarily by its success outside of this region. But it is precisely in the non-European world that one is most struck by the occurrence of major ideological transformations. Surely the most remarkable changes have occurred in Asia. Due to the strength and adaptability of the indigenous cultures there, Asia became a battleground for a variety of imported Western ideologies early in this century. Liberalism in Asia was a very weak reed in the period after World War I; it is easy today to forget how gloomy Asia's political future looked as recently as ten or fifteen years ago. It is easy to forget as well how momentous the outcome of Asian ideological struggles seemed for world political development as a whole.

The first Asian alternative to liberalism to be decisively defeated was the fascist one represented by Imperial Japan. Japanese fascism (like its German version) was defeated by the force of American arms in the Pacific war, and liberal democracy was imposed on Japan by a victorious United States. Western capitalism and political liberalism when transplanted to Japan were adapted and transformed by the Japanese in such a way as to be scarcely recognizable.[12] Many Americans are now aware that Japanese industrial organization is very different from that prevailing in the United States or Europe, and it is questionable what relationship the factional maneuvering that takes place with the governing Liberal Democratic Party bears to democracy. Nonetheless, the very fact that the essential elements of economic and political liberalism have been so successfully grafted onto uniquely Japanese traditions and institutions guarantees their survival in the long run. More important is the contribution that Japan has made in turn to world history by following in the footsteps of the United States to create a truly universal consumer culture that has become both a symbol and an underpinning of the universal homogenous state. V. S. Naipaul travelling in Khomeini's Iran shortly after the revolution noted the omnipresent signs advertising the products of Sony, Hitachi, and JVC, whose appeal remained virtually irresistible and gave the lie to the regime's pretensions of restoring a state based on the rule of the *Shariah*. Desire for access to the consumer culture, created in large measure by Japan, has played a crucial role in fostering the spread of economic liberalism throughout Asia, and hence in promoting political liberalism as well.

The economic success of the other newly industrializing countries (NICs) in Asia following on the example of Japan is by now a familiar story. What is important from a Hegelian standpoint is that political liberalism has been following economic liberalism, more slowly than many had hoped but with seeming inevitability. Here again we see the victory of the idea of the universal homogenous state. South Korea had developed into a modern, urbanized society with an increasingly large and well-educated middle class that could not possibly be isolated from the larger democratic trends around them. Under these circumstances it seemed intolerable to a large part of this population that it should be ruled by an anachronistic military regime while Japan, only a decade or so ahead in economic terms, had parliamentary institutions for over forty years. Even the former socialist regime in Burma, which for so many decades existed in dismal isolation from the larger trends dominating Asia, was buffeted in the past year by pressures to liberalize both its economy and political system. It is said that unhappiness with strongman Ne Win began when a senior Burmese officer went to Singapore for medical treatment and broke down crying when he saw how far socialist Burma had been left behind by its ASEAN neighbors.

But the power of the liberal idea would seem much less impressive if it had not infected the largest and oldest culture in Asia, China. The simple existence of communist China created an alternative pole of ideological attraction, and as such constituted a threat to liberalism. But the past fifteen years have seen an almost total discrediting of Marxism-Leninism as an economic system. Beginning with the famous third plenum of the Tenth Central Committee in 1978, the Chinese Communist party set about decollectivizing agriculture for the 800 million Chinese who still lived in the country-side. The role of the state in agriculture was reduced to that of a tax collector, while production of consumer goods was sharply increased in order to give peasants a taste of the universal homogenous state and thereby an incentive to work. The reform doubled Chinese grain output in only five years, and in the process created for Deng Xiao-ping a solid political base from which he was able to extend the reform to other parts of the economy. Economic statistics do not begin to describe the dynamism, initiative, and openness evident in China since the reform began.

China could not now be described in any way as a liberal democracy. At present, no more than 20 percent of its economy has been marketized, and most importantly it continues to be ruled by a self-appointed Communist party which has given no hint of wanting to devolve power. Deng has made none of Gorbachev's promises regarding democratization of the political system and there is no Chinese equivalent of *glasnost*. The Chinese leadership has in fact been much more circumspect in criticizing Mao and Maoism than Gorbachev with respect to Brezhnev and Stalin, and the regime continues to pay lip service to Marxism-Leninism as its ideological underpinning. But anyone familiar with the outlook and behavior of the new technocratic elite now governing China knows that Marxism and ideological principle have become virtually irrelevant as guides to policy, and that bourgeois consumerism has a real meaning in that country for the first time since the revolution. The various slowdowns in the pace of reform, the campaigns against "spiritual pollution" and crackdowns on political dissent are more properly seen as tactical adjustments made in the process of managing what is an extraordinarily difficult political transition. By ducking the question of political reform while putting the economy on a new footing, Deng has managed to avoid the breakdown of authority that has accompanied Gorbachev's *perestroika*. Yet the pull of the liberal idea continues to be very strong as economic power devolves and the economy becomes more open to the outside world. There are currently over 20,000 Chinese students studying in the U.S. and other Western countries, almost all of them the children of the Chinese elite. It is hard to believe that when they return home to run the country they will be content for China to be the only country in Asia unaffected by the larger democratizing trend. The student demonstrations in Beijing that broke out first in December 1986 and recurred recently on the occasion of Hu Yao-bang's death were only the beginning of what will inevitably be mounting pressure for change in the political system as well.

What is important about China from the standpoint of world history is not the present state of the reform or even its future prospects. The central issue is the fact that the People's Republic of China can no longer act as a beacon for illiberal forces around the world, whether they be guerrillas in some Asian jungle or middle class students in Paris. Maoism, rather than being the pattern for Asia's future, became an anachronism, and it was the mainland Chinese who in fact were decisively influenced by the prosperity and dynamism of their overseas co-ethnics—the ironic ultimate victory of Taiwan.

Important as these changes in China have been, however, it is developments in the Soviet Union—the original "homeland of the world proletariat"—that have put the final nail in the coffin of the Marxist-Leninist alternative to liberal democracy. It should be clear that in terms of formal institutions, not much has changed in the four years since Gorbachev has come to power: free markets and the cooperative movement represent only a small part of the Soviet economy, which remains centrally planned; the political system is still dominated by the Communist party, which has only begun to democratize internally and to share power with other groups; the regime continues to assert that it is seeking only to modernize socialism and that its ideological basis remains Marxism-Leninism; and, finally, Gorbachev faces a potentially powerful conservative opposition that could undo many of the changes that have taken place to date. Moreover, it is hard to be too sanguine about the chances for success of Gorbachev's proposed reforms, either in the sphere of economics or politics. But my purpose here is not to analyze events in the short-term, or to make predictions for policy purposes, but to look at underlying trends in the sphere of ideology and consciousness. And in that respect, it is clear that an astounding transformation has occurred.

Emigres from the Soviet Union have been reporting for at least the last generation now that virtually nobody in that country truly believed in Marxism-Leninism any longer, and that this was nowhere more true than in the Soviet elite, which continued to mouth Marxist slogans out of sheer cynicism. The corruption and decadence of the late Brezhnev-era Soviet state seemed to matter little, however, for as long as the state itself refused to throw into question any of the fundamental principles underlying Soviet society, the system was capable of functioning adequately out of sheer inertia and could even muster some dynamism in the realm of foreign and defense policy. Marxism-Leninism was like a magical incantation which, however absurd and devoid of meaning, was the only common basis on which the elite could agree to *rule* Soviet society.

What has happened in the four years since Gorbachev's coming to power is a revolutionary assault on the most fundamental institutions and principles of Stalinism, and their replacement by other principles which do not amount to liberalism *per se* but whose only connecting thread is liberalism. This is most evident in the economic sphere, where the reform economists around Gorbachev have become steadily more radical in their support for free markets, to the point where some like Nikolai Shmelev do not mind being compared in public to Milton Friedman. There is a virtual consensus among the currently dominant school of Soviet economists now that central planning and the command system of allocation are the root cause of economic inefficiency, and that if the Soviet system is ever to heal itself, it must permit free and decentralized decision-making with respect to investment, labor, and prices. After a couple of initial years of ideological confusion, these principles have finally been incorporated into policy with the promulgation of new laws on enterprise autonomy, cooperatives, and finally in 1988 on lease arrangements and family farming. There are, of course, a number of fatal flaws in the current implementation of the reform, most notably the absence of a thoroughgoing price reform. But the problem is no longer a *conceptual* one: Gorbachev and his lieutenants seem to understand the economic logic of marketization well enough, but like the leaders of a Third World country facing the IMF, are afraid of the social consequences of ending consumer subsidies and other forms of dependence on the state sector.

In the political sphere, the proposed changes to the Soviet constitution, legal system, and party rules amount to much less than the establishment of a liberal state. Gorbachev has spoken of democratization primarily in the sphere of internal party affairs, and has shown little intention of ending the Communist party's monopoly of power; indeed, the political reform seeks to legitimize and therefore strengthen the CPSU's rule.[13] Nonetheless, the general principles underlying many of the reforms—that the "people" should be truly responsible for their own affairs, that higher political bodies should be answerable to lower ones, and not vice versa, that the rule of law should prevail over arbitrary police actions, with separation of powers and an independent judiciary, that there should be legal protection for property rights, the need for open discussion of public issues and the right of public dissent, the empowering of the Soviets as a forum in which the whole Soviet people can participate, and of a political culture that is more tolerant and pluralistic—come from a source fundamentally alien to the USSR's Marxist-Leninist tradition, even if they are incompletely articulated and poorly implemented in practice.

Gorbachev's repeated assertions that he is doing no more than trying to restore the original meaning of Leninism are themselves a kind of Orwellian doublespeak. Gorbachev and his allies have consistently maintained that intraparty democracy was somehow the essence of Leninism, and that the various liberal practices of open debate, secret ballot elections, and rule of law were all part of the Leninist heritage, corrupted only later by Stalin. While almost anyone would look good compared to Stalin, drawing so sharp a line between Lenin and his successor is questionable. The essence of Lenin's democratic centralism was centralism, not democracy; that is, the absolutely rigid, monolithic, and disciplined dictatorship of a hierarchically organized vanguard Communist party, speaking in the name of the *demos*. All of Lenin's vicious polemics against Karl Kautsky, Rosa Luxemburg, and various other Menshevik and Social Democratic rivals, not to mention his contempt for "bourgeois legality" and freedoms, centered around his profound conviction that a revolution could not be successfully made by a democratically run organization.

Gorbachev's claim that he is seeking to return to the true Lenin is perfectly easy to understand: having fostered a thorough denunciation of Stalinism and Brezhnevism as the root of the USSR's present predicament, he needs some point in Soviet history on which to anchor the legitimacy of the CPSU's continued rule. But Gorbachev's tactical requirements should not blind us to the fact that the democratizing and decentralizing principles which he has enunciated in both the economic and political spheres are highly subversive of some of the most fundamental precepts of both Marxism and Leninism. Indeed, if the bulk of the present economic reform proposals were put into effect, it is hard to know how the Soviet economy would be more socialist than those of other Western countries with large public sectors.

The Soviet Union could in no way be described as a liberal or democratic country now, nor do I think that it is terribly likely that *perestroika* will succeed such that the label will be thinkable any time in the near future. But at the end of history it is not necessary that all societies become successful liberal societies, merely that they end their ideological pretensions of representing different and higher forms of human society. And in this respect I believe that something very important has happened in the Soviet Union in the past few years: the criticisms of the Soviet system sanctioned by Gorbachev have been so thorough and devastating that there is very little chance of going back to either Stalinism or Brezhnevism in any simple way. Gorbachev has finally permitted people to say what they had privately understood for many years, namely, that the magical incantations of Marxism-Leninism were nonsense, that Soviet socialism was not superior to the West in any respect but was in fact a monumental failure. The conservative opposition in the USSR, consisting both of simple workers afraid of unemployment and inflation and of party officials fearful of losing their jobs and privileges, is outspoken and may be strong enough to force Gorbachev's ouster in the next few years. But what both groups desire is tradition, order, and authority; they manifest no deep commitment to Marxism-Leninism, except insofar as they have invested much of their own lives in it.[14] For authority to be restored in the Soviet Union after Gorbachev's demolition work, it must be on the basis of some new and vigorous ideology which has not yet appeared on the horizon.

If we admit for the moment that the fascist and communist challenges to liberalism are dead, are there any other ideological competitors left? Or put another way, are there contradictions in liberal society beyond that of class that are not resolvable? Two possibilities suggest themselves, those of religion and nationalism.

The rise of religious fundamentalism in recent years within the Christian, Jewish, and Muslim traditions has been widely noted. One is inclined to say that the revival of religion in some way attests to a broad unhappiness with the impersonality and spiritual vacuity of liberal consumerist societies. Yet while the emptiness at the core of liberalism is most certainly a defect in the ideology—indeed, a flaw that one does not need the perspective of religion to recognize[15]—it is not all clear that it is remediable through politics. Modern liberalism itself was historically a consequence of the weakness of religiously based societies which, failing to agree on the nature of the good life, could not provide even the minimal preconditions of peace and stability. In the contemporary world only Islam has offered a theocratic state as a political alternative to both liberalism and communism. But the doctrine has little appeal for non-Muslims, and it is hard to believe that the movement will take on any universal significance. Other less organized religious impulses have been successfully satisfied within the sphere of personal life that is permitted in liberal societies.

The other major "contradiction" potentially unresolvable by liberalism is the one posed by nationalism and other forms of racial and ethnic consciousness. It is certainly true that a very large degree of conflict since the Battle of Jena has had its roots in nationalism. Two cataclysmic world wars in this century have been spawned by the nationalism of the developed world in various guises, and if those passions have been muted to a certain extent in postwar Europe, they are still extremely powerful in the Third World. Nationalism has been a threat to liberalism historically in Germany, and continues to be one in isolated parts of "post-historical" Europe like Northern Ireland.

But it is not clear that nationalism represents an irreconcilable contradiction in the heart of liberalism. In the first place, nationalism is not one single phenomenon but several, ranging from mild cultural nostalgia to the highly organized and elaborately articulated doctrine of National Socialism. Only systematic nationalisms of the latter sort can qualify as a formal ideology on the level of liberalism or communism. The vast majority of the world's nationalist movements do not have a political program beyond the negative desire of independence *from* some other group or people, and do not offer anything like a comprehensive agenda for socio-economic organization. As such, they are compatible with doctrines and ideologies that do offer such agendas. While they may constitute a source of conflict for liberal societies, this conflict does not arise from liberalism itself so much as from the fact that the liberalism in question is incomplete. Certainly a great deal of the world's ethnic and nationalist tension can be explained in terms of peoples who are forced to live in unrepresentative political systems that they have not chosen.

While it is impossible to rule out the sudden appearance of new ideologies or previously unrecognized contradictions in liberal societies, then, the present world seems to confirm that the fundamental principles of socio-political organization have not advanced terribly far since 1806. Many of the wars and revolutions fought since that time have been undertaken in the name of ideologies which claimed to be more advanced than liberalism, but whose pretensions were ultimately unmasked by history. In the meantime, they have helped to spread the universal homogenous state to the point where it could have a significant effect on the overall character of international relations.

IV

What are the implications of the end of history for international relations? Clearly, the vast bulk of the Third World remains very much mired in history, and will be a terrain of conflict for many years to come. But let us focus for the time being on the larger and more developed states of the world who after all account for the greater part of world politics. Russia and China are not likely to join the developed nations of the West as liberal societies any time in the foreseeable future, but suppose for a moment that Marxism-Leninism ceases to be a factor driving the foreign policies of these states—a prospect which, if not yet here, the last few years have made a real possibility. How will the overall characteristics of a de-ideologized world differ from those of the one with which we are familiar at such a hypothetical juncture?

The most common answer is not very much. For there is a very widespread belief among many observers of international relations that underneath the skin of ideology is a hard core of great power national interest that guarantees a fairly high level of competition and conflict between nations. Indeed, according to one academically popular school of international relations theory, conflict inheres in the international system as such, and to understand the prospects for conflict one must look at the shape of the system—for example, whether it is bipolar or multipolar—rather than at the specific character of the nations and regimes that constitute it. This school in effect applies a Hobbesian view of politics to international relations, and assumes that aggression and insecurity are universal characteristics of human societies rather than the product of specific historical circumstances.

Believers in this line of thought take the relations that existed between the participants in the classical nineteenth-century European balance of power as a model for what a deideologized contemporary world would look like. Charles Krauthammer, for example, recently explained that if as a result of Gorbachev's reforms the USSR is shorn of Marxist-Leninist ideology, its behavior will revert to that of nineteenth-century imperial Russia.[16] While he finds this more reassuring than the threat posed by a communist Russia, he implies that there will still be a substantial degree of competition and conflict in the international system, just as there was say between Russia and Britian or Wilhelmine Germany in the last century. This is, of course, a convenient point of view for people who want to admit that something major is changing in the Soviet Union, but do not want to accept responsibility for recommending the radical policy redirection implicit in such a view. But is it true?

In fact, the notion that ideology is a superstructure imposed on a substratum of permanent great power interest is a highly questionable proposition. For the way in which any state defines its national interest is not universal but rests on some kind of prior ideological basis, just as we saw that economic behavior is determined by a prior state of consciousness. In this century, states have adopted highly articulated doctrines with explicit foreign policy agendas legitimizing expansionism, like Marxism-Leninism or National Socialism.

The expansionist and competitive behavior of nineteenth-century European states rested on no less ideal a basis; it just so happened that the ideology driving it was less explicit than the doctrines of the twentieth century. For one thing, most "liberal" European societies were illiberal insofar as they believed in the legitimacy of imperialism, that is, the right of one nation to rule over other nations without regard for the wishes of the ruled. The justifications for imperialism varied from nation to nation, from a crude belief in the legitimacy of force, particularly when applied to non-Europeans, to the White Man's Burden and Europe's Christianizing mission, to the desire to give people of color access to the culture of Rabelais and Molière. But whatever the particular ideological basis, every "developed" country believed in the acceptability of higher civilizations ruling lower ones—including, incidentally, the United States with regard to the Philippines. This led to a drive for pure territorial aggrandizement in the latter half of the century and played no small role in causing the Great War.

The radical and deformed outgrowth of nineteenth-century imperialism was German fascism, an ideology which justified Germany's right not only to rule over non-European peoples, but over *all* non-German ones. But in retrospect it seems that Hitler represented a diseased bypath in the general course of European development, and since his fiery defeat, the legitimacy of any kind of territorial aggrandizement has been thoroughly discredited.[17] Since the Second World War, European nationalism has been defanged and shorn of any real relevance to foreign policy, with the consequence that the nineteenth-century model of great power behavior has become a serious anachronism. The most extreme form of nationalism that any Western European state has mustered since 1945 has been Gaulism, whose self-assertion has been confined largely to the realm of nuisance politics and culture. International life for the part of the world that has reached the end of history is far more preoccupied with economics than with politics or strategy.

The developed states of the West do maintain defense establishments and in the postwar period have competed vigorously for influence to meet a worldwide communist threat. This behavior has been driven, however, by an external threat from states that possess overtly expansionist ideologies, and would not exist in their absence. To take the "neorealist" theory seriously, one would have to believe that "natural" competitive behavior would reassert itself among the OECD states were Russia and China to disappear from the face of the earth. That is, West Germany and France would arm themselves against each other as they did in the 1930s, Australia and New Zealand would send military advisers to block each others' advances in Africa, and the U.S.–Canadian border would become fortified. Such a prospect is, of course, ludicrous: minus Marxist-Leninist ideology, we are far more likely to see the "Common Marketization" of world politics than the disintegration of the EEC into nineteenth-century competitiveness. Indeed, as our experience in dealing with Europe on matters such as terrorism or Libya prove, they are much further gone than we down the road that denies the legitimacy of the use of force in international politics, even in self-defense.

The automatic assumption that Russia shorn of its expanisionist communist ideology should pick up where the czars left off just prior to the Bolshevik Revolution is therefore a curious one. It assumes that the evolution of human consciousness has stood still in the meantime, and that the Soviets, while picking up currently fashionable ideas in the realm of economics, will return to foreign policy views a century out of date in the rest of Europe. This is certainly not what happened to China after it began its reform process. Chinese competitiveness and expansionism on the world scene have virtually disappeared: Beijing no longer sponsors Maoist insurgencies or tries to cultivate influence in distant African countries as it did in the 1960s. This is not to say that there are not troublesome aspects to contemporary Chinese foreign policy, such as the reckless sale of ballistic missile technology in the Middle East; and the PRC continues to manifest traditional great power behavior in its sponsorship of the Khmer Rouge against Vietnam. But the former is explained by commercial motives and the latter is a vestige of earlier ideologically-based rivalries. The new China far more resembles Gaullist France than pre–World War I Germany.

The real question for the future, however, is the degree to which Soviet elites have assimilated the consciousness of the universal homogenous state that is post-Hitler Europe. From their writings and from my own personal contacts with them, there is no question in my mind that the liberal Soviet intelligentsia rallying around Gorbachev has arrived at the end-of-history view in a remarkably short time, due in no small measure to the contacts they have had since the Brezhnev era with the larger European civilization around them. "New political thinking," the general rubric for their views, describes a world dominated by economic concerns, in which there are no ideological grounds for major conflict between nations, and in which, consequently, the use of military force becomes less legitimate. As Foreign Minister Shevardnadze put it in mid-1988:

> The struggle between two opposing systems is no longer a determining tendency of the present-day era. At the modern stage, the ability to build up material wealth at an accelerated rate on the basis of front-ranking science and high-level techniques and technology, and to distribute it fairly, and through joint efforts to restore and protect the resources necessary for mankind's survival acquires decisive importance.[18]

The post-historical consciousness represented by "new thinking" is only one possible future for the Soviet Union, however. There has always been a very strong current of great Russian chauvinism in the Soviet Union, which has found freer expression since the advent of *glasnost*. It may be possible to return to traditional Marxism-Leninism for a while as a simple rallying point for those who want to restore the authority that Gorbachev has dissipated. But as in Poland, Marxism-Leninism is dead as a mobilizing ideology: under its banner people cannot be made to work harder, and its adherents have lost confidence in themselves. Unlike the propagators of traditional Marxism-Leninism, however, ultranationalists in the USSR believe in their Slavophile cause passionately, and one gets the sense that the fascist alternative is not one that has played itself out entirely there.

The Soviet Union, then, is at a fork in the road: it can start down the path that was staked out by Western Europe forty-five years ago, a path that most of Asia has followed, or it can realize its own uniqueness and remain stuck in history. The choice it makes will be highly important for us, given the Soviet Union's size and military strength, for that power will continue to preoccupy us and slow our realization that we have already emerged on the other side of history.

V

The passing of Marxism-Leninism first from China and then from the Soviet Union will mean its death as a living ideology of world historical significance. For while there may be some isolated true believers left in places like Managua, Pyongyang, or Cambridge, Massachusetts, the fact that there is not a single large state in which it is a going concern undermines completely its pretensions to being in the vanguard of human history. And the death of this ideology means the growing "Common Marketization" of international relations, and the diminution of the likelihood of large-scale conflict between states.

This does not by any means imply the end of international conflict *per se*. For the world at that point would be divided between a part that was historical and a part that was post-historical. Conflict between states still in history, and between those states and those at the end of history, would still be possible. There would still be a high and perhaps rising level of ethnic and nationalist violence, since those are impulses incompletely played out, even in parts of the post-historical world. Palestinians and Kurds, Sikhs and Tamils, Irish Catholics and Walloons, Armenians and Azeris, will continue to have their unresolved grievances.

This implies that terrorism and wars of national liberation will continue to be an important item on the international agenda. But large-scale conflict must involve large states still caught in the grip of history, and they are what appear to be passing from the scene.

The end of history will be a very sad time. The struggle for recognition, the willingness to risk one's life for a purely abstract goal, the worldwide ideological struggle that called forth daring, courage, imagination, and idealism, will be replaced by economic calculation, the endless solving of technical problems, environmental concerns, and the satisfaction of sophisticated consumer demands. In the post-historical period there will be neither art nor philosophy, just the perpetual caretaking of the museum of human history. I can feel in myself, and see in others around me, a powerful nostalgia for the time when history existed. Such nostalgia, in fact, will continue to fuel competition and conflict even in the post-historical world for some time to come. Even though I recognize its inevitability, I have the most ambivalent feelings for the civilization that has been created in Europe since 1945, with its north Atlantic and Asian offshoots. Perhaps this very prospect of centuries of boredom at the end of history will serve to get history started once again.

NOTES

1. Kojève's best-known work is his *Introduction à la lecture de Hegel* (Paris: Editions Gallimard, 1947), which is a transcript of the *Ecole Practique* lectures from the 1930s. This book is available in English entitled *Introduction to the Reading of Hegel* arranged by Raymond Queneau, edited by Allan Bloom, and translated by James Nichols (New York: Basic Books, 1969).

2. In this respect Kojève stands in sharp contrast to contemporary German interpreters of Hegel like Herbert Marcuse who, being more sympathetic to Marx, regarded Hegel ultimately as an historically bound and incomplete philosopher.

3. Kojève alternatively identified the end of history with the postwar "American way of life," toward which he thought the Soviet Union was moving as well.

4. This notion was expressed in the famous aphorism from the preface to the *Philosophy of History* to the effect that "everyhting that is rational is real, and everything that is real is rational."

5. Indeed, for Hegel the very dichotomy between the ideal and material worlds was itself only an apparent one that was ultimately overcome by the self-conscious subject; in his system, the material world is itself only an aspect of mind.

6. In fact, modern economists, recognizing that man does not always behave as a *profit*-maximizer, posit a "utility" function, utility being either income or some other good that can be maximized: leisure, sexual satisfaction, or the pleasure of philosophizing. That profit must be replaced with a value like utility indicates the cogency of the idealist perspective.

7. One need look no further than the recent performance of Vietnamese immigrants in the U.S. school system when compared to their black or Hispanic classmates to realize that culture and consciousness are absolutely crucial to explain not only economic behavior but virtually every other important aspect of life as well.

8. I understand that a full explanation of the origins of the reform movements in China and Russia is a good deal more complicated than this simple formula would suggest. The Soviet reform, for example, was motivated in good measure by Moscow's sense of *insecurity* in the technological-military realm. Nonetheless, neither country on the eve

of its reforms was in such a state of *material* crisis that one could have predicted the surprising reform paths ultimately taken.

9. It is still not clear whether the Soviet peoples are as "Protestant" as Gorbachev and will follow him down that path.

10. The internal politics of the Byzantine Empire at the time of Justinian revolved around a conflict between the so-called monophysites and monothelites, who believed that the unity of the Holy Trinity was alternatively one of nature or of will. This conflict corresponded to some extent to one between proponents of different racing teams in the Hippodrome in Byzantium and led to a not insignificant level of political violence. Modern historians would tend to seek the roots of such conflicts in antagonisms between social classes or some other modern economic category, being unwilling to believe that men would kill each other over the nature of the Trinity.

11. I am not using the term "fascism" here in its most precise sense, fully aware of the frequent misuse of this term to denounce anyone to the right of the user. "Fascism" here denotes any organized ultra-nationalist movement with universalistic pretensions—not universalistic with regard to its nationalism, of course, since the latter is exclusive by definition, but with regard to the movement's belief in its right to rule other people. Hence Imperial Japan would qualify as fascist while former strongman Stoessner's Paraguay or Pinochet's Chile would not. Obviously fascist ideologies cannot be universalistic in the sense of Marxism or liberalism, but the structure of the doctrine can be transferred from country to country.

12. I use the example of Japan with some caution, since Kojève late in his life came to conclude that Japan, with its culture based on purely formal arts, proved that the universal homogenous state was not victorious and that history had perhaps not ended. See the long note at the end of the second edition of *Introduction à la Lecture de Hegel*, 462–63.

13. This is not true in Poland and Hungary, however, whose Communist parties have taken moves toward true power-sharing and pluralism.

14. This is particularly true of the leading Soviet conservative, former Second Secretary Yegor Ligachev, who has publicly recognized many of the deep defects of the Brezhnev period.

15. I am thinking particularly of Rousseau and the Western philosophical tradition that flows from him that was highly critical of Lockean or Hobbesian liberalism, though one could criticize liberalism from the standpoint of classical political philosophy as well.

16. See his article, "Beyond the Cold War," *New Republic*, December 9, 1988.

17. It took European colonial powers like France several years after the war to admit the illegitimacy of their empires, but decolonialization was an inevitable consequence of the Allied victory which had been based on the promise of a restoration of democratic freedoms.

18. *Vestnik Ministerstva Inostrannikh Del SSSR* no. 15 (August 1988), 27–46. "New thinking" does of course serve a propagandistic purpose in persuading Western audiences of Soviet good intentions. But the fact that it is good propaganda does not mean that its formulators do not take many of its ideas seriously.

S T E P H E N   E R I C   B R O N N E R

Into the Future

Revolution was anathema in 1989. Contemporary historians like Francois Furet and Simon Schama were virtually seeking to invalidate the term; traditionalists like Hannah Arendt and Crane Brinton, associated with the claim that all revolutions produce a terror apparatus, were widely hailed; Edmund Burke and Alexis de Tocqueville were back in fashion. So it was that, just at the moment when politicians everywhere were scurrying to distance themselves from the preparations under way for the Bicentennial in Paris, a specter from the past was inspiring the present. Infused with a commitment to constitutionalism and the rule of law, without either a centralized power apparatus or institutionalized violence,[1] a genuine international revolution occurred which exploded old assumptions and gave fresh meaning to the liberal doctrine of resistance. A previously unacknowledged possibility became actual; the *novum*, once again, emerged and evidenced its radical content precisely through its ties to the past.

Justifying the claim that history has ended thus first demands a theory of history.[2] And such a theory, if history has truly come to an end, must reject the possibility of either a new stage emerging or backsliding into preliberal political forms. By definition, Hegel viewed the culmination of history within the modern state as precluding any possible retreat into prior modes of political organization.[3] That is because the final stage of historical development was seen as having already incorporated or "sublated" (*aufgehoben*) the progressive moments within all previous forms of political organization: the democratic *as well as* the aristocratic and the monarchical. Hegel could thus view history as coming to an end within a constitutional monarchy; indeed, published in 1831, his last written work involved an examination of the important democratic developments of a year earlier, "On the English Reform Bill."

Perhaps Fukuyama might deny that he is presenting a teleological theory of history. It doesn't matter. Substantiating his claims makes it incumbent upon him to illuminate a logic of historical development. Unfortunately, he doesn't. Maintaining that progress emerges from conflicts within a cultural complex is simply inadequate. Hegel was never so vague; no less than Marx, who believed that the priority of the economic "moment" was specific only to the capitalist phase of development, he always sought to determine the various ways in which religion, art, and philosophy aligned in order to define the cultural character of different historical periods. Indeed, for both Hegel and Marx, such concern with "determinacy" only makes sense since the increasing ability to specify an extension of freedom constitutes the mark of historical progress.[4]

"Truth," said Hegel, "is concrete." Although he never provided a definition of particular governmental types like Aristotle, from his theory, the idea of freedom remains "abstract" without reference being made to the institutional forms it will take. Reason thus only becomes fully manifest when conflicts between diverse interests can be adjudicated through the "neutral" bureaucratic order defining a constitutional monarchy; a similar ability to reconcile the economic pursuit of private interests with the exigencies of the public good, through institutions democratically accountable to the working class, was also originally seen as the "rational" justification of socialism.

Fukuyama, however, is unconcerned with institutions. He never delineates the "determinate" forms which liberal democracy can assume or the aims it should seek to realize. Serious structural differences exist between democracies with one-party regimes, two-party systems in which the winner takes all, and various forms of proportional representation. Each has a different impact on the ability of the disadvantaged to gather information, coordinate their efforts, present their demands, challenge the manner in which priorities are set, and render institutions democratically accountable. And so, if only because some forms provide a more just or "rational" mode of adjudicating between diverse interests than others, Fukuyama's theoretical inadequacy becomes a matter of some importance. Indeed, setting up a rigid dichotomy between representative government and "dictatorship" is simply insufficient.

Of course, fundamental political and economic similarities exist between western states; questions regarding civil liberties aside, in general, even the most reactionary capitalist democracy has been able to deliver a degree of material satisfaction that would be substantially threatened by a sustained revolutionary assault on the existing order. All such states, furthermore, give formal democratic rights to workers; this, in turn, involves providing conditions for bureaucratic bargaining wherein normative and long-term will turn into calculable and short-term demands. The need for overt coercion is thus lessened. No doubt, especially for the technocratic intelligentsia, this combination of relative material satisfaction with noncoercive institutional mechanisms to ensure consent is precisely what made western capitalist democracy so attractive to so many in Eastern Europe.

But democracy is not merely a formal matter pertaining to civil liberties and the will of the majority. Reagan's America is neither politically nor economically identifiable with a democratic socialist Sweden. It makes a *qualitative* difference whether there is public control over investment, full employment, free child care, national health insurance, publicly funded higher education, a progressive tax policy, along with a host of other social services. It also matters what ideological values are promulgated and what institutions exist to render power accountable. Remaining on the same plane of "indeterminacy" as his ultraleftist adversaries,[5] however, Fukuyama cannot take into account the divergent ways in which either political or economic power is unequally distributed between classes. Indeed, this becomes crucial when dealing with the institution of *capital*.

According to the existing logic of accumulation, workers are economically dependent upon the private decisions of capitalist firms. Employment depends on investment which, in turn, is itself dependent on the maintenance of a satisfactory rate of profit. Should instability exist, should workers make "exorbitant" demands, or any set of circumstances arise in which profits are threatened, capital will either disinvest or move elsewhere. Such structurally induced dependency will, in turn, obviously influence the demands that labor's representatives can make even before they sit down at the bargaining table. Nevertheless, even within a capitalist frame of reference, certain conditions are more conducive to furthering the demands of workers than others.

Administrative constraints on unions, laws regulating business activity, strong parties, institutions to deal with various labor grievances, and democratic socialist traditions all play a significant role. The analyst who claims to deal with the modern state must deal with such factors. Fukuyama does not. Nor does he recognize how different regimes inhibit or foster participation. And that is crucial since, ultimately, there is no substitute for the civic involvement of working people. Workers' councils can exist under a variety of regimes, laws on the books can go unenforced, the most progressive instutional arrangements can petrify, and political traditions can wither. There are no organizational or ideological tricks to supplant the fact that overcoming the subaltern conditions of workers is possible only through their organized involvement in the political process. The power of capital still rests on the degree of unity exhibited by workers.[6] And the degree to which regimes allow for the organization of such unity will differ radically.

Attempts to limit the economic intervention of *republican states* have historically been connected with attempts to constrain the development of an organized politics from below. The concerted attack on the interventionist state in America during the 1980s involved an assault on unions as well as the legislative advances made by minorities and other previously excluded groups. Even so, the "free market" is dead. The welfare state no less than central planning was a response to the failure of classical liberal economics; the counterrevolution of the 1980s itself occurred within boundaries defined by mixed economies and state intervention. Calls for the reinstitution of *laissez-faire* thus actually retain a political and ideological purpose.

And that is true in the East no less than the West. Eric Foner, the renowned American historian, has in this vein correctly suggested that the vision of a "free market" currently so popular there serves less as a serious economic strategy than as a "protest ideal" against prior communist authoritarianism. But the ideological problem is still real. Such talk distorts economic reality. It also veils the fact that the high standard of living experienced in the West was the result of contingent political activities by working-class organizations and popular movements as well as structural developments. Luckily, with the breakdown of communist rule, independent worker organizations have begun to form in Eastern Europe. The question is whether they will recognize quickly enough that it is not merely the specific degree of mix between a free market and traditional forms of state planning which is at issue in the present debate; it is also the future of democracy itself. . . .

The map of Europe looked very different less than a hundred years ago, and there is no reason why it shouldn't look very different a hundred years from now. Conflicts will continue to exist between nation-states and regionalist institutions, between regionalist institutions and the United Nations. Inflamed by traditionalist ideologies, the most exploited areas will suffer fragmentation and conflict as a reduction of regions into wealthier and poorer nations takes place all over the globe. Even as this occurs, however, it is also possible to envision the emergence of more decentralized and democratic forms of organization—perhaps nonauthoritarian variants of Singapore or political structures, less integrated than nation-states while more so than commonwealth, like "confederations." Democracy inherently retains an experimental quality; it is no more fixed or finished than freedom itself.

Internationalism is no different. It can stagnate and assume purely ideological, even reactionary, forms. Without institutional accountability, and plans to transform conditions in the ever more marginalized nations, the use of arbitrary economic power by powerful nations under the cloak of internationalism will increase and the concept will lose its emancipatory appeal. Economic justice is a moment of internationalism. But, as Kant already knew, so is the commitment to republican values and the genuine sense of neighborliness inherent within cosmopolitanism.[7] Internationalism thus implies a rejection of all institutional threats to civil liberties, especially those of ethnic minorities, as well as of attempts to create a "fortress Europe" or turn "national identity" into a campaign issue.[8]

Internationalism is not reducible to any set of national beliefs or loyalties;[9] it is a phenomenon *sui generis*. The claim that only nationalism can grip the hearts of citizens is nonsense; the partisans of Judaism, Islam, and the Catholic Church knew better. Also, whether the failures, enormous sacrifices—often sacrifices of national identity—took place in all three of the Internationals that marked the modern labor movement. Internationalism has its own history which extends from Grotius and Kant to Paine and Marx, from Jaurès and Rosa Luxemburg to Monnet and Dag Hammarskjold. Economic, political, and cultural conditions demand the reappropriation of that legacy. But no longer is it possible to believe with Hegel that "when all the conditions of an event are present, it will come to pass."

Nuclear disarmanent and the radical reduction of conventional forces in Europe by the United States are clearly taking place. Unless disarmament agreements include a ban on sales to the Third World, however, discarded military hardware picked up by new powers can have a drastic and dangerous impact on the balance of power and world peace. New international unions, building on attempts to establish a European Charter of Social Rights, will also have to meet the challenge of ecologically sound production, changes in migration patterns, and the need to ensure equitable wages as well as transnational standards of health and safety.[10] A reinvigorated Socialist International may thus have a role to play. In any event, however, international organizations will often need to intervene in the activities of national states in order to ensure "human rights" and social justice.

Left at a purely technocratic or economic level, internationalism will fail—and the proverbial "lowly and insulted" will suffer the most. Even while fashionable theorists decry totalizing standpoints and fasten their eyes on particularist concerns, the need grows ever greater for an articulation of democratic principles as well as the socialist content of a modern internationalism. Neoconservatives will not prove helpful for the new undertaking; they were mistaken on Eastern Europe, they ignored the emergence of transnationalism, they initially joked about human rights, and they always forget the price of a "free" market. No doubt, philosophical ostriches will stick their heads in the sand or grow melancholy over the "end of art" and the "end of philosophy," the end of hope and the end of human innovation—all as real *history* passes them by.

Progress is not yet a worthless concept. Economic justice, democracy, and internationalism were originally understood as interconnected moments of the socialist project. Teleology no longer guarantees their actualization; no party any longer serves as their revolutionary vehicle; they have been ripped from their context by intellectuals who claim that a coherent context is impossible to affirm. But their relevance will remain; ignoring one might even ultimately involve endangering all three. An ethical choice, perhaps grounded only in the hatred of any arbitrary exercise of institutional power, looms on the horizon. A new moment of decision thus confronts us. The triumph of those who could freeze time or turn back the clock will also pass. The future is not over; indeed, it has barely begun.

NOTES

1. Ulrich K. Preuss, *Revolution, Fortschritt und Verfassung: Zu einem neuen Verfassungsverständnis* (Berlin, 1990), pp. 10, 59ff.
2. The point is to comprehend both the result and the process for the one is justified by the other; indeed, "the naked result is the corpse of the system which has left its guiding tendency behind it." G. W. F. Hegel, *The Phenomenology of Mind*, trans J. B. Baillie (New York, 1931), p. 3ff.
3. "Every contemporary and future state and judicial order must presuppose the universal principle of freedom derived from the [French] Revolution"; indeed, the argument that Hegel is a thinker of the European "Restoration" is undercut by Joachim Ritter, *Hegel und die französische Revolution* (Frankfurt, 1972), pp. 30ff.
4. For the rather self-serving and "indeterminate" claim that all language, and so every theory, is equally indeterminate see Jacques Derrida, *Writing and Difference* (Chicago, 1978).
5. Alex Callinicos, *The Revenge of History: Marxism and the European Revolutions* (University Park, Pa.: 1991), pp. 91–94.
6. Categories like the "class ideal," which strives to identify the common interests of working people in all social movements while privileging none, thus become necessary for shaping a new package of socio-economic reforms and a new set of public priorities in the next century. Note the discussion in my *Socialism Unbound* (New York, 1990), pp. 161–69.
7. Note, in this regard, the third article of the essay "Perpetual Peace," in *Kant's Political Writings*, ed. Hans Reiss (New York, 1970), pp. 105ff.
8. See the analysis of Simon Gunn, *Revolution of the Right: Europe's New Conservatism* (London, 1989).

9. "Universal history does not suppress the histories of individual nations, but tries to understand them as contributions to history in general. Just as one loses sight of the history of Sardinia after that kingdom had fought for the unity of Italy, so the histories of Belgium, Holland, and Luxemburg will soon have a merely provincial interest, and even the histories of greater countries will be submerged in the history of the development of the Common Market." Henry Pachter, *The Fall and Rise of Europe: A Political, Social, and Cultural History of the Twentieth Century* (New York, 1975), p. xi.

10. John Palmer, "Europe 1992: A Socialist Perspective" in *New Politics* 2.4 (Winter 1990), pp. 59ff.

SELECTED BIBLIOGRAPHY

THE LIBERAL IDEA

Ackerman, Bruce. *The Future of Liberal Revolution*. New Haven: Yale University Press, 1992.

Berlin, Isaiah. *Four Essays on Liberty*. New York: Oxford University Press, 1969.

Bobbio, Norberto. *The Future of Democracy: A Defense of the Rules of the Game*. Minneapolis: University of Minnesota Press, 1987.

Dahl, Robert. *Democracy and Its Critics*. New Haven: Yale University Press, 1989.

Finkelkraut, Alain. *The Defeat of the Mind*. Trans. Judith Friedlander. New York: Columbia University Press, 1995.

Ferry, Luc, and Alain Renault. *Political Philosophy*. 3 vols. Chicago: University of Chicago, 1993.

Gilbert, Alan. *Democratic Individuality*. New York: Cambridge University Press, 1990.

Gutmann, Amy. *Liberal Equality*. New York: Cambridge University Press, 1980.

Hartz, Louis. *The Liberal Tradition in America*. New York: Harcourt, Brace, 1955.

Manning, David John. *Liberalism*. New York: St. Martin's Press, 1976.

Moore, Barrington, Jr. *Injustice: The Social Bases of Obedience and Revolt*. New York: M. E. Sharpe, 1978.

Pateman, Carole. *The Sexual Contract*. Cambridge, U.K.: Polity Press, 1988.

Rawls, John. *A Theory of Justice*. Cambridge, Mass.: Harvard University Press, 1971.

Schlesinger, Arthur M., Jr. *The Vital Center: The Politics of Freedom*. Boston: Houghton Mifflin, 1949.

COMMUNITARIANISM AND CULTURE

Avineri, Shlomo, ed. *Communitarianism and Individualism*. Oxford: Oxford University Press, 1992.

Barber, Benjamin R. *Strong Democracy: Participatory Politics for a New Age*. Berkeley: University of California Press, 1984.

Bell, Daniel. *Communitarianism and Its Critics*. Oxford: Clarendon Press, 1993.

Benhabib, Seyla. *Situating the Self: Gender, Community and Postmodernism in Contemporary Ethics*. New York: Routledge, 1992.

Bulhall, Stephen, and Adam Swift. *Liberals and Communitarians*. London: Basil Blackwell, 1992.

Kymlicka, Will. *Liberalism, Community and Culture*. Oxford: Clarendon, 1991.

MacIntyre, Alisdair. *After Virtue*. Notre Dame, Ind.: University of Notre Dame Press, 1981.

McWilliams, Wilson Carey. *The Idea of Fraternity in America*. Berkeley: University of California Press, 1973.

Phillips, Derek L. *Looking Backward: A Critical Appraisal of Communitarian Thought*. Princeton: Princeton University Press, 1995.

Putnam, Robert. *Making Democracy Work: Civic Traditions in Modern Italy*. Princeton: Princeton University Press, 1994.

Sandel, Michael J. *Liberalism and the Limits of Justice*. New York: Cambridge University Press, 1982.

Taylor, Charles. *The Ethics of Authenticity*. Cambridge, Mass.: Harvard University Press, 1991.

Walzer, Michael. *Spheres of Justice: A Defense of Pluralism and Equality*. New York: Basic Books, 1984.

THE CONSERVATIVE DISPOSITION

Bennett, William J. *The De-valuing of America*. New York: Summit Books, 1992.

Bloom, Allan. *The Closing of the American Mind*. New York: Simon & Schuster, 1988.

Ehrman, John. *The Rise of Neo-conservatism: Intellectuals and Foreign Affairs, 1954–1994*. New Haven: Yale University Press, 1995.

Himmelfarb, Gertrude. *The De-Moralization of Society*. New York: Alfred A. Knopf, 1995.

Habermas, Jürgen. *The New Conservatism: Cultural Criticism and the Historians' Debate*. Ed. and trans. Shierry Weber Nicholsen. Cambridge, Mass.: MIT Press, 1992.

Hirschman, Albert O. *The Rhetoric of Reaction: Perversity, Futility, Jeopardy*. Cambridge, Mass.: Harvard University Press, 1991.

Hondrick, Ted. *Conservatism*. Boulder, Colo.: Westview Press, 1991.

Kirk, Russel, ed. *The Portable Conservative Reader*. New York: Penguin, 1982.

Mannheim, Karl. *Conservatism: A Contribution to the Sociology of Knowledge*. New York: Routledge, 1986.

Murray, Charles. *Losing Ground*. Reprint, New York: Basic Books, 1995.

Nozick, Robert. *Anarchy State and Utopia*. New York: Basic Books, 1977.

Sowell, Thomas. *The Vision of the Anointed: Self-Congratulation as a Basis for Social Policy*. New York: Basic Books, 1995.

White, Reginald James, ed. *The Conservative Tradition*. New York: New York University Press, 1957.

Wilson, James Q. *The Moral Sense*. New York: The Free Press, 1993.

Anarchism and Freedom

Avrich, Paul. *Anarchist Voices: An Oral History of Anarchism in America*. Princeton: Princeton University Press, 1995.

Brown, Susan L. *The Politics of Individualism: Liberalism, Feminism, and Anarchism*. Montreal: Black Rose Books, 1993.

Cohn-Bendit, Daniel. *Obsolete Communism: The Left Wing Alternative*. New York: McGraw- Hill, 1968.

Gans, Chaim. *Philosophical Anarchism and Political Disobedience*. New York: Cambridge University Press, 1992.

Goldman, Emma. *Anarchism and Other Essays*. New York: Mother Earth Publishing Association, 1911.

Goodway, David. *For Anarchism: History, Theory and Practice*. New York: Routledge, 1989.

Guérin, Daniel. *Anarchism: From Theory to Practice*. Trans. Mary Klopper. New York: Monthly Review Press, 1970.

Joll, James. *The Anarchists*. Boston: Little, Brown, 1964.

Kropotkin, Peter. *Memoirs of a Revolutionist*. Ed. James Allen Rogers. New York: Doubleday, 1962.

Miller, David. *Anarchism*. London: J. M. Dent, 1984.

Nomad, Max. *Dramas, Dynamiters, and Demagogues*. New York: Walden Press, 1964.

Orwell, George. *Homage to Catalonia*. New York: Harcourt, Brace, 1952.

Read, Sir Herbert. *The Philosophy of Anarchism*. London: Freedom Press, 1947.

Woodcock, George. *Anarchism: A History of Libertarian Ideas and Movements*. New York: World Publishing Co., 1962.

Democratic Socialism

Abendroth, Wolfgang. *A Short History of the European Working Class*. Trans. Nicholas Jacobs and Brian Trench. London: New Left Books, 1972.

Beilharz, Peter. *Postmodern Socialism: Romanticism, City, and State*. Melbourne: Melbourne University Press, 1994.

Boggs, Carl. *The Socialist Tradition: From Crisis to Decline*. New York: Routledge, 1995.

Braunthal, Julius. *History of the Internationals 1864–1968*. 3 vols. Trans. Henry Collins et al. New York and Boulder, Colo.: Praeger and Westview, 1980.

Bronner, Stephen Eric. *Socialism Unbound*. New York: Routledge, 1990.

Fromm, Erich, ed. *Socialist Humanism: An International Symposium*. New York: Anchor, 1966.

Harrington, Michael. *Socialism: Past and Future*. Penguin: New York, 1992.

Joll, James. *The Second International 1889–1914*. New York: Harper & Row, 1966.

Kolakowski, Leszek. *Main Currents of Marxism*. 3 vols. New York: Oxford University Press, 1978.

Lichtheim, George. *Marxism: An Historical and Critical Study*. New York: Praeger, 1961.

Osborne, Peter, ed. *Socialism and the Limits of Liberalism.* London: Verso, 1991.

Pierson, Christopher. *Socialism After Communism: The New Market Socialism.* University Park, Pa.: Penn State University Press, 1995.

Roemer, John E. *A Future for Socialism.* Cambridge, Mass.: Harvard University Press, 1994.

COMMUNISM AND REVOLUTION

Borkenau, Franz. *World Communism: A History of the Communist International.* Ann Arbor: University of Michigan Press, 1962.

Conquest, Robert. *The Great Terror: Stalin's Purge of the Thirties.* New York: Macmillan, 1968.

Crossman, Richard, ed. *The God That Failed.* Reprint, New York: Bantam, 1965.

Deutscher, Isaac. *Stalin.* Reprint, New York: Oxford University Press, 1966.

Ehrenberg, John. *The Dictatorship of the Proletariat: Marxism's theory of Socialist Democracy.* New York: Routledge, 1992.

Gramsci, Antonio. *Selections from the Prison Notebooks.* Ed. and trans. Quintin Hoare and Geoffrey Nowell Smith. New York: International Publishers, 1971.

Gruber, Helmut, ed. *International Communism in the Era of Lenin: A Documentary History.* New York: Doubleday, 1972.

Gruber, Helmut, ed. *Soviet Russia Masters the Comintern: International Communism in the Era of Stalin's Ascendancy.* New York: Doubleday, 1974.

James, C. L. R. *World Revolution 1917–1936: The Rise and Fall of the Communist International.* Atlantic Highlands, N.J.: Humanities Press International, 1993.

Lowenthal, Richard. *World Communism: The Disintegration of a Secular Faith.* New York: Oxford University Press, 1964.

Merleau-Ponty, Maurice. *Humanism and Terror.* Trans. John O'Neill. Boston: Beacon Press, 1969.

Trotsky, Leon. *The Revolution Betrayed: What Is the Soviet Union and Where Is It Going?* Trans. Max Eastman. Reprint, New York: Pathfinder, 1972.

THE FASCIST WORLDVIEW

Arendt, Hannah. *The Origins of Totalitarianism.* Cleveland: Meridian Press, 1951.

Bloch, Ernst. *Heritage of Our Times.* Trans. Neville and Stephen Plaice. Berkeley: University of California Press, 1990.

Bullock, Alan. *Hitler: A Study in Tyranny.* New York: Harper Torchbooks, 1962.

Fromm, Erich. *Escape from Freedom.* New York: Bantam, 1941.

Hamilton, Alistair. *The Appeal of Fascism: A Study of Intellectuals and Fascism 1919–1945.* New York: Macmillan, 1971.

Hibbert, Christopher. *Il Duce: The Life of Benito Mussolini.* Boston: Little, Brown, 1962.

Kogon, Eugen. *The Theory and Practice of Hell.* Trans. Heinz Nordan. New York: Berkley, 1950.

Mosse, George L. *The Crisis of German Ideology: Intellectual Origins of the Third Reich.* New York: Grosset & Dunlap: 1964.

Neumann, Franz. *Behemoth: The Structure and Practice of National Socialism 1933–1944.* Reprint, New York: Harper & Row, 1963.

Nolte, Ernst. *Three Faces of Fascism: Action Francaise, Italian Fascism, National Socialism*.
    Trans. Leila Vennowitz. Reprint, New York: New American Library, 1965.

Sternhell, Zev. *The Birth of Fascist Ideology: From Cultural Rebellion to Political Revolution*.
    Trans. David Maisel. Princeton: Princeton University Press, 1996.

Tannenbaum, Edward R. *The Fascist Experience: Italian Society and Culture, 1922–1945*.
    New York: Basic Books, 1972.

Forever in the Shadow of Hitler: The Controversy Concerning the Singularity of the Holocaust.
    Trans. James Knowlton and Truett Cates. Atlantic Highlands, N.J.: Humanities
    Press International, 1993.

CRITICAL THEORY

Arato, Andrew, and Eike Gebhardt, eds. *The Essential Frankfurt School Reader*. New York:
    Continuum Press, 1982.

Bronner, Stephen Eric. *Of Critical Theory and Its Theorists*. Oxford: Basil Blackwell, 1994.

Dubiel, Helmut. *Theory and Politics: Studies in the Development of Critical Theory*. Trans.
    Benjamin Gregg. Cambridge, Mass.: MIT Press, 1985.

Held, David. *Introduction to Critical Theory*. Berkeley: University of California Press, 1985.

Horkheimer, Max, and Theodor W. Adorno. *Dialectic of Enlightenment*. Trans. John
    Cumming. New York: Herder & Herder, 1971.

Jay, Martin. *The Dialectical Imagination: A History of the Frankfurt School and the Institute of
    Social Research 1923–1950*. Boston: Little, Brown, 1973.

Jay, Martin. *Marxism and Totality: The Adventures of a Concept from Lukács to Habermas*.
    Berkeley: University of California Press, 1984.

Kellner, Douglas. *Critical Theory, Marxism and Modernity*. Cambridge, U.K.: Polity
    Press, 1989.

Korsch, Karl. *Marxism and Philosophy*. Trans. Fred Halliday. London: New Left Books, 1970.

Lukács, Georg. *History and Class Consciousness: Studies in Marxist Dialectics*. Trans. Rodney
    Livingstone. Cambridge, Mass.: MIT Press, 1972.

Tar, Zoltan. *The Frankfurt School: The Critical Theories of Max Horkheimer and Theodor W.
    Adorno*. New York: Schocken, 1985.

Wiggershaus, Rolf. *The Frankfurt School*. Cambridge, Mass.: MIT Press, 1994.

POSTMODERNISM AND POSTSTRUCTURALISM

Bauman, Zygmunt. *Legislators and Interpreters: On Modernity, Postmodernity, and
    Intellectuals*. London: Cambridge University Press, 1987.

Best, Steven, and Douglas Kellner. *Postmodern Theory: Critical Interrogations*. New York:
    Guilford, 1991.

Callinicos, Alex. *Against Postmodernism*. New York: St. Martin's Press, 1990.

Deleuze, Gilles, and Felix Guattari. *Anti-Oedipus: Capitalism and Schizophrenia*. Trans.
    Robert Hurley, et al. New York: Viking, 1977.

Derrida, Jacques. *Of Grammatology*. Trans. Gayatri Chakravorty Spivak. Baltimore: Johns
    Hopkins University Press, 1976.

Dews, Peter. *Logics of Disintegration*. New York: Verso, 1987.

Habermas, Jürgen. *The Philosophical Discourse of Modernity: Twelve Lectures*. Trans.
    Frederick Lawrence. Cambridge, Mass.: MIT Press, 1987.

Harvey, David. *The Condition of Postmodernity*. London: Basil Blackwell, 1989.

Hutcheon, Linda. *The Politics of Postmodernism*. New York: Routledge, 1989.

Jameson, Fredric. *Postmodernism*. Durham, N.C.: Duke University Press, 1992.

Kroker, Arthur, and David Cook. *The Postmodern Scene*. New York: St. Martin's Press, 1986.

Poster, Mark. *Critical Theory and Poststructuralism: In Search of a Context*. Ithaca, N.Y.: Cornell University Press, 1989.

Rabinow, Paul, ed. *The Foucault Reader*. New York: Pantheon, 1984.

POSTCOLONIAL POLITICAL THEORY

Achebe, China. *Hopes and Impediments: Selected Essays*. New York: Doubleday, 1988.

Anzaldua, Gloria. *Borderlands/La Frontera: The New Mestiza*. San Francisco: Aunt Lute Books, 1987.

Asante, Molefi Kete. *Afrocentricity*. Trenton, N.J.: Africa World Press, 1988.

Bernal, Martin. *Black Athena: The Afroasiatic Roots of Classical Civilization*. New Brunswick, N.J.: Rutgers University Press, 1987.

Cesaire, Aime. *Discourse on Colonialism*. New York: Monthly Review Press, 1972.

Fanon, Frantz. *Black Skin, White Masks*. New York: Grove Weidenfeld, 1967.

Memmi, Albert. *Dominated Man*. Boston: Beacon Press, 1969.

Said, Edward. *Culture and Imperialism*. New York: Alfred A. Knopf, 1933.

Saldivar, Ramon. *Chicano Narrative: The Dialectics of Difference*. Madison: University of Wisconsin Press, 1990.

Senghor, Leopold. *African Socialism*. New York: American Society for African Culture, 1959.

Spivak, Gayatri Chakravorty. *In Other Worlds*. New York: Routledge, 1989.

Suleri, Sara. *Meatless Days*. Chicago: University of Chicago Press, 1989.

Taylor, Charles. *Multiculturalism and "The Politics of Recognition."* Princeton: Princeton University Press, 1992.

Williams, Patrick, ed. *Colonial Discourse/Postcolonial Theory*. New York: Columbia University Press, 1994.

THE AFRICAN-AMERICAN HERITAGE

Baldwin, James. *The Fire Next Time*. New York: Vintage, 1962.

Bell, Derrick. *Faces at the Bottom of the Well: The Permanence of Racism*. New York: Basic Books, 1992.

Carmichael, Stokeley, and Charles V. Hamilton. *Black Power: The Politics of Liberation in America*. New York: Vintage, 1967.

Cruse, Harold. *The Crisis of the Negro Intellectual*. New York: William Morrow, 1967.

DuBois, W. E. B. *The Souls of Black Folk*. New York: New American Library, 1969.

hooks, bell. *Black Looks: Race and Representation*. Boston: South End Press, 1992.

D'Souza, Dinesh. *The End of Racism*. New York: The Free Press, 1995.

Gates, Henry Louis. *Loose Canons: Notes on the Culture Wars*. New York: Oxford University Press, 1991.

Gould, Stephen Jay. *The Mismeasure of Man*. New York: W. W. Norton, 1981.

Myrdal, Gunnar. *An American Dilemma: The Negro Problem and Modern Democracy*. 2 vols. New Brunswick, N.J.: Transaction Publishers, 1995.

Sowell, Thomas. *Race and Culture: A Worldview*. New York: Basic Books, 1994.

Williams, Patricia. *The Alchemy of Race and Rights*. Cambridge, Mass.: Harvard University Press, 1991.

Wright, Richard. *White Man, Listen!* Conn.: Greenwood Press, 1957.

X, Malcolm, and Alex Haley. *The Autobiography of Malcolm X*. New York: Ballantine, 1964.

GENDERED EXPERIENCES

Collins, Patricia Hill. *Black Feminist Thought: Knowledge, Consciousness, and the Politics of Empowerment*. New York: Routledge, 1990.

Eisenstein, Zillah R. *The Radical Future of Liberal Feminism*. New York: Longman, 1981.

Friedan, Betty. *The Feminine Mystique*. New York: W. W. Norton, 1963.

Gilligan, Carol. *In a Different Voice*. Cambridge, Mass.: Harvard University Press, 1982.

Grant, Judith. *Fundamental Feminism*. New York: Routledge, 1993.

Haraway, Donna J. *Simians, Cyborgs, and Women: The Reinvention of Nature*. New York: Routledge, 1991.

Hartsock, Nancy. *Money, Sex, and Power: Toward a Feminist Historical Materialism*. New York: Longman, 1983.

Hirsch, Marianne, and Evelyn Fox Keller. *Conflicts in Feminism*. New York: Routledge, 1990.

Irigaray, Luce. *Speculum of the Other Woman*. Trans. Gillian C. Gill. Ithaca, N.Y.: Cornell University Press, 1974.

MacKinnon, Catharine A. *Toward a Feminist Theory of the State*. Cambridge, Mass.: Harvard University Press, 1989.

Moraga, Cherrie, and Gloria Anzaldua. *This Bridge Called My Back: Writings by Radical Women of Color*. New York: Kitchen Table/Women of Color Press, 1981.

Rich, Adrienne. "Compulsory Heterosexuality and Lesbian Existence." *Signs* 5 (Summer 1980).

Rubin, Gayle. "The Traffic in Women: Notes on the Political Economy of Sex." In Rayna R. Reiter, ed., *Toward an Anthropology of Women*. New York: Monthly Review Press, 1975.

ECOLOGICAL VISIONS

Biehl, Janet. *Rethinking Ecofeminist Politics*. Boston: South End Press, 1994.

Bookchin, Murray. *Remaking Society: Pathways to a Green Future*. Boston: South End Press, 1993.

Diamond, Irene. *Fertile Ground: Women, Earth and the Limits of Control*. Boston: Beacon Press, 1994.

Dobson, Andrew, and Paul Lucardie. *The Politics of Nature: Explorations in Green Political Theory*. New York: Routledge, 1995.

Feenberg, Andrew, ed. *Critical Theory of Technology*. New York: Oxford University Press, 1991.

Ferry, Luc. *The New Ecological Order*. Trans. Carol Volk. Chicago: University of Chicago Press, 1995.

Jonas, Hans. *The Imperative of Responsibility: Search for an Ethic for the Technological Age.* Trans. Hans Jonas with David Merr. Chicago: University of Chicago Press, 1984.

Luhmann, Niklas. *Ecological Communication.* Trans. John Bednarz. Chicago: University of Chicago Press, 1989.

Martell, Luke. *Ecology and Society: An Introduction.* Amherst: University of Massachusetts Press, 1994.

Merchant, Carolyn. *Radical Ecology: The Search for a Livable World.* New York: Routledge, 1992.

Morrison, Roy. *Ecological Democracy.* Boston: South End Press, 1995.

Murphy, Raymond. *Rationality and Nature: A Sociological Inquiry into a Changing Relationship.* Boulder, Colo.: Westview Press, 1994.

Thomashow, Mitchell. *Ecological Identity: Becoming a Reflective Environmentalist.* Cambridge, Mass.: MIT Press, 1995.

CONCLUSION: THE END OF HISTORY?

Attali, Jacques. *Millennium: Winners and Losers in the Coming World Order.* Trans. Leila Conners and Nathan Gardels. New York: Random House, 1991.

Becher, Jeremy, et al., eds. *Global Visions: Beyond the New World Order.* Boston: South End Press, 1993.

Beck, Ulrich. *Risk Society: Towards a New Modernity.* Trans. Mark Ritter. London: Sage Publications, 1992.

Beck, Ulrich, Anthony Giddens, and Scott Lash. *Reflexive Modernization: Politics, Tradition and Aesthetics in the Modern Social Order.* Stanford: Stanford University Press, 1994.

Giddens, Anthony. *Beyond Left and Right: The Future of Radical Politics.* Stanford: Stanford University Press, 1994.

Gúehenno, Jean-Marie. *The End of the Nation State.* Minneapolis: University of Minnesota Press, 1995.

Kennedy, Paul. *Preparing for the Twenty-First Century.* New York: Vintage, 1993.

Latouche, Serge. *In the Wake of Affluent Society: An Exploration of Post-Development.* Trans. Martin O'Connor and Rosemary Arnoux. London: Zed Books, 1993.

Melzer, Arthur M., et al, eds. *History and the Idea of Progress.* Ithaca, N.Y.: Cornell University Press, 1995.

O'Brien, Conor Cruise. *On the Eve of the Millennium: The Future of Democracy through an Age of Unreason.* New York: The Free Press, 1995.

Preuss, Ulrich K. *Constitutional Revolution: The Link Between Constitutionalism and Progress.* Trans. Deborah Lucas Schneider. Atlantic Highlands, N.J.: Humanities Press International, 1995.

Waters, Malcolm. *Globalization.* New York: Routledge, 1995.

SOURCES

Jaspers, Karl; *The Future of Mankind*, trans. E. B. Ashton (Chicago: University of Chicago Press, 1961), pp. 291–99.

Rawls, John; *Philosophy and Public Affairs*, vol. 14, no. 3 © 1985 by Princeton University Press. Reprinted by permission of Princeton University Press.

Dewey, John; "The Search for the Great Community" © Copyright 1984 by the Board of Trustees, Southern Illinois.

Arendt, Hannah; *The Human Condition* (Chicago: University of Chicago Press, 1958), pp. 68–78.

Sandel, Michael J.; *Political Theory*, vol, 12, no. 1, pp. 81–96 © 1994 by Sage Publications. Reprinted with permission by Sage Publications.

Oakeshott, Michael; from *Rationalism in Politics and Other Essays*, by Michael Oakeshott. © 1962 Michael Oakeshott. Reprinted by permission of HarperCollins Publishers, Inc.

Podhoretz, Norman; © 1986 by Norman Podhoretz. Reprinted by permission of Georges Borchardt, Inc. for the author.

Souchy, Augustin; *Beware Anarchist! A Life for Freedom* © 1993 by Charles H. Kerr. Reprinted with permission.

Buber, Martin; *Paths to Utopia*, © 1958 Beacon Press. Reprinted with permission of the Estate of Martin Buber.

Jaurès, Jean; trans. by I. A. Langas; ed. Irving Howe; *The Essential Works of Socialism*, Yale University Press © Copyright 1986. Used with permission.

Luxemburg, Rosa; Copyright © 1970 by Pathfinder Press. Reprinted by permission.

Rosselli, Carlo; *Liberal Socialism*. Copyright © 1994 by Princeton University Press. Reprinted by permission of Princeton University Press.

Pachter, Henry M.; from *Socialism in History* by Henry Pachter. Copyright © 1984 by Columbia University Press. Reprinted with permission of the publisher.

Lenin, V. I.; Robert Daniels, "What Is to Be Done," from *A Documentary on Communism*, © 1960 by Robert Daniels, University of Vermont by permission University Press of New England.

Gramsci, Antonio; an extract "The Revolution against *Capital*" by Antonio Gramsci from *Selections from the Political Writings 1910–1920* by Quetin Hoare (ed) Lawrence and Wishart, London 1977.

Stalin, Josef; *Foundations of Leninism* © 1939. Used by Permission of International Publishers Co.

Tse-tung, Mao; *Selected Readings*, Foreign Language Press: Beijing © 1971. Used by permission of the publisher.

Barrès, Maurice; *The French Right from de Maistre to Maurras*, ed. J. S. McClellend. © Jonathan Cape: London, 1970. Used by permission of the publisher.

CONTRIBUTORS

THEODOR W. ADORNO (1903–1969) Born in Frankfurt, Adorno was a leading member of the Institute for Social Research and co-author of the *Dialectic of Enlightenment*. His own works, which span the intellectual spectrum, include *Prisms*, *Anti-Epistemology*, *Minima Moralia*, *Aesthetic Theory*, *Negative Dialectic*, *The Jargon of Authenticity*, *Notes on Literature*, and *The Philosophy of Modern Music*.

HANNAH ARENDT (1906–1975) One of the most influential of the German exiles from Hitler, a student of Karl Jaspers and Martin Heidegger, Arendt taught at the University of Chicago and the New School for Social Research in New York. Her major works include *The Origins of Totalitarianism*, *The Human Condition*, *On Revolution*, *Eichmann in Jerusalem*, and *The Life of the Mind*.

AUGUSTE MAURICE BARRÈS (1862–1923) A publicist and novelist, a leading figure in the early years of the Third Republic, and a founder of the fascist *Action Française*, Barrès is the author of the three-volume *The Cult of the Self* and *The Deracinated*.

SIMONE DE BEAUVOIR (1908–1986) Born to a bourgeois family and educated at the École Normale Superieure, where she met Jean-Paul Sartre (who would become her lifelong companion), de Beauvoir was close to the Communist Party in the aftermath of World War II and became a founder of modern feminism. She wrote novels, essays, and various works of social theory as well as a set of diaries, which constitute a record of political and social life in twentieth-century France. Her most important works are *The Second Sex*, *The Mandarins*, *The Ethics of Ambiguity*, *The Prime of Life*, and *The Force of Circumstance*.

ULRICH BECK (1944–) Editor of *Social World*, Professor of Sociology at the University of Munich, and a leading figure in German social science, Beck is the author of *Risk Society* and *The Reinvention of Politics*.

WALTER BENJAMIN (1892–1940) One of the most fascinating figures associated with the "Frankfurt School." A literary critic, philosopher, and social theorist, Benjamin committed suicide while fleeing fascism. His essay collection *Illuminations* is a classic work, and his correspondence with Gershom Scholem constitutes one of the extraordinary documents of the century.

MARTIN BUBER (1879–1965) Born in Vienna, professor of religion and ethics at the University of Frankfurt and (from 1938–51) professor of social philosophy at the Hebrew University in Jerusalem, Buber was a towering figure in modern Jewish intellectual culture and existential philosophy. His works include *I and Thou*, *Moses*, *Paths in Utopia*, and *Tales of the Hassidim*.

JUDITH BUTLER (1957–) A leading interpreter of postmodern feminism and the author of *Gender Trouble: Feminism and the Subversion of Identity*, Butler is Professor of Rhetoric and Comparative Literature at the University of California, Berkeley.

BENEDETTO CROCE (1886–1952) A major idealist philosopher of history who served in the Italian Senate and successive cabinet posts until the seizure of power by Mussolini, Croce is the author of *The Philosophy of the Spirit* and *History as the Story of Liberty*.

JOHN DEWEY (1859–1952) A seminal proponent of pragmatism with William James and Charles Sanders Peirce, a major public intellectual, and an innovative educational theorist, Dewey taught at the University of Chicago and Columbia University. In 1937, he headed the commission investigating the charges made against Leon Trotsky during the infamous Moscow Trials and published its finding under the title *Not Guilty*. His major works include *Studies in Logical Theory*, *The School and Society*, *Democracy and Education*, *Experience and Nature*, *Reconstruction in Philosophy*, and *A Common Faith*.

WILLIAM EDWARD BURGHARDT DUBOIS (1868–1963) After completing his doctorate at Harvard in 1895, DuBois completed the first major empirical sociological study of African-American life in the United States, *The Philadelphia Negro* (1899). An organizer of the Niagara Movement and an activist his whole life, he moved to Ghana at the age of 93 and began work on *The Encyclopedia Africana*. His most popular work remains *The Souls of Black Folk*.

FRANTZ FANON (1925–1961) Born in Martinique, Fanon became a psychiatrist in France and served in a hospital in Algeria before dying of cancer at the age of 36. His works include the classic *Wretched of the Earth* and *Black Skins, White Masks*.

MICHEL FOUCAULT (1926–1984) Born in Poitiers and educated at the École Normale Superieure, Foucault taught philosophy at the University of Clermont-Ferrand and then at Vincennes until 1970, when he became professor of history and systems of thought at the Collège de France. His most important works include *Madness and Civilization*, *Discipline and Punish*, and *The Archaeology of Knowledge*.

JO FREEMAN (1945–) A lawyer and political scientist, a feminist scholar, and an important figure in the women's liberation movement, Freeman is the author of *The Politics of Women's Liberation* and the editor of *Social Movements of the Sixties and Seventies* and *Women: A Feminist Perspective.*

FRANCIS FUKUYAMA (1945–) A deputy director of the State Department's policy-planning staff and senior social scientist at the Rand Corporation, Fukuyama is the author of *Trust: The Social Virtues and the Creation of Prosperity.*

MOHANDAS KARAMCHJAND GANDHI (1869–1948) Born to a middle-class Indian family, Gandhi studied law in England, moved to South Africa, and became the leader of the movement for the independence of India. His theory of nonviolent resistance and his emphasis on the spiritual foundations of political action had a worldwide impact. A Hindu, Gandhi became a symbol of tolerance and integrity before his tragic assassination at the hands of Moslem extremists.

ANDRE GORZ (1924–) Born in Vienna, Gorz grew up in France, where he still lives as a philosopher and journalist. An important theorist of workers' self-management during the 1960s, he has became a major figure in the international environmental movement. His works include *Socialism and Revolution*, *Farewell to the Working Class*, *Ecology and Politics*, and the *Critique of Economic Reason.*

ANTONIO GRAMSCI (1891–1937) A founder of the Italian Communist Party and one of the seminal figures in the unorthodox tradition of "Western Marxism," Gramsci composed his legendary *Prison Notebooks* and *Letters from Prison* while he was incarcerated by Mussolini's police.

ERNESTO CHE GUEVARA (1928–1967) Once a major figure in the Cuban Revolution, theorist and tactician of guerilla warfare, Minister of Economics, and international revolutionary, Guevara was killed while fostering revolution in Bolivia. His works include *Man and Socialism in Cuba* and *Guerilla Warfare.*

JÜRGEN HABERMAS (1929–) A leading figure in the tradition of critical theory and the former director of the Max Planck Institute, Habermas is currently Professor Emeritus at the Johann Wolfgang University in Frankfurt. His major works include *Knowledge and Human Interests*, *Theory and Practice*, *On the Logic of the Social Sciences*, and *The Theory of Communicative Action.*

ADOLF HITLER (1889–1945) Born in Austria, Hitler attempted a career as an artist and served on the front lines in World War I before becoming the leader of the German National Socialist Workers Party. While in prison following his attempted coup of 1923 in Munich, he wrote his autobiography, *Mein Kampf.* The year 1933 saw his ascension to power in Germany, and in 1941, he called for the implementation of the "Final Solution" against the European Jews. He died in a Berlin bunker as World War II drew to a close.

MAX HORKHEIMER (1895–1973) The most important director of the Institute for Social Research at Frankfurt and the co-author of the seminal *Dialectic of Enlightenment*, Horkheimer edited the *Journal for Social Research*, in which many of the writings of the Institute's associates appeared. He moved the Institute to the United States following Hitler's seizure of power, but he returned to Germany after the war and became Rector of the University of Frankfurt. His major works include *Critical Theory* and *The Eclipse of Reason*.

KARL JASPERS (1883–1969) initially studied medicine and psychiatry. The author of a seminal work in psychopathology, Jaspers would become a principal exponent of modern existentialism. Professor of philosophy at Heidelberg University until 1937, when he was removed by Hitler, he was reinstated in 1945 and taught at the University of Basel in Switzerland from 1948 on. His major works include *Reason and Existenz*, *The Perennial Scope of Philosophy*, *Way to Wisdom*, and the three-volume *Philosophy*.

JEAN JAURÈS (1859–1914) One of the greatest figures of international socialism prior to World War I. A leading proponent of internationalism and liberalism, a humanist, and a critic of anti-Semitism and every form of prejudice, Jaurès is the author of *The Origins of German Socialism*, one of the first inquiries into the influence of the idealist tradition upon Marx and socialism, and the nine-volume *Socialist History of the French Revolution*.

MARTIN LUTHER KING, JR. (1929–1968) Born in Atlanta, the son of a pastor, King recieved his Ph.D. from Boston University in 1955. Leader of the Southern Christian Leadership Conference, which served as the institutional base for the civil rights movement, he organized the legendary march on Washington in 1963 and the Selma march to Montgomery in 1965. Linking his commitment to civil rights with opposition to the Vietnam War, King was in the midst of organizing a new "poor people's movement" when he was assassinated in Memphis while speaking to sanitation workers.

VLADIMIR ILYICH ULYANOV LENIN (1870–1924) The guiding force of the Russian Revolution and the founder of Bolshevism. Lenin's major works include *The Development of Capitalism in Russia*, *What Is To Be Done?*, *Imperialism: The Last Stage of Capitalism*, and *State and Revolution*.

AUDRE LORDE (1934–1992) Lorde is an acclaimed poet and essayist and a major figure of Black lesbian feminism. Her major works include *From the Land Where Other People Live*, *A Burst of Light*, and *Sister, Outsider*.

ROSA LUXEMBURG (1871–1919) A leading interpreter of Marxism and a humanist and prominent socialist activist in Germany and Eastern Europe, Luxemburg authored *Mass Strike, The Party, and Trade Unions*; *The Accumulation of Capital*; and a host of extraordinary essays before she was killed in the Spartacus Revolt in Berlin.

JEAN-FRANÇOIS LYOTARD (1924–) A major theorist of postmodernism, Lyotard is both Professor Emeritus of Philosophy at the Université de Paris and Professor of Philosophy at the

University of California, Irvine. His works include *Driftworks*, *The Differend*, *Heidegger and the "Jews"*, and *The Postmodern Condition*.

HERBERT MARCUSE (1898–1979) Born in Berlin, a participant in the Spartacus events of 1919, Marcuse studied philosophy at Freiburg University with Martin Heidegger. A prominent representative of the Frankfurt School, he worked for the Organization for Strategic Services in the United States during World War II and later taught at Brandeis University and the University of California, San Diego. A leading figure in the student movement of the 1960s and a superb essayist, Marcuse is the author of *Eros and Civilization*, *One-Dimensional Man*, *Negations*, *Counter-Revolution and Revolt*, and *The Aesthetic Dimension*.

CAROLYN MERCHANT (1936–) Currently Professor of Environmental History, Philosophy, and Ethics at the University of California, Berkeley, Merchant is the author of *Radical Ecology: The Search for a Livable World*, *Ecological Revolutions: Nature, Gender, and Science in New England*, and *The Death of Nature: Women, Ecology, and the Scientific Revolution*.

BENITO MUSSOLINI (1883–1945) Born in the Romagna, Mussolini became a left-wing socialist and journalist before founding his own fascist movement. Known as *Il Duce* (the leader), he took power in 1922 and held it until the final defeat of Italy and his execution by partisans of the Resistance.

MICHAEL OAKESHOTT (1901–1994) Educated at Cambridge, Oakeshott was chair of political science at the London School of Economics. His most important books include *Rationalism in Politics* and *On Human Conduct*.

HENRY M. PACHTER (1907–1980) Born in Berlin, Pachter received his doctorate in history from the University of Berlin in 1931. He went on to help form the first anti-Nazi resistance group after Hitler took power and then to serve as a publicist for loyalist forces during the Spanish Civil War. A social theorist and historian with wide-ranging interests, ultimately a professor of political science at the New School for Social Research and the City College of New York, Pachter is the author of *Paraclesus: Magic Into Science*, *Modern Germany*, *The Fall and Rise of Europe*, *Weimar Etudes*, and *Socialism in History*.

NORMAN PODHORETZ (1930–) The editor of *Commentary* (one of the most influential conservative magazines) since 1960, this leading public intellectual is the author of *The Present Danger* and *Breaking Ranks: A Political Memoir*.

JOHN RAWLS (1921–) A preeminent American political theorist, Rawls taught at Princeton, Cornell, and MIT before moving to Harvard, where he has taught since 1962. His major works are *A Theory of Justice* and *Political Liberalism*.

JOSE ANTONIO PRIMO DE RIVERA (1903–1936) The son of a former dictator of Spain and a theoretician and leader of the fascist *Falange*, Rivera inspired and helped initiate the uprising of Generalissimo Franco against the Spanish Republic. He was captured by loyalist troops and then executed after a sensational trial.

CARLO ROSSELLI (1899–1937) Born to a Jewish family with liberal roots, Rosselli was an important figure in the socialist labor movement and a founder of the anti-fascist group known as Justice and Liberty. He was imprisoned and later murdered by henchmen of Mussolini.

SHEILA ROWBOTHAM (1943–) Born in Leeds, Rowbotham is an activist with the Trade Union Council of London and the European Union, a playwright, historian, and theorist, and one of the most important figures in British feminism. Her works include *Hidden from History*, *Dutiful Daughters*, *Women, Resistance, and Revolution*, and *Beyond the Fragments*.

EDWARD W. SAID (1935–) Born in Jersualem, Said received his doctorate at Harvard University in 1964 and taught at several universities before taking a position as Professor of English Literature at Columbia University. His major works include *Orientalism*, *The Question of Palestine*, and *Culture and Imperialism*.

MICHAEL J. SANDEL (1953–) Sandel is a professor of government at Harvard University whose major works include *Democracy's Discontent*, *Liberalism and the Limits of Justice*, and *Liberalism and Its Critics*.

AUGUSTIN SOUCHY (1892–1986) A leading figure in the European anarchist movement whose work as an activist led him all over the world, Souchy wrote for a number of anarchist journals and became best known for his autobiography, *Beware Anarchist!: A Life for Freedom*.

JOSEF STALIN (1879–1953) Born in Georgia, eventually an expert on the nationalities question, Stalin would become the undisputed successor of Lenin in his epic battle with Leon Trotsky for control of the Soviet Union. A ruthless tyrant whose secret police killed millions and created a genuinely totalitarian state, the "cult of the personality" turned him into a major theorist. His major work was *Questions of Leninism*.

LEO STRAUSS (1899–1973) Born in Germany, Strauss received his Ph.D. from the University of Hamburg in 1921 and emigrated in 1938 to the United States, where he became one of the most influential political theorists while teaching at the University of Chicago. Co-editor of the *History of Political Philosophy*, Strauss is the author of *On Tyranny*, *Natural Right and History*, and *What Is Political Philosophy?*

MAO TSE-TUNG (ZEDONG) (1893–1976) A founder of the Chinese Communist Party, a writer, and a teacher, Mao led the civil war against the forces of Chiang Kai-shek, resulting in the creation of the Chinese People's Republic in 1949. His emphasis on the peasantry, his break with Stalin, and his experimentalism with regard to policy make Mao among the most important figures in the Leninist tradition.

ROBERT PAUL WOLFF (1933–) Currently a professor of philosophy and African-American Studies at the University of Massachusetts, Amherst. Wolff's major works include *The Poverty of Liberalism*, *The Idea of the University*, *In Defense of Anarchism*, and *About Philosophy*.

MALCOLM X (1925–1965) Born in Omaha, Malcolm X converted to the Nation of Islam while in jail for theft and became one of its most important spokesmen. A founder of black nationalism and a fiery orator who broke with Elijah Muhammed, he is best known for his autobiography.

INDEX